William Bell

A handbook of freethought

Containing in condensed and systematized form a vast amount of evidence against

the superstitious doctrines of Christianity

William Bell

A handbook of freethought
Containing in condensed and systematized form a vast amount of evidence against the superstitious doctrines of Christianity

ISBN/EAN: 9783337284251

Printed in Europe, USA, Canada, Australia, Japan

Cover: Foto ©Lupo / pixelio.de

More available books at **www.hansebooks.com**

A HANDBOOK OF FREETHOUGHT.

Containing in Condensed and Systematized Form a Vast Amount of Evidence Against the Superstitious Doctrines of Christianity.

Selected by W. S. BELL.

New York:
THE TRUTH SEEKER COMPANY,
28 Lafayette Place.

PREFACE.

I have aimed in preparing this work to put into compact and orderly form a large amount of irrefragable evidence against the superstitions of the church. I have often felt the need of such a work for my own use. The matter herewith presented has been culled from some of the ablest writers living and dead. As a book of reference I hope it may be a valuable aid to all investigators and truthseekers. Its running head lines, chapter heads, subheads, and classified subjects make it a "handbook."

SAN FRANCISCO.
 January 10, 1890.

CREATION.

In the beginning God created the heaven and the earth. (Gen. 1: 1.)

No sooner do we read this sentence than we find our minds full of perplexing questions. Quite naturally we ask in the "beginning" of what? It could not mean in the beginning of God, for it is supposed that he had no beginning; it could not mean the beginning of eternity, as that is without commencement or end, and it could not have been in the beginning of matter as it is eternal. If then matter is eternal, the story about the creation of the heaven and the earth is nothing more than a myth—a childish story that has come down to us from the dark ages of the remote past.

The indestructibility of matter is the corner-stone of modern philosophy, and the indestructibility of matter implies its eternal existence, that is, it never was created and it never will cease to exist. Theologians have taught for centuries that God created matter out of nothing. Enlightened people have to smile when they hear these stories repeated. Some theologians who have discovered the folly of such empty traditions have tried to reconstruct them by means of new interpretations. The Rev. De Witt Talmage, of Brooklyn, has discovered that God created matter out of a piece of omnipotence. This discovery is important, and may lead to grand results; still there are some people who doggedly refuse to accept this invention, and maintain that omnipotence is nothing more than an attribute, and that one could with as much propriety speak of God's creating matter out of omniscience, or omnipresence.

There are others who do not claim that matter was made out of nothing, but that it was in a chaotic state, and that at a certain time (before time was), God formed it into the universe in six days of creation.

But this explanation does not help us out of our difficulties. For if God did not create matter out of nothing then it is eternal, and there could be no such thing as creation, or Creator. There is nothing in this old story at all, if it proves on examination that the "Creator" did not create matter; for in that case matter is co-eternal with God, and like him, is uncaused. When this old definition of creation fails the theological superstructure built upon it totters and falls to the ground. For if the Creator did not originate the universe from nothing, then matter is eternal, and God is not omnipotent, is not infinite, is not God. Thus we see that we have no reason whatever to think that there ever was a beginning to matter, or that creation of matter is at all thinkable. The words "beginning" and "creation," as thus used are without meaning.

It is a marvel how long the mind of man has been subject to this childish fable. Surely the wise men of the different ages who heard it perceived its unreasonableness. But the wise men were few and the unwise were many, and the superstructure built over their heads in the form of theocracies and theologies, laid upon the foundations of this myth were too formidable to admit of free thought. The prophets must prophesy according to the traditions of the fathers. New interpretations were never welcome in this world. A radical idea is always a source of pain to the superficial or bigoted mind. And above all heresy was the worst of all things, and everything new was heresy. And because human reason was all the time making discoveries which revealed better things than had been known, and because reason exposed the weakness and falsity of traditions and superstitions, therefore reason itself was condemned and put under ban and was called "carnal reason," and in order to overcome it, faith, blind belief, was set up as the greatest of all human virtues. And so strong was reason in its persistent attempts to get at the truth, it became necessary to preach faith all the time and to make salvation in another world depend upon it. And, as if this was not enough, he was constantly reminded that the sentence, "believe or be damned" did not relate wholly to another world Damnation often began in this world. The persecutions, inquisitions, crusades, St. Bartholomew massacres all show how hard it is with those who have faith to have kindness of heart.

"And God said let there be light and there was light." But how do we know he said so? Who was the reporter at that early date? In fact even if it were true, how could any one have ever found it out? And if any one had found it how could we know it? The same question might be asked in reference to creation. Who discovered the fact? How could we know that some one had learned it even if it were true?

"And God saw the light that it was good." From this expression, we should infer that he did not know beforehand whether the light he was about experimentally to originate would be a good thing or not; but after having spoken it into existence and contemplating it for a while, he pronounced it good. The approval is spoken of it much after the manner of men. For instance we see a painter after having put the finishing touches on his picture step back and with satisfaction look at it, and say, "it is the greatest effort of my life."

"And God divided the light from the darkness." The originator of this story had not the slightest idea of the nature of light. He supposed it to be a substance that could be separated from darkness, which he also imagined a substance, as white beans may be separated from black beans.

In his imagination he probably saw God throwing pieces and chunks of darkness on one side and rays and beams of light on the other. It is hard for a man who has been born but once to understand these things. ("Mistakes of Moses," Ingersoll.)

"And God called the light day, and the darkness he called night; and the evening and the morning were the first day."

Bible expounders have found it difficult to reconcile the word "day" with the teachings of geology. According to common chronology the creation of this universe out of nothing took place four thousand and four years before the birth of Christ, which would make the universe about six thousand years old. The testimony of geology is that the formation of this earth as it now is, must have a record of millions of years. And astronomy demonstrates that there are stars so far from this earth that it would take an indefinitely long time for the light from them to reach this earth.

Here then are two witnesses against this story which makes the earth about six thousand years old. These witnesses cannot be impeached.

What shall be done with the record? Oh, put a new interpretation upon it. "A person who is not a critic," says Huxley, "and is not a Hebrew scholar, can only stand up and admire the marvelous flexibility of the language which admits of such adverse interpretations."

The great expounders who explain the inexplicable things assure us that the six days of creation spoken of in the book of Genesis do mean literal days of twenty-four hours, but that the word "day" is here used to mean an indefinite period, "a great while." But there are so many, and such great difficulties in the way of our accepting this explanation that we are forced to reject it.

In the first place the record says "days," and says nothing in connection with the word that would lead us to think the writer meant anything by the word more than it usually signifies; while on the other hand all the uses of the word seem to imply that a day in every instance where the the word is used, means a period of twenty-four hours.

Hugh Miller, and an eminent geologist, attempted to reconcile Genesis with geology, and after a laborious effort to achieve this end committed suicide. He attempted an impossible task.

There is not the slightest grounds for supposing the writer of Genesis to mean by the word "day" anything more than we mean by the same word. The language, "the evening and the morning were the first day," can admit of but one interpretation, and that is the duration of twenty-four hours. We shall find that the writer uses the word "day" where, by no possible flexibility of interpretation, can the word mean anything other than this, and gives no hint that he means anything different in the use of the word in the latter case from its signification in its previous use.

"And on the seventh day God ended his work which he had made, and he rested on the seventh day from all his work which he had made. And God blessed the seventh day and sanctified it, because that in it he had rested from all his work."

"For in six days the Lord made heaven and earth, the sea and all that in them is, and rested the seventh day, wherefore the Lord blessed the Sabbath day and hallowed it."

"It is a sign between me and the children of Israel forever; for in six days the Lord made heaven and earth and on the seventh day he rested and was refreshed."

And still another instance may be given to show that the word "day" has no double meaning: "And God made two great lights, the greater to rule the day and the lesser to rule the night." The word "day" obviously means what we mean by it when we use it in connection with night.

These proofs settle the question of the meaning of the word "day." It means in Genesis just what it means when we use it. The account given of creation in speaking of "days" meant literally twenty-four hours; and geology and astronomy prove such statements to be childish and foolish. If we should admit that the word "day" in this narrative meant millions of years, then the first Sabbath upon which the Lord rested and was refreshed also meant millions of years. If this be so then it is safe to infer that he is still resting. This may in some degree account for the fact that the ministers are trying to run the world in his name. For if God exerts his power over the world to guide and control it according to his own sovereign will it is nothing less than high handed presumption if not rebellious usurpation on the part of the clergy to attempt to take the management out of his hands.

In the second chapter of Genesis, Adam is said to have been made before the animals were created. After Adam had given names to all the animals as they passed before him in grand review, there was no helpmeet found among them for him, and as an afterthought God formed a woman for him out of a rib. But here was a very long period between the creation of Adam and Eve. According to the first chapter of Genesis Adam and Eve were created at the same time, and before the creation of the animal kingdom, but in the second chapter man was the first creature made and woman the last. This would make Adam millions of years older than Eve, if the word "day" means millions of years in the first chapter of Genesis.

"And God said, Let there be a firmament in the midst of the waters, and let it divide the waters. And God made the firmament and divided the waters which were under the firmament from the waters which were above the firmament; and it was so. And God called the firmament heaven."

According to this writer's ideas heaven and earth were two flat spheres, upon each of which were vast quantities of water. The firmament in which were set the sun, moon, and stars was in some way supported at a short distance above the earth.

The Hebrew term *rakia* so translated, is generally regarded as expressive of simple expansion, and is so rendered in the margin of the A. V. (authorized version). (Gen. 1: 6.) The root means to expand by beating whether by the hand, the foot, or any other instrument. It is especially used of beating out metals into thin plates. (Ex. 39: 3, and Num. 16: 39.) The sense of solidity is combined with the ideas of expansion and tenuity in the term. The same idea of solidity runs through all the references to the *rakia*. In Exodus 24: 10, it is represented as a solid floor. So again in Ezekiel 1: 22-26, the "firmament" is the floor on which the throne of the Most High is placed. Further, the office of the *rakia* in the economy of the world demanded strength and substance. It was to serve as a division between the waters above and the waters below. (Gen. 1: 7.) In keeping with this view the *rakia* was provided with "windows" (Gen. 7: 11, Isa. 24: 18, Mal. 3: 10), and "doors" (Ps. 78: 23) through which the rain and the snow might descend. A secondary purpose which the *rakia* served was to support the heavenly bodies, sun, moon, and stars (Gen. 1: 14), in which they were fixed as nails, and from which consequently, they might be said to drop off. (Isa. 14: 12-34, Mat. 24: 29.) In all these particulars we recognize the same view as was entertained by the Greeks, and to a certain extent by the Latins. If it be objected to the Mosaic account that the view embodied in the word *rakia* does not harmonize with strict philosphical truth, the answer to such an objection is, that the writer describes things as they appear rather than as they are. (Smith's "Abridged Bible Dictionary," Firmament.)

One not acquainted with the wonderful flexibility of biblical interpretation, might conclude after reading this explicit definition of the *rakia* that the story of creation was an inspired revelation, but not true. We ourselves are inclined to this opinion, and we accept the conclusion that the Mosaic description of the firmament "does not harmonize with strict philosophical truth; and possibly we shall conclude that all parts of the Mosaic cosmogony will show that the writer who attempts to give a history of the beginning of the universe, did nothing more than describe things as they appeared to his mind's eye, rather than as they actually were.

"And God said, Let the earth bring forth grass, and the herb yielding seed, and the fruit tree yielding fruit, after his kind, whose seed is in itself, upon the earth, and it was so."

This was on the third day, and we read that on the fifth day, "God created great whales and every living creature that moveth which the waters brought forth abundantly after their kind." But in the evolution of life upon this earth, grasses, trees and plants do not precede the evolution of marine animals. Here again we come upon one of those instances where the account given does not harmonize with strict philosophical truth; but the answer to such objections is that "the writer describes things as they appear rather than as they are." In modern language we should say he was merely guessing at the riddle of existence.

"And God made two great lights, and the greater to rule the day and the lesser to rule the night; and he made the stars also."

The creation of the sun and the moon was on the fourth day. But it is not made clear how there could have been a morning and an evening of three previous days, in the absence of the sun. Then again there is no poselble explanation for the existence of vegetation without sunlight.

Grasses, trees, and plants will not grow without sunlight. And still another difficulty meets us in the same passage. The writer says God made two great lights, the greater to rule the day and the lesser to rule the night. And this also is lacking in harmony with "strict philosophical truth," for there is only one great light; the moon has no light, but merely reflects the sun's rays. It is true it seems to be a light, and as "the writer describes things as they appear rather than as they are," we can hold him responsible only for the revelation he makes as a matter of inspiration and not for its truth.

Before the sun was created, the writer gives us to understand that the dry land appeared—or to put it more definitely, God commanded saying, "Let the dry land appear." But to whom was it to appear when there was no eye yet created to look upon it, and if there had been, there was no sunlight, and therefore if the world had been full of eyes the land would not have appeared! This is a problem. Did the waters lie on the mountain tops, and refuse to run down to the valleys, until they were commanded?

For how was it possible for a writer who describes things as they *appear*, to attempt to give us a glimpse of things which certainly could not have *appeared*, only to a mind diseased? But not wishing to appear captious we will let this pass, only however with the explicit understanding that the writer, in this case certainly attempted to describe things as they could not appear.

We find our perplexities increasing as we proceed. Especially when we attempt to read the stone book of geology in company with the Hebrew book of Genesis.

Whoever he may have been, and there can be no doubt of the sex of the writer, as the book everywhere betrays the spirit of the "lord of creation," man, he seems to think that the earth was created before the sun, when the truth is the earth is the child of the sun. One could as well speak of a son being older than his father as to talk of the creation of the sun, after the earth had been created.

Thus, statement after statement of the story about creation falls for lack of support—and like bubbles the airy word pictures burst at the first touch of science.

What gross ignorance the writer betrays in speaking of the vast universe. It is nothing; it needs no extended description, five words are enough to describe the creation of an infinite universe, and hence to the writer it was quite sufficient to merely say, "He made the stars also." And two of these words are supplied by the transcribers. As it seemed to this original cosmogonist the work of getting up a universe was not a matter of very great importance.

We are not disposed to credit this story for the reason that, the author makes it necessary for God to take five days to create the solar system, but for the infinite universe beyond, he needed less than one day. The Mosaic cosmogonist had no soul for astronomy or he would have seen the necessity of more time in the creation of the starry systems. We could have no patience with his description if it were not for the fact of which we are so well assured by Smith's Bible Dictionary, that he is not giving us matter of fact but is "describing things as they appear rather than as they are."

But no sooner do we quit one difficulty than we are beset with another. In looking over the leaves of the stone book of geology we find fossils of animals which existed untold ages before man, and as they had eyes there must therefore have been light, the sun must have existed an indefinitely long period before man.

And last of all on the sixth day late on Saturday afternoon, God created man in his own image. And as he stepped back and surveyed the week's work which was before him he pronounced himself satisfied with it all. Everything was just as he would have it. Everything was perfect. "And God saw everything that he had made, and behold it was *very good.*" In fact there was not a single thing he could see a chance to make any improvement on; for it is impossible for us to think of a perfect creator making an imperfect creature. And if by any mistake he had made anything not just as it ought to be, and as he intended, we should think that knowing the fact he would make the necessary improvement; and if he would not, then we must conclude that he is not infinitely good. Thus every turn we make in this story drives us to the conclusion that it is not true, that it is only an ancient myth. It is the brass of ignorance which has been palmed off upon us for the gold of truth.

"So God created man in his own image," and yet in the next breath the writer informs us that after Adam and Eve had eaten of the forbidden fruit, they became more like God, and if they had been permitted to eat of the tree of life they would have become still more like him. But it is hard for one who has not been born again to understand how Adam and Eve could become more and more like God, when they were created in his image and pronounced *very good*.

The command given them was, "Ye shall not eat of it, neither shall ye touch it lest ye die." But the serpent said unto the woman, "Ye shall not surely die; for God doth know that in the day ye eat thereof, then your eyes shall be opened, and ye shall be as gods knowing good and evil."

And this was just how it turned out. After they had eaten of this prohibited tree, they became more like the gods than they had been. But we are led to immediately to ask, could they have been made in the first place like them? And unless they were both counterfeits we cannot imagine how an image can be improved—that is, become more of an image.

And the Lord God said, "Behold the man has become as one of us, (just as the serpent had foretold) to know good and evil." Here is a clear contradiction of terms. And in order to explain the matter at all satisfactorily to ourselves we have to recur to the assurance of authority that it is not claimed that the narration is literal history of fact, but merely the writer's opinions of how it seemed to him it ought to be.

"Behold I have given you every herb bearing seed, which is upon the face of all the earth, and, every tree which is the fruit of a tree yielding seed, to you it shall be for meat."

Here is an explicit statement of Adam's right to eat of any fruit he might find. But in the third chapter of this wonderful book, we find that there are two trees whose fruit he is prohibited from eating, "Of the fruit of the tree which is in the midst of the garden, God hath said he shall not eat of it." Then after Adam and Eve had refreshed themselves from the fruit of the tree of knowledge, which made them as the gods knowing good and evil, the Lord God said, "Now lest he put forth his hand and take also of the tree of life and eat and live forever, therefore the Lord sent him forth from the garden of Eden to till the ground from whence he was taken."

We fail to see any reason for the apparent change of plan in the mind of the Lord. He first grants Adam and Eve the privilege of eating any fruit they chose, and afterward prohibited them from eating of the fruit of two trees, which would have most benefited them. Certainly we can see no good reason for prohibiting them from acquiring knowledge, especially of good and evil, since the gods had this sort of knowledge themselves. In fact we would naturally suppose that the more accurate man's knowledge of good and evil is the better off he would be; he would certainly be more moral. But let us imagine that it was not desirable for Adam and Eve to have such knowledge and morality and thus to resemble so closely the gods themselves, is there any good reason why they should not have partaken of the fruit of the tree of life, and thereby lived forever? Why should the fact that they had become more like the gods be a sufficient reason for preventing them from sharing in the immortal life? Would not it have been altogether probable that Adam and Eve would continue to become more and more like the gods, seeing that they had begun so persistently to acquire the godlike virtues?

"And when the woman saw the tree was good for food, and that it was pleasant to the eyes, and a tree to be desired to make one wise," etc. We see that it was wisdom that was prohibited, and not murder, robbery, or drunkenness. Why was knowledge and wisdom forbidden to man when these above all things else he needed most? Why is it that religion has always condemned learning, discoveries, inventions, reforms, etc.? Knowledge is the forbidden fruit of all the gardens of the gods. But how could these celestial creators expect to prevent man from gaining knowledge after they had created him with a brain to think? To think is to have knowledge, and to have some knowledge is to thirst for more, and thus it was absolute madness to create man with a brain and command him not think. As well throw a bird into the air, and shoot it for flying, or spear a fish for swimming in the water, as to damn a human being for coming into possession of the knowledge of good and evil.

The story seems to imply many contradictions which are not explicitly expressed. For Adam and Eve must have been moral beings to have understood the supposed commands of God. If they were moral then they already knew what good and evil was. The way in which this primitive couple acquired knowledge reminds one of the description of the creation of the sun. In the first chapter of this wonderful book, we find light created, and on the fourth day afterward the sun is made. This is reversing the order of cause and effect, as in this effect comes before cause. There is this explanation, however, that the world was new and had not got fairly into working order.

In the case of Adam and Eve, we have no such explanation to offer. We find them from the very first moment, rational beings, and of course having a knowledge of good and evil; but the historian who gives us the account, declares that they came into the possession of knowledge not by virtue of their brains; but because of their eating of certain fruit. The effect is made to be the cause.

There is only one way out of the dilemma. The writer described things "as they seemed rather than as they are."

Even so great a man as the Hon. W. E. Gladstone has to betake himself to specious arguments in attempting to refute the testimony of science when opposed to Genesis. His logic is kindred to that quoted from Smith's Bible Dictionary, wherein the writer says of the author of Genesis that he "describes things as they appear, rather than as they are." Mr. Gladstone in the "Order of Creation," says:

Proceeding, on what I hold to be open ground, to state my own idea of the key to the meaning of the Mosaic record (Genesis), I suggest that it was intended to give moral, and not scientific instruction to those for whom it was written.

Who was it that "intended to give moral, and not scientific instruction?" If it was the author of Genesis who intended it for only moral instruction, then it cannot be claimed to be a *revleation from God*; but if on the other hand it was God who intended to give only moral instruction, then he is responsible for making the author of Genesis record that which is not true. What a sight for gods and men! To see the ex-premier of England pettifogging at the bar of Reason for a dying, nay dead superstition; for certainly Genesis as a revelation is dead so far as reason and science are concerned.

But this hostility to knowledge instituted in the garden of Eden has been perpetuated through all the ages. Faith has been held up as the all-important virtue, as by it the priests could get the people to believe anything. Somewhere Goethe says, "Belief is not the beginning but the end of knowledge." In the early days of the church it was found necessary to abandon reason. The world had too many philosophers who stood prepared to expose the superstitions which set themselves up with authority. The injunction given to and heeded by chiefly the low and ignorant was, "Do not examine; only believe and thy faith will make thee blessed." "Wisdom is a bad thing in life, foolishness is to be preferred." But this sentiment was older than that date, for we find in the writings of Paul the same teaching, "If any man among you seemeth to be wise, let him become a fool that he may be wise." At another time he insists that, "We are fools for Christ's sake."

My advice is to eat of the fruit of knowledge, and have your eyes opened to the truth no matter what it is. It may be that some delusive Santa Claus may fade away in the distance before your clearer vision. Let it go. Nothing is so expensive as error. Seek to know the truth, and struggle to throw off such prejudices as tempt you to fashion truth to your own intellectual myopia or moral obliquities. Eat and become more truly a man; eat and become more beautifully a woman.

"And to every beast of the earth, and to every fowl of the air, and to everything that creepeth upon the earth wherein there is life I have given every herb for meat."

This writer never visited a menagerie. His knowledge of the habits of the animal kingdom are as innocent as if he had never sought for knowledge, had never examined natural history, or else he would have known that such animals as lions, tigers, and wolves could not feed on grass. The vultures of the air do not live upon seeds or hay, but must have fish or flesh. Daniel going into a den of lions fed on hay, would be about as brave as a milk maid's going into the stall to milk a cow. We cannot conjecture what state of mind the Mosaic cosmogonist could have been in when he described the lion as a herbivorous animal. It is so wide a departure from the most common knowledge of the habits of animals that our confidence in the accuracy of the historian is greatly shaken.

It is commonly believed that if man had not eaten of the forbidden fruit he would have been immortal. Now the very fact that Adam and Eve ate at all, proves them to have been mortal. For eating implies a nutritive system, which means growth, maturity, and decay of the organism. Death is natural, and not a penalty—not a curse pronounced upon the primitive pair for disobedience. They would have died even if they had partaken of the tree of life.

And in connection with this erroneous idea of the loss of immortality is another respecting labor. It has been a doctrine taught by the church that labor is a curse pronounced upon the family of man in consequence of Adam's transgression, and proof often quoted is, "In the sweat of thy face shalt thou eat bread."

This is the consequence of cherishing an ambition to become more like the gods. Because he was foolish enough to disobey in the matter of tasting some tempting fruit which attracted his eye, he and all his posterity must toil hard to get a mere subsistence, and then go to hell and roast forever. To an ordinary man this seems rather rough for so small an offense—to sweat in this life is bad enough, but to roast in another is too much, and we utter our righteous protest against it. And since we now have our choice between hell, hades, sheol or gehenna I, for one, prefer hades as its temperature is lower.

But this story like many others lacks consistency. For we read that before Adam transgressed the commandment, "The Lord took the man and put him into the garden of Eden to dress it and to keep it." This looks like work, and gardeners and farmers would look upon all such arrangements as work, especially would they thus regard it, if the garden was large and it was the duty of one person to take the entire care of it, to that is, do all the work.

Labor therefore was natural to man and did not come upon him as a curse. It was not in consequence of his eating prohibited apples that the necessity of toil was imposed upon him as a curse, but because mental and physical activity are natural, and he could not exist without them.

Labor is natural and honorable. The hands and brain of man imply labor, as necessarily as the lungs imply air, or the gills of the fish imply water. Man could not exist without it; but the great evil which has arisen is the abuse of labor. Some have been enabled to get possession of wealth and thereby have the power to control the laborer and take such a share out of the profits of his toil as they see fit. The stronger prey upon the weaker. Our present civilization does not civilize, because it does not remove this relic of barbarism which allows the rich to rob the poor of the profits of their labor. The laborer who produces the wealth of the country is the one who does not get its benefits. The old form of European civilization which justifies and aids the rich in becoming richer and making the poor poorer is beginning to show traces of its existence in this country. And we must say we cannot see how or when this sort of civilization with gilded top and rotten base is to come to an end. Surely there is no way out of our barbarous degradation except by the development of the individual through his intelligence into liberty, morality, and manhood.

"And out of the ground the Lord God formed every beast of the field, and every fowl of the air, and brought them unto Adam to see what he would name them." Some animals, as the Armadillo, and Sloth of South America would consume more time in going from South America to the garden of Eden, than Adam's life covered. And how could the polar bear and the humming bird of the tropics pass through the different temperatures to reach the garden of Eden? and how long could they survive if they were even there, and how could they find their way back to their former habitats? Did the fish all swim up to the shore and range themselves in a row to be named?

We wish to call attention to the grand review of the animals, to point out the implication that Adam could not find a helpmeet among them. We read:

"And out of the ground the Lord God formed every beast of the field, and every fowl of the air, and brought them to Adam to see what he would name them. And whatsoever Adam called every living creature that was the name thereof. And Adam gave names to all the cattle, to the fowl of the air, to every beast of the field, but for Adam there was not found an helpmeet for him."

Now the very words, "was not found," imply that search was made for a helpmeet, but none could be found. And because none could be found, therefore the Lord God went immediately to work to make a woman for him. The Creator threw him into a deep sleep, and while in that unconscious condition and unable to do or say a thing in his own defense, the Lord took out a rib, or as Ingersoll says, "a cutlet," while Dr. Talmage insists that God took out Adam's "side" and reformed it into a woman; and as the text reads, "Brought her unto the man." Was he not there right on the spot? Was it necessary for the Lord after taking out the rib to go off a distance by himself that he might finish the work undisturbed? Unless something of the kind was necessary we do not see the force of the sentence, "Brought her unto the man."

The Greenlanders have a story that relates the creation of woman from man's thumb. This is significant and much more probable. There is wisdom in this even if it be regarded as a myth. The bare fact that woman has always been under man's thumb shows some kinetic relation. The masculine gender has not been reluctant to manifest a disposition to preserve the gentler sex in this position. He calls her by pet names, and bestows compliments upon her, and declares upon the honor of a despot that there is no name so sacred as mother, and that there is no virtue so precious as that possessed by woman—he will even die for her, but still he prefers to keep her in subjection under his thumb. Liberty will come to woman when she becomes tired of being a mere plaything, a pet, a favorite slave, and then, and not till then may she rise into the full dignity of womanhood, and throw off thumb authority and all allegiance to the legends which give the thumb its authority. Woman needs again to eat of the tree of knowledge of good and evil, even if she be driven out of the social garden and ostracised therefrom with the flaming sword of respectability guarding the gates against her return. Her first rebellion brought knowledge and progress to man, and her second rebellion must be against both God and man.

"And the serpent said unto the woman, ye shall not surely die." Never in the history of snakes was there a match for this first one. It is highly probable that his snakeship did not have a protracted existence after this emeute of the garden. In fact we never hear of him more. Some historians say he changed his name and went west, and some have gone so far as to say that Satan, who attacked Job many centuries after the seduction of Adam and Eve was nothing more than the old Serpent under a new name.

One thing is certain, and that is, that the snake in the garden of Eden immortalized himself in a short time. But we can hardly comprehend the curse pronounced upon it for so laudable a work. This was the curse: "Above all cattle, and above every beast of the field; upon thy belly shalt thou go and dust shalt thou eat all the days of thy life." It would seem from this, that the serpent did not go naturally upon his belly, but some how or other he diddled along on the tip end of his tail. We fail to see any reason for this sort of locomotion unless it was to help him look out for other snakes. And we are perplexed to understand why he should be sentenced to eat dust. If he was cursed, it seems that the curse is quite conveniently borne by him; for he finds it just to his gait to go upon his belly, and as for eating dust, he never did and never will. He is defiant, rebellious, and successful.

The more we study the character of this original **snake** the more we find to admire in him.

It is true we do not always understand just how things could happen as they did, but we take them as they read and make the best of them. For instance we can form no idea of how it was possible for the serpent to talk to Eve, and reason with her like a philosopher. He talked to her the same as if he had had vocal organs, and a brain similar but superior to man's. Unless he had a mouth and head like a human being we cannot see how he could have talked; and if his head was of that type we cannot see how he could have been called a snake. There was a great many suggestions prompted by reading the account of this wonderful serpent. We cannot understand why he should have been made. Or why, if it were necessary to have him, he was not placed under some restraint? Why was he not created so that God himself could govern him? Or why after seeing he had made him a little too wise, and a trifle too devilish he did not kill him? Or if that were impracticable or impossible, why did he not put up signs on all the fences around Eden, "Adam and Eve beware of snakes!"

"And Adam and his wife hid themselves from the presence of the Lord God amongst the trees of the garden. And the Lord God called unto Adam and said unto him, where art thou?" But we are amazed at the very thought that it was possible for them to get out of sight of the omniscient eye! We read in many books, and have heard it all our lives that God sees all things, but according to this account, his first creatures, fresh from his plastic hands, and very near to him got beyond his omniscient sight. How could this be, when "the eyes of the Lord are in every place beholding the evil and the good?"

"For his eyes are upon the ways of man and he seeth all his goings."

"For the eyes of the Lord run to and fro throughout the whole earth."

And yet, notwithstanding he made all things, and sees all things, and knows all things, Adam and Eve were able to get behind the trees and hide away out of his sight.

On another occasion it is recorded that the Lord had come down from heaven to see whether the reports which were brought up to him were true or not. "And the Lord came down to see the city and the tower which the children of men builded." And in still another place it is written: "And the Lord said because of the city of Sodom and Gomorrah is great and because their sin is grievous I will go down now and see whether they have done according to the cry of it, which is come up before me, and if not I will know."

And yet other equally inspired writers, describing things as they appeared rather than as they are, solemnly declare that "all things are naked and open to him with whom we have to do."

But we pass on leaving Adam behind the tree, hid away from the presence of the Lord, to notice other sacred passages which are not in harmony with strict philosophical truth.

"Unto the woman he said, I will greatly multiply thy sorrow; in sorrow shalt thou bring forth children, and thy desire shall be to thy husband and he shall rule over thee." Now there is no reason to suppose that the pain of childbirth has ever been increased in woman. Her physiological structure has in no way undergone a radical change. Besides, all animals bearing offspring bear pains. Did the curse upon woman extend to the females of animals bearing offspring? But wherein does the male suffer his share in this divine punishment?

"And he shall rule over thee." This is a matter of fact —and is equally true of those people who know nothing of Israel or Israel's god. Man has ruled over woman in all times and in all countries, and will continue to reign over her until she aspires to and contends for her rights.

The path of woman's future is steep, slippery, and long. Many ages will pass before she attains the glory and beauty possible to womanhood, but with prophetic eyes we see that time coming. With joy we labor and wait, that at some future day this world will be made happy and grand through the evolution of truth, love, and liberty in the elevation of woman.

Another part of the curse is that, "Thorns and thistles shall it (the ground) bring forth," but geology shows that thorns and thistles were as plentiful in the primeval world as they are now. Hence there must be some mistake on the part of the writer in setting down the origin of thorns and thistles for that particular date.

"And Adam called his wife Eve because she was the mother of all living."

This is another astonishing statement. Eve was the mother of all (human beings) living, and there were none living but herself and Adam! If she was the mother of all living, she was not only Adam's mother, but her own mother too.

It is true that when Cain grew to manhood and slew his brother, there were some people down in the land of Nod, but what God made them we have no means of knowing. They were not a people of much consequence as no notice is taken of them by our author, and besides they permitted Cain to come and live among them and take a wife. Perhaps these people were before Adam and Eve, for it is stated that in the city there were workers of iron and brass. Brass is a compound of copper and zinc, and these workers must have had a knowledge of the arts of mining and compounding metals. The mark, too, was set upon Cain that "whosoever" might not slay him; then there must have been a "whosoever." It is very likely that if Cain built a city he must have had the aid of carpenters and workmen, and it may be that he found his wife in the land of Nod among the "whosoever" "workers in of iron and brass." I think the clergy will agree that there was a "whosoever." It would have been needless to put a mark on Cain to preserve his life from a "whosoever" if there were no "whosoever," and my opinion is that Mr. Cain married some of the daughters of Mr. "Whosoever" in the land of Nod.

"And Adam called his wife Eve because she was the mother of all living!" That eclipses everything. And we were about concluding that nothing of the kind had ever been known before, but we remember the story about Ahaziah, and that he was two years older than his father.

Thirty and two years old was he (Jehoram) when he began to reign, and he reigned eight years in Jerusalem.

And Ahaziah his son reigned in his stead.

Two and twenty years old was Ahaziah when he began to reign. (Kings 8: 17, 24, 26.)

In the book of Chronicles we have another account.

Thirty and two years old was he (Jehoram) when he began to reign and he reigned in Jerusalem eight years. And the inhabitants of Jerusalem made Ahaziah his youngest son king in his stead. Forty and two years old was Ahaziah when he began to reign. (2 Chron. 21: 20, and 2 Chron. 20: 1, 2.)

Jehoram was thirty-two years old when he came to the throne, and he reigned eight years, which made him forty years old at his death, and his son Ahaziah who took up the reins of government which dropped from the hands of his father, was forty-two years old—just two years older than his father, and the youngest son at that.

"Unto Adam also and to his wife did the Lord God make coats of skins and clothed them."

There is no description of the style of these dresses, and we are left without data for judging of their fitness, only we are inclined to the opinion that the country where it was just the temperature for the natives to go naked, skin coats would be a trifle too winterish in style. We fail too see the necessity for such heavy clothing, or in fact for any clothing at all, inasmuch as they were created to go naked. For we read that, "They were both naked the man and his wife, and were not ashamed." Or if they must have some protection for their modesty why were not fig-leaf aprons quite sufficient for that climate? And still further we can see no necessity for the Lord to turn tailor and make their clothes when Adam and Eve had already learned to sew; for "they sewed fig-leaves together and made themselves aprons," and as the seasons changed they could easily have learned to make garments of comfort for themselves, and also to set the fashions for the rest of the world. The origin of the universe is an insoluble mystery. And yet to the uninformed mind it seems to be no problem at all. We daily hear such people reasoning in this way: "There must have been a First Cause of all things, and that First Cause we call God." It is only because the mind of man is uninformed, that he reasons in this way. It requires only a little reflection to see that there could have been no First Cause. It is clear that every cause must have an effect, for unless it produces an effect it cannot be a cause. Hence we cannot infer that there can be an effect which of itself does not become a cause, producing other effects, so that it is absolutely impossible in the nature of cause and effect, for a last cause or a first cause to exist. As a last cause would be a cause only when it produced an effect, and the last effect would be an effect only when it became a cause. It is equally true that there could be no First Cause; for whatever is, is the result of some previous cause. We can view causation only as a chain in form of a circle.

"If we apply to this question the notion of *time* we see the limit of our thought, because if we try to think of an absolute creative power *before* creation, we discover that the idea is unthinkable, as infinite and absolute creative power in the presence of inactivity and nothing are incompatible. It could not have been creative power without creating something. We are therefore unable to think of absolute creative power as inert—we are equally unable to think of it inactive in the presence of chaos, and as impotent to conceive of its existence as absolute. We cannot think of it existing *after* creation, as rest and inactivity are again incompatible with the notion of force."

We may look at this subject in whatever way we choose we shall find that in no way whatever can we form any idea of a First Cause, an infinite and absolute Creator. Let us see. "The First Cause cannot be absolute, that is, it cannot exist out of all relation to the universe. Whereas a cause not only sustains some relation to its effect, but exists as a cause only by virtue of such relations. Suppress the effect and the cause has ceased to be a cause. Absolute cause, therefore, is like the phrase, circular triangle. The two words stand for conceptions which cannot be made to unite. We attempt, says Mr. Mansel, to escape from this apparent contradiction by introducing the succession of time. The absolute exists first by itself and afterward becomes a cause. But here we are checked by the third conception of the infinite. How can the infinite become that which it has not from the first." ("Fisk's Cosmic Philos,.")

Look at it whatever way we may the finite mind cannot grasp the conception of the infinite. Nay, cannot know of the existence of the infinite. Hence all efforts to explain the First Cause, the absolute, and the infinite, are more artificial and unreal than painted ships upon a painted sea.

We may view the subject in still another light. If God reasons, his knowledge is limited and he is finite. Man reasons because his knowledge is circumscribed. If he knew everything he would have no doubts, and hence would not need to investigate, experiment, recollect, and compare. He would not be compelled to lay down certain definite data, and follow their implications through rules of logic, and through scientific experiment in order to reach conclusions. The end would be as clearly before his mind as the beginning; in fact there would be to such a mind no beginning and no end. But we cannot imagine an infinite being who needs to recollect past events. But if we deny that in the mind of God there is the faculty of memory, we thereby deny that he reasons. The same may be said of doubt, for if the mind of God is never troubled with doubts, it is simply because he does not reason. Much of the mind's activity is employed in doubts. Doubt and inquiry are necessary elements of thought. Does God doubt? Does he investigate, compare, and test matters by experiment? If he does then he is not infinite, and if he does not, then he does not reason. Has he imagination? If he exercises this important function of the mind then he deals in unrealities, idealizes, has dreams, cherishes visions, builds air castles. If he does not thus exercise imagination he cannot be said to reason.

It is an old argument that design implies a designer. The essential weakness of this argument lies in what is called "proofs of design." And in support of this idea it is commonly urged that there are everywhere apparent in nature evidences of order, harmony, and adaptation. But to put this argument into a sentence, the maggot in the cheese could offer the same arguments to show there was a design in his position in the cheese. He could argue that everything about him showed order, harmony, and adaptation. It was just the cheese for him.

But even if we should admit this statement, it would not prove the existence of God, for if an intelligent mind had created the universe, it is certain that that mind itself must have been governed by law which yields to order, harmony, and adaptation, and if these imply a designer in one case they must also in the other, and therefore every designer must have had a designer.

The Difference Between the Two Cosmogonies as Given in the First Two Chapters of Genesis.

In the first, the earth emerges from the waters and is therefore saturated with moisture. (Gen. 1: 9, 10.) In the second, the whole face of the ground requires to be moistened. (Gen. 2: 6.)

In the first, the birds and beasts are created *before* man. (Gen. 1: 20, 24, 26.) In the second, man is created before the birds and beasts. (Gen. 2: 7, 9.)

In the first, all the "fowls that fly" are made out of the *waters*. (Gen. 1: 20.) In the second, the "fowls of the air" are made out of the *ground*. (Gen. 2: 19.)

In the first, man is made lord of the whole earth. (Gen. 1: 28.) In the second, he is merely placed in the garden of Eden to dress it and to keep it. (Gen. 2: 8, 15.)

In the first, man and woman are created together. (Gen. 1: 28.) In the second, the beasts and birds are created *between the man and woman*. (Gen. 2: 7, 8, 15, 22.)—Bishop Colenso.

Evidence of the Vast Age of the Universe.

"I have looked *further into space than ever human being did before me*. I have observed stars, of which the light, it can be proved, must take two millions of years to reach this earth. Nay more, if those distant bodies had ceased to exist two million of years ago, we should still see them, as the light would travel after the body was gone. * * *

"The light from the nearest star requires some three years to reach the earth. From a star one thousand three hundred and forty-four times farther it would require about four thousand years, and for such a cluster as we have imagined, no less than six thousand years are needed." (Sir Wm. Herschell, "Life and Works of Sir Wm. Herschell" by Edward S. Holden.)

Sir Wm. Thomson, in Encyclopedia Britannica, article, Geology, showed from data available at the time, "that the superficial consolidation of the globe (this earth) could not have occurred less than twenty millions of years ago."

"And as any table of the earth's crust will show you there are rocks above and below the chalk, for the production of which millions heaped upon millions of years were required." (Clodd's "Childhood of Religions.")

Such eminent scientists as Sir Wm. Thomson, Helmholtz, Newcomb, Croll, Bishop, Reade, Lyell, Darwin, and others think it would have taken many millions of years for the original nebulæ to condense to the present dimensions of the sun.

PROPHECY.

"A *prophecy*, in the ordinary acceptation of the term, signifies a prediction of future events, which could not have been foreseen by human sagacity, and the knowledge of which was supernaturally communicated to the prophet. It is clear, therefore, that in order to establish the claim of anticipatory statement, promise, or denunciation, to the rank of a prophecy, four points must be ascertained with *precision*; namely, (1.) what the event was to which the alleged prediction was intended to refer; (2.) that the prediction was uttered *in specific, not vague, language* before the event; (3.) that the event took place specifically, not loosely, as predicted; (4.) and that it could not have been foreseen by human sagacity. * * *

"It is probably not too much to affirm that we have no instance in the prophetical books of the Old Testament of a prediction, in the case of which we possess, at once and combined, clear and unsuspicious proof of the date, the precise event predicted, the exact circumstances of the event, and the inability of human sagacity to foresee it.

The state of the case appears to be this: That all the Old Testament prophesies have been *assumed* to be genuine inspired predictions; and, when falsified *in their obvious meaning and received interpretation*, by the event, have received immediately a new interpretation, and been supposed to *refer to some other event*. When the result has disappointed expectation, the conclusion has been, not that the prophecy was false, but the interpretation was erroneous.

It is obvious that a mode of reasoning like this is peculiar to theological inquirers. * * *

"In justification of this idea of a double sense, he (Dr. Arnold) continues: 'The notion of a double sense in prophecy has been treated by some persons with contempt. Yet it may be said that it is almost necessarily involved in the idea of prophecy. Every prophecy has according to the very definition of the word, a double source; it has, if I may venture so to speak, two authors, the one human, the other divine. . . . If uttered by the tongue of man, it must also, unless we suppose him to be a mere instrument (in the same sense as a flute or a harp), be colored by his own mind. The prophet expresses in words certain truths conveyed to his mind; but his mind does not fully embrace them, nor can it; for how can man fully comprehend the mind of God? Every man lives in time, and belongs to time; the present must be to him clearer than the future. . . . But with God there is no past, nor future; every truth is present to him in all its extent, so that his expression, if I may so speak, differs essentially from that which can be *comprehended* by the mind, or uttered by the tongue of man. Thus every prophecy as uttered by man (that is, by an intelligent and not a mere mechanical instrument), and at the same time as inspired by God, must, so far as appears, have a double sense; one, *the sense entertained by the human mind of the writer; the other, the sense infused into it by God.*' We must confess our amazement at the obvious and extreme unsoundness of this whole passage. Not only does it painfully remind us of the double meaning so often and so justly charged upon the Pagan oracles—but it assumes the strange and contradictory improbabilities: *first*, that God was unable to convey his meaning to the mind of the prophet; *secondly*, that he infused this meaning into the words which were uttered, although he could not infuse it into the mind of the man who uttered them; and *thirdly*, that we can see further into the mind and meaning of God than those to whom he spoke; that they in expressing the ideas which he had put into their minds, mistook or imperfectly conceived those ideas,—but that to us is given to discover a thought which those words contained, but did not express, or which, if they did express it, they were not understood by the writer to express. Now, either the ideas which God wished to communicate were conveyed to the mind of the prophet, or they were not; if they were so conveyed, then the prophet must have comprehended them, and intended to express them correctly—for it is monstrous to suppose that God would infuse ideas into a man's mind for the purpose of being communicated to the public; which ideas he yet did not enable him to communicate; and then all the above confused subtleties fall to the ground. If, on the other hand, these ideas were not so conveyed to the prophet's mind, then it must have been the *words* and not the *ideas* which were inspired, and God used the prophet simply as a flute (a supposition scouted by Dr. Arnold) and we are thus driven to the equally monstrous supposition that God used words which did not convey his meaning, even to the very favored individual to whom and through whom he spoke." (Greg's "Creed of Christendom," pp. 76, 92.)

"We have already had ample proof that the Jewish writers not only did not scruple to narrate past events as if predicting future ones—to present history in the form of prophecy, but that they habitually did so. The original documents from which the books of Moses were compiled, must have been written, as we have seen in the time of the earliest kings, while the book of Deuteronomy was not composed, and the whole Pentateuch did not assume its present form till, probably, the reign of Josiah; yet they abound in such anticipatory narrative—in predictions of events long past. The instances are far too numerous to quote." (Greg's "Creed of Christendom," p. 86.)

"There is not throughout the whole Bible any word that describes to us what we call a poet, nor any word that describes what we call poetry. The case is, that the word *prophet*, to which latter times have affixed new ideas, was the Bible word for poet, and the word *prophesying* meant the art of making poetry. It also meant the art of playing poetry to a tune upon any instrument of music.

"We read of prophesying with pipes, tabrets, and horns —of prophesying with harps, with psalteries, with cymbols, and with every other instrument of music then in fashion. Were we now to speak of prophesying with a fiddle, or with a pipe and tabor, the expression would have no meaning, or would appear ridiculous, and to some people contemptuous, because we have changed the meaning of the word.

"We are told of Saul being among the *prophets*, and also that he prophesied, but we are not told what *they prophesied*, nor what *he prophesied*. The case is, there was nothing to tell; for these prophets were a company of musicians and poets, and Saul joined in the concert, and this was called prophesying."—Thomas Paine on the Prophecies.

"There is no reason to think that a prophet ever received a revelation which was not spoken directly and pointedly to his own time. (Ency. Brit. "Bible.")

"It is plain, however, that the whole work (the Pentateuch) is not the uniform production of one pen, but that in some way a variety of records of different ages, and styles have been combined to form a single narrative. Accordingly, Jewish tradition bears evidence that Moses wrote the Pentateuch, Joshua the book named after him, Samuel the book of Judges, and so forth. *As all Hebrew history is anonymous*, a sure sign that people had not yet learned to lay weight on questions of authorship, it is not probable that this tradition rests on any surer ground than conjecture." (Ency. Brit., "Bible.")

"I have now fully and fairly analyzed and exposed many of the most important prophecies or pretended prophecies of the whole Bible, I have shown that very few of them are real prophecies at all; that those which are real prophecies, very few ever have been, or ever can be fulfilled; that the very few which seem to have been fulfilled were written after the occurrence of the events claimed to be their fulfilments, and that, whether fulfilled or unfulfilled, none of these prophecies ever have been, or ever can be, of any service to the world. And thus fall all the prophetic props of priestcraft. Not one of them can bear the test of fair examination." (Kelso's "Bible Analayzed.")

MIRACLES.

"At the very outset of inquiry into the origin and true character of Christianity we are brought face to face with the supernatural. Christianity professes to be a Divine Revelation of truths which the human intellect could not otherwise have discovered. It is not a form of religion developed by the wisdom of man and appealing to his reason, but a system miraculously communicated to the human race, the central doctrines of which are either supernatural or untenable. If the truths said to be revealed were either of an ordinary character, or naturally attainable they would at once discredit the claim to divine origin. No one could maintain that a system discoverable by reason would be supernaturally communicated. The whole argument for Christianity turns upon the necessity of such a revelation, and the consequent probability that it would be made. * *

"The spontaneous offer of miraculous evidence, indeed, has always been advanced as a special characteristic of Christianity logically entitling it to acceptance in contradistinction to all other religions. 'It is an acknowledged historical fact,' says Bishop Butler, 'that Christianity offered itself to the world, and demanded to be received, upon the allegation, that is, as unbelievers would speak, upon the pretence of miracles, publicly wrought to attest the truth of it. in such an age; . . . and Christianity, including the dispensation of the Old Testament, seems distinguished by this from all other religions.'

"Having then ascertained that miracles are absolutely necessary to attest the reliability of a Divine Revelation we may proceed to examine them more closely, and for the present we shall confine ourselves to the representation of these phenomena which are in the Bible. Throughout the Old Testament the doctrine is inculcated that supernatural communications must have supernatural attestation. God is described as arming his servants with power to perform wonders, in order that they may thus be accredited as his special messengers. The Patriarchs and the people of Israel generally are represented as demanding 'a sign' of the reality of the communications said to come from God, without which, we are led to suppose, they not only would not have believed, but would have been justified in disbelieving, that the messengers actually came from him. Thus Gideon asks for a sign that the Lord talked with him.

'And the Lord said unto him, Surely I will be with thee, and thou shalt smite the Midianites as one man.'

'And he (Gideon) said unto him, If now I have found grace in thy sight, then show me a sign that thou talkest with me.' (Judges 6: 16, 17.)

"And Hezekiah demands proof of the truth of Isaiah's prophecy that he should be restored to health.

'And Hezekiah said unto Isaiah, What shall be the sign that the Lord will heal me, and that I shall go up unto the house of the Lord the third day?' (2 Kings 20: 8.)

"It is, however, unnecessary to refer to instances, for it may be affirmed that upon all occasions, miraculous evidence of an alleged divine mission is stated to have been required and accorded.

"The startling information is at the same time given, however, that miracles may be wrought to attest what is false as well as to accredit what is true. In one place, it is declared that if a prophet actually gives a sign or wonder and it comes to pass, but teaches the people on the strength of it, to follow other gods, they are not to hearken to him, and the prophet is to be put to death.

'If there arise among you a prophet, or a dreamer of dreams, and giveth thee a sign or wonder, and the sign or wonder come to pass, whereof he spake unto thee, saying, Let us go after other gods which thou hast not known, and let us serve them; thou shalt not hearken unto the words of that prophet or that dreamer of dreams.' (Deut. 13: 1. 2, 3.)

"The false miracle is here attributed to God himself.

'For the Lord your God proveth you, to know whether you love the Lord your God with all your heart and with all your soul.' (Deut. 13: 3.)

"In the book of the prophet Ezekiel the case is stated in a still stronger way, and God is represented as directly deceiving the prophet.

'And if the prophet be deceived when he hath spoken a thing, I the Lord have deceived that prophet, and I will stretch out my hand upon him, and will destroy him from the midst of my people Israel.' (Ezek. 14: 9.)

"The narrative of God's hardening Pharaoh's heart in order to bring more plagues upon the land of Egypt is in this vein. God, in fact, is represented as exerting his almighty power to deceive a man and then destroying him for being deceived. In the same spirit is the passage in which Micaiah describes the Lord as putting a lying spirit into the mouths of the prophets who incited Ahab to go to Ramothgilead. (1 Kings 22: 14-23.)

"The miracles wrought by the Egyptians sorcerers in competing with Moses were done by another power than God. We have notable instances of the belief in *signs* and *wonders* wrought by this other power. Jesus is represented as warning his disciples against false prophets, who work signs and wonders.

'Many will say to me in that day, Lord, Lord, have we not prophesied in thy name? and in thy name cast out devils? and in thy name done many wonderful works? of whom he should say, I never knew you, depart from me, ye that work iniquity.' (Mat. 7: 22, 23.)

And again in another place:

'For false prophets shall arise, and shall work signs and wonders, to seduce, if it were possible, the elect.' (Mark 13: 22.)

Also, when the Pharisees accuse him of casting out devils by Beelzebub, the prince of the devils, Jesus asks: 'By whom do your children cast them out?' a reply which would lose all its point if they were not admitted to be able to cast out devils. In another passage John is described as saying: 'Master, we saw one casting out devils in thy name, who followeth not us, and we forbade him.' Without multiplying instances, however, there can be no doubt of the fact that the reality of false miracles and lying wonders is admitted in the Bible. The obvious deduction from this representation of miracles is that the source and purpose of such supernatural phenomena must always be exceedingly uncertain. Their evidential value is, therefore, profoundly affected, 'it being,' as Dr. Newman has said of ambiguous miracles, 'antecedently improbable that the Almighty should rest the credit of his Revelation upon events which but obscurely implied his immediate presence.' As it is affirmed that other supernatural beings exist, as well as an assumed personal God, by whose agency miracles are performed, it is impossible to argue with reason that such phenomena are at any time especially due to the intervention of the Deity. Dr. Newman recognizes this, but passes over the difficulty with masterly lightness of touch. After advancing the singular argument that our knowledge of spirits is only derived from scripture, and that their existence cannot be deduced from nature, whilst he asserts that the being of a God—a personal God be it remembered—can be so discovered, and that, therefore, miracles can only properly be attributed to him, he proceeds: 'Still it may be necessary to show that on our own principles we are not open to inconsistency. That is, it has been questioned whether, in admitting the existence and power of the spirits on the authority of Revelation, we are not in danger of invalidating the evidence upon which that authority rests.

For the cogency of the argument for miracles depends on the assumption, that interruptions in the course of nature must ultimately proceed from God; which is not true, if they may be effected by other beings without his sanction. And it must be conceded, that, explicit as scripture is in considering miracles as signs of divine agency, it still does seem to give created spirits some power of working them; and even, in its most literal sense, intimates the possibility of their working them in opposition to the true doctrine (Deut. 13: 1–3; Mat. 24: 24; 2 Thes. 2: 9-11).' (Dr. Newman's Two Essays on Miracles, p. 31.)

"Dr. Newman repudiates the attempts of various writers to overcome this difficulty by making a distinction between great miracles and small, many miracles and few, or by referring to the nature of the doctrine attested in order to determine the author of the miracles, or by denying the power of spirits altogether, and explaining away scripture statements of demoniacal possession and the narrative of the Lord's temptation 'Without having recourse to any of these dangerous modes of answering the objection,' he says, 'it may be sufficient to reply, that, since, agreeably to the antecedent sentiment of reason, God has adopted miracles as the seal of a divine message, we believe he will never suffer them to be so counterfeited as to deceive the humble inquirer.' (Ibid. p. 51.)

"This is the only reply which even so powerful a reasoner as Dr. Newman can give to an objection based on distinct statements of scripture itself. He cannot deny the validity of the objection, he can only hope or believe in spite of it. Personal belief independent of evidence is the most common and the weakest of arguments; at best it is prejudice masked in the garb of reason. It is perfectly clear that miracles being thus acknowledged to be common both to God and to other spirits they cannot be considered a distinctive attestation of divine intervention; and as Spinoza finely argued, not even the mere existence of God, can be inferred from them; for as a miracle is a limited act and never expressed more than certain and limited power, it is certain that we cannot from such an effect, conclude even the existence of a cause whose power is infinite.

"This dual character obviously leads to many difficulties in defining the evidential function and force of miracles, and we may best appreciate the dilemma which is involved by continuing to follow the statements and arguments of divines themselves. To the question whether miracles are absolutely to command the obedience of those in whose sight they are performed, and whether upon their attestation, the doer and his doctrine are to be accepted as of God, Archbishop French unhesitatingly replies: 'It cannot be so, for side by side with the miracles which serve for the furthering of the kingdom of God runs another line of wonders, the counter-workings of him who is ever the ape of the Most High.' (Dr. French's 'Notes on the Miracles of Our Lord.') Eighth ed., p. 22.

"'This fact,' he says, 'that the kingdom of lies has its wonders no less than the kingdom of truth, is in itself sufficient evidence that miracles cannot be appealed to absolutely and finally, in proof of the doctrine which the worker of them proclaims.'

"This being the case, it is important to discover how miracles perform their function as the indispensible evidence for a Divine Revelation, for with this disability they do not seem to possess much potentiality. Archbishop French, then offers the following definition of the function of miracles: 'A miracle does not prove the truth of a doctrine or the divine mission of him that brings it to pass. That which alone it claims for him at the first is a right to be listened to; it puts him in the alternative of being from heaven or from hell. The doctrine must first commend itself to the conscience as being *good*, and only then can the miracle seal it as *divine*.' But the first appeal is from the doctrine to the conscience, to the moral nature of man. Under certain circumstances, he maintains their evidence is utterly to be rejected. 'But the purpose of the miracle' he says, 'being as we have seen, to confirm that which is good, so, upon the other hand, where conscience and mind witness against the doctrine, not all the miracles in the world have a right to demand submission to the word which they seal. On the contrary, the great act of faith is to believe, against, and in despite of them all, in what God has revealed to, and implanted in the soul of the holy and the true; not to believe another gospel, though an angel from heaven, or one transformed into such should bring it (Deut. 13: 3; Gal. 1: 8); and instead of compelling assent, miracles are then rather warnings to us that we keep aloof, for they tell us that not merely lies are here, for to that the conscience bore witness already, but that he who utters them is more than a common deceiver, is eminently a liar and anti-Christ, a false prophet; standing in more immediate connection than other deceived and evil men to the kingdom of darkness, so that Satan has given him his power (Rev. 13: 2); is using him to be an especial organ of his, and to do a special work for him.' And he lays down the distinct principle that: 'The miracle must witness for itself, and then, and then only, the first is capable of witnessing for the second.'

"These opinions are not peculiar to the Archbishop of Dublin, but are generally held by divines, although Dr. French expresses them with unusual absence of reserve. Dr. Mozley emphatically affirms the same doctrine when he says: 'A miracle cannot oblige us to accept any doctrine which is contrary to our moral nature or a fundamental principle of religion.' Dr. Mansel speaks to the same effect: 'If a teacher claiming to work miracles proclaims doctrines contrary to previously established truths, whether to the conclusions of natural religion or to the teaching of a former revelation, such a contradiction is allowed even by the most zealous defenders of the evidential value of miracles, to invalidate the authority of the teacher. But the right conclusion from this admission is not that true miracles are invalid as evidences, but that the supposed miracles in this case are not true miracles at all; that is, are not the effects of divine power, but of human deception or of some other agency.' A passage from a letter written by Dr. Arnold, which is quoted by Dr. French in support of his views, both illustrates the doctrine and the necessity which has led to its adoption. 'You complain,' says Dr. Arnold, writing to Dr. Hawkins, 'of those persons who judge of a revelation not by its evidence, but by its substance. It has always seemed to me that its substance is a most essential part of its evidence; and that miracles wrought in favor of what was foolish or wicked would only prove Manicheism. We are so perfectly ignorant of the unseen world, that the character of any supernatural power can only be judged by the moral character of the statements which it sanctions. Thus only can we tell whether it be a revelation from God or from the Devil.' In another place Dr. Arnold declares: 'Miracles must not be allowed to overrule the gospel; for it is only through our belief in the gospel that we accord our belief in them.'

"It is obvious that the mutual dependence which is thus established between miracles and the doctrines in connection with which they are wrought destroys the evidential force of miracles, and that the first and final appeal is made to reason. The doctrine in fact proves the miracles instead of the miracle attesting the doctrine. Divines, of course, attempt to deny this, but no other deduction from their own statements is logically possible. Miracles according to scripture itself, are producible by various supernatural beings and may be satanic as well as divine: man on the other hand, is so ignorant of the unseen world that avowedly, he cannot, from the miracle itself, determine the agent by whom it was performed; the miracle, therefore, has no intrinsic evidential value. How, then, according to divines, does it attain any potentiality? Only through a favorable decision on the part of reason on the 'moral nature of man' regarding the character of the doctrine. The result of the appeal to reason respecting the morality and credibility of the doctrine determines the evidential status of the miracle. The doctrine therefore, is the real criterion of the miracle which, without it, is necessarily an object of doubt and suspicion.

We have already casually referred to Dr. Newman's view of such a relation between miracle and doctrine, but may here more fully quote his suggestive remarks. 'Others by referring to the nature of the doctrine attested,' he says, 'in order to determine the author of the miracle, have exposed themselves to the plausible charge of adducing, first the miracle to attest the divinity of the doctrine, and then the doctrine to prove the divinity of the miracle.' This argument he characterizes as one of the 'dangerous modes' of removing a difficulty, although he does not himself point out a safer, and in a note, he adds: 'There is an appearance of doing honor to the Christian doctrines in representing them as *intrinsically* credible, which leads many into supporting opinions which, carried to their full extent, supercede the need of miracles altogether. It must be recollected, too, that they who are allowed to praise have the privilege of finding fault, and may reject, according to their *a priori* notions, as well as receive. Doubtless the divinity of a clearly immoral doctrine could not be evidenced by miracles; for our belief in the moral attributes of God, is much stronger than our conviction of the negative proposition, that none but he can interfere with the system of nature. But there is always the danger of extending this admission beyond its proper limits, of supposing ourselves judges of the *tendency* of doctrines; and because, unassisted reason informs us what is moral and immoral in our own case, of attempting to decide on the abstract morality of actions. . . . These remarks are in nowise inconsistent with using (as was done in a former section) our actual knowledge of God's attributes, obtained from a survey of nature and human affairs, in determining the probability of certain professed miracles having proceeded from him. It is one thing to infer from the experience of life another to imagine the character of God from the gratuitous conceptions of our own minds.' Although Dr. Newman apparently fails to perceive that he himself thus makes reason the criterion of miracles and therefore incurs the condemnation with which our quotation opens, the very indicision of his argument illustrates the dilemma in which divines are placed. Dr. Mozley, however, still more directly condemns the principle we are discussing, that the doctrine must be the criterion of the miracle, although he also, as we have seen elsewhere, substantially affirms it. He says: 'The position that the revelation proves the miracle, and not the miracles the revelation, admits of a good qualified meaning; but taken literally, it is a double offense against the rule, that things are properly proved by the proper proof of them; for a supernatural fact *is* the proper proof of supernatural doctrine, while a supernatural doctrine on the other hand is certainly *not* a proper proof of a supernatural fact.'

"This statement is obviously true, but it is equally undeniable that, their origin being uncertain, miracles have no evidential force. How far then, we may inquire in order thoroughly to understand the position, can doctrines prove the reality of miracles or determine the agency by which they are performed? In the case of moral truths within the limits of reason, it is evident that doctrines, which are in accordance with our idea of what is good and right do not require miraculous evidence at all. They can secure acceptance by their own merits alone. At the same time it is universally admitted that the truth or goodness of a doctrine could not attest the divine origin of a miracle. Such truths, however, have no proper connection with revelation at all. '*These* truths,' to quote the words of Bishop Atterbury, 'were of themselves sufficiently obvious and plain, and needed not a divine testimony to make them plainer. But the truths which are necessary in this manner to be attested, are those which are of positive institution; those which if God had not pleased to reveal them, human reason could not have discovered; and those, which, even now, they are revealed, human reason cannot fully account for, and perfectly comprehend.' How is it possible then that reason, or the 'moral nature of man' can approve as good, or appreciate the fitness of, doctrines which in their very nature are beyond the criterion of reason. What reply, for instance, can reason give to any appeal to it regarding the doctrine of the trinity or of the incarnation? If doctrines, the truth and goodness of which are apparent, do not afford any evidence of divine revelation, how can doctrines which reason can neither discover nor comprehend attest the divine origin of miracles? Dr. Mozley clearly recognizes that they cannot do so. 'The proof of a revelation,' he says, and we may add, the proof of a miracle—itself a species of revelation— 'which is contained in the substance of a revelation has this inherent check or limit in it; namely: that it cannot reach to what is undiscoverable by reason.' 'Internal evidence is itself an appeal to reason, because at every step the test is our own appreciation of such and such an idea or doctrine, our own perception of its fitness; but human reason cannot in the nature of the case prove that which, by the very hypotheses, lies beyond reason.' It naturally follows that no doctrine which lies beyond reason, and therefore requires the attestation of miracles, can possibly afford that indication of the source and reality of miracles which is necessary to endow them with evidential value, and the supernatural doctrine must, therefore, be rejected in the absence of miraculous evidence of a decisive character.

"Canon Mozley labors earnestly, but unsuccessfully, to restore to miracles as evidence some part of that potentiality of which these unfortunate limitations have deprived them. 'Whilst on the one hand' he says, 'we must admit indeed an inherent modification in the function of a miracle as an instrument of proof,' he argues that this is only a limitation, and no disproof of it, and he contends that: 'The evidence of miracles is not negatived because it has conditions.' His reasoning, however, is purely apologetic, and attempts by the unreal analogy of supposed limitations of natural principles and evidence to excuse the disqualifying limitations of the supernatural. He is quite conscious of the serious difficulty of the position: 'The question' he says, 'may at first sight create a dilemma.—If a miracle is nugatory on the side of one doctrine, what cogency has it on the side of another? Is it legitimate to accept its evidence when we please and reject it when we please?' The only reply he seems able to give to these very pertinent questions is the remark which immediately follows them: 'But in truth a miracle is never without an argumentative force, although that force may be counterbalanced.' In other words, a miracle is always an argument, although it is often a bad one. It is scarcely necessary to go to the supernatural for bad arguments.

"It might naturally be expected that the miraculous evidence selected to accredit a divine revelation should possess certain unique and marked characteristics. It must at least, be clearly distinctive of divine power and exclusively associated with divine truth. It is inconceivable that the Deity, deigning thus to attest the reality of a communication from himself of truths beyond the criterion of reason, should not make the evidence simple and complete, because the doctrines proper to such a revelation, not being appreciable from internal evidence, it is obvious that the external testimony for them,—if it is to be of any use—must be unmistakable and decisive. The evidence which is actually produced, however, so far from satisfying these legitimate anticipations, lacks every one of the qualifications which reason antecedently declares necessary. Miracles are not distinctive of divine power but are common to Satan, and they are admitted to be performed in support of falsehood as well as in the service of truth. They bear, indeed, so little upon them the impress of their origin and true character, that they are dependent for their recognition upon our judgment of the very doctrines to attest which they are said to have been designed.

"Even taking the representation of miracles, therefore, which divines themselves give, they are utterly incompetent to perform their contemplated functions. If they are superhuman they are not supersatanic, and there is no sense in which they can be considered miraculously evidential of anything. To argue as theologians do, that the ambiguity of their testimony is intended as a trial of our faith is absurd, for reason being unable to judge of the nature either of supernatural fact or of supernatural doctrine it would be mere folly and injustice to subject to such a test beings avowedly incapable of sustaining it. Whilst it is absolutely necessary, then, that a divine revelation should be attested by miraculous evidence to justify our believing it the testimony so called seems in all respects unworthy of the name, and presents anomalies much more suggestive of human invention than divine orignality. We are, in fact, prepared by the scriptural accountof miracles to expect that further examination will supply an explanation of such phenomena which will wholly remove them from the region of the supernatural.

"We have seen that a divine revelation is such only by virtue of communicating to us something which we could not know without it, and which is in fact undiscoverable by human reason; and that miraculous evidence is absolutely requisite to establish its reality. It is admitted that no other testimony could justify our believing the specific revelation which we are considering, the very substance of which is supernatural and beyond the criterion of reason, and that its astounding announcements, if not demonstrated to be miraculous truths, must inevitably be pronounced 'the wildest delusions.' On examining the supposed miraculous evidence, however, we find that not only is it upon general grounds antecedently incredible, but that the testimony by which its realty is supported, so far from establishing the inferences drawn from the supposed supernatural phenomena, is totally insufficient even to certify the actual occurrence of the events narrated.

"Even if the reality of miracles could be substantiated, their value as evidence for the divine revelation is destroyed by the necessary admission that miracles are not limited to one source, but that there are miracles satanic which are to be disbelieved, as well as divine and evidential ones to be believed.

"Similar miracles to those which are supposed to attest it are reported long antecedent to the promulgation of Christianity, and continued to be performed for centuries after it.

"A stream of miraculous pretension, in fact, has flowed through all human history, deep and broad as it has passed through the darker ages, but dwindling down to a thread as it has entered days of enlightenment.

"The true character of miracles is at once betrayed by the fact that their supposed occurrence has been confined to ages of ignorance and superstition, and that they are absolutely unknown in any time or place where science has provided witnesses fitted to appreciate and ascertain the nature of such exhibitions of supernatural power.

"There is no uncertainty as to the origin of belief in supernatural interference with nature. The assertion that spurious miracles have sprung up round a few instances of genuine miraculous power has not a single valid argument to support it.

"When we turn from more general arguments to examine the documentary evidence for the reality of the supposed miraculous occurrences, and of the divine revelation which they accredit, we meet with the characteristics which might have been expected. We do not find any trace even of the existence of our gospels for a century and a half after the events they record. They are anonymous narratives, and there is no evidence of any value connecting these works with the writers to whom they are popularly attributed. The miraculous evidence upon which alone, it is admitted, we could be justified in believing its astounding doctrines being thus nugatory, the claims of Christianity to be considered a divine revelation must necessarily be disallowed, and its supernatural elements, which are, in fact, the very substance of the system, inevitably sharing the same fate as the supposed miraculous evidence, must, therefore, be rejected as incredible and opposed to reason and complete induction." ("Supernatural Religion," p. 698.)

"A miracle as evidence can establish no fact, for the reason that the miracle does not exist. The miracle itself must be attested. As we have no evidence of miracles, we are not called on to believe them, but to believe the story which relates them. 'But the miracle is above and beyond reason.' To this we reply: It is absurd to assume what is beyond reason, to account for what is opposed to reason." (Ibid.)

David Hume's Argument on Miracles.

"A miracle is a violation of the laws of nature; and as a firm and unalterable experience has established these laws, the proof against a miracle, from the very nature of the fact, is as entire as any argument from experience can possibly be imagined. Why is it more than probable that all men must die; that lead cannot of itself remain suspended in the air; that fire consumes wood, and is extinguished by water; unless it be that these events are found agreeable to the laws of nature, and there is required a violation of these laws, or, in other words, a miracle, to prevent them? Nothing is esteemed a miracle if it ever happen in the common course of nature. It is no miracle that a man seemingly in good health should die suddenly; because such a kind of death, though more unusual than any other, has yet been frequently observed to happen. But it is a miracle that a dead man should come to life; because that has never been observed in any age or country. There must, therefore, be a uniform experience against every miraculous event, otherwise the event would not merit that appellation. And as a uniform experience amounts to a proof there is here a direct and full *proof*, from the nature of the fact, against the existence of any miracle; nor can such a proof be destroyed or the miracle rendered credible but by an opposite proof which is superior. (2.)

The plain consequence is (and it is a general maxim worthy of our attention), 'that no testimony is sufficient to establish a miracle, unless the testimony be of such a kind that its falsehood would be more miraculous than the fact which it endeavors to establish; and even in that case there is a mutual destruction of arguments, and the superior only gives us an assurance suitable to that degree of force which remains after deducting the inferior.' When any one tells me that he saw a dead man restored to life, I immediately consider with myself whether it be more probable that this person should either deceive or be deceived, or that the fact which he relates should really have happened. I weigh the one miracle against the other, and according to the superiority which I discover I pronounce my decision, and always reject the greater miracle. If the falsehood of his testimony would be more miraculous than the event which he relates, then, and not till then, can he pretend to command my belief or opinion.

"In the foregoing reasoning we have supposed that the testimony upon which a miracle is founded may possibly amount to an entire proof, and that the falsehood of that testimony would be a real prodigy; but it is easy to show that we have been a great deal too liberal in our concession, and that there never was a miraculous event established on so full an evidence.

"For, *first*, there is not to be found, in all history, any miracle attested by a sufficient number of men of such unquestioned good sense, education, and learning, as to secure us against all delusion in themselves; of such undoubted integrity as to place them beyond all suspicion of any design to deceive others; of such credit and reputation in the eyes of mankind as to have a great deal to lose in case of their being detected in any falsehood; and, at the same time, attesting facts performed in such a public manner, and in so celebrated a part of the world, as to render the detection unavoidable; all which circumstances are requisite to give us a full assurance in the testimony of men.

"*Secondly.* We may observe in human nature a principle which, if strictly examined, will be found to diminish extremely the assurance which we might, from human testimony, have in any kind of prodigy. The maxim by which we commonly conduct ourselves in our reasonings is, that the objects of which we have no experience resemble those of which we have; that what we have found to be most usual is always most profitable, and that where there is an opposition of argument we ought to give the preference to such as are founded on the greatest number of past observations; but though, in proceeding by this rule, we readily reject any fact which is unusual and incredible in an ordinary degree, yet in advancing further the mind observes not always the same rule, but when anything is affirmed utterly absurd and miraculous it rather the more readily admits of such a fact, upon account of that very circumstance which ought to destroy all its authority. The passion of *surprise* and *wonder* arising from miracles, being an agreeable emotion, gives a sensible tendency toward the belief of those events from which it is derived. And this goes so far, that even those who can not enjoy this pleasure immediately, nor can believe those miraculous events of which they are informed, yet love to partake of the satisfaction at secondhand or by rebound, and take pride and delight in exciting the admiration of others.

"With what greediness are the miraculous accounts of travelers received, their descriptions of sea and land monsters, their relations of wonderful adventures, strange men and uncouth manners! But if the spirit of religion joins itself to the love of wonder, there is an end of common sense, and human testimony, in these circumstances, loses all pretensions to authority. A religionist may be an enthusiast, and imagine he sees what has no reality; he may know his narrative to be false, and yet persevere in it with the best intentions in the world, for the sake of promoting so holy a cause; or even where this delusion has not place, vanity, excited by so strong a temptation, operates on him more powerfully than on the rest of mankind in any other circumstances, and self-interest with equal force. His auditors may not have, and commonly have not, sufficient judgment to canvass his evidence; what judgment they have, they renounce by principle, in these sublime and mysterious subjects; or if they were ever so willing to employ it, passion and a heated imagination disturb the regularity of its operations. Their credulity increases his impudence, and his impudence overpowers their credulity.

"Eloquence, when at its highest pitch, leaves little room for reason or reflection, but, addressing itself entirely to the fancy or the affections, captivates the willing hearers and subdues their understanding. Happily, this pitch it seldom attains. But what a Tully or a Demosthenes could scarcely effect over a Roman or Athenian audience, every Capuchin, every itinerant or stationary teacher, can perform over the generality of mankind, and in a higher degree, by touching such gross and vulgar passions.

"The many instances of forged miracles and prophecies, and supernatural events, which in all ages have either been detected by contrary evidence or which detect themselves by their absurdity, prove sufficiently the strong propensity of mankind to the extraordinary and the marvelous, and ought reasonably to beget a suspicion against all relations of this kind. This is our natural way of thinking, even with regard to the most common and most credible events. For instance, there is no kind of report which rises so easily and spreads so quickly, especially in country places and provincial towns, as those concerning marriages: insomuch that two young persons of equal condition never see each other twice but the whole neighborhood immediately join them together. The pleasure of telling a piece of news so interesting, of propagating it, and of being the first reporters of it, spreads the intelligence. And this is so well known that no man of sense gives attention to these reports till he finds them confirmed by some greater evidence. Do not the same passions, and others still stronger, incline the generality of mankind to believe and report, with the greatest vehemence and assurance, all religious miracles?

"*Thirdly.* It forms a strong presumption against all supernatural and miraculous relations that they are observed chiefly to abound among ignorant and barbarous nations; or if a civilized people has ever given admission to any of them, that people will be found to have received them from ignorant and barbarous ancestors, who transmitted them with that inviolable sanction and authority which always attend received opinions. When we peruse the first histories of all nations, we are apt to imagine ourselves transported into some new world, where the whole frame of nature is disjointed, and every element performs its operations in a different manner from what it does at present. Battles, revolutions, pestilence, famine, and death, are never the effect of those natural causes which we experience. Prodigies, omens, oracles, judgments, quite obscure the few natural events that are intermingled with them. But as the former grow thinner every page, in proportion as we advance nearer the enlightened ages, we soon learn that there is nothing mysterious or supernatural in the case, but that all proceeds from the usual propensity of mankind toward the marvelous; and that though this inclination may at intervals receive a check from sense and learning, it can never be thoroughly extirpated from human nature.

"*It is strange*, a judicious reader is apt to say upon the perusal of those wonderful historians, that such *prodigious* events never happen in *our* days. But it is nothing strange, I hope, that men should lie in all ages. You must surely have seen instances enough of that frailty. You have yourself heard many such marvelous relations started, which, being treated with scorn by all the wise and judicious, have at least been abandoned even by the vulgar. Be assured that those renowned lies, which have spread and flourished to such a monstrous height, arose from like beginnings; but being sown in a more proper soil, shot up at last into prodigies almost equal to those which they relate.

"It was a wise policy in that false prophet Alexander, who, though now forgotten, was once so famous, to lay the first scene of his impostures in Paphlagonia, where, as Lucian tells us, the people were extremely ignorant and stupid, and ready to swallow even the grossest delusion. People at a distance who are weak enough to think the matter at all worth inquiry have no opportunity of receiving better information. The stories come magnified to them by a hundred circumstances. Fools are industrious in propagating the imposture; while the wise and learned are contented, in general, to deride its absurdity, without informing themselves of the particular facts by which it may be distinctly refuted. And thus the imposture above mentioned was enabled to proceed, from his ignorant Paphlagonians, to the enlisting of votaries even among the Grecian philosophers and men of the most eminent rank and distinction in Rome; nay, could engage the attention of that sage emperor Marcus Aurelius, so far as to make him trust the success of a military expedition to his delusive prophecies.

"The advantages are so great of starting an imposture among an ignorant people that, even though the delusion should be too gross to impose on the generality of them, which, though *seldom*, is *sometimes* the case, it has a much better chance for succeeding in remote countries than if the first scene had been laid in a city renowned for arts and knowledge. The most ignorant and barbarous of these barbarians carry the report abroad. None of their countrymen have a large correspondence of sufficient credit and authority to contradict and beat down the delusion. Men's inclination to the marvelous has full opportunity to display itself. And thus a story, which is universally exploded in the place where it was first started, will pass for certain at a thousand miles distant. But had Alexander fixed his residence at Athens, the philosophers of that renowned mart of learning would have spread, throughout the whole Roman empire, their sense of the matter; which, being supported by so great an authority, and displayed by all the force of reason and eloquence, would have entirely opened the eyes of mankind. It is true Lucian, passing by chance through Paphlagonia, had an opportunity of performing this good office. But though much to be wished, it does not always happen that every Alexander meets with a Lucian ready to expose and detect his impostures.

"I may add as a *fourth* reason which diminishes the authority of prodigies, that there is no testimony for any, even those which have not been expressly detected, that is, not opposed by any infinite number of witnesses; so that not only the miracle destroys the credit of testimony, but the testimony destroys itself. To make this the better understood, let us consider that in matters of religion, whatever is different is contrary; and it is impossible that the religions of ancient Rome, of Turkey, of Siam, and of China, should all of them be established on any solid foundation. Every miracle, therefore, pretended to have been wrought in any of those religions (and all of them abound in miracles), as its direct scope is to establish the particular system to which it is attributed, so has it the same force, though more indirectly, to overthrow every other system. In destroying a rival system, it likewise destroys the credit of those miracles on which that system was established; so that all the prodigies of different religions are to be regarded as contrary facts; and the evidences of these prodigies, whether weak or strong, as opposite to each other. According to this method of reasoning, when we believe any miracle of Mahomet or his successors, we have for our warrant the testimony of a few barbarous Arabians: and on the other hand, we are to regard the authority of Titus, Livius, Plutarch, Tacitus, and, in short, of all the authors and witnesses—Grecian, Chinese, and Roman Catholic, who have related any miracle in their particular religion; I say we are to regard their testimony in the same light as if they had mentioned that Mahometan miracle, and had in express terms contradicted it, with the same certainty as they have for the miracle they relate. This argument may appear over subtile and refined; but is not in reality different from the reasoning of a judge who supposes that the credit of two witnesses, maintaining a crime against any one is destroyed by the testimony of two others who affirm him to have been two hundred leagues distant at the same instant when the crime is said to have been committed.

"One of the best-attested miracles in all profane history is that which Tacitus reports of Vespasian, who cured a blind man in Alexandria by means of his spittle, and a lame man by the mere touch of his foot, in obedience to a vision of the god *Serapis*, who had enjoined them to have recourse to the emperor for these miraculous cures. The story may be seen in the works of that historian (Hist. lib. v. cap. 8. Suetonius gives nearly the same account in Vitia Vesp.), where every circumstance seems to add weight to the testimony, and might be displayed at large with all the force of argument and eloquence, if any one were now concerned to enforce the evidence of that exploded and idolatrous superstition: The gravity, solidity, age, and probity of so great an emperor, who, through the whole course of his life conversed in a familiar manner with his friends and courtiers, and never affected those extraordinary airs of divinity assumed by Alexander and Demetrius. The historian, a contemporary writer, noted for candor and veracity, and, withal, the greatest and most penetrating genius perhaps of all antiquity, and so free from any tendency to credulity that he even lies under the contrary imputation of Atheism and profaneness. The persons from whose authority he related the miracle, of established character for judgment and veracity, as we may well presume; eye witnesses of the fact, and confirming their testimony after the *Flavian* family was despoiled of the empire, and could no longer give any reward as the price of a lie. *Utrumque, qui interfuere, nunc quoque memorant, postquam nullum, mendacio pretium.* To which if we add the public nature of the facts as related, it will appear that no evidence can well be supposed stronger for so gross and palpable a falsehood.

"There is also a memorable story related by Cardinal de Retz, which may well deserve our consideration. When that intriguing politician fled into Spain to avoid the persecution of his enemies, he passed through Saragossa, the capital of Arragon, where he was shown, in the cathedral, a man who had served seven years as a doorkeeper, and was well known to everybody in town that had ever paid his devotions at that church. He had been seen, for so long a time, wanting a leg; but recovered that limb by the rubbing of holy oil upon the stump; and the cardinal assures us that he saw him with two legs. This miracle was vouched by all the canons of the church; and the whole company in town were appealed to for a confirmation of the fact; whom the cardinal found by their zealous devotion, to be thorough believers of the miracle. Here the relater was also contemporary to the supposed prodigy, of an incredulous and libertine character, as well as of great genius, the miracle of so *singular* a nature as could scarcely admit of a counterfeit, and the witnesses very numerous, and all of them, in a manner spectators, of the fact to which they gave their testimony. And what adds mightily to the force of the evidence, and may double our surprise on this occasion, is that the cardinal himself, who relates the story, seems not to give any credit to it, and consequently can not be suspected of any concurrence in the holy fraud. He considered, justly, that it was not requsite, in order to reject a fact of this nature, to be able accurately to disprove the testimony, and to trace its falsehood through all the circumstances of knavery and credulity which produced it. He knew that as this was commonly altogether impossible at any small distance of time and place, so was it extremely difficult, even where one was immediately present, by reason of the bigotry, ignorance, cunning, and roguery of a great part of mankind. He therefore concluded, like a just reasoner, that such an evidence carried falsehood upon the very face of it, and that a miracle supported by any human testimony was more properly a subject of derision than of argument.

"There surely never was a greater number of miracles ascribed to one person than those which were lately said to have been wrought in France upon the tomb of Abbe *Paris*, the famous Jansenist, with whose sanctity the people were so long deluded. The curing of the sick, giving hearing to the deaf, and sight to the blind, were everywhere talked of as the usual effects of that holy sepulcher. But, what is more extraordinary, many of the miracles were immediately proved upon the spot, before judges of unquestioned integrity, attested by witnesses of credit and distinction, in a learned age, and on the most eminent theater that is now in the world. Nor is this all: a relation of them was published and dispersed everywhere; nor were the Jesuits, though a learned body, supported by the civil magistrate, and determined enemies to those opinions in whose favor the miracles were said to have been wrought, ever able distinctly to refute or detect them. (3.) Where shall we find such a number of circumstances agreeing to the corroboration of one fact? And what have we to oppose to such a cloud of witnesses but the absolute impossibility or miraculous nature of the events which they relate? And this, surely, in the eyes of all reasonable people, will alone be regarded as a sufficient refutation.

"Is the consequence just, because some human testimony has the utmost force and authority in some cases —when it relates the battle of Phillipi or Pharsalia, for instance—that therefore all kinds of testimony must, in all cases, have equal force and authority? Suppose that the Cæsarean and Pompeian factions had, each of them, claimed the victory in these battles, and that the historians of each party had uniformly ascribed the advantage to their own sides; how could mankind, at this distance, have been able to determine between them? The contrariety is equally strong between the miracles related by Herodotus or Plutarch, and those delivered by Mariana, Bede, or any monkish historian.

"The wise lend a very academic faith to every report which favors the passion of the reporter, whether it magnifies his country, his family, or himself, or in any other way strikes in with his natural inclinations and propensities. But what greater temptation than to appear a missionary, a prophet, an embassador from heaven. Who would not encounter many dangers and difficulties in order to obtain so sublime a character. Or if, by the help of vanity and a heated imagination, a man has first made a convert of himself and entered seriously into the delusion, who ever scruples to make use of pious frauds in support of so holy and meritorious a cause.

"The smallest spark may here kindle into the greatest flame: because the materials are always prepared for it. The *avidum genus auricularum* (Lucrtius)—the gazing populace receive greedily, without examination, whatever soothes superstition and promotes wonder.

"How many stories of this nature have, in all ages, been detected and exploded in their infancy. How many more have been celebrated for a time and have afterward sunk into neglect and oblivion. Where such reports, therefore, fly about, the solution of the phenomenon is obvious; and we judge in conformity to regular experience and observation when we account for it by the known and natural principles of credulity and delusion. And shall we, rather than have recourse to so natural a solution, allow of a miraculous violation of the most established laws of nature?

"I need not mention the difficulty of detecting a falsehood in any private or even public history at the place where it is said to happen; much more when the scene is removed to ever so small a distance. Even a court of judicature, with all the authority, accuracy, and judgment which they can employ, find themselves often at a loss to distinguish between truth and falsehood in the most recent actions. But the matter never comes to any issue if trusted to the common method of altercation and debate and flying rumors, especially when men's passions have taken part on either side.

"In the infancy of new religions the wise and learned commonly esteem the matter too inconsiderable to deserve their attention or regard. And when afterward they would willingly detect the cheat, in order to undeceive the deluded multitude, the season is now past, and the records and witnesses which might clear up the matter have perished beyond recovery.

"No means of detection remain but those which must be drawn from the very testimony itself of the reporters; and these, though always sufficient with the judicious and knowing, are commonly too fine to fall under the comprehension of the vulgar.

"Upon the whole, then, it appears that no testimony for any kind of miracle has ever amounted to a probability, much less to a proof; and that even supposing it amounted to a proof, it would be opposed by another proof, derived from the very nature of the fact which it would endeavor to establish. It is experience only which gives authority to human testimony; and it is the same experience which assures us of the laws of nature. When, therefore, these two kinds of experience are contrary, we have nothing to do but subtract the one from the other, and embrace an opinion, either on one side or the other, with that assurance which arises from the remainder. But according to the principle here explained, this subtraction, with regard to all popular religions, amounts to an entire annihilation; and therefore we may establish it as a maxim, that no human testimony can have such force as to prove a miracle, and make it a just foundation for any such system of religion.

"I beg the limitations here made may be remarked when I say that a miracle can never be proved, so as to be the foundation of a system of religion. For I own that, otherwise, there may possibly be miracles or violations of the usual course of nature, of such a kind as to admit of proof from human testimony; though perhaps it will be impossible to find any such in all the records of history. Thus, suppose all authors, in all languages, agree that from the first of January, 1600, there was a total darkness over the whole earth for eight days; suppose that the tradition of this extraordinary event is still strong and lively among the people; that all travelers who return from foreign countries bring us accounts of the same tradition, without the least variation or contradiction—it is evident that our present philosophers, instead of doubting the fact, ought to receive it as certain, and ought to search for the causes whence it might be derived. The decay, corruption, and dissolution of nature is an event rendered probable by so many analogies, that any phenomenon which seems to have a tendency toward that catastrophe comes within the reach of human testimony, if that testimony be very extensive and uniform.

"But suppose that all the historians who England treat of should agree that on the first day of January, 1600, Queen Elizabeth died; that both before and after her death she was seen by her physicians and the whole court, as is usual with persons of her rank; that her successor was acknowledged and proclaimed by the parliament; and that after being interred a month she again appeared, resumed the throne, and governed England for three years—I must confess that I should be surprised at the concurrence of so many odd circumstances, but should not have the least inclination to believe so miraculous an event. I should not doubt of her pretended death, and of those other public circumstances that followed it; I should only assert it to have been pretended, and that it neither was nor possibly could be real. You would in vain object to me the difficulty, and almost impossibility, of deceiving the world in an affair of such consequence. The wisdom and solid judgment of that renowned queen, with the little or no advantage she could reap from so poor an artifice—all this might astonish me; but I would still reply that the knavery and folly of men are such common phenomena, that I should rather believe the most extraordinary events to arise from their concurrence than admit of so signal a violation of the laws of nature.

"But should this miracle be ascribed to any new system of religion, men in all ages have been so much imposed on by ridiculous stories of that kind that this very circumstance would be a full proof of a cheat, and sufficient with all men of sense not only to make them reject the fact, but even reject it without further examination. Though the being to whom the miracle is ascribed be in this case Almighty, it does not upon that account become a whit more probable, since it is impossible for us to know the attributes or actions of such a being otherwise than from the experience which we have of his productions in the usual course of nature. This still reduces us to past observation, and obliges us to compare the instances of the violation of truth in the testimony of men with those of the violation of the laws of nature by miracles, in order to judge which of them is most likely and probable. As the violations of truth are more common in the testimony concerning religious miracles than in that concerning any other matter of fact, this must diminish very much the authority of the former testimony, and make us form a general resolution never to lend any attention to it, with whatever specious pretense it may be covered.

"Lord Bacon seems to have embraced the same principles of reasoning. 'We ought,' says he, 'to make a collection or particular history of all monsters and prodigious births or productions, and, in a word, of everything new, rare, and extraordinary in nature. But this must be done with the most severe scrutiny, lest we depart from truth. Above all, every relation must be considered as suspicious which depends in any degree upon religion, as the prodigies of Livy: and, no less so, every thing that is to be found in the writers of natural magic or alchemy, or such authors who seem, all of them, to have an unconquerable appetite for falsehood and fable.' (Nov. Org. lib. 2, aph. 9.)

"I am the better pleased with the method of reasoning here delivered, as I think it may serve to confound those dangerous friends or disguised enemies to the Christian religion who have undertaken to defend it by the principles of human reason. Our most holy religion is founded on *faith*, not on reason; and it is a sure method of exposing it to put it to such a trial as it is by no means fitted to endure. To make this more evident, let us examine those miracles related in scripture; and, not to lose ourselves in too wide a field, let us confine ourselves to such as we find in the Pentateuch, which we shall examine according to the principles of these pretended Christians, not as the word or testimony of God himself, but as the production of a mere human writer and historian. Here, then, we are first to consider a book, presented to us by a barbarous and ignorant people, written in an age when they were still more barbarous, and in all probability long after the facts which it relates, corroborated by no concurring testimony, and resembling those fabulous accounts which every nation gives of its origin. Upon reading this book, we find it full of prodigies and miracles. It gives an account of a state of the world and of human nature entirely different from the present: of our fall from that state; of the age of man extended to near a thousand years; of the destruction of the world by a deluge; of the arbitrary choice of one people as the favorites of heaven, and that people the countrymen of the author; of their deliverance from bondage by prodigies the most astonishing imaginable: I desire any one to lay his hand upon his heart, and, after a serious consideration, declare whether he thinks that the falsehood of such a book, supported by such a testimony, would be more extraordinary and miraculous than all the miracles it relates; which is, however, necessary to make it be received according to the measures of probability above established.

"What we have said of miracles may be applied, without any variation, to prophecies; and, indeed, all prophecies are real miracles, and as such only can be admitted as proofs of any revelation. If it did not exceed the capacity of human nature to foretell future events, it would be absurd to employ any prophecy as an argument for a divine mission or authority from heaven; so that upon the whole we may conclude that the Christian religion not only was at first attended with miracles, but even at this day cannot be believed by any reasonable person without one. Mere reason is insufficient to convince us of its veracity; and whoever is moved by *faith* to assent to it is conscious of a continued miracle in his own person which subverts all the principles of his understanding, and gives him a determination to believe what is most contrary to custom and experience."

"For hundreds of years, miracles were about the only things that happened. They were wrought by thousands of Christians, and testified to by millions. The saints and martyrs, the best and greatest, were the witnesses and workers of wonders. Even heretics, with the assistance of the Devil, could suspend the 'laws of nature.' Must we believe these wonderful accounts because they were written by 'good men,' by Christians, 'who made their statements in the presence and expectation of death?' The truth is that these 'good men' were mistaken. They expected the miraculous. They breathed the air of the marvelous. They fed their minds on prodigies, and their imaginations feasted on effects without causes. They were incapable of investigating. Doubts were regarded as 'rude disturbers of the congregation.' Credulity and sanctity walked hand in hand. Reason was danger. Belief was safety. As the philosophy of the ancients was rendered almost worthless by the credulity of the common people, so the proverbs of Christ, his religion of forgiveness, his creed of kindness, were lost on the mist of miracle and the darkness of superstition." (Ingersoll's Reply to Black.)

"Believers in miracles should not try to explain them. There is but one way to explain anything, and that is to account for it by natural agencies. The moment you explain a miracle it disappears. You should depend not upon explanation, but assertion. You should not be driven from the field because the miracle is shown to be unreasonable. You should reply that all miracles are unreasonable. Neither should you be in the least disheartened if it is shown to be impossible. The possible is not miraculous. You should take the ground that if miracles were reasonable, and possible, there would be no reward for believing them. The Christian has the goodness to believe, while the sinner asks for evidence. It is enough for God to work miracles without being called upon to substantiate them for the benefit of unbelievers." (Ingersoll's "Mistakes of Moses," p. 146.)

"So when we are told that wine was made out of water, and bread and fish out of nothing in large quantities, we know that we are listening to statements that simply go out of the field of credible testimony into the realm of supreme credulity. Such assertions require you to believe not only what you have not seen, but what all reason and experience tell you, you never can see. They ask you not only to believe in a past event, but in a past event outside of all reason, unsupported by nature, opposed to all natural laws, beneath the realm of reason, out of the light of experience, under the shadow of superstition. The great electric light of the intellect is turned off at the church door." (Helen H. Gardener, "Men, Women, and Gods.")

Some Extra Miracles.

A snake *talks*, reasons, and has more knowledge than Adam and Eve. See third chapter of Genesis.

God *talks* to the snake in the same chapter. On another occasion God spoke to a fish. "And the Lord spake unto the fish, and it vomited out Jonah upon dry land." (Jonah 2: 10.)

Balaam's ass seems to have been able to talk, and to see angels. "And the Lord opened the mouth of the ass, and she said unto Balaam, What have I done unto thee, that thou hast smitten me these three times?" (Numbers 22: 28.)

The Great Quail Story.

"And there went forth a wind from the Lord, and brought quails from the sea, and let them fall by the camp, as it were a day's journey on this side (thirty-three and one-fifth miles), and as it were a day's journey (thirty-three and one-fifth miles) on the other side, round about the camp and as it were two cubits (three feet and four inches) high upon the face of the earth. And while the flesh was yet between their teeth, ere it was chewed the wrath of the Lord was kindled against the people, and the Lord smote the people with a very great plague." (Numbers 11: 31, 33.) And the people quailed before the Lord; that is they quailed outwardly, but not inwardly.

A Suit of Clothes Lasting Forty Years, and even then Not Old.

"Yea forty years didst thou sustain them in the wilderness, so that they lacked nothing; their clothes waxed not old, and their feet swelled not." (Neh. 9: 21.)

Lot's Wife turned into a Pillar of Salt.

The Boston Transcript knows of an erudite clergyman who spoke of the unfortunate woman of Sodom as "Lot's lady who was transformed into a monolith of chloride of sodium."

Cattle which were Killed Several Times After they were Dead.

"And the Lord did that thing on the morrow, and all the cattle of Egypt died, but of the cattle of the children of Israel died not one." (Ex. 9: 6.)

This is the first time they were killed, so far as we know of. The immediate cause of their taking off is ascribed to "Murrain." In the twenty-fifth verse of the same chapter it is fully implied that they were killed again: "And the hail smote throughout all the land of Egypt all that was in the field, both man and beast; and the hail smote every herb of the field, and brake every tree of the field." Now it is fair to infer that a hail which "brake every tree of the field" was destructive enough to kill animals. This makes the second time they were killed.

In the twelfth chapter of Exodus and twenty-ninth verse we read that some of the same cattle were killed again, making three times that they died: "And it came to pass that at midnight the Lord smote all the first born of the land of Egypt, from the first born of Pharaoh that sat upon the throne unto the first born of the captive in the dungeon; and the first born of cattle." After these repeated deaths of the cattle, we find Pharaoh and his horsemen in full pursuit of the fleeing Hebrews, and Pharaoh and his horsemen and horses, were drowned in the sea. Of course it is difficult for one who is carnally minded, to understand how cattle can be killed so many times. Possibly the "Society for the Prevention of Cruelty to Dumb Animals" might have done good service had it been in full working order in those days.

People Get Up in the morning Dead.

"And when they arose, behold they were all dead corpses." (Isaiah 37: 36.)

Elisha Returns to Life.

"And it came to pass, as they were burying a man, that, behold, they spied a band of men; and they cast the man unto the sepulcher of Elisha: and when the man (the corpse) was let down, and touched the bones of Elisha, he revived, and stood up on his feet." (2 Kings 13: 21.)

It would have been a great consolation to us, if the writer had only added a few lines more, and told us what Elisha did after he stood up on his feet. Of course if he stood up, he could not stand on any one else's feet than his own, but did he climb out of the sepulcher and go on his way rejoicing? Execrable historian to leave us in the dark when we so greatly need light! We fear the writer of Matthew had this story in his mind, when speaking of the earthquake at the crucifixion of Christ. He says, "And the graves were opened; and many bodies of the saints which slept, arose, and came out of the graves after his resurrection, and went into the holy city, and appeared unto many."—"Came out of the graves *after his resurrection*"; but they arose at the time of the earthquake, and the resurrection did not take place until the third day afterward. What were they doing all this time? Standing up in their graves, dressed in their funeral wardrobe? If they appeared unto many there is no mention of the fact made by either Jew or Gentile.

HEAVEN.

Elijah Went to Heaven in a Chariot of Fire.

"And it came to pass as they still went on, and talked, that behold, there appeared a chariot of fire, and horses of fire, and parted them both asunder; and Elijah went up by a whirlwind into heaven." (2 Kings 2: 11.)

The writer of Luke, has given us almost a literal copy of this story in telling of Jesus' ascent to heaven:

"And he led them out as far as Bethany, and he lifted up his hands, and blessed them; and it came to pass while he blessed them, he was parted from them and carried up into heaven." (Luke 24: 50, 51.)

"So then after the Lord had spoken unto them, he was received up into heaven, and sat on the right hand of God." (Mark 16: 19.)

To these writers heaven was only a few miles away. They had not the faintest conception of the distance of the nearest fixed star:

"And he (Jacob) dreamed and behold a ladder set up on the earth and the top of it reached to heaven: and behold the angels of God ascending and descending on it." (Gen. 28: 12.)

The tower of Babel was another method of reaching heaven. The writers of the gospels have no better ideas than the ancient Jews had.

I give below, a few out of many passages which show that the writers of the New Testament regarded heaven as only a few miles away.

"And, lo, the heavens were opened." (Mat. 3: 16.)

"He saw the heavens opened." (Mark 1: 10.)

"There came a voice from heaven saying." (Mark 1: 11.)

"And lo, a voice from heaven saying." (Mat. 3: 17.)

"For the angel of the Lord descended from heaven, and came and rolled back the stone from the door, and sat on it." (Mat. 28: 2.)

"And there appeared an angel unto him from heaven." (Luke 22: 43.)

"Then came there a voice from heaven saying." (John 12: 28.)

"I heard another voice from heaven saying." (John 18: 4.)

All these and many more passages which might be cited go to show that these writers supposed heaven to be but a short distance away. There was a constant and familiar intercourse between the gods above and men below.

The Christian idea of heaven is but another form of the Greek notion of Mt. Olympus—it is not only borrowed, but vague and mythical in the extreme—it is childish and has much of the flavor of Santa Claus stories.

Deluge.

The great flood in which the waters piled up at the rate of about eight hundred feet per day for forty days was another of the extraordinary occurrences of Bible record. In these degenerate times a downfall of three inches of rain, for one day is usually sufficient to satisfy everybody. But think of about eight hundred feet per day!

A river turned into blood after it had just been transformed into blood: "And Moses and Aaron did so, as the Lord commanded; and he lifted up the rod, and smote the waters that were in the river, in the sight of Pharaoh, and in sight of his servants, and all the waters that were in the river were turned into blood. And the fish that was in the river died; and the river stank, and the Egyptians could not drink of the water of the river; and there was blood throughout all the land of Egypt. And the magicians of Egypt did so with their enchantments." (Ex. 7: 20, 21, 22.) The magicians turned a river of blood into blood, and killed dead fish, eh?

The Ass and the Calf.

"And he took the (golden) calf which they had made, and burnt it in the fire, and ground it to powder, and strewed it upon the waters, and made the children of Israel drink of it." (Ex. 32: 20.)

But as gold does not burn in a fire, nor can it be ground to powder, or strewed upon the waters, or drunk, we are forced to conclude that the author of this little golden calf story, must have been an ass.

JESUS CHRIST.

The Genealogy of Jesus.

"Matthew (1: 17) says, 'So all the generations from Abraham to David are fourteen generations; and from the carrying away into Babylon are fourteen generations; and from the carrying away into Babylon unto Christ are fourteen generations.'

"Luke (3: 23-38) relates Christ's genealogy, and gives forty-three generations between David and Christ, these two persons being included. Here then in the genealogy of the same person is an utterly irreconcilable discrepancy of fifteen generations. This is truly a bad beginning. Although these two accounts may both be false they cannot possibly both be true. If 'all the generations,' from David to Jesus, were only 'twenty-eight,' as given by Matthew, there could not possibly have been at the same time, 'forty-three' of them as given by Luke. The case becomes much worse, however, when we discover that, with the exception of Jesus, Joseph, and David, these two authors give entirely different sets of of men. Since it is utterly impossible for the same individual to have descended through both of these lines of ancestors, it is equally impossible for both of these accounts to be true." (J. R. Kelso's "Bible Analyzed.")

"On the first glance these genealogies, as given by Matthew and Luke, are so evidently different that it has been the ordinary, if not invariable practice of Christian harmonists and commentators to represent the former Evangelist as recording the descent of Joseph, while the latter Evangelist is said to have given the pedigree of Mary. We will say nothing of the plausibility of this explanation, which acknowledges the genealogies to be wholly different, and supposes they belong to two persons. Our questions must rather effect the truthfulness of this mode of explaining away the difficulty. Let the reader bear in mind how Matthew states that 'Jacob begat Joseph the husband of Mary,' and how Luke's words are 'Joseph which was the son of Heli,' and then let the reader say whether it is truthful to allege that these different genealogies belong to different individuals. Is it not plain that each of them professes to trace the lineal descent of one and the same man, Joseph? If we are still to be told that when Matthew professes to give the descent of Joseph, he is to be understood as giving the descent of Mary, then we simply rejoin that such an explanation is nothing more nor less than an abandonment of the idea of inspirational infallibility; for it represents the Bible as saying one thing and meaning another." (McNaught, "Doctrine of Inspiration.")

When was Jesus Born?

As to the time when Jesus was born, we have no positive information. Matthew says he was born in Herod's time, and that Herod caused all the little children to be killed on account of him. Luke says Jesus was born in the time of Cyrenius, when Augustus Cæsar gave orders that all the people should be taxed. Now, Cyrenius succeeded Archelaus, who reigned ten years after the death of Herod. Here is a contradiction that cannot be explained away. The exact day of Herod's death can be almost arrived at, as shown by Josephus, who says that on the night preceding the death of Herod there was an eclipse of the moon. In calculating back to the time of this eclipse, it is found to have occurred on the fourth of March, four years before Christ; another perplexing discrepancy. Matthew says he was born in the days of Herod, and John says it was in the days of Cyrenius, fourteen years afterward. Again, Mark and Luke say Jesus began to be thirty years of age in the fifteenth year of the reign of Tiberius, the very day of whose accession is known; and by counting back, we find that Jesus must have been born four years before the Christian era, which disagrees entirely with the statement of Matthew.

Professor John Fiske remarks that while the Jesus of the dogma is the best known, the Jesus of history is the least known of all the eminent names in history. "Persons who had given much attention to the subject affirmed that there were not less than one hundred and thirty-two different opinions as to the year in which the Messiah appeared." ("Conflict Between Religion and Science," p. 184.)

Dr. Adam Clarke, on observations of Luke 2: 8, in his Commentary says: "The nativity of Jesus in December should be given up. The Egyptians placed it in January; Wagenseil in February; Bochart in March. Some mentioned by Clemens Alexandrine in April; others in May. Epiphanius speaks of some who placed it in June, and others supposed it to have been in July. Wagenseil, who was not sure of February, fixed it as probably in August; Lightfoot on the fifteenth of September. But the Latin church [Catholic], supreme in power and infallible in judgment, placed it on the twenty-fifth of December, the very day on which the ancient Romans celebrated the feast of their goddess, Bruma. Pope Julius I. (in the fourth century) made the first alteration, and it appears to have been done for this reason." The Christians often aim to make an argument that the chronology of the Christian era is established by the confirmation that is given by the years being numbered from the supposed birth of Jesus, but it is no proof at all. The idea of counting the years from the advent of Jesus was not thought of for several centuries after the time when the vague legends said he was supposed to have lived. The plan of numbering the years from that apocryphal event was first invented by a monk, Dionysius Exiguus, about 530 after Christ. It was introduced into Italy not long afterward, and was propagated by Bede, who died in 735. It was ordered to be used by the bishops in the Council of Chalcedon in 816, but it was not generally employed for several centuries afterward. It was not legalized until the year 1000. Charles III. of Germany was the first sovereign who added "In the year of our Lord" to his reign, in 879. (See Haydn's Dictionary of Dates, and Encyclopedia of Chronology.)

Now, in recapitulation, let us see how much, by the common sense method of interpreting the gospels, we have been forced to reject as incredible.

First, we have seen that Joseph's dream concerning the immaculate conception was, after all, only a dream, and that wonderful dreams are not uncommon; Samson's mother having had one which is so identical with Joseph's, that we are persuaded that the dream of the latter is but a copy of the dream of the former; that almost all men of distinction in ancient times were reported to have had wonderful prodigies attending their conception and birth,—and that there is no evidence in the gospels of the resurrection of Jesus. Paul saw him in a vision, that is, in his mind's eye, but does not claim to have seen him in the flesh. And of the ascension, it is a self-evident fiction.

The miracles are not only incredible from their being incompatible with and contrary to human experience, but the manner in which they are related proves that they never were performed. (See "Miracles.") And concerning the moral teachings of Jesus we find great imperfection. He did not come to save all men, but only the lost sheep of the house of Israel; he taught that the end of the world was nigh at hand, when a great physical revolution should usher in the kingdom of heaven, but it did not come. We find also that Jesus did not respect the rights of property; that he despised this world; that he condemned the rich because they were rich, and made great promises to the poor because they were poor; that he professed to pardon sin, and on one occasion pardoned a person's sins for washing his feet; that he exhibited an imperfect sense of justice in a great many instances; and, lastly, we find that there is no history of him excepting the gospels, and in these there is no unquestionable record of the time when or the place where he was born. We are forced to conclude that if ever there was such a person as Jesus of Nazareth, we have no trustworthy sources of positive knowledge concerning him.

Christianity Rests Upon a Dream.

"Now the birth of Jesus Christ was on this wise: When as his mother Mary was espoused to Joseph, before they came together, she was found to be with child of the Holy Ghost. Then Joseph her husband, being a just man and not willing to make her a public example, was minded to put her away privily. But while he thought on these things, behold, the angel of the Lord appeared to him in a dream, saying, Joseph thou son of David, fear not to take unto thee Mary thy wife, for that which is conceived in her is of the Holy Ghost." (Mat. 1: 18-20.)

"Before they came together, she was found to be with child of the Holy Ghost."

1. How could any one but Mary say who the father of the child was?

2. If the conception was miraculous then neither Mary nor any one else could know ought of the paternity of the child.

3. Mary says nothing about the overshadowing of the Holy Ghost.

4. Who found out that Joseph had had such a dream?

5. Was it duly reported and verified then and there?

6. The book that relates the dream is anonymous and does not appear in history until A. D. 180-182.

7. The writers of the other three gospels know nothing of this dream.

8. There is no evidence that the writer of the first gospel ever personally knew Mary.

9. Luke (1: 30) says that it was to Mary that the angel of the Lord appeared.

10. Only a dream! The corner-stone of Christianity rests upon a dream! Take away this dream and Christianity has nothing left.

THE GOLDEN RULE.

The moral teachings of the Bible are not original. Back of the pyramids in pre-historic times mothers taught their children to be kind to each other. Not from heaven but out of the human heart came the golden rule. A mother's love was sufficient to reveal this best rule of life. Human inspiration is the only inspiration needed to call forth the expression—"Do unto others as ye would have them do unto you."

Sixty years before the Christian era, Hellel, a Jewish rabbi wrote: "Do not do to others, what you would not like others to do to you."

Two hundred and eighty years before Christ, Epicurus said: "It is more blessed to give than to receive."

Three hundred and fifty years before Christ, Socrates said: "Act toward others as you desire them to act toward you."

Three hundred and seventy years before Christ, Aristippus said: "Cherish reciprocal benevolence, which will make you as anxious for another's welfare as your own."

Three hundred and eighty-five years before Christ, Aristotle wrote: "We should conduct ourselves toward others, as we would have them act toward us."

Four hundred years before Christ, Sextus said: "What you wish your neighbors to be to you, such be also to them."

Four hundred and twenty years before Christ, Plato wrote: "May I do to others as I would have them do to me."

Five hundred years before Christ, Confucius taught: "Do unto another what you would have him do to you, and do not to another what you would not have him do unto you: it is the foundation principle of all the rest." (24th Maxim Confucius.) Jesus concludes by saying, "For this is the law and the prophets," and Confucius closes his rule by observing, "Thou only needst this law alone; it is the foundation and principle of all the rest."

And it should not be overlooked that Jesus, in thus attributing the golden rule to "the law and the prophets," disclaims its authorship. Confucius does the same.

Six hundred years before Christ, Thales said: "Avoid doing what you would blame others for doing."

Six hundred and fifty years before Christ, Pittacus taught: "Do not do to your neighbor what you would take ill from him."

"That the system of morals propounded in the New Testament contains no maxim which had not been previously enunciated, and that some of the most beautiful passages in the apostolic writings are quotations from Pagan authors, are well known to every scholar; and so far from supplying, as some suppose, an objection against Christianity, it is a strong recommendation of it, as indicating the intimate relation between the doctrines of Christ and the moral sympathies of mankind in different ages. But to assert that Christianity communicated to man moral truths previously unknown, argues on the part of the assertor, either gross ignorance or else wilful fraud." (Buckle, "History of Civilization," vol. 1, p. 129.)

"Did space admit, I could cite numerous passages from Enoch in close correspondence with the New Testament scripture, in many cases almost word for word. In that book, as in the Talmud, and as was held by the Jews in general (saving the Sadducees), may be found the exact doctrines taught by Jesus relative to the Son of Man coming in the clouds of heaven, the resurrection of the dead, the day of judgment, the punishment of the wicked in everlasting fire, and the reward of the righteous in heaven. The eschatology of Jesus is borrowed in toto from that prevalent in Judea during his lifetime. Not one single new idea respecting the 'four final things,' death, judgment, heaven, and hell, can be found in Jesus' teachings as embodied in the gospels."—Wm. Emmette Coleman.

Jesus an Essene.

"Of the resemblance between the Essenes and the followers of Christ in their principles and practices, I will let a Christian writer speak—Christian D. Ginsburg, LL.D., who is a leading contributor to Alexander's new edition of Kitto's Cyclopedia, the most orthodox of the chief English Bible dictionaries. I will read a few extracts from an essay entitled, 'The Essenes Their History and Doctrines.' Dr. Ginsburg says: "The identity of many of the precepts and practices of Essenism and Christianity is unquestionable. Essenism urged on its disciples to seek first the kingdom of God and his righteousness; so did Christ. (Mat. 6: 33, and Luke 12: 31.) The Essenes forbade the laying up of treasures upon earth; so did Christ. (Mat. 6: 19, 21.) The Essenes demanded of those who wished to join them, to sell all their possessions, and to divide it among the poor brethren; so Christ. (Mat. 19: 21, and Luke 12: 33.) The Essenes had all things in common, and appointed one of the brethren as steward to manage the common bag; so the primitive Christians. (Acts 2: 44, 45; 4: 32, 34, and John 12: 6; 13: 29.) Essenism regarded all its members on the same level, forbidding the exercise of authority of one over the other, and enjoining mutual service; so Christ. (Mat. 20: 25-28, and Mark 9: 35, 37; 10: 42, 45.) Essenism commanded its disciples to call no man master upon the earth; so Christ. (Mat. 23: 8, 9.) Essenism laid the greatest stress on being meek and lowly in spirit; so Christ. (Mat. 5: 5, 29.)

'Christ commended the poor in spirit, those who hunger after righteousness, the merciful, the pure in heart and the peacemakers; so the Essenes. . . . Christ combined the healing of the body with that of the soul; so the Essenes.

Like the Essenes, Christ declared that the power to cast out evil spirits, to perform miraculous cures, etc., should be possessed by his disciples as signs of their belief. (Mark 16: 17; comp. also Mat. 10: 8, and Luke 9: 1, 2; 10: 9.) Like the Essenes, Christ commanded his disciples not to swear at all, but to say yea, yea, and nay, nay. The manner in which Christ directed his disciples to go on their journey (Mat. 10: 9, 10) is the same which the Essenes adopted when they started on a mission of mercy. The Essenes, though repudiating offensive war, yet took weapons with them when they went on a perilous journey: Christ enjoined his disciples to do the same thing. (Luke 22: 36.) Christ commended that elevated spiritual life, which enables a man to abstain from marriage for the kingdom of heaven's sake, and which cannot be attained by all men save those to whom it is given (Mat. 19: 10-12; comp. also 1 Cor. 8); so the Essenes, who, as a body, in waiting for the kingdom of heaven, abstained from connubial intercourse. The Essenes did not offer animal sacrifices, but strove to present their bodies a living sacrifice, holy and acceptable, unto God, which they regarded as a reasonable service; the apostle Paul exhorts the Romans to do the same. (Rom. 12: 1.) It was the great aim of the Essenes to live such a life of purity and holiness as to be the temples of the holy spirit and to be able to prophesy; the apostle Paul urges the Corinthians to covet to prophesy. (1 Cor. 14: 1, 39.) When Christ pronounced John to be Elias (Mat. 11: 14), he declared that the Baptist had already attained to that spirit and power which the Essenes strove to obtain in their highest stage of purity. It will therefore hardly be doubted that our Savior himself belonged to this holy brotherhood. This will especially be apparent when we remember that the whole Jewish community, at the advent of Christ, was divided into three parties, the Pharisees, the Sadducees, and the Essenes, and that every Jew had to belong to one of these sects. Jesus, who in all things conformed to Jewish law, who was holy, harmless, undefiled, and separate from sinners, would naturally associate himself with that order of Judaism which was most congenial to his holy nature. Moreover, the fact that Christ, with the exception of once, was not heard of in public till his thirtieth year, implying that he lived in seclusion with this fraternity, and that though he frequently rebuked the Scribes, Pharisees, and Sadducees, he never denounced the Essenes, strongly confirms this conclusion. . . The accounts given by Josephus first mentioned their existence in the days of Jonathan the Maccabaean, B.C. 166; and they most unquestionably show that the Essenes existed at least two centuries before the Christian era, and that they at first lived among the Jewish community at large. Their residence at Jerusalem is also evident from the fact that there was a gate named after them. When they ultimately withdrew themselves from the rest of the Jewish nation, the majority of them settled on the northwest shore of the Dead Sea, sufficiently distant to escape its noxious exhalations, and the rest lived in scattered communities throughout Palestine and Syria. Both Philo and Josephus estimated them to be above four thousand in number. This must have been exclusive of women and children. We hear very little of them after this period (that is, 40 A.D.); and there can hardly be any doubt that, owing to the great similarity which existed between their precepts and practices, and those of the primitive Christians, the Essenes, as a body, must have embraced Christianity.'"—Underwood, in Underwood-Marples Debate.

Jesus' Teachings Not up to the Moral Standard of To-day.

1. Jesus failed to explicitly teach any of the cardinal human virtues. If he taught kindness and forgiveness it was usually at the expense of justice.

2. He nowhere explains and inspires self-reliance and individual liberty.

3. He nowhere condemns kingcraft, priestcraft and tyranny. He opposes their abuses, but not the radical evils out of which they spring.

4. He has no just ideas of marriage and divorce.

5. He nowhere explains the nature of heaven and hell.

6. He does not teach the value of economy and thrift, but turns people loose with the notion that they must take no thought for the morrow.

The following saying of Jesus exhibits the lack of a high moral sense of justice, and also the fact that he does not pretend to be the savior of the whole human race. He said to his own countrymen: "Unto you it is given to know the mystery of the kingdom of God, but unto them that are without, all these things are done in parables; that seeing they may see, and not perceive; and hearing they may hear, and not understand; lest at any time they should be converted, and their sins be forgiven them. (Mark 4: 11.)

From this we learn that Jesus did not desire to save the Gentiles; the parabolical style was used in order to prevent them from becoming converted and having their sins pardoned.

In addition to this imperfection of the moral sense, Jesus was sometimes unforgiving in his spirit and practice. He says on one occasion: "Whosoever shall deny me before men, him will I also deny before my father which is in heaven." (Mat. 10: 33.)

It is true that he taught his disciples to love their enemies, but it is a precept he did not observe himself; he allowed himself to speak of those who did not accept his teachings as, "fools," "hypocrites," "thieves," "serpents," "vipers," and many other abusive epithets, which clearly exhibit on his part anger and hatred. We have another instance of his unforgiving spirit in that myth of the dying thief on the cross. It is there recorded that Jesus prayed for the forgiveness of his enemies, but had he been consistent with that prayer, he would not have pardoned one thief without also pardoning the other. When he could ask God to forgive his enemies, it would have been demanded by his own rule, that he also forgive them; but, on the contrary, he only forgives the malefactor who spoke words in his praise. This spirit is carried out in the doctrine of future rewards and punishments.

Jesus Exhibits an Imperfect Sense of Justice.

In failing to recognize the rights of property; in his denunciation of the rich; in his teachings of submission to wrong; in his professing to pardon sin, even before it is asked for, Jesus errs. This moral sense is lacking in his teachings concerning God. Take this as an illustration: "Which of you shall have a friend, and shall go unto him at midnight, and say unto him, Friend, lend me three loaves; for a friend of mine in his journey is come to me, and I have nothing to set before him. And he from within shall answer and say, Trouble me not; the door is now shut, and my children are with me in bed; I cannot rise and give thee. I say unto you, Though he will not rise and give him, because he is his friend, yet because of his importunity he will rise and give him as many as he needeth." (Luke 11: 15.)

And so it is with God, he leads us to believe, for though he is our friend he will not grant our requests; but if we annoy and tease him, at last, worn out, he will answer our prayers to get rid of us. Therefore, "Ask and it shall be given you; for every one that asketh receiveth."

The parable of the unfortunate widow is another instance in point: "There was in a city a judge who feared not God, neither regarded man [same kind of judges in our cities now]. And there was a widow in that city, and she came unto him, saying, Avenge me of mine adversary. And he would not for a while; but afterwards he said within himself, Though I fear not God, nor regard man, yet because this widow troubleth me, I will avenge her, lest by her continual coming she weary me." (Luke 18: 2-6.) It is just so in praying to God. He may not hear you or heed you at first, yet by a "continual coming and troubling him," he must of necessity at last become weary and grant you the desires of your heart, in order to escape being troubled.

At one time the scribes and Pharisees brought a woman to Jesus who had been taken in the act of adultery, and asked for his judgment. He said: "He that is without sin among you let him first cast a stone at her." This was a well-directed rebuke, and they felt it, and they "went out one by one, beginning at the eldest even unto the last." Then Jesus, standing alone with the woman, asks, "Woman where are those thine accusers? hath no man condemned thee? She said, No man, Lord. And Jesus said unto her, Neither do I condemn thee; go and sin no more." (John 8: 7-11.)

In all parts of the Bible adultery is condemned, and by all civil laws it is now prohibited, and all religious teaching forbids it, and there is no reason in this case why Jesus should not have condemned the act, even while he showed mercy to the actor. Here as elsewhere Jesus shows mercy at the expense of justice. Were these principles carried out in life, the criminal would go untried and unpunished.

"Go into the village over against you, and straightway you shall find an ass tied, and a colt with her; loose them and bring them unto me. And if any man say aught unto you, ye shall say, The Lord hath need of them, and staightway he will send them. All this was done, that it might be fulfilled which was spoken by the prophet, saying, Tell ye the daughter of Zion, Behold, thy king cometh unto thee, meek, and sitting upon an ass, and a colt, the foal of an ass. And the disciples went and did as Jesus commanded them, and brought the ass, and the colt, and put on their clothes, and set him thereon." (Mat. 21: 2-7.)

The writer would have us believe that Jesus rode upon two asses at once; but the prophet who could invent such a story must have been an ass himself to suppose that Jesus could ride upon two donkeys of such unequal size at one time. It was not the prophet, however, who perpetrated this outrage upon common sense, but the writer of Matthew, whoever he was. Mark, Luke, and John mentioned the affair, and all agree in speaking of one ass only. Had the writer read the prophet aright, he would have quoted it differently, "Behold thy King cometh unto thee, . . lowly, and sitting upon an ass; even a colt, the foal of an ass." (Zech. 9: 9.)

Another instance of this disregard of the interests of others is exhibited by Jesus where he casts the devils out of two men and permits them to enter the swine, "and the swine ran down a steep place into the sea and perished in the waters." Mark (5: 12) says there were about two thousand head, but there is not a word said about the equity of the proceeding. In this case Jesus does not offer any compensation for the destruction of property which had been caused by him.

He does not make even an apology or an explanation. No wonder, then, that the people became alarmed at this and asked him to go on his journey with as little delay as possible: "The whole city came out to meet Jesus: and when they saw him, they besought him that he would depart out of their coasts." (Mat. 8: 34.)

Another instance of this lack of the sense of justice is displayed in the parable of Dives and Lazarus. The one goes to heaven, that is, to Abraham's bosom, because he was poor, and the other to hell, because he was rich. Say what we may our civilization is built upon wealth. Civilization, the highest and noblest estate of man, is achieved by the utter repudiation of poverty. The legitimate love of money is the spur of all human progress. Civilization would speedily degenerate into barbarism if this respect for property was removed.

His views of poverty are in harmony with his teachings on other human interests: "Lay not up for yourselves treasures upon earth;" "Take no thought for the morrow; for the morrow shall take thought for the things of itself." How evident it is that one of the most essential virtues of life is here repudiated.

Thoughtfulness about the future is a distinguishing trait of a wise man. To take no thought for the morrow would be as foolish as for one to bind himself hand and foot on the approach of his enemy. Science inspires man with earnest inquiry about the morrow, and also enables him by his perception of it how better to live to-day.

"Give to him that asketh thee, and from him that would borrow of thee, turn not thou away." (Mat. 5: 42.) Society as it now exists would not last a single day if his command were obeyed. Borrowing and lending is poor business, even as it is now carried on, but what it would become under the universal practice it would be impossible to guess.

"And if ye lend to them of whom ye hope to receive, what thank have ye? For sinners also lend to sinners, to receive as much again. But love ye your enemies, and do good, and lend, hoping for nothing again." (Luke 6: 34.) So impracticable a precept is this, that no people have ever practiced it, nor could it be carried out without the demoralization and overthrow of civilization.

Jesus Teaches the Duty of Submission to Wrong.

The general doctrines of resignation and contentment are incompatible with strength of character and progress in life. The most worthy members of society everywhere are just those people who have the least resignation and contentment. Jesus does not seem to have cherished these conditions himself. He was neither contented nor resigned to the social status about him. "The powers that be" did not seem to him to be from above, but from beneath, and he accordingly waged war upon the existing social evils. But Jesus also teaches the duty of submission to wrong: "And unto him that smiteth thee on the one cheek, offer also the other; and him that taketh away thy cloak forbid not to take thy coat also. Give to every man that asketh of thee; and of him that taketh away thy goods, ask them not again." (Luke 6: 29, 30.) Just think of it! "And of him that taketh away thy goods, ask them not again." Society would be overthrown in a day if this command was carried out. We should have no commerce, no law protecting our various interests, no civilized society. Paul echoes the same notion when he says, "Now, therefore, there is utterly a fault among you, because ye go to law one with another. Why do ye not rather take wrong? Why do ye not rather suffer yourselves to be defrauded?" (1 Cor. 6: 7.)

Suffer yourselves to be defrauded! If human life has any virtue at all, it surely consists in some degree in doing the very opposite, that is, in not suffering ourselves to be defrauded. It is true that love seems at first sight to be an all-important virtue, and one incapable of abuse; but such love as induces us to submit to wrong is spurious. In the world as it exists about us, we are culpable when we suffer ourselves to be defrauded. The common virtues which are recognized by all men are courage and resistance to wrong. Everywhere our eyes turn, we look to see the hero who nobly resists the wrongs and frauds which the powerful perpetrate upon the weak and helpless. "Resistance to tyrants is the will of God" is the modern conception of duty. And in accordance therewith we have laws prohibiting wrong and fraud. Besides there is no manliness, self-reliance, or self-respect compatible with such craven submission, which is spiritless and purposeless. John Stuart Mill observes of Christianity: "Its ideal is negative rather than positive; passive rather than active; innocence rather than nobleness; abstinence from evil rather than energetic pursuit of good. In its precepts (as has been well said), 'thou shalt not' predominates over 'thou shalt.'"

Immoral Teachings of Jesus.

"Suppose ye that I am come to give peace on earth? I tell you nay; but rather division." (Luke 12: 51.)

"For I am come to set a man at variance against his father, and a daughter against her mother, and the daughter-in-law against her mother-in-law." (Mat. 10: 35.)

"I am come to send fire on earth; and what will I, that it be already kindled." (Luke 12: 49.)

"For from henceforth there shall be five in one house divided, three against two, and two against three.

"The father shall be divided against the son, and the son against the father; the mother against the daughter, and the daughter against the mother; the mother-in-law against her daughter-in-law, and the daughter-in-law against the mother-in-law." (Luke 12: 52, 53.)

"If any man come to me, and hate not his father and mother, and wife and children, and brethren and sisters, yea, and his own life also, he cannot be my disciple." (Luke 14: 26.)

"Think not that I am come to send peace on earth. I come not to send peace, but a sword." (Mat. 10: 34.)

"And the brother shall deliver up the brother to death, and the father the child: and the children shall rise up against their parents, and cause them to be put to death." (Mat. 10: 21.)

"And they said unto him, Lord, behold here are two swords. And he said unto them, It is enough." (Luke 22: 38.)

"He that hath no sword let him sell his garment and buy one." (Luke 22: 36.)

Bitter and Unreasonable Denunciations of Jesus.

"All that ever came before me are thieves and robbers." (John 10: 8.)

"Ye are of your father, the Devil, and the lusts of your father ye will do." (John 8: 44.)

"Ye serpents, ye generation of vipers, how can ye escape the damnation of hell?" (Mat. 23: 33.)

"O, generation of vipers, how can ye, being evil, speak good things?" (Mat. 12: 34.)

"But he turned and said unto Peter, Get thee behind me, Satan." (Mat. 16: 23.)

"Depart from me ye cursed, into everlasting fire, prepared for the Devil and his angels." (Mat. 25: 41.)

"He that believeth and is baptized shall be saved; but he that believeth not shall be damned." (Mark 16: 16.)

Jesus a False Prophet.

"But when they persecute you in this city, flee ye into another: for verily I say unto you, Ye shall not have gone over the cities of Israel till the Son of man be come." (Mat. 10: 23.)

"Verily I say unto you, There be some standing here, which shall not taste of death, till they see the Son of man coming in his kingdom." (Mat. 16: 28.)

"Immediately after the tribulation of those days, shall the sun be darkened, and the moon shall not give her light, and the stars shall fall from heaven and the powers of the heavens shall be shaken.

"And then shall appear the sign of the Son of man in heaven: and then shall all the tribes of the earth mourn, and they shall see the Son of man coming in the clouds of heaven with power and great glory.

"And he shall send his angels with a great sound of a trumpet, and they shall gather together his elect from the four winds, from one end of heaven to the other.

"Now learn a parable of the fig tree; When his branch is yet tender, and putteth forth leaves, ye know that summer is nigh. So likewise ye, when ye shall see all these things, know that it is near, even at the doors.

"Verily I say unto you, *This* generation *shall not* pass till *all* these things be *fulfilled*." (Mat. 24: 29-34.)

"But I tell you of a truth, there be some standing here, which shall not taste of death, till they have seen the kingdom of God." (Luke 9: 27.)

"And he said unto them, Verily, I say unto you, That there be some of them, that stand here, which shall not taste of death, till they have seen the kingdom of God come with power." (Mark 9: 1.)

"Now learn a parable of the fig tree: When her branch is yet tender, and putteth forth leaves, Ye know that the summer is near: So ye in like manner, when ye shall see these things come to pass know that it is nigh, even at the doors. Verily, I say unto you, That this generation shall not pass till all these things be done." (Mark 13: 28-30.)

"And there shall be signs in the sun, and in the moon, and in the stars; and upon the earth distress of nations, with perplexity; the sea and the waves roaring; Men's hearts failing them for fear, and for looking after those things which are coming on the earth: for the powers of heaven shall be shaken. And then shall they see the Son of man coming in a cloud, with power and great glory.

"And when these things begin to come to pass, then look up, and lift up your heads: for your redemption draweth nigh.

"And he spake to them a parable; Behold the fig tree, and all the trees; When they now shoot forth, ye see and know of your ownselves that summer is now nigh at hand. So likewise ye, when ye see these things come to pass, know ye that the kingdom of heaven is nigh at hand." (Luke 21: 25-31.)

"If I will that he tarry till I come what is that to thee?" (John 21: 23.)

It is unnecessary to call attention to the fact that the foregoing passages imply that the end of the world was at hand. Jesus was a false prophet.

Jesus Curses the Fig Tree.

"The Jesus of the four gospels is alleged to have been God, all-wise; being hungry, he went to a fig tree, when the season of figs was not yet come. Of course there were no figs on the tree, and Jesus then caused the tree to wither away. This is an interesting account to a true orthodox trinitarian. Such a one will believe: first, that Jesus was God, who made the tree and prevented it from bearing figs; second, that, God the all-wise, who is not subject to human passions being hungry went to the fig tree, on which he knew there were no figs, expecting to find some there; third, that God the all-just then punished the tree because it did

not bear figs in opposition to God's eternal ordination."—
Charles Bradlaugh

Contemporaneous Historians are Silent Concerning the Resurrection of Jesus.

Philo, Josephus, Seneca, Pliny the elder, and Pliny the younger, Diogenes, Socrates, Pausanias, Suetonius, Tacitus, Adrian, Marcus Aurelius, Lucian, and others have not one word to say about it.

In answer to this a certain minister replies that: "Seneca, Diogenes, Laertes, Pausanias, Tacitus, and Marcus Aurelius, were Pagans, who certainly in works of stoic philosophy, travels, and geography would not discourse of Jesus." In answer to this I maintain that it is altogether probable, if not certain, that some of these writers would have recorded the "darkness over all the earth," which lasted some three hours (Luke 23: 44) and the opening of the graves out of which many of the dead came and went into the city and showed themselves unto many: besides, there were several earthquakes. (Mat. 27: 51, and 28: 2, also Acts 16: 26.) Such marvels, especially the darkness over all the earth, and the earthquakes could not have escaped the pen of all such historians and philosophers.

"Each of these philosophers (Pliny the Second and Seneca) in a laborious work, has recorded all the great phenomena of nature, earthquakes, meteors, comets, and eclipses which his indefatigable curiosity could collect; neither of them has mentioned or even alluded to the miraculous darkness at the crucifixion."—Gibbon.

The Resurrection of Jesus.

Comparing now the several narratives of the resurrection with one another, we find this general result:

In Mark Jesus is said to have appeared three times.
1. To Mary Magdalene.
2. To two disciples.
3. To the disciples at meat.

Two such appearances only are recorded in Matthew:

1. To the women.
2. To the eleven in Galilee.

In Luke he appears:
1. To Cleopas and his companion.
2. To Peter.
3. To the eleven and others.

In the last chapters of John the appearances amount to four:
1. To Mary Magdalene.
2. To the disciples without Thomas.
3. To the disciples with Thomas.
4. To several disciples on the Tiberias lake.

Paul extends them to six:
1. To Peter.
2. To the twelve.
3. To more than five hundred.
4. To James
5. To all the apostles.
6. To Paul.

"Upon this most momentous question every one of the Christian writers is at variance with every other." (Amberley's "Analysis of Religious Belief," p. 273.)

They differ as to the number of women who visited the sepulcher. John mentions only *one*; Matthew names *two*, Mary Magdalene and the other Mary. Mark says there were *three*, the two Marys and Salome. Luke says there were *more* than three, the two Marys, Joanna, and certain others with them. They differ as to the number of persons in white seen at the sepulcher. Mark mentions *one*, "a young man." Matthew speaks of *one*, an angel. Luke says there were *two* men, and John that there were *two* angels. They disagree as to what was said by the persons in white. According to Matthew and Mark, they spoke of the resurrection of Jesus and his departure into Galilee, and sent a message to his disciples commanding them to follow him thither. In Luke they simply said that he was risen, and referred to a former prediction of his to this effect. In John they simply asked Mary, "Woman! why weepest thou?"

Discrepancies as to where Jesus went after his resurrection. Matthew, dismissing Jesus from history with these words, "Go ye therefore and teach all nations, baptizing them in the name of the Father, Son, and Holy Ghost" (28: 19), seems to know nothing of the ascension; for it is utterly incompatible with the assumption that he is an honest and faithful historian. He could not possibly neglect recording so important an event had he known it, and the plain inference—the irresistible conclusion is that if he did not record it, it was because no such thing had occurred.

See with what brevity Mark concludes the career of Jesus. Mark gives these as the parting words of Jesus: "So then after the Lord had spoken unto them he was received up into heaven, and sat on the right hand of God." (16: 19.)

How brief is the description of this wonderful scene! No writer that had witnessed such a sight could possibly condense his thoughts and feelings concerning it into one sentence. He would have had much to say; namely, of his own thoughts and emotions on the occasion, and what other witnesses said and did at the time the event occurred. Writers who go into particulars on less marvelous affairs would not be likely to dash off the most wonderful event that had ever happened before human eyes in one sentence. The thing is utterly improbable and incredible. "He was received up into heaven" reveals the credulity and superstition of the times. How could the writer know where he had gone, if he had once passed away from his sight? Moreover, he knew nothing of a local heaven or of a personal God, yet he says that Jesus "sat (down) on the right hand of God," as though the Infinite Power which pervades the universe had two hands and was made in the image of man!

The only rational explanation we can put upon such language is to suppose it written by one who was not present at the time referred to, but had heard of it and had undertaken to give his version of what he heard, perhaps in the attempt trying to reconcile two or three different versions of the story, and at the same time weave in his own opinion on the subject. At any rate, whoever wrote it, the writer does not claim to have been an eye-witness, and the legendary character of the account proves that the myth had been handed down to him.

Luke (24: 50, 51) says: "And he led them out as far as to Bethany, and he lifted up his hands and blessed them; and it came to pass while he blessed them, he was parted from them and carried up into heaven." This version leaves out the sitting on the right hand of God—yet it has the same superstition of a local heaven—of which the writer speaks as if he had as positive and distinct knowledge as he claims to have of Jesus and his resurrection.

If Matthew closes without giving us anything of the after life and death of Jesus—if he breaks off abruptly without giving us any insight into the feelings of the disciples, Luke does not. He says that after they had witnessed the departure of Jesus they worshiped him and returned to Jerusalem with *great joy.* (24: 52.) But this is totally unnatural. We cannot imagine disciples rejoicing in the loss of their friend. It is not human nature to be glad on such occasions. We always grieve in parting with friends. The father grieves when he parts with his son, the mother weeps when she gives the parting kiss to her daughter. It may be said in reply that the disciples had faith that Jesus had gone to heaven. But this will not meet the difficulty, for Christian mothers believe when they part with their sweet, innocent babes that they go straight to heaven, but does this belief dry their tears or soothe their anguished hearts? No, these mothers are frequently tormented to frenzy and even madness by the intense grief occasioned by loss of their dear ones. It is human nature to grieve upon the loss of friends, but here we find disciples who do not mourn when their dearest friend has departed from them.

They were glad of it, and so they "returned to Jerusalem with *great joy*." Such a paragraph as this could have been inserted in the story by some subsequent writer, but never could have been written by one who had witnessed such an event. Another feature of this description, as given by Luke, is that it seems to be a slightly varied copy of the account given of Elijah. "And it came to pass, as they still went on, and talked, that behold there appeared a chariot of fire and horses of fire and parted them both asunder; and Elijah went up by a whirlwind into heaven." (2 Kings 2: 11.)

How closely Luke's account seems to resemble this! "And he led them out as far as to Bethany, and he lifted up his hands and blessed them. And it came to pass while he blessed them he was parted from them and carried up into heaven." (Luke 24: 50, 51.) "And when he had spoken these things, while they beheld, he was taken up; and a cloud received him out of their sight." (Acts 1: 9.)

How suggestive is the fact that the writers do not undertake to tell how he was translated! The writer of the book of Kings gives us a "chariot of fire" and "a whirlwind" as the *modus operandi* of translating Elijah from one world to the other (?), but here there are no agencies mentioned, and so far as the writers are concerned, there seems to be nothing incomplete or unreasonable in the statements that he "was carried up into heaven," and "was taken up and a cloud received him out of their sight." We must suppose that persons witnessing such an extraordinary event would have some notions as to the *means* used in translating Jesus above the clouds, and that they could not fail to express them in giving an account of what they had seen. Their silence on this point, and the utter incredibility of the story make it apparent that the writer is merely recording myths.

The last chapters of John are silent concerning the ascension. Now, as it is generally admitted by the best biblical critics that the last twelve verses of the last chapter of Mark are spurious, we have then only one of the four biographers of Jesus who mentions the ascension. It is utterly improbable that these three other writers should deliberately refuse to give an account of the greatest event they had ever seen. We must consider the discrepancies of the writers concerning the number of days that Jesus remained on earth after his resurrection.

According to Luke's account, he did not remain on earth *one day*. "To-day shalt thou be with me in paradise" (Luke 23: 43)—that is, in heaven; see 2 Cor. 12: 4. In this same twenty-third chapter of Luke, Jesus does not ascend until the *third day* after his crucifixion; and in Acts 1: 3, it is recorded that he was "seen of them *forty days*."

Another slight discrepancy occurs in relation to the length of time Jesus was in the grave. Matthew says (12: 40), "For as Jonas was three nights in the whale's belly, so shall the Son of man be three days and three nights in the heart of the earth." But as Jesus was only two nights and one day in the grave there is no analogy between the two, hence the statement is radically erroneous.

An orthodox clergyman critic explains this seeming contradiction in this way: "In regard to Jesus being only one day and two nights in the grave, the very same quantity of time 'three days and three nights,' and which according to our computation was one whole day, parts of two others and two whole nights, is termed three days and three nights in the book of Esther. There is no impropriety in this interpretation." The word "interpretation" as here used is slightly equivocal, as is also the phrase "according to our computation." It is peculiar to mathematics that it does not change *according to our computation* or any kind of *interpretation*. It is always true that two and two make four whether the book of Esther acknowledges the fact or not. And it not only damages the gospels to bring forth this sort of evidence, but it seriously derogates from the inspiration of the book of Esther, which thus attempts in defiance of arithmetic to make one day and two nights into three days and three nights.

THE RESURRECTION OF JESUS.

No one saw Jesus come from the grave. When Mary Magdalene came to the sepulcher, "Behold there was a great earthquake, for the angel of the Lord descended from heaven, and came and rolled back the stone from the door and sat upon it. His countenance was like lightning and his raiment white as snow. And for fear of him the keepers did shake and become as dead men. And the angel answered and said unto the women, Fear not ye, for I know that ye seek Jesus, which was crucified. *He is not here,* for he is risen as he said. Come see the place where the Lord lay." (Mat. 28: 2-6.)

We have here the stone at the door of the sepulcher, and yet the body of Jesus had risen and departed from the tomb. There would seem to be no need in closing the grave after he had risen. But a more serious criticism must be made upon the fact that it is not pretended that there was any eye-witness of Jesus coming from the sepulcher. We have only the word of an angel, but as a story abounding with conversations of angels is legendary we are not permitted to take their testimony. Besides, we have serious contradictions concerning the number of angels seen. Matthew says there was one angel, and that he rolled back the stone from the door and sat upon it. Mark says that when Mary Magdalene and Mary the mother of James and Salome, had brought sweet spices, that they might come and anoint him; and very early in the morning, etc. "And they said among themselves, Who shall roll us away the stone from the door of the sepulcher? And when they looked, they saw that the stone *was rolled away,* for it was very great. And entering, they saw a *young man* sitting on the right side, clothed in a long white garment, and they were affrighted." (16: 1-3.)

Luke also says the stone was rolled away when the women came to the sepulcher, and upon entering in, behold "**two** men" *stood* by them in shining garments. John says Mary saw **two** angels in white *sitting*, the one at the head and the other at the feet where the body of Jesus had lain. Besides, she sees the stone rolled away from the door. Matthew records the descent of an angel from heaven; the other biographers of Jesus know nothing of this starting point of the angel. Matthew here says that the angel rolled away the stone from the door, but Mark, Luke, and John say that the stone *was rolled* from the door of the sepulcher when Mary Magdalene came to it. Matthew here relates that Mary Magdalene saw an angel sitting upon the stone at the door outside of the sepulcher, but Mark says she saw a young man sitting down *inside* the sepulcher. Luke avers that she saw two men *standing* inside of it, and John affirms that Mary Magdalene sees two men *sitting*, "one at the head and the other at the feet where the body of Jesus had lain;" but they do not tell her that Jesus had risen, as did the angel in Matthew, and the young man in Mark, and the two men in Luke.

According to John, Jesus first appeared to Mary Magdalene. But according to Luke Jesus did not first appear to Mary Magdalene, but to two persons traveling from Jerusalem to Emmaus: the name of one of them we are told was Cleopas. (Luke 24: 13.) But this appearance of Jesus to brethren who were not apostles is clearly legendary. The other synoptics seem to know nothing of it. It is wholly improbable that Jesus should, after his resurrection, appear first of all to two unknown Christians after this manner and accompany them upon such a journey.

Now all the attendant circumstances of this event are mysterious, inexplicable, and improbable; and the closing paragraph removes the account beyond sober history. "And it came to pass as he sat at meat with them, he took bread and blessed it and broke and gave to them. And their eyes were opened and they knew him, and he vanished out of their sight." (Luke 24: 30, 31.)

"Their eyes were holden," is superstitious, and as for his vanishing out of sight, we have the most unmistakable traces of legend—the fruit of ignorance and childish imagination.

We are called upon to believe that with feet, the bones of which were broken and crushed with the spikes driven through them on the cross, he traveled back to Jerusalem about as rapidly as did the two persons with whom he journeyed to Emmaus. How could he walk upon feet thus crippled? His hands were yet unhealed, although his fellow-travelers did not perceive such wounds, nor did they notice that he stepped haltingly.

He possessed the same *material* body which he had before his death. He could be *seen* and *touched*. All of which shows that he not only possessed a physical organization, but that it was the same body he had before his death. And yet this body could vanish from the two unknown brethren at Emmaus, it could travel rapidly, it could come in through closed doors, it could ascend from earth out of sight contrary to the laws of gravitation; he had flesh and bones, and could eat and drink. "And when he had thus spoken he showed them his hands and his feet, and while they believed not for joy and wondered, he said unto them, Have ye any meat? And they took and gave him a piece of broiled fish and honeycomb, and he took it and *did eat* before them." (Luke 24: 41–43.)

It is useless to attempt any explanation of this difficulty by calling his body a spiritual body. The disciples on this occasion, when Jesus suddenly appeared among them, thought they had seen a *spirit*, but Jesus wishing to disabuse their minds, said, "Behold my hands and my feet, that it is I myself; handle me and see; for a spirit *hath not flesh and bones*, as ye see me have." (Luke 24: 39.)

If we accept this plain declaration, then, we are forced to enquire what became of this physical body. It surely must have died. It is certain that if he ate and drank, he had a nutritive system—a human organism—subject to death. And what became of this "corruptible body?" Matthew and John do not pretend to know anything about the matter. Mark has no knowledge of the final disposition of his body, for the last twelve verses of Mark are generally regarded as spurious. Why should not all these writers have possesed the same information that Luke pretends to have? They do not write to complement and supplement the writings of one another, but each claims to give the important features of Jesus' biography independently. Is not the end of Jesus' career on earth important, in order to understand his life and character? Three of the four biographers by their silence say either that there is no importance to be attached to the ascension of Jesus, or that it was unknown to them; in other words, that it did not occur.

Passing this, we encounter irreconcilable contradictions between different writers as to the locality *where* Jesus appeared to his disciples after his resurrection. Matthew says the angel at the sepulcher informed the woman to "go quickly and tell his disciple that he is risen from the dead, and behold he goeth before you into Galilee; there ye shall see him." (28: 7.) "And as they went to tell his disciples, behold, Jesus met them and said, All hail!" (28: 9.) But as the angel had instructed them to go into Galilee, so also does Jesus give the same command, "Go tell my brethren that they go into Galilee, and there shall they see me." (28: 10.)

Mark gives a very similar account of the woman coming to the tomb and seeing the "young man," who said, "Be not affrighted; ye seek Jesus of Nazareth, which was crucified; he is risen; he is not here; behold the place where they laid him. But go your way and tell his disciples that he goeth before you into Galilee, there ye shall see him, as he said unto you." (16: 6, 7.)

The writers of the third and fourth gospels know nothing of any command to go into Galilee; but on the contrary, Luke relates the command of Jesus to his disciples to remain where they *were* until they should receive blessings from God. "Tarry ye in the city of Jerusalem until ye be endued with power from on high." (24: 49.) Here is manifestly an entire unconsciousness of any necessity of the disciples for going into Galilee. For, after giving this command, Luke goes on to say, "He led them out as far as Bethany, and he lifted up his hands and blessed them. And it came to pass while he blessed them, he was parted from them, and carried up into heaven." (24: 50, 51.)

The two gospels of Mark and Luke make no mention of any journey; but on the contrary, the immediate ascension of Jesus precludes the possibility of it. Matthew, who knows nothing of any ascension, gives this very equivocal statement of the affair: "Then the eleven disciples went away into Galilee into a mountain where Jesus had appointed them, and when they saw him they worshiped him, *but some doubted.*" (28: 16, 17.) But this is too vague; the point which would most interest us to know is what they doubted and who it was that doubted. Another equally vague expression is found in the fourth gospel, where it is related of Peter and John that they went into the sepulcher, "Then went in also that other disciple which came first to the sepulcher, and they *saw* and *believed*" (20: 8); but *what* they saw and believed is not made plain, except that they saw an empty tomb, or at least one which contained only the "linen clothes;" but what they *believed* concerning this empty grave we are not informed. If their belief maintained any correspondence with what they saw, they believed that they had seen an empty grave. But our difficulties do not cease; we are surprised that these early visitors of sepulchers do **not** see anything of the material in which Jesus was embalmed. It is recorded that "there came also Nicodemus which at the first came to Jesus by night, and brought a mixture of myrrh and aloes, about an hundred pound weight." (John 19: 39.)

It is but natural to suppose that if the linen clothes were laid off, the myrrh and aloes also would be found lying with them, for there is no probability that Jesus would go abroad *a la mummy.* We might ask where the clothes came from that he wore after coming out of the sepulcher. His own garments had been taken by the soldiery when he died, that the *scripture* might be *fulfilled* (?), but where is the scripture fulfilled which informs us whence came his resurrection garments? He did not go into society nude, and yet we have no evidence that any provisions were made for a new suit of clothes. Some have supposed that when Mary saw him and mistook him for the gardener her mistake arose from the fact that he may have been clothed in the garments of the gardener. But how did he get possession of them?

We must return to the contradictions in regard to the embalmment of Jesus. Matthew's version excludes the myrrh and aloes. He says, "And when Joseph had taken the body, he wrapped it in a clean linen cloth and laid it in his own new tomb." (27: 59, 60.)

The fourth gospel, as we have seen, relates that when Joseph of Arimathea and Nicodemus had received the body of Jesus, they embalmed it in "a mixture of myrrh and aloes, about an hundred pound weight." Mark knows nothing of this, and his account wholly excludes it. Joseph "bought fine linen and took him down and wrapped him in the linen and laid him in the sepulcher." (15: 46.) "And when the Sabbath was past, Mary Magdalene and Mary the mother of James, and Salome, had bought sweet spices that they might come and anoint him." (16: 1.) If the women came on the third day to embalm the body, they certainly knew nothing of its embalmment on the day of his death. Luke's version also excludes the version of the fourth gospel. As in Mark, so in Luke, they came on the first day of the week to perform this rite of embalmment. "And they [the women] returned and prepared spices and ointments . . . and upon the first day of the week, very early in the morning, they came unto the sepulcher, bringing the spices which they had prepared." (23: 56, and 24: 1.)

Some *exegetes* have *interpreted* this, by saying that "the women came to embalm the body of Jesus, being wholly ignorant of what Joseph and Nicodemus had done."

This might be sufficient if it were not for the fact that the women saw Jesus after he was put in the tomb. "And Mary Magdalene and Mary the mother of Jesus beheld where he was laid." (Mark 15: 47.) Matthew corroborates this: "And there was Mary Magdalene and the other Mary, sitting over against the sepulcher" (27: 61) when Jesus was placed in it.

The obvious meaning of these texts is that they saw him wrapped in "the fine linen" and laid away in the tomb. Here, then, are the contradictory statements. The writer of the fourth gospel relates how Jesus was embalmed on the day of his death; the writers of the second and third gospels state that the women came on the third day to perform this service, wholly unconscious of such embalmment having taken place on the day of Jesus' death; while the writer of the first gospel knows nothing of the embalmment on the day of his death, nor of the intended embalmment on the third day. He speaks of the early visit of the women as coming merely to *see* the grave. "In the end of the Sabbath, as it began to dawn, toward the first day of the week, came Mary Magdalene and the other Mary to *see* the sepulcher." (28: 1.)

Further contradictions are found in the statements of the writers as to the *time* when the women prepared the spices. Mark says (16: 11), that when the "*Sabbath* was *past*" the women bought spices with which to anoint the body of Jesus. Luke says they bought them before the Sabbath; "And they returned and prepared spices and ointments, and rested on the Sabbath day." (23: 56.)

Jesus Foretells his Resurrection.

There are a number of passages in the gospels which show that Jesus told his disciples over and over again that he should rise on the third day, and there are other passages which as plainly show that they had no thought of any such resurrection when the third day came. If he repeatedly told his followers that he was to be put to death in Jerusalem and rise again the third day, we must conclude that his disciples would remember his sayings and that at least some of them would wait for the third day to come, expecting to see the miracle transpire. But we are astounded to read over and over again of this "rising again the third day," and yet find no friend remembering or expecting the event when the third day came. It is urged that Jesus' followers did not understand his words, but this will not meet the case. If several of these disciples were intelligent enough to write the biography of their Master they could not have been so stupid as not to understand such plain words; besides, we must remember that his enemies understood him.

The Pharisee said to Pilate, "Sir, we remember that the deceiver said while he was yet alive, After three days I will rise again."

Pilate said, "Ye have a watch, go your way, make it sure as ye can." The disciples could not have failed to understand him, because it was a special effort on the part of Jesus to show that he must die and rise again on the third day.

"But their eyes were holden that they should not know him." (Luke 24: 16.)

This miraculous blindness is too irrational to discuss. It is certain that if their eyesight was good enough to see what was in the tomb "when it was yet *dark*" (John 20: 1), they would surely recognize an intimate friend if they journeyed with him in the highway in the middle of the afternoon.

"From that time forth began Jesus to show unto his disciples how that he must go up to Jerusalem, and suffer many things of the elders and chief priests and scribes and be killed, and be raised again the third day." (Mat. 16: 21.)

"And while they abode in Galilee, Jesus said unto them, The Son of man shall be betrayed into the hands of men: And they shall kill him, and the third day he shall rise again." (Mat. 27: 22, 23.)

"And Jesus going up to Jerusalem took the twelve disciples apart in the way and said unto them, Behold we go up to Jerusalem and the Son of man shall be betrayed unto the chiefs and priests and unto the scribes, and they shall condemn him to death, and shall deliver him to the Gentiles to mock, and to scourge, and to crucify him: and the *third day* he shall *rise* again." (Mat. 20: 17–19.)

"And he began to teach them, that the Son of man must suffer many things, and be rejected of the elders, and of the chief priests and scribes, and be killed, and after *three days rise* again. And he spoke that saying *openly*." (Mark 8: 31.)

There is not a chance to refer this prediction to the *esoteric* teachings of Jesus, for he "*spake* that saying *openly*."

"For he taught his disciples, and said unto them, The Son of man is delivered into the hands of men, and they shall kill him, and after that he is killed he shall rise the third day." (Mark 9: 31.)

"And he took again the twelve and began to tell them what things should happen unto him, saying, Behold, we go up to Jerusalem, and the Son of man shall be delivered unto the chief priests and unto the scribes, and they shall condemn him to death, and shall deliver him to the Gentiles, and they shall mock him, and shall scourge him; and shall spit upon him; and the third day he shall rise again." (Mark 10: 32, 33.)

"The Son of man must suffer many things, and be rejected of the elders and chief priests and scribes, and be slain, and be raised the *third day*." (Luke 9: 22.)

"Then he took unto him the twelve, and said unto them, Behold, we go up to Jerusalem, and all things that are written concerning the Son of man shall be accomplished. For he shall be delivered unto the Gentiles, and shall be mocked and spitefully entreated and spitted upon; and they shall scourge him, and put him to death, and the *third day* he shall *rise* again." (Luke 18: 31–33.)

These teaching are so plain and repeated so often that it is inconceivable that his disciples should not comprehend his meaning. If these passages had been as enigmatical as the following, there might have been some grounds for the claim of ignorance or dullness on the part of the disciples: "For as Jonas was three days and three nights in the whale's belly, so shall the Son of man be three days and three nights in the heart of the earth." (Mat. 12: 40.)

But the above predictions have nothing dark or obscure about them. The time of his resurrection is always specified as the *third day.*"

None of the Disciples Looking for a Resurrection.

With these numerous predictions of his resurrection before us, let us see whether they can be made to harmonize with other statements on the subject. When immediately after the transfiguration Jesus warns his disciples not to reveal what they had seen until after he had risen from the dead, we are told that they questioned among themselves "what *rising* from the *dead* should mean." (Mark 9: 2.)

How is it possible that such doubt and surprise could be expressed by men who had first witnessed the resurrection of Moses and Elias, and who had also seen the resurrection of the daughter of Jairus, the son of the widow of Nain and Lazarus!

Now it is plain that if they had ever witnessed these miraculous resurrections, they could not possibly have wondered "what the rising from the dead should mean." Both statements cannot be true, for if they thus *wondered*, it is proof enough that they had never seen the dead raised to life; and if they did not so express themselves, then the gospels are unhistorical. That they never queried in this manner among themselves is evident from the fact that the resurrection from the dead was at that time a doctrine generally accepted by the Jews. It is evident that those who undertook the embalmment of Jesus had no thought of his resurrection within forty-eight hours. But suppose it conceded that Jesus was deserted by his immediate friends, and his body handed over to Joseph and Nicodemus, who embalmed it in "a mixture of myrrh and olives about one hundred pound," possibly being ignorant of the repeated predictions of his resurrection on the third day, which were made to the disciples; still this is unavailing, as the disciples are also ignorant of any rising from the dead to take place on the *third day*. The women undertook the task of embalming the body of Jesus, but they seem not to have got fully prepared for the task until the third day. When his body was taken down from the cross and wrapped in linen and put in the sepulcher, "the women also which came with him from Galilee followed after, and beheld the sepulcher and how his body was laid, and they returned and prepared spices and ointments, and rested the Sabbath day according to the commandment. Now upon the first day of the week, very early in the morning, they came unto the sepulcher, *bringing the spices* which they had *prepared.*" (Luke 23: 55, 56, and 24: 1.)

"In the end of the Sabbath as it began to dawn toward the first day of the week, came Mary Magdalene, and the other Mary to *see* the *sepulcher.*" (Mat. 27: 61.)

These two writers, while not agreeing on the object of the women's visiting the sepulcher, nevertheless do agree that they did not go expecting to see the sepulcher empty.

This early visit was made ostensibly to anoint or embalm the body of Jesus. Mary Magdalene and the other women did not even dream of a resurrection—she did not come expecting to find the tomb empty, but was concerned to know how they should remove the stone from the mouth of the tomb. It is evident that if she had heard Jesus say repeatedly that on the third day after his death he would rise again, she would not have forgotten it; and if she had, she must have recollected his predictions when she found the grave empty. In fact she never once thinks of a resurrection, but when she sees the empty grave, exclaims, "They have taken away the Lord out of the sepulcher, and we know not where they have laid him." (John 20: 2.)

Luke says that, "As the women were much perplexed thereabout, behold two men stood by them in shining garments, and as they were afraid, and bowed themselves to the earth [people usually run away when they are frightened] they said unto them, Why seek ye the living among the dead? He is not here, but is risen; remember how he spoke unto you when he was yet in Galilee, saying: The Son of man must be delivered into the hands of sinful men, and be crucified, and the third day rise again. And they remembered his words." (Luke 24: 5-8.)

This is evidently an afterthought, an effort to fill out an imperfect record, but the patch is too perceptible; for had it been that the women needed only to have their memory jogged to recollect the prediction of Jesus concerning his rising from the dead on the third day, we may infer that a similar reminder would refresh the memory of the eleven, but on the contrary they scouted the idea of such a thing. The women "returned from the sepulcher and told all these things unto the eleven, and the rest . . And their words seemed to them as idle tales, and they believed them *not*." (24: 9, 11.)

Mark also says that the eleven did not believe the story of Mary Magdalene: "She went out and told them that had been with him, as they mourned and wept. And they, when they had heard that he was alive, and had been seen of her, *believed not*." (16: 10, 11.)

They also had not so much as a dream of the resurrection of Jesus. They were not waiting and watching for the third day to come that they might see the predictions of Jesus fulfilled and their hearts filled to overflowing with joy at the sight. They were not at the sepulcher, as we might naturally expect. True, it was not too early for the women impelled by human love to be there with ointments and spices; but the eleven who were baptized with heavenly love (John 20: 22), **entertained not the first thought of visiting** the grave. And even when the marvelous scenes witnessed by the women are clearly stated to the eleven who had heard him teach that he must go up to Jerusalem and be killed and the third day rise again—who had heard this teaching and prediction repeatedly and openly, and in the plainest language, and yet did not believe anything in it or in the report of the women—all this is simply incredible. We are forced to conclude that if they were not at the tomb on the third day, and scouted the story of the women—for "their words seemed to them as idle tales"—they had never once heard Jesus say he would rise from the dead on the third day.

Luke says, that of the eleven only Peter went to the sepulcher, and that stooping down "he saw the linen clothes laid by themselves, and departed wondering in himself at that which had come to pass." (24: 12.)

He wonders, but expresses no thought of a resurrection. The writer of the fourth gospel contradicts Luke in saying that there were two persons who went to the sepulcher on that occasion. "Peter therefore went forth, and that other disciple, and came to the sepulcher . . . Then went in also that other disciple, which came first to the sepulcher, and he saw and believed. For as yet they knew not the Scripture, that he must rise again from the dead." (John 20: 3, 9, 10.)

"He saw and believed," but we are not told *what* he believed. He did not certainly believe in the resurrection of Jesus. "For as yet they knew not the Scripture, that he must rise again." This passage is plainly legendary. It belongs to a later age when the dogma began to control the minds of Christians; for it is true that the early Christians did not insist so much upon the evidence of miracles as they did upon the prophecies. It must have been written long after that time, for it is not the "scriptures" they needed to *know* to be informed concerning his resurrection, but the plain language of Jesus which he had with special effort, and in an open manner uttered in their ears but a few days before. It was wholly needless for them to know the scriptures in order to recollect these prophetic predictions. Regard these statements as we may, they are certainly unhistorical. For if Jesus so frequently spoke of his death and subsequent resurrection, then it is certain that they would have remembered his words, and if they had not cherished them with faith, yet when they had heard from the women of the empty grave, they would without doubt, have recalled his predictions, and claimed their fulfillment. But they do no such thing. They said of the women's story what was probably true, that "their words seemed to them as idle tales, and [therefore] they believed them not."

The Evidence of Paul on the Resurrection of Jesus.

He gives his testimony in this form: "For I delivered unto you first of all that which I also *received*, that Christ died for our sins according to the Scriptures, and was buried, and that he rose again the third day according to the Scriptures. And that he was seen by Cephas, then by the twelve. After that he was seen of above five hundred brethren at once, of whom the greater part remain unto this present, but some are fallen asleep. After that he was seen by James, then by all the Apostles. And last of all he was seen of me also, as of one born out of due time." (1 Cor. 15: 4–8.)

In this statement Paul does not pretend to have witnessed the event himself, but preaches it as a doctrine which he had "received." He speaks of it as a tradition, "that Christ died for our sins according to the Scriptures, and that he was buried, and that he rose again the third day *according to the Scriptures.*"

This language betrays the influence of the dogma of a later date; for the writer in speaking of the five hundred by whom Jesus was said to have been seen says, "of whom the greater part remain unto this present [day] but some are fallen asleep." "Unto this present" [day] shows that the writer is making his record long after the event.

THE RESURRECTION OF JESUS. 111

Paul wrote probably about twenty-five years after the date of the events he records. And the writers of the gospels also wrote at a late date. Matthew says, "And this saying is commonly reported among the Jews *until this day*." (28: 15.)

The phrase "until this day" points out the fact that the gospel records were not completed until long after the time of their occurrence. In addition to this, there were many gospels recording the life and doings of Jesus. "Forasmuch as *many* have taken in hand to set forth in order a declaration of those things which are most surely believed among us." (Luke 1: 1.) "*Believed* among us"—he did not *know*, but merely *believed* these things. Now suppose we had these other gospels, what harmony could we expect to find among the imaginary five hundred if they had left a record of what was "most surely *believed*."

"He was seen by Cephas." It is significant of Paul's independence, that while the writers of the four gospels all explicitly declare that Jesus first appeard to Mary Magdalene, Paul knows nothing of such an appearance. That he makes no mention of this first appearance of Jesus is evidence that he wrote independently of others, as he said he did, and also that he wrote before the evangelists wrote. He had no honors to bestow upon women, as his writings show, and if he had ever heard of this appearance to Mary Magdalene, he concluded that it was "an idle tale." (Luke 24: 11.)

It is noticeable also that although this doctrine is "received" as a prediction of the scriptures, yet no one is recorded in either of the gospels or writings of Paul as having seen Jesus rise from the sepulcher. Even though it is affirmed that Mary Magdalene and the other Mary had seen the angel from heaven *roll back the stone* from the mouth of the sepulcher, yet they did not witness any resurrection.

All that Paul "received" on this subject was the current traditions. As a Pharisee, he believed in the doctrine of a **general resurrection, and it was most natural for him to** accept such tradition into his belief. That he wrote under the influence of a later age, when the dogma began to assume character, is manifest in the recourse he has to scripture evidences. "And that he rose again the third day *according* to the *Scriptures.*" (1 Cor. 15: 4.) But the passages usually cited as proof-predictions that Jesus should rise from the dead, when examined, cannot be regarded as Messianic at all; for the idea of a *suffering* Messiah was wholly foreign to the Jewish mind. The scriptures usually cited are Isaiah 53; Psalms 22 and 69; Psalms 16: 10; Hosea 6: 2.

As illustrating the free use made of the scriptures, we have only to compare Matthew 12: 40 with parallel passages of Mark and Luke. Mark (8: 11), says, "And the Pharisees came forth and began to question with him, seeking of him a sign from heaven, tempting him. And he sighed deeply in his spirit and saith, Why doth this generation seek after a sign? Verily I say unto you, there shall no sign be given unto this generation."

Luke (11: 29-31) states that "when the people were gathered thick together, he began to say, This is an evil generation; they seek a sign; and there shall no sign be given it, but the sign of Jonas the prophet. For as Jonas was a sign unto the Ninevites, so shall the Son of man be to this generation."

Matthew gives two versions of this incident, "A wicked and adulterous generation seeketh after a sign, and there shall be no sign but the sign of the prophet Jonas." (16: 4.) "Certain of the scribes and of the Pharisees answered, saying, Master, we would see a sign from thee. But he answered and said unto them, An evil and adulterous generation seeketh after a sign, and there shall no sign be given to it, but the sign of the prophet Jonas. For as Jonas was three days and three nights in the whale's belly so shall the Son of man be three days and three nights in the heart of the earth." (Mat. 12: 38-41.)

Here it will be observed is an illustration of the growth of the dogma and myth in adding this reference to Jonas. And it is highly significant that the application of the myth of Jonas is wholly fanciful, as the passage referred to (Jonah 1: 17.) has not the slighest character of prophecy. That the scriptures are evidently tortured is obvious from the fact that Jesus was only one day and two nights in the heart of the earth, and, as before said, the passage is not prophetic; besides, its varied form in the gospels plainly shows it to be a myth.

"He was seen by Cephas, then by the twelve, and after that he was seen by above five hundred brethren at once." But there were only *eleven* Apostles until after the ascension, when Matthias was elected to fill the vacancy occasioned by the death of Judas. "And they gave forth their lots, and the lot fell upon Matthias; and he was numbered with the *eleven* apostles." (Acts 1: 26.)

This election of Matthias took place after the ascension. He could not therefore have been seen by the "twelve" *after* his *ascension* (and there were not twelve until after the ascension), only by the "eye of faith."

That Jesus was seen by above five hundred is nothing more than naked statement. Paul does not claim to have been one of that number. This episode, moreover, is not mentioned in any of the four gospels. It is remarkable that so great an event should be passed over by other writers also, for not a trace of it can be found elsewhere. It is difficult for us to understand how this marvelous scene could so completely perish out of sight of all writers except one who was not present, but merely heard of it afterward. That Paul may have believed the story we do not deny— and that he believed that the greater part of the witnesses "remain unto this present" time. Now if these survivors remained he does not mention the names of any of them. And besides, they were not within reach of the Corinthians who might wish to hear and investigate their testimony, for the Corinthians did not accept the resurrection of Jesus as a matter of fact.

How could five hundred disciples come together immediately at one time, when some time after the ascension the number of disciples at Jerusalem was only one hundred and twenty? (Acts 1: 15.)

We need to know something of the character of those who gave Paul this information, and the sources of their knowledge. For it is all-important to our inquiry to know from whom Paul *received* these traditions and what evidences his informants had of the truth of the story they told. To believe in the reality of these appearances simply because Paul states that he has "received" his information from others and believes it to be true, without inquiring as to the character of his informers, is the blindest credulity. Who were the five hundred? What did they think of the event? How did Paul or any other person know what they thought, if there were no written statements by them? Where and when did the five hundred see the risen Jesus?

"Last of all he was seen by me." In another place he says, "Have I not seen Jesus Christ our Lord?" (1 Cor. 9: 1.)

Elsewhere he relates: "But when he was pleased, God, who separated me from my mother's womb, and called me through his grace to reveal his son in me, that I might preach him among the heathen, immediately I conferred not with flesh and blood, but I went into Arabia and returned again to Damascus." (Gal. 1: 15–17.)

"For neither did I receive it from men nor was taught it, but through the *revelation* of Jesus Christ." (Gal. 1: 11.) We shall find as we proceed that Paul saw Jesus *subjectively*. It is quite natural to so understand his words. "reveal his son in me." Especially does this seem obvious when we remember that Paul was a man who firmly believed in visions and revelations. In relating his own experience he states this fact plainly. "I knew a man in Christ above fourteen years ago (whether in the body I cannot tell—God knoweth), such a one caught up to the third heaven. And I knew such a man (whether in the body or out of the body, I cannot tell—God knoweth) how that he was caught up into paradise and heard unspeakable words, which it is not lawful for man to utter. Of such an one will I glory." (2 Cor. 12: 2-4.)

In Acts there are three contradictory accounts of his seeing Jesus in a vision. "And as he journeyed, he came near Damascus: and suddenly there shined round about him a *light* from *heaven*. And he fell to the earth and heard a voice saying unto him, Saul, Saul, why persecutest thou me? And he said, Who art thou, Lord? And the Lord said I am Jesus, whom thou persecutest: it is hard for thee to kick against the pricks. And he, trembling and astonished, said, Lord, what wilt thou have me to do? And the Lord said unto him, Arise, and go into the city, and it will be told thee what thou must do. And the men which journeyed with him stood speechless, hearing a voice, but seeing no man." (Acts 9: 3-7.)

A second version is in this form: "And it came to pass that as I made my journey and was come nigh unto Damascus about noon, suddenly there shone from heaven a great light round about me. And I fell unto the ground, and heard a voice saying unto me Saul, Saul, why persecutest thou me? And I answered, Who art thou, Lord? And he said unto me, I am Jesus of Nazareth, whom thou persecutest. And they that were with me *saw* indeed the *light* and were afraid, but they heard not the voice of him that spoke to me. And I said, Lord, what wilt thou have me do? And the Lord said unto me, Arise, and go into Damascus, and there it shall be told thee of all the things which are appointed for thee to do." (Acts 22: 6-10.)

The third account of the affair is given thus: "Whereupon as I went to Damascus with authority and commission from the chief priests, at mid-day, O king, I saw in the way a light from heaven, above the brightness of the sun, shining round about me. And when we were all fallen to the earth, I heard a voice speaking unto me, saying, in the Hebrew tongue, Saul, Saul, why persecutest thou me? it is hard for thee to kick against the pricks. And I said, Who art thou, Lord? And he said, I am Jesus of Nazareth, whom thou persecutest . . . Whereupon, O king, I was not disobedient unto the heavenly *vision*." (Acts 26: 9–19.)

According to the first account the companions of Paul "*stood* speechless" (9: 7); in the third they "*all fall* to the *earth*." (26: 14.) Then again, in the first account it is said that the men "stood speechless, *hearing* the *voice*, but seeing no one." In the second it is stated that "they that were with me saw indeed the light, but they *heard not* the voice." These contradictions do not seem to clothe the vision of Paul with the acceptable form of harmony.

It will be observed that even in this *vision* Paul is not described as *seeing* Jesus. He *sees* a *light* and falls to the ground, and when he rises he is blind. "And they led him by the hand and brought him to Damascus. And he was three days without sight." (9: 8.)

In the continuation of this account Paul has another vision: "And it came to pass that when I was come again to Jerusalem, even while I prayed in the temple, I was in a trance, and saw him saying unto me, Make haste and get thee out of Jerusalem." (22: 17, 18.)

In connection with these visions and revelations it is highly significant that Paul never claims to have seen Jesus in the flesh, and he never speaks of the resurrection as material, but as spiritual. "It is sown a natural body, it is raised a spiritual body." (1 Cor. 15: 44.) "Who shall change our vile bodies that it may be fashioned like unto his glorious body," (Phil. 3: 21.) Evidently there *is no claim* for seeing Jesus *in the body* made by *Paul* in any of his writings. He preaches the doctrine of the resurrection, but this doctrine he, as a Pharisee, believed before he became a Christian. Paul claims that in a vision he saw Jesus. Luke says that this was also the manner in which

Mary Magdalene and the other women saw Jesus. "And when they found not his body, they came, saying, that they had also seen a *vision* of angels, which said that he was alive." (24: 2, 3.)

This gives force to the claim of Paul, that his seeing or *vision* of Jesus was of the same class as the visions of all the others who had seen him.

Thus, after a careful examination of the writings attributed to the immediate followers of Jesus, we find that not one of them says, "I saw Jesus rise from the grave;" or "I saw Jesus in the flesh after his resurrection." In legendary style it is frequently repeated that he "appeared" first to this and then to that one, but there is not the slightest evidence that any one saw him. And in this connection it is worthy of remark that Jesus did not appear to any persons except his friends. This gives better occasion for suspicion that the story is mythical.

"Him God raised up the third day, and showed him openly, not to all the people, but unto witnesses chosen before of God, even to us who did eat and drink with him." (Acts 10: 41.) To appear to a few private friends for *one day* does not seem much like bringing life and immortality to light to the whole world. The method is too narrow and exclusive. And even of these few friends not one has left the record for us of what he saw. The writers who have recorded the current traditions of their time, agree in saying that Mary Magdalene found the grave empty: further than this the writers do not corroborate one another.

How soon the resurrection of the physical body became popular we have no means of knowing. It was not certainly until some time after the writings of Paul were given to the churches, for he, as we have seen, speaks, of it as a *spiritual* resurrection. So also does Peter (1 Peter 3: 18), speak of Jesus "being slain in the flesh, but made alive again in the *spirit.*"

The legend became more and more marvelous as it spread abroad. Enthusiasm inflamed the minds of the ignorant and superstitious until the subjective visions of Paul became crystalized into objective realities. His visions, and the visions, revelations and messages of the angels of others were reduced in popular belief to historical facts.

CHRISTIANITY WITHOUT HISTORICAL BASIS.

1. No one of the four gospels is mentioned in any other part of the New Testament. [This assuredly would not have been the case had they been the oldest, and the foundation on which the whole was built.]

2. No work of art of any kind has ever been discovered, no painting or engraving, no sculpture or other relic of antiquity which may be looked upon as furnishing additional evidence of the existence of those gospels, and which was executed earlier than the latter part of the second century. Even the explorations of the Christian catacombs failed to bring to light any evidence of that character.

3. The four gospels were written in Greek, and there was no translation of them into other languages earlier than the third century.

4. No manuscript of the gospels are in existence dating further back than the fourth century. Of that century, or the next, there are three or four, and some twenty or thirty, more than a thousand years old.

5. No autograph manuscript of any of the gospels has ever been known, so far as there is any authentic record, nor has any credible witness ever claimed to have seen such a manuscript. No one has ever claimed to have seen such a manuscript of either of the four gospels in the hand-writing of Luke, Mark, Matthew, or John. If the autograph manuscripts had ever existed they would have been preserved among the most sacred relics of the church.

6. During the first two centuries tradition was esteemed of more value and better evidence of the gospel history, than any written books or manuscripts.

7. The dialect in which the New Testament books were written, a sort of Hebraistic Greek, has been considered evidence of their antiquity. But this dialect prevailed three centuries after Christ, and was in full use during the second century. The same or similar Hebraisms abound in the apocryphal gospels of that age.

8. The canonical gospels were selected by the bishops from a large number then in circulation.

In taking a general review of the first hundred and seventy years of the Christian religion the first thing that strikes the mind is the dearth of material from which to construct a reliable history. It is seen at once how much must rest upon probability in its different degrees—how much must be relegated to the province of speculation. The works of the only church historian who wrote during that period, lost or destroyed the few fragments that are left being of comparatively no value—the writings of Porphyry and others who wrote against Christianity, and those of the heretic Christians, all destroyed—there remain only the works of some of the orthodox fathers, and the text of those in a mutilated and corrupted condition.

Such is the material at the hands of the historian. Of course he cannot rely implicitly upon the unsupported assertion of any such writer for the truth of any historical fact whatever. In every instance he is obliged to scrutinize carefully, and endeavor to ascertain whether any ulterior motives may have prompted whatever statement may be under consideration. If he can find none, and the fact stands uncontradicted by other writers, it is cautiously accepted. Under such circumstances progress is slow and uncertain. The most that any writer can hope to accomplish is to place in proper shape what is already known, and to establish here and there a landmark for the benefit of subsequent historians.

In conclusion, as the result of this investigation, it may be repeated that no evidence is found of the existence in the first century of either of the following doctrines: the immaculate conception—the miracles of Christ—the material resurrection. No one of these gospels is found in the epistles of the New Testament, nor have we been able to find them in other writings of the first century.

As to the four gospels, in coming to the conclusion that they were not written in the first century, we have but recorded the conviction of the most advanced scholars of the present day, irrespective of their religious views in other respects; with whom as now presented, is, How early in the second century were they composed. Discarding as inventions of the second century, having no historical foundation, the three doctrines above named, and much else which must necessarily stand or fall with them, what remains of the Christian religion? (C. B. Waite, "History of the Christian Religion to the year 200.")

The Canon.

"The infancy of the canon was cradled in an uncritical age and rocked with traditional ease. Conscientious care was not directed from the first to the well authenticated testimony of eye-witnesses. Of the three fathers who contributed most to its early growth, Irenæus was credulous and blundering; Tertullian passionate and one-sided; and Clement, of Alexandria, imbued with the treasures of Greek wisdom, was mainly occupied with ecclesiastical ethics.

"Irenæus agrees that the gospels should be four in number, neither more nor less, because there are four universal winds and four quarters of the world. The Word or Architect of all things gave the gospel in a four-fold shape. According to this father the apostles were fully informed concerning all things, and had a perfect knowledge after their Lord's ascension.

"He says, 'Matthew wrote his gospels while Peter and Paul were preaching in Rome, and founding the church.' Such assertions show both ignorance and exaggeration.

"Tertullian affirms that the tradition of the apostolic churches guarantees the four gospels, and refers his readers to the churches of Corinth, Philippi, Ephesus, etc., for the authentic epistles of Paul. What is this but the rhetoric of an enthusiast?

"Clement contradicts himself in making Peter authorize Mark's gospel to be read in the churches, while in another place he says the apostles 'neither forbade nor encouraged it.'

"The three fathers of whom we are speaking had neither the ability nor inclination to examine the genesis of documents surrounded with an apostolic halo. No analysis of their authenticity and genuineness was seriously attempted. In its absence, custom, accident, taste, practical needs, directed the tendency of tradition. All the rhetoric employed to throw the value of their testimony as far back as possible, even up to or very near to the apostle John, is of the vaguest sort. Appeals to the continuity of tradition and of church doctrine, to the exceptional veneration of these fathers for the gospels, to their opinions being formed earlier than the composition of the works in which they are expressed, possess no force.

"The ends which the fathers in question had in view, their polemic motives, their uncritical, inconsistent assertions, their want of sure data, detract from their testimony. Their decisions were much more the result of pious feeling, biased by the theological speculations of the times, than the conclusions of a sound judgment. The *very arguments* they use to establish certain conclusions show *weakness* of perception. What are the manifestations of spiritual feeling compared with the result of logical reasoning?" (Davidson on the Canon.)

Thus we have the testimony of one of the ablest and clearest minds that has ever written upon the canon which the fathers most depended upon to establish the authenticity of the small books forming it, were "ignorant," "credulous," "blundering," "passionate," "one-sided," "uncritical," "inconsistent," "possessed undue enthusiasm with contradictions;" "not possessing ability or inclination to examine;" "attempting no analysis of genuineness;" "an unreasonable apostolic reverence." "Custom, accident, taste, and the tendency of tradition taking the place of careful examination;" "a disposition to misrepresent;" "exceptional veneration of the fathers for the gospels older than the composition;" "want of data; "their decisions the result of pious feeling based upon [incorrect] theological speculations;" "unsound judgment;" "weakness of perception;" "lack of logical reasoning." These are the characteristics of the fathers depended upon to establish the authenticity of a gospel story which has no solid foundation to rest upon and which is clearly of an apocryphal character. ("Answers to Christian Questions" pp. 69-70, by D. M. Bennett.)

"One hundred and seventy years from the coming of Christ elapsed before the collection assumed a form that carried with it the idea of *holy* and inspired." (Davidson on the Canon, p. 106.)

"It is clear that the earliest church fathers did not use the books of the New Testament as sacred documents clothed with divine authority, but followed for the most part, at least till the middle of the second century, apostolic tradition orally transmitted." (Ibid, p. 107.)

"Their decisions (the fathers) were much more the result of pious feeling biased by the theological speculations of the times, than the conclusions of a sound judgment. The very arguments they use to establish certain conclusions show weakness of perception." (Ibid p. 124.)

"The men who first canonized them (the gospels) had no certian knowledge of their authors." (Ibid p. 127.)

"That Luke did not write the gospel of Luke." (Ibid 2, p. 25.)

"The canon was not the work of the Christian Church so much as of the men who were striving to form the church." (Ibid p. 129.)

"Professor Davidson says that the Gospel of Matthew, as we have it now could not have been written by Matthew. Intro. New Test. 1, p. 484. He says that the present Gospel of Mark was not written by Mark and that its author is unknown." (Ibid 2, p. 83, 84.)

Of John's Gospel he says:

"Its existence before 140 A. D. is incapable either of decision or probable showing. The Johannine authorship has receded before the tide of modern criticism, and though this tide is arbitrary at times, it is here irresistible.

"No certain traces of the existence of the fourth gospel can be found till after Justin Martyr, that is till after the middle of the second century." (Ibid 2, p. 520.)

The Value of Papias' Testimony.

"Suppose Papias is referring to our present gospel of Mark, what testimony have we to the authenticity of Jesus' words as contained in it? Just this: Eusebius says that Papias said that John the presbyter said that Mark said that Peter said that Jesus said thus and so." (Keeler's "Short History of the Bible," p. 19.)

Ignorance and Dishonesty of the Early Fathers.

That the charge of *ignorance* justly attaches to many of the fathers of the church, and that of *dishonesty* as well, there is abundant evidence, but a small portion of this can be given here. Mosheim, in part 2 chapter 3 of his "Ecclesiastical History," says:

"'The interest of virtue and true religion suffered yet more grievously by the monstrous errors that were universally adopted in this century, and became a source of innumerable calamities and mischiefs of succeeding ages. The first of these maxims was *that it was an act of virtue to deceive and lie* when by that means the interest of the church might be promoted; and the second, equally horrible, though in another point of view, was "that errors in religion, when maintained and adhered to after proper admonition were punishable with civil penalties and corporal tortures." The former of these erroneous maxims was now of long standing. It had been adopted for long ages past, and had produced an incredible number of ridiculous fables, fictitious prodigies, and pious frauds to the remarkable detriment to that glorious cause in which they were employed. And it must be frankly confessed that the greatest men and the most eminent saints of this century [the fourth] were more or less tainted with the infection of this corrupt principle, as will appear evident to such as look with an attentive eye to their writings and actions. We would willingly except from this charge Ambrose, and Hiliary Augustine, Gregory Nazianzen, and Jerome; but truth, which is more respectable than these venerable fathers, obliges us to involve them in the general accusation."

At another time he says, as translated by Vidal:

"At the time when he [Hermas] wrote, it was an established maxim with many Christians to avail themselves of fraud and deception, if it was likely they would conduce toward the attainment of any considerable good."

He again says:

"It was considered that they who made it their business to deceive, with a view of promoting the cause of truth, were deserving rather of commendation than censure."

The French Protestant writer, Casaubon, talks in a similar way, thus:

"It mightily affects me to see how many there were in the earliest times of the church who considered it a capital exploit to lend to heavenly truth the help of their own inventions in order that the new doctrine might be received by the wise among the Gentiles. These officious lies, they said, were devised for a good end."

Le Clerc, corroborating these opinions, says:

"Dissemblers of truth are nowhere to be met with in such abundance as among the writers of church history."

M. Daille, another learned and impartial French writer, in his celebrated work, the "Use of the Fathers," says:

"We find them saying things which they did not themselves believe. They are mutually witnesses against each other, that they are not to be believed absolutely on their bare word."

In book 1, chapter 6, he states upon the authority of St. Jerome, that:

"Origin, Methodius, Eusebius, Apollonaris, have written largely against Celsus and Porphyry. Do but observe their manner of arguing, and what slippery problems they used. They alleged against the Gentiles, not what they believed, but what they thought necessary."

Jerome himself adds:

"I forbear mentioning the Latin writers, as Tertullian, Cyprian, Minutius, Victorinus, Lactantius, Hiliary, lest I should rather seem to accuse others than defend myself."

Daille adds of the fathers:

"They made no scruple to forge whole books."

An able writer in the Eclectic Review of 1814, page 179, speaks of the fathers in this way:

"When we consider the number of gospels, acts, epistles, revelations, traditions, and constitutions which were put in circulation during the first three centuries, and which are unquestionably spurious, we find sufficient reason for examining with care and receiving with extreme caution productions attributed to eminent men in the primitive church. Some of the early Christians do not seem to have possessed in some points a nice sense of moral obligation. The writing of books under false names, and the circulating of fables, were not accounted violations of duty; or, if the impropriety of such conduct was felt, the end proposed—the promotion of the Christian cause—was thought to justify the means employed for the accomplishment. (From D. M. Bennett's "Answers to Christian Questions," p. 78–80.)

Jesus Not a Historical Character.

The following very pertinent argument is made use of by the Rev. S. Baring-Gould in his "Lost and Hostile Gospels": "It is somewhat remarkable that no contemporary, or even early account of the life of our Lord exists, except from the pen of Christian writers. That we have none by Greek or Roman writers is not, perhaps, to be wondered at; but it is singular that neither Philo, Josephus, nor Justus of Tiberius, should ever have alluded to Christ or to primitive Christianity. Philo was born at Alexandria about twenty years before Christ. In the year A. D. 40 he was sent by the Alexandrian Jews on a mission to Caligula, to entreat the emperor not to put in force his order that his statue should be erected in the temple of Jerusalem and in all the synagogues of the Jews. Philo was a Pharisee. He traveled in Palestine, and speaks of the Essenes he saw there; but he says not a word about Jesus Christ or his followers. It is possible that he may have heard of the new sect, but he probably concluded it was but insignificant, and consisted merely of the disciples, poor and ignorant, of a Galilean rabbi, whose doctrines he, perhaps did not stay to inquire into, and supposed they did not differ fundamentally from the traditional teaching of the rabbis of his day."

The Spurious Passage in Josephus.

"At this time lived Jesus, a wise man [if indeed he ought to be called a man]; for he performed wonderful works [he was a teacher of men who received the truth with gladness]; and he drew to him many Jews and also many Greeks. [This was the Christ.] But when Pilate, at the instigation of our chiefs, had condemned him to crucifixion, they who at first loved him did not cease; [for he appeared to them on the third day again; for the divine prophets had foretold this, together with many other wonderful things concerning him], and even to this time the community of Christians called after him, continues to exist."

That this passage is *spurious* has been almost universally acknowledged. One may be accused perhaps of killing dead birds, if one again examines and discredits the passage; but as the silence of Josephus on the subject which we are treating is a point on which it will be necessary to insist, we cannot omit as brief a discussion as possible of the celebrated passage.

The passage is first quoted by Eusebius (fl. A.D. 315) in two places (Hist. Eccl. lib. 1. c. 11; Demonst. Evang. lib. 3.), but it was unknown to Justin Martyr (fl. A.D. 140.), Clement of Alexandria (fl. A.D. 192), Tertullian (fl. A.D. 193), and Origen (fl. A.D. 230.) Such a testimony would certainly have been produced by Justin in his apology, or in his controversy with Trypho the Jew, had it existed in the copies of Josephus at his time. The silence of Origen is still more significant. Celsus in his book against Christianity introduces a Jew. Origen attacks the arguments of Celsus and his Jew. He could not have failed to quote the words of Josephus, whose writings he knew, had the passage existed in the genuine text. He indeed distinctly affirms that Josephus did not believe in Christ. (Contra. Celsus 1.)

Again the paragraph interrupts the chain of ideas in the original text. Before this passage comes an account of how Pilate, seeing there was a want of pure drinking water in Jerusalem, conducted a stream into the city from a spring two hundred stadia distant, and ordered that the cost should be defrayed out of the treasury of the Temple. This occasioned a riot. Pilate disguised Roman soldiers as Jews, with swords under their cloaks, and sent them among the rabble, with orders to arrest the ringleaders. This was done. The Jews finding themselves set upon by other Jews, fell into confusion; one Jew attacked another, and the whole company of rioters melted away. "And in this manner," says Josephus, "was this insurrection suppressed." Then follows the paragraph about Jesus, beginning, "At this time lived Jesus, a wise man, if indeed one ought to call him a man," etc., and the passage is immediately followed by, "About this time another misfortune threw the Jews into disturbance; and in Rome an event happened in the temple of Isis which produced great scandal." And then he tells an indelicate story of religious deception which need not be repeated here. The misfortune which befell the Jews was, as he afterward relates, that Tiberius drove them out of Rome. The reason of this was, he says, that a noble Roman lady who had become a proselyte, had sent gold and purple to the temple at Jerusalem. But this reason is not sufficient. It is clear from what precedes—a story of sacerdotal fraud—that there was some connection between the incidents in the mind of Josephus. Probably the Jews had been guilty of religious deceptions in Rome, and had made a business of performing cures and expelling demons, with talismans, and incantations, and for this had obtained rich payment.

From the connection that exists between the passage about the "other misfortune which befell the Jews," and the former one about the riot suppressed by Pilate, it appears evident that the whole of the paragraph concerning our Lord is an interpolation. That Josephus could not have written the passage as it stands, is clear enough, for only a Christian would speak of Jesus in the terms employed. Josephus was a Pharisee and a Jewish priest; he shows in all his writings that he believes in Judaism.

It has been suggested that Josephus may have written about Christ as in the passage quoted, but that the portions within brackets are the interpolations of a Christian copyist. But when these portions within brackets are removed, the passage loses all its interest and is a dry statement utterly unlike the sort of notice Josephus would have been likely to insert. He gives color to his narratives; his incidents are always sketched with vigor; this account would be meagre besides those of the riot of the Jews and the rascality of the priests of Isis. Josephus asserts, moreover, that in his time there were four sects among the Jews —the Pharisees, the Sadducees, the Essenes, and the sect of Judas of Gamala. He gives tolerably copious particulars about these sects, and their teachings, but of the Christian sect he says not a word. Had he wished to write about it, he would have given full details, likely to interest his readers, and not have dismissed the subject in a couple of lines.

It was perhaps felt by the early Christians that the silence of Josephus, so famous a historian and a Jew, on the life, miracles, and death of the founder of Christianity was extremely inconvenient; the fact could not fail to be noticed by their adversaries. Some Christian transcriber may have argued, either Josephus knew nothing of the miracles performed by Christ—in which case he is a weighty testimony against them—or he must have heard of Jesus, but not having deemed his acts, as they were related to him, of sufficient importance to find a place in history. Arguing thus, the copyist took the opportunity of rectifying the omission, written from the stand point of a Pharisee, and therefore designated the Lord as merely a wise man. (D. M. Bennett in "Jesus Christ.")

That this paragraph, concerning the Lord Jesus Christ, is not Josephus's but an interpolation, is argued from these several following considerations:

1. It is not quoted or referred to by any Christian writer before Eusebius, who flourished at the beginning of the fourth century, and afterward.

2. This paragraph was wanting in the copies of Josephus which were seen by Photius, in the ninth century.

3. It interrupts the course of the narration.

4. It is unsuitable to the general character of Josephus, who is allowed not to have been a Christian.

5. If Josephus were the author of this paragraph, it would be reasonable to expect in him frequent mention of Christ's miracles; whereas he is everywhere else silent about them.

6. The word Christ or Messiah appears not in any place in all the works of Josephus, excepting two; namely, the paragraph which we have been considering, which is now in the eighteenth book of his Antiquities; and another in the twentieth book of the same Antiquities where is mention

made of James, the brother Jesus who is called 'Christ.' (Works of N. Lardner, vol. 7, pp. 14, 15.)

EUSEBIUS.

The Father of Church History.

In referring to his work of writing a history of the church up to his own times, he says:

"We are attempting a kind of trackless and unbeaten path."

Again he says of Philo Judæus that he was a very "learned man." Among many other things which contradict this estimate, is the fact that Philo takes more than one hundred pages in showing how that dreams are sent from God.

Again, Eusebius does not say that the last works of Hegesippus, Papias and Dionysius of Corinth, contain anything concerning the canonical gospels; therefore, they contained none.

We give the opinion of a few well-known writers upon this "father of church history":

In Draper's Intellectual Development of Europe, p. 197, Bunsen and Niebuhr are quoted—the one (Bunsen) as saying that he purposely "perverted chronology for the sake of making synchronisms," and the other (Niebuhr) declaring "he is a very dishonest writer."

"Eusebius had a peculiar faculty of diverging from the truth." ("History of Christian Religion," p. 7.)

"The gravest of the ecclesiastical historians, Eusebius, himself, indirectly confesses that he has related whatever might redound to the glory, and has suppressed all that could tend to the disgrace of religion." (Gibbon's "Rome," vol. 1, p. 493.)

"In one of the most learned and elaborate works that antiquity has left us, the thirty-second chapter of the twelfth book of his evangelical preparation, bears for its title this scandalous proposition: 'How it may be lawful and fitting to use falsehood as a medicine and for the benefit of those who want to be deceived.'" (Gibbon's "Vindication," p. 76.)

"But Eusebius, the father of church history, capped the climax by fabricating the celebrated passage about "Jesus, a wise man, if it be lawful to call him such." ("Anti-Christ, p. 28.)

"He (Eusebius) has frankly told us that his principle in writing history was to conceal the facts that were injurious to the reputation of the church." (Lecky's "European Morals," vol. 1, p. 492.)

"Eusebius, who would never lie or falsify except to promote the glory of God." (Taylor's Diegesis, p. 345.)

Eusebius pronounces a panegyric upon Constantine. The following is the list of Constantine's murders as given by Robert Taylor:

Maximinian, his wife's father..	A. D. 310
Bassianus, his sister Anastacia's husband...................	" " 314
Licinianus, his nephew by Constantina.........................	" " 319
Fausta, his wife...	" " 320
Sopater, his former friend...	" " 321
Licinius, his sister Constantina's husband...................	" " 325
Crispus, his own son...	" " 326

And the church still continues to regard these two persons as holy men of God, raised up for a wise purpose—the one an open, wholesale murderer, and the other a cowardly, cunning and corrupt priest. The vast injury they have done the human race can never be computed. They poisoned the fountains of civilization, and all christendom has been drinking its poisoned waters ever since. If there are anywhere in history two men who have done their fellow men more positive harm and wrong, I do not know them. Their names should be held up to eternal scorn.

Baronius, a sincere advocate of the Christian faith, calls Eusebius: "the great falsifier of ecclesiastical history, a wily sychophant, a consummate hypocrite, a time serving persecutor, who had nothing in his known life or writings to support the belief that he himself believed in the Christian system."

Eusebius is the source from whom all have drawn their material. Of him Dean Milman in a note to Gibbon's Rome says: "It is deeply to be regretted that the history of this period rests so much on the loose, and, it must be admitted, by no means scrupulous authority of Eusebius." (Page 85.)

Spurious Writings of the Early Church.

"Not long after Christ's ascension into heaven, several histories of his life and doctrines, full of pious frauds and fabulous wonders, were composed by persons whose intentions, perhaps, were not bad, but whose writings discovered the greatest superstition and ignorance." (Mosheim's "Ecclesiastical History.")

"Christian churches had scarcely been gathered and organized when here and there men rose up who, not being contented with the simplicity and purity of that religion which the apostles taught, attempted innovations, and fashioned religion according to their own liking." (Mosheim's "Ecclesiastical History," vol. 1, c. 5.)

"To avoid being imposed upon, we ought to treat tradition as we do a notorious and known liar, to whom we give no credit, unless what he says is confirmed to us by some person of undoubted veracity." (Extract from Bower's "Lives of the Popes.")

"This opinion has always been in the world, that to settle a certain and assured estimation upon that which is good and true, it is necessary to remove out of the way whatever may be an hindrance to it. Neither ought we to wonder that even those of the honest, innocent, primitive times made use of these deceits, seeing for a good end they made no scruple to forge whole books." (Daille on the Use of the Fathers, b. 1, c. 3.)

The Bible Not an Inspired Revelation.

"What would be the characteristics of a revelation? 1st. A revelation would be free from inherent contradictions. Does the New Testament revelation stand this test? 2d. A revelation would not contradict natural laws, for nature is the only undisputed revelation to man. 3d. A revelation would be so authenticated that it would be more reasonable to admit than to deny its claims. The history of thousands of years proves that, so far, no revelation has been made that compels the mind's assent, as thousands of thinking men reject the so-called revelation of the New Testament. The New Testament does not claim infallibility for itself; and proving that a book is infallible does not prove that it was inspired, else we might claim inspiration for the problems of Euclid." (Anon.)

"When Moses told the children of Israel that he received the two tables of commandments from the hands of God, they were not obliged to believe him, because they had no other authority for it, than his telling them so; and I have no authority for it than some historian telling me so. The commandments carry no internal evidence of divinity with them; they contain some good moral precepts, such as any man qualified to be a lawgiver or a legislator, could produce himself without having recourse to supernatural intervention." (Thomas Paine's "Age of Reason.")

"Revelation is a communication of something which the person, to whom that thing is revealed, did not know before. For if I have done a thing, or seen it done, it needs no revelation to tell me I have done it, or seen it, nor to enable me to tell it, or to write it." (Thomas Paine's "Age of Reason.")

"If it was worth God's while to make a revelation to man at all, it was certainly worth his while to see to it that it was correctly made. He would not have allowed the ideas and mistakes of pretended prophets and designing priests to become so mingled with the original text that it is impossible to tell where he ceased and where the priests and prophets began. Neither will it do to say that God adapted his revelation to the prejudices of mankind. Of course it was necessary for an infinite being to adapt his revelation to the intellectual capacity of man; but why should God confirm a barbarian in his prejudices? Why should he fortify a heathen in his crimes? If a revelation is of any importance whatever, it is to eradicate prejudices from the human mind. It should be a lever with which to raise the human race. Theologians have exhausted their ingenuity in finding excuses for God. It seems to me that they would be better employed in finding excuses for men. They tell us that the Jews were so cruel and ignorant that God was compelled to justify, or nearly to justify, many of their crimes, in order to have any influence with them whatever. They tell us that if he had declared slavery and polygamy to be criminal, the Jews would have refused to receive the ten commandments. They insist that, under the circumstances, God did the best he could; that his real intention was to lead them along slowly, step by step, so that, in a few hundred years they would be induced to admit that it was hardly fair to steal a babe from its mother's breast. It has always seemed reasonable that an infinite God ought to have been able to make man grand enough to know, even without a special revelation, that it is not altogether right to steal the labor, or the wife, or the child of another. When the whole question is thoroughly examined, the world will find that Jehovah had the prejudices, the hatreds, and superstitions of his day.

"If there is anything of value, it is liberty. Liberty is the air of the soul, the sunshine of life. Without it the world is a prison and the universe an infinite dungeon.

"If Christ was in fact God, he knew all the future. Before him, like a panorama, moved the history yet to be. He knew exactly how his words would be interpreted. He knew what crimes, what horrors, what infamies, would be committed in his name. He knew that the fires of persecution would climb around the limbs of countless martyrs. He knew that brave men would languish in dungeons, in darkness, filled with pain; that the church would use the instruments of torture, and that his followers would appeal to whip and chain. He must have seen the horizon of the future red with the flames of the *auto da fe*. He knew all the creeds that would spring like poisoned fungi from every text. He saw the sects waging war against each other. He saw thousands of men, under the orders of priests, building dungeons for their fellow men. He saw them using instruments of pain. He heard the groans, saw the faces white with agony, the tears, the blood—heard the shrieks and sobs of all the moaning, martyred multitudes. He knew that commentaries would be written on his words with swords, to be read by the light of faggots. He knew that the Inquisition would be born of teachings attributed to him. He saw all the interpolations and falsehoods that hypocrisy would write and tell. He knew that above these fields of death, these dungeons, these burnings, for a thousand years would float the dripping banner of the cross. He knew that in his name his followers would trade in human flesh, that cradles would be robbed, and woman's breasts unbabed for gold, and yet he died with voiceless lips. Why did he fail to speak? Why did he not tell his disciples, and through them the world, that man should not persecute, for opinion's sake, his fellow man? Why did he not cry, You shall not persecute in my name; you shall not burn and torment those who differ from you in creed? Why did he not plainly say, I am the Son of God? Why did he not explain the doctrine of the trinity? Why did he not tell the manner of baptism that was pleasing to him? Why did he not say something positive, definite, and satisfactory about another world? Why did he not turn the tear-stained hope of heaven to the glad knowledge of another life? Why did he go dumbly to his death, leaving the world to misery and to doubt?

"You may ask, And what of all this? I reply, As with everything in nature, so with the Bible. It has a different story for each reader. Is, then, the Bible a different book to every human being who reads it? It is. Can God, through the Bible, make precisely the same revelation to two persons? He cannot. Why? Because the man who reads is not inspired. God should inspire readers as well as writers.

"You may reply: God knew that his book would be understood differently by each one, and intended that it should be understood as it is understood by each. If this is so, then my understanding of the Bible is the real revelation to me. If this is so, I have no right to take the understanding of another. I must take the revelation made to me through my understanding, and by that revelation I must stand. Suppose, then, that I read this Bible honestly, fairly, and when I get through am compelled to say, 'The book is not true.' If this is the honest result, then you are compelled to say, either that God has made no revelation to me, or that the revelation that it is not true is the revelation made to me, and by which I am bound. If the book and my brain are both the work of the same infinite God, whose fault is it that the book and the brain do not agree? Either God should have written a book to fit my brain, or should have made my brain to fit his book. The inspiration of the Bible depends upon the credulity of him who reads. There was a time when its geology, its astronomy, its natural history, were thought to be inspired: that time has passed. There was a time when its morality satisfied the men who ruled the world of thought: that time has passed.

"These are the passages that have liberated woman!

"According to the Old Testament, woman had to ask pardon, and had to be purified, for the crime of having borne sons and daughters. If in this world there is a figure of perfect purity, it is a mother holding in her thrilled and happy arms her child. The doctrine that the woman is the slave, or serf, of man—whether it comes from heaven or from hell, from God or a demon, from the golden streets of the New Jerusalem or from the very Sodom of perdition—is savagery, pure and simple.

"In no country in the world had women less liberty than in the Holy Land, and no monarch held in less esteem the rights of wives and mothers than Jehovah of the Jews. The position of woman was far better in Egypt than in Palestine. Before the pyramids were built, the sacred songs of Isis were sung by women, and women with pure hands had offered sacrifices to the gods. Before Moses was born, women had sat upon the Egyptian throne. Upon ancient tombs the husband and wife are represented as seated in the same chair. In Persia women were priests, and in some of the oldest civilizations 'they were reverenced on earth, and worshiped afterward as goddesses in heaven.' At the advent of Christianity, in all Pagan countries women officiated at the sacred altars. They guarded the eternal fire. They kept the sacred books. From their lips came the oracles of fate. Under the domination of the Christian church, woman became the merest slave for at least a thousand years. It was claimed that through woman the race had fallen, and that her loving kiss had poisoned all the springs of life. Christian priests asserted that but for her crime the world would have been an Eden still. The ancient fathers exhausted their eloquence in the denunciation of woman, and repeated again and again the slander of St. Paul. The condition of woman has improved just in proportion that man has lost confidence in the inspiration of the Bible.

"The old argument that if Christianity is a human fabrication its authors must have been either good men or bad men, takes it for granted that there are but two classes of persons—the good and the bad. There is, at least, one other class—*the mistaken*, and both of the other classes may belong to this. Thousands of most excellent people have been deceived, and the history of the world is filled with instances where men have honestly supposed that they had received communications from angels and gods." (Ingersoll's Reply to Black.)

"But an infinite being must know not only the real meaning of the words, but the exact meaning they will convey to every reader and hearer. He must know every meaning that they are capable of conveying to every mind. He must also know what explanations must be made to prevent misconception. If an infinite being cannot, in making a revelation to man, use such words that every person to whom a revelation is essential, will understand distinctly what that revelation is, then a revelation from God, through the instrumentality of language is impossible, or it is not essential that all should understand it correctly.

"After all, the real question is, not whether the Bible is inspired, but whether it is true. If it is true, it does not need to be inspired. If it is true, it makes no difference whether it was written by a man or a god. The multiplication table is just as useful, just as true as though God had arranged the figures himself. If the Bible is really true, the claim of inspiration need not be urged; and if it is not true, its inspiration can hardly be established. As a matter of fact, the truth does not need to be inspired. Nothing needs inspiration except a falsehood or a mistake." (Ingersoll's "Mistakes of Moses," p. 59.)

"It may be argued that millions have not the capacity to understand a revelation, although expressed in plainest words. To this it seems a sufficient reply, to ask, why a being of infinite power should create men so devoid of intelligence, that he cannot by any means make known to them his will?" (Ingersoll's "Mistakes of Moses," p. 90.)

"Millions have declared this book to be infinitely holy, to prove that they were right have imprisoned, robbed and burned their fellow men. The inspiration of this book has been established by famine, sword, and fire, by dungeon, chain, and whip, by dagger and by rack, by force and fear and fraud, and generations have been frightened by threats of hell, and bribed with promises of heaven.

"Had we been born in Turkey, most of us would have **been** Mohammedans and believed in the inspiration of the

Koran. We should have believed that Mohammed actually visited heaven and became acquainted with an angel by the name of Gabriel who was so broad between the eyes that it required three hundred days for a very smart mule to travel the distance. If some man had denied this story we should have denounced him as a dangerous person, one who was endeavoring to undermine the foundations of society, and to destroy all distinctions between virtue and vice. We should have said to him ' What do you propose to give us in place of this angel? We cannot afford to give up an angel of that size for nothing.' We would have insisted that the wisest and best men believed the Koran." (Ingersoll's "Mistakes of Moses," p. 36.)

The Pentateuch.

"The Pentateuch is affirmed to have been written by Moses under the influence of divine inspiration. Considered thus a record vouchsafed and dictated by the Almighty, it commands not only scientific but universal consent.

"But here in the first place it may be demanded, who or what is it that has put forth this great claim in its behalf?

"Not the work itself. It nowhere claims the authorship of one man, or makes the impious declaration that it is the writing of Almighty God." (Draper's "Conflict Between Religion and Science."

The Bible Not Inspired.

1. The Bible is full of errors:

"In 1847, the American Bible Society appointed a committee of its members to prepare a standard edition of King James's version, free from typographical errors. They prepared such an edition, correcting, as they stated, twenty-four thousand errors; but alarmed at the attacks made upon it, it was withdrawn; and the American Bible Society continues to this day to circulate for the word of God a book having in it twenty-four thousand acknowledged errors." ("Common Sense Thoughts on the Bible," Wm. Denton.)

2. The Bible sanctions cruelties. The wars of extermination waged by the Jews upon surrounding nations afford ample proof.

3. The Bible indorses immorality. It indorses war, slavery, polygamy, intemperance, and superstition.

4. The writers of the gospels do not claim to be inspired.

5. We do not know when, where, or by whom, either the gospels or the books supposed to be written by Moses, were composed.

6. Paul says: "All scripture is given by inspiration of God; but there is (1.) no definite meaning attached to the word inspiration. (2.) He does not refer to the gospels for they had no existence when he wrote.

7. Inspiration is not a success. There are a thousand different sects quarreling about the meaning of the "inspired scriptures."

8. Inspiration should be pure. The Bible abounds in obscenity.

9. The Bible undergoes revisions, improvements, etc. An infallible book cannot be improved.

10. The Bible has no plan or system, and hence has no definite object. Millions upon millions of Christians have differed regarding its teachings.

11. The Bible is a fetich. Millions of people have a slavish regard for the Holy Bible who have little or no respect for Humanity, Truth, or Justice.

God's Ways are Not Our Ways.

"Now this God either did or he did not believe in and command murder and rapine in the days when he used to sit around evenings and chat with Abraham and Moses and the rest of them. His especial plans and desires were 'revealed' or they were not. The ideas of justice and right were higher in those days than they are now, or else we are wiser and better than God, or else the Bible is not his revealed will. You can take your choice. My choice is to keep my respect for divine justice and honor, and let the Bible bear the burden of its own mistakes.

"If religion is a revelation, then it is not a growth, and it would have been most perfect in design and plan when it was nearest its birth. Now accepting the Bible theory of Jehovah, we find that when the communications of God were immediate and personal there could have been no mistake as to his will. To deal with it as a growth or evolution toward better things is to abandon the whole tenet of a revealed law of God. But to deal with it as a revelation is to make God a being too repulsive and brutal to contemplate for one moment with respect.

"He either did or did not tell those men those things. Which will you accept?" (Helen Gardener's "Men, Women, and Gods.")

"Revelation when applied to religion, means something communicated *immediately* from God to man. No one will deny or dispute the power of the Almighty to make such a communication, if he pleases. But admitting, for the sake of a case, that something has been revealed to a certain person, and not revealed to any other person, it is revelation to that person only. When he tells it to a second person, a second to a third, a third to a fourth, and so on, it ceases to be a revelation to all those persons. It is a revelation to the first person only, and *hearsay* to every other, and, consequently, they are not obliged to believe it.

"It is a contradiction in terms and ideas, to call anything a revelation that comes to us at second-hand, either verbally or in writing. Revelation is necessarily limited to the first communication—after this, it is only an account of something which that person says was a revelation made to him; and though he may find himself obliged to believe it, it cannot be incumbent upon me to believe it in the same manner; for it was not a revelation made to *me*, and I have only his word for it that it was made to him.

"When I am told that the Koran was written in heaven, and brought to Mahomet by an angel, the account comes too near the same kind of hearsay evidence and secondhand authority as the former.* I did not see the angel myself, and, therefore, I have a right not to believe it.

"When also I am told that a woman called the Virgin Mary, said, or gave out, that she was with child without any cohabitation with a man, and that her betrothed husband, Joseph, said that an angel told him so, I have a right to believe them or not; such a circumstance required a much stronger evidence than their bare word for it; but we have not even this—for neither Joseph nor Mary wrote any such matter themselves; it is only reported by others that *they said so*—it is hearsay upon hearsay, and I do not choose to rest my belief upon such evidence.

"It is, however, not difficult to account for the credit that was given to the story of Jesus Christ being the Son of God. He was born when the heathen mythology had still some fashion and repute in the world, and that mythology had prepared the people for the belief of such a story. Almost all the extraordinary men that lived under the heathen mythology were reputed to be the sons of some of their gods. It was not a new thing at that time, to believe a man to have been celestially begotten; the intercourse of gods with women was then a matter of familiar opinion. Their Jupiter, according to their accounts, had cohabited with hundreds; the story therefore had nothing in it either new, wonderful, or obscene; it was conformable to the opinions that then prevailed among the people called Gentiles, or Mythologists, and it was those people only that believed it. The Jews who had kept strictly to the belief of one God, and no more, and who had always rejected the heathen mythology, never credited the story.

"It is curious to observe how the theory of what is called the Christian church, sprung out of the tail of heathen mythology. A direct incorporation took place in the first instance, by making the reputed founder to be celestially begotten. The trinity of gods that then followed

——*Referring to the story of Moses receiving the two tables of commandments. See page 134.

was no other than a reduction of the former plurality, which was about twenty or thirty thousand; the statue of Mary succeeded the statue of Diana of Ephesus, the deification of heroes changed into the canonization of saints; the mythologists had gods for everything; the Christian mythologists had saints for everything; the church became as crowded with the one, as the pantheon had been with the other; and Rome was the place of both. The Christian theory is little else than the idolatry of the ancient mythologists, accommodated to the purposes of power and revenue; and it yet remains to reason and philosophy to abolish the amphibious fraud.

"Nothing that is here said can apply even with the most distant disrespect, to the *real* character of Jesus Christ. He was a virtuous and an amiable man. The morality that he preached and practiced was of the most benovolent kind; and though similar systems of morality had been preached by Confucius, and by some of the Greek philosophers, many years before; by the Quakers since; and by many good men in all ages, it has not been exceeded by any.

"Jesus Christ wrote no account of himself, of his birth, parentage, or anything else; not a line of what is called the New Testament is of his own writing. The history of him is altogether the work of other people; and as to the account given of his resurrection and ascension, it was the necessary counterpart to the story of his birth. His historians, having brought him into the world in a supernatural manner, were obliged to take him out again in the same manner, or the first part of the story must have fallen to the ground.

"The first part, that of the miraculous conception, was not a thing that admitted of publicity; and therefore the tellers of this part of the story had this advantage, that though they might not be credited, they could not be detected." (Thomas Paine's "Age of Reason.")

SELF-CONTRADICTIONS OF THE BIBLE.

THEOLOGICAL DOCTRINES.

God is Satisfied with his Works.

And God saw everything that he had made, and behold it was very good. (Gen. 1: 31.)

God is Dissatisfied with his Works.

And it repented the Lord that he had made man on the earth, and it grieved him at his heart. (Gen. 6: 6.)

God Dwells in Chosen Temples.

And the Lord appeared to Solomon by night, and said unto him: I have heard thy prayer, and have chosen this place to myself for a house of sacrifice. . . . For now have I chosen and sanctified this house, that my name may be there forever: and mine eyes and my heart shall be there perpetually. (2 Chr. 7: 12, 16.)

God Dwells Not in Temples.

Howbeit the Most High dwelleth not in temples made with hands. (Acts 7: 48.)

God Dwells in Light.

Dwelling in the light which no man can approach unto. (1 Tim. 6: 16.)

God Dwells in Darkness.

The Lord said that he would dwell in the thick darkness. (1 Kings 8: 12.)

He made darkness his secret place. (Ps. 18: 11.)

Clouds and darkness are round about him. (Ps. 97: 2.)

God is Seen and Heard.

And I will take away my hand, and thou shalt see my back parts. (Ex. 33: 23.)

And the Lord spake unto Moses face to face, as a man speaketh unto his friend. (Ex. 33: 11.)

And the Lord called unto Adam, and said unto him, Where art thou? And he said I heard thy voice in the garden, and I was afraid. (Gen. 3: 9, 10.)

For I have seen God face to face, and my life is preserved. (Gen. 32: 30.)

In the year that King Uzziah died, I saw, also, the Lord sitting upon a throne, high and lifted up. (Is. 6: 1.)

Then went up Moses and Aaron, Nadab and Abihu, and seventy of the elders of Israel. And they saw the God of Israel. . . . They saw God, and did eat and drink. (Ex. 24: 9, 10, 11.)

God is Invisible and Cannot be Heard.

No man hath seen God at any time. (John 1: 18.)

Ye have neither heard his voice, at any time, nor seen his shape. (John 5: 37.)

And he said, thou canst not see my face; for there shall no man see me and live. (Ex. 33: 20.)

God is Tired and Rests.

For in six days the Lord made heaven and earth, and on the seventh day he rested, and was refreshed. (Ex. 31: 17.)

I am weary with repenting. (Jer. 15: 6.)

Thou hast wearied me with thine iniquities. (Is. 43: 24.)

God is Never Tired and Never Rests.

Hast thou never heard that the everlasting God, the Lord, the Creator of the ends of the earth, fainteth not, never is weary? (Is. 40: 28.)

God is Omnipresent, Sees and Knows all Things.

The eyes of the Lord are in every place. (Prov. 15: 3.)

Whither shall I flee from thy presence? If I ascend up into heaven, thou art there; if I make my bed in hell, behold, thou art there. If I take the wings of the morning, and dwell in the uttermost parts of the sea, even there shall thy hand lead me, and thy right hand shall hold me. (Ps. 139: 7–10.)

There is no darkness nor shadow of death where the workers of iniquity may hide themselves. For his eyes are upon the ways of man, and he seeth all his goings. (Job 34: 22, 21.)

God is Not Omnipresent, Neither Sees nor Knows all Things.

And the Lord came down to see the city and the tower. (Gen. 11: 5.)

And the Lord said, Because the cry of Sodom and Gomorrah is great, and because their sin is very grievous, I will go down now and see whether they have done altogether according to the cry of it, which is come unto me; and, if not, I will know. (Gen. 18: 20, 21.)

And Adam and his wife hid themselves from the presence of the Lord God, amongst the trees of the garden. (Gen. 3: 8.)

God Knows the Hearts of Men.

Thou, Lord, which knowest the hearts of all men. (Acts 1: 24.)

Thou knowest my down-sitting and mine up-rising; thou understandest my thought afar off. Thou compassest my path and my lying down, and art acquainted with all my ways. (Ps. 139: 2, 3.)

For he knoweth the secrets of the heart. (Ps. 44: 21.)

God Tries Men to Find Out what is in their Hearts.

The Lord, your God, proveth you, to know whether ye love the Lord your God, with all your heart and with all your soul. (Deut. 13: 3.)

The Lord thy God led thee these forty years in the wilderness, to humble thee, and to prove thee, to know what was in thy heart. (Deut. 8: 2.)

For now I know that thou fearest God, seeing thou hast not withheld thy son, thine only son, from me. (Gen. 22: 12.)

God is All-Powerful.

Behold, I am the Lord, the God of all flesh; is there anything too hard for me? . . . There is nothing too hard for thee. (Jer. 32: 27, 17.)

With God all things are possible. (Mat. 19: 26.)

God is Not All-Powerful.

And the Lord was with Judah, and he drave out the inhabitants of the mountain; but could not drive out the inhabitants of the valley, because they had chariots of iron. (Judges 1: 19.)

God is Unchangeable.

With whom is no variableness, neither shadow of turning. (James 1: 17.)

For I am the Lord; I change not. (Mal. 3: 6.)

I, the Lord, have spoken it; it shall come to pass, and I will do it. I will not go back, neither will I spare, neither will I repent. (Ezekiel 24: 14.)

God is not a man that he should lie, neither the son of man that he should repent. (Num. 23: 19.)

God is Changeable.

And it repented the Lord that he had made man on the earth, and it grieved him at his heart. (Gen. 6: 6.)

And God saw their works, that they turned from their evil way; and God repented of the evil that he had said that he would do unto them, and he did it not. (Jonah 3: 10.)

Wherefore the Lord God of Israel saith, I said indeed, that thy house, and the house of thy father, should walk before me forever; but now the Lord saith, Be it far from me. . . . Behold, the days come that I will cut off thine arm, and the arm of thy father's house. (1 Sam. 2: 30, 31.)

In those days was Hezekiah sick unto death. And the prophet Isaiah, the son of Amoz, came to him, and said unto him, Thus saith the Lord, Set thy house in order; for thou shalt die, and not live. . . . . And it came to pass afore Isaiah was gone out into the middle court, that the word of the Lord came unto him, saying, Turn again and tell Hezekiah, the captain of my people, Thus saith the Lord, . . . I have heard thy prayer, . . . and I will add unto thy days, fifteen years. (2 Kings 20: 1, 4, 5, 6.)

And the Lord said unto Moses, Depart and go up hence, thou and the people. . . . For I will not go up in the midst of thee. . . . And the Lord said unto Moses, I will do this thing, also, that thou hast spoken. . . . My presence *shall* go with thee, and I will give thee rest. (Ex. 33: 1, 3, 17, 14.)

God is Just and Impartial.

The Lord is upright, . . . and there is no unrighteousness in him. (Ps. 92: 15.)

Shall not the Judge of all the earth do right? (Gen. 18: 25.)

A God of truth, and without iniquity, just and right is he. (Deut. 32: 4.)

There is no respect of persons with God. (Rom. 2: 11.)

Ye say the way of the Lord is not equal. Hear now, O house of Israel; is not my way equal? (Ezek. 18: 25.)

He doth execute the judgment of the fatherless and widow, and loveth the stranger, in giving him food and raiment. Love ye, therefore, the stranger. (Deut. 10: 18, 19.)

God is Unjust and Partial.

Cursed be Canaan; a servant of servants shall he be unto his brethren. (Gen. 9: 25.)

For I, the Lord thy God, am a jealous God, visiting the iniquity of the fathers upon the children unto the third and fourth generation. (Ex. 20: 5.)

For the children being not yet born, neither having done any good or evil, that the purpose of God, according to election, might stand, . . . it was said unto her, The elder shall serve the younger. As it is written, Jacob have I loved, but Esau have I hated. (Rom. 9: 11, 12, 13.)

For whosoever hath, to him shall be given, and he shall have more abundance; but whosoever hath not, from him shall be taken away even that he hath. (Mat. 13, 12.)

Ye shall not eat of anything that dieth of itself; thou shalt give it unto the stranger that is in thy gates, that he may eat it; or thou mayest sell it unto an alien. (Deut. 14: 21.)

And David spake unto the Lord when he saw the angel that smote the people, and said, Lo, I have sinned, and I have done wickedly; but these sheep, what have *they* done? (2 Sam. 24: 17.)

God is Not the Author of Evil.

The law of the Lord is perfect. . . . The statutes of the Lord are right. . . . The commandment of the Lord is pure. (Ps. 19: 7, 8.)

God is not the author of confusion. (1 Cor. 14: 33.)

A God of truth and without iniquity, just and right is he. (Deut. 32: 4.)

For God cannot be tempted with evil, neither tempteth he any man. (James 1: 13.)

God is the Author of Evil.

Out of the mouth of the Most High proceedeth not evil and good? (Lam. 3: 38.)

Thus saith the Lord, Behold I frame evil against you and devise a device against you. (Jer. 18: 11.)

I make peace and create evil. I, the Lord, do all these things. (Is. 45: 7.)

Shall there be evil in a city, and the Lord hath not done it? (Amos 3: 6.)

Therefore I gave them also statutes that were not good, and judgments whereby they should not live. (Ezek. 20: 25.)

God Gives Freely to those who Ask.

If any of you lack wisdom, let him ask God, that giveth to all men liberally and upbraideth not, and it shall be given him. (James 1: 5.)

For every one that asketh receiveth, and he that seeketh findeth. (Luke 11: 10.)

God Withholds his Blessings and Prevents their Reception.

He hath blinded their eyes and hardened their heart that they should not see with their eyes, nor understand with their heart, and be converted, and I should heal them. (John 12: 40.)

For it was of the Lord to harden their hearts, that they should come against Israel in battle, that he might destroy them utterly, and that they might have no favor. (Josh. 11: 20.)

O Lord, why hast thou made us to err from thy ways and hardened our heart? (Is. 63: 17.)

God is to be Found by Those who Seek him.

Every one that asketh receiveth, and he that seeketh findeth. (Mat. 7: 8.)

Those that seek me early shall find me. (Prov. 8: 17.)

God is Not to be Found by Those who Seek him.

Then shall they call upon me but I will not answer; they shall seek me early, but shall not find me. (Prov. 1: 28.)

And when ye spread forth your hands, I will hide mine eyes from you; yea, when ye make many prayers I will not hear. (Is. 1: 15.)

They cried, but there was none to save them; even unto the Lord, but he answered them not. (Ps. 18: 41.)

God is Peaceful.

The God of peace. (Rom. 15: 33.)

God is not the author of confusion, but of peace. (1 Cor. 14: 33.)

God is Warlike.

The Lord is a man of war. (Ex. 15: 3.)

The Lord of Hosts is his name. (Is. 51: 15.)

Blessed be the Lord, my strength, which teacheth my hands to war and my fingers to fight. (Ps. 144: 1.)

God is Kind, Merciful, and Good.

The Lord is very pitiful and of tender mercy. (James 5: 11.)

For he doth not afflict willingly, nor grieve the children of men. (Lam. 3: 33.)

For his mercy endureth forever. (1 Chron. 16: 34.)

I have no pleasure in the death of him that dieth, saith the Lord God. (Ezek. 18: 32.)

The Lord is good to all, and his tender mercies are over all his works. (Ps. 145: 9.)

Who will have all men to be saved, and to come unto the knowledge of the truth. (1 Tim. 2: 4.)

God is love. (1 John 4: 16.)

Good and upright is the Lord. (Ps. 25: 8.)

God is Cruel, Unmerciful, Destructive, and Ferocious.

I will not pity, nor spare, nor have mercy, but destroy them. (Jer. 13: 14.)

And thou shalt consume all the people which the Lord thy God shall deliver thee; thine eye shall have no pity upon them. (Deut. 7: 16.)

Now go and smite Amalek, and utterly destroy all that they have, and spare them not, but slay both man and woman, infant and suckling. (1 Sam. 15: 2, 3.)

Because they had looked into the ark of the Lord, even he smote of the people fifty thousand, and three score and ten men. (1 Sam. 6: 19.)

The Lord thy God is a consuming fire. (Deut. 4: 24.)

The Lord cast down great stones from heaven upon them, . . and they died. (Josh. 10: 11.)

God's Anger is Slow, and Endures but for a Moment.

The Lord is merciful and gracious, slow to anger and plenteous in mercy. (Ps. 103: 8.)

His anger endureth but a moment. (Ps. 30: 5.)

God's Anger is Fierce, Frequent, and Endures Long.

And the Lord's anger was kindled against Israel, and he made them wander in the wilderness forty years, until all the generation that had done evil in the sight of the Lord was consumed. (Num. 32: 13.)

And the Lord said unto Moses, Take all the heads of the people, and hang them up before the Lord against the sun, that the fierce anger of the Lord may be turned away from Israel. (Num. 25: 4.)

For ye have kindled a fire in mine anger which shall burn forever. (Jer. 17: 4.)

God is angry ["*with the wicked,*" interpolated by the translators] every day. (Ps. 7: 11.)

And the Lord met him and sought to kill him. (Ex. 4: 24.)

God Commands, Approves of, and Delights in Burnt Offerings, Sacrifices, and Holy Days.

Thou shalt offer every day a bullock for a sin offering for atonement. (Ex. 29: 36.)

On the tenth day of this seventh month there shall be a day of atonement; it shall be a holy convocation unto you, and ye shall afflict your souls and offer an offering made by fire unto the Lord. (Lev. 23: 27.)

And thou shalt burn the whole ram upon the altar; . . . it is a sweet savor; an offering made by fire unto the Lord. (Ex. 29: 18.)

And the priest shall burn all on the altar to be a burnt sacrifice, an offering made by fire, of a sweet savor unto the Lord. (Lev. 1: 9.)

God Disapproves of, and has no Pleasure in, Burnt Offerings, Sacrifices, and Holy Days.

For I spake not unto your fathers, nor commanded them in the day that I brought them out of the land of Egypt, concerning burnt offerings or sacrifices. (Jer. 7: 22.)

Your burnt offerings are not acceptable, nor your sacrifices sweet unto me. (Jer. 6: 20.)

Will I eat of the flesh of bulls, or drink the blood of goats? Offer unto God *thanksgiving*, and pay thy *vows* unto the Most High. (Psalm 50: 13, 14.)

Bring no more vain oblations; incense is an abomination unto me; the new moons and sabbaths, the calling of assemblies I cannot away with; it is iniquity, even the solemn meeting. . . . To what purpose is the multitude of your sacrifices unto me? saith the Lord. I am full of the burnt offerings of rams, and the fat of fed beasts, and I delight not in the blood of bullocks, or of lambs, or of he goats. When ye come to appear before me, who hath required this at your hand? (Is. 1: 13, 11, 12.)

God Forbids Human Sacrifice.

Take heed to thyself that thou be not snared by following them [the Gentile nations;] . . . for every abomination to the Lord which he hateth have they done unto their gods; for even their sons and their daughters have they burnt in the fire to their gods. (Deut. 12: 30, 31.)

God Commands and Accepts Human Sacrifices.

No devoted thing that a man shall devote unto the Lord of all that he hath, both of *man* and of beast, and of the field of his possession, shall be sold or redeemed; every devoted thing is most holy unto the Lord. None devoted, which shall be devoted of *men*, shall be redeemed, but shall surely be put to *death*. (Lev. 27: 28, 29.)

The king [David] took the two sons of Rizpah, . . . and the five sons of Michael; . . . and he delivered them into the hands of the Gibeonites, and they hanged them in the hill before the Lord. . . . And after that God *was entreated* for the land. (2 Sam. 21: 8, 9, 14.)

And he [God] said, Take now thy son, thine only son Isaac, whom thou lovest, and get thee into the land of Moriah, and offer him there for a burnt offering. (Gen. 22: 2.)

And Jephthah vowed a vow unto the Lord, and said, If thou shalt without fail deliver the children of Ammon into my hands, then it shall be, that whatsoever cometh forth of the doors of my house to meet me when I return in peace from the children of Ammon, shall surely be the Lord's, and I will offer it up for a burnt offering. So Jephthah passed over unto the children of Ammon to fight against them; and the Lord delivered them into his hands. . . . And Jephthah came to Mizpeh unto his house and behold, his daughter came out to meet him. . . . And he sent her away for two months; and she went with her companions and bewailed her virginity upon the mountains. And it came to pass at the end of two months that she returned unto her father, who did according to his vow which he had vowed. (Judges 11: 30, 31, 32, 34, 38, 39.)

God Tempts No Man.

Let no man say when he is tempted, I am tempted of God; for God cannot be tempted with evil, neither tempteth he any man. (James 1: 13.)

God Does Tempt Men.

And it came to pass after these things that God did tempt Abraham. (Gen. 22: 1.)

And again the anger of the Lord was kindled against Israel, and he moved David against them to say, Go number Israel and Judah. (2 Sam. 24: 1.)

And the Lord said unto Satan, Hast thou considered my servant Job, that there is none like him in the earth, a perfect and an upright man, one that feareth God and escheweth evil? And still he holdeth fast his integrity, although thou movedst me against him, to destroy him without cause. (Job. 2: 3.)

O Lord, thou hast deceived me, and I was deceived, [marginal reading, *enticed*.] (Jer. 20: 7.)

Lead us not into temptation. (Mat. 6: 13.)

God Cannot Lie.

God is not a man, that he should lie. (Num. 23: 19.)
It was impossible for God to lie. (Heb. 6: 18.)

God Lies; He Sends Forth Lying Spirits to Deceive.

Ah, Lord God! surely thou hast greatly deceived this people. (Jer. 4: 10.)

Wilt thou be altogether unto me as a liar? (Jer. 14: 18.)

For this cause God shall send them strong delusion, that they should believe a lie. (2 Thes. 2: 11.)

Now, therefore, behold, the Lord hath put a lying spirit in the mouth of all these thy prophets, and the Lord hath spoken evil concerning thee. (1 Kings 22: 23.)

Then God sent an evil spirit. (Judges 9: 23.)

And if the prophet be deceived when he hath spoken a thing, I the Lord have deceived that prophet. (Ezek. 14: 9.)

Because of Man's Wickedness God Destroys him.

And God saw that the wickedness of man was great in the earth, and that every imagination of the thoughts of his heart was only evil continually. . . . And the Lord said, I will destroy man whom I have created. (Gen. 6: 5, 7.)

Because of Man's Wickedness God will Not Destroy him.

And the Lord said in his heart, I will not again curse the ground any more for man's sake; for the imagination of man's heart is evil from his youth; neither will I again smite any more every living thing. (Gen. 8: 21.)

God's Attributes are Revealed in his Works.

For the invisible things of him from the creation of the world are clearly seen, being understood by the things that are made, even his eternal power and Godhead. (Rom. 1: 20.)

God's Attributes Cannot be Discovered.

Canst thou, by searching, find out God? (Job. 11: 7.)

There is no searching of his understanding. (Is. 40: 28.)

There is but One God.

The Lord our God is one Lord. (Deut. 6: 4.)

There is none other God but one. (1 Cor. 8: 4.)

There is a Plurality of Gods.

And God said, Let us make man in our image. (Gen. 1: 26.)

And the Lord God said, Behold the man is become as one of us. (Gen. 3: 22.)

And the Lord appeared unto him [Abraham] in the plains of Mamre. . . . And he lifted up his eyes and looked, and lo, three men stood by him; and when he saw them he ran to meet them from the tent door, and bowed himself toward the ground, and said, My Lord, if now I have found favor in thy sight, pass not away, I pray thee, from thy servant. (Gen. 18: 1, 2, 3.)

For there are three that bear record in heaven, the Father, the Word, and the Holy Ghost. (1 John 5: 7.)

MORAL PRECEPTS.

Robbery Commanded.

When ye go, ye shall not go empty; but every woman shall borrow of her neighbor, and of her that sojourneth in her house, jewels of silver and jewels of gold, and raiment; and ye shall put them upon your sons and upon your daughters; and ye shall spoil the Egyptians. (Ex. 3: 21, 22.)

And they borrowed of the Egyptians jewels of silver, and jewels of gold, and raiment. . . . And they spoiled the Egyptians. (Ex. 12: 35, 36.)

Robbery Forbidden.

Thou shalt not defraud thy neighbor, neither rob him. (Lev. 19: 13.)

Thou shalt not steal. (Ex. 20: 15.)

Lying Commanded, Approved, and Sanctioned.

And the Lord said unto Samuel, . . . I will send thee to Jesse, the Bethlemite; for I have provided me a king among his sons. And Samuel said, How can I go? If Saul hear it he will kill me. And the Lord said, Take a heifer with thee, and say, I am come to sacrifice to the Lord. (1 Sam. 16: 1, 2.)

And the woman [Rahab] took the two men and hid them and said thus: There came men unto me, but I wist not whence they were; and it came to pass about the time of shutting of the gate, when it was dark, that the men went out; whither the men went I wot not; pursue after them quickly, for ye shall overtake them. But she had brought them up to the roof of the house and hid them with the stalks of flax. (Josh. 2: 4, 5, 6.)

Was not Rahab, the harlot, *justified* by works, when she had received the messengers, and had them sent out another way? (James 2: 25.)

And the king of Egypt called for the midwives, and said unto them, Why have ye done this thing, and have saved the men-children alive? And the midwives said unto Pharoah, Because the Hebrew women are not as the Egyptian women; for they are lively, and are delivered ere the midwives come in unto them. *Therefore God dealt well* with the midwives. (Ex. 1: 18–20.)

And there came forth a spirit, and stood before the Lord, and said, I will persuade him. . . I will go forth and will be a lying spirit in the mouth of all his prophets. And he said, Thou shalt persuade him and prevail also; go forth and do so. (1 Kings 22: 21, 22.)

Ye shall know my breach of promise. (Num. 14: 34.)

For if the truth of God hath more abounded through my lie unto his glory, why yet am I also judged as a sinner? (Rom. 3: 7.)

Being crafty, I caught you with guile. (2 Cor. 12: 16.)

Lying Forbidden.

Thou shalt not bear false witness. (Ex. 20: 16.)

Lying lips are an abomination to the Lord. (Prov. 12: 22.)

All liars shall have their part in the lake which burneth with fire and brimstone. (Rev. 21: 8.)

Killing Commanded and Sanctioned.

Thus saith the Lord God of Israel, Put every man his sword by his side, and go in and out from gate to gate throughout the camp, and slay every man his brother, and every man his companion, and every man his neighbor. (Ex. 32: 27.)

So Jehu slew all that remained of the house of Ahab. . . . And the Lord said unto Jehu, Because thou hast done well in executing that which is right in mine eyes, and hast done unto the house of Ahab according to all that was in my heart, thy children of the fourth generation shall sit on the throne of Israel. (2 Kings 10: 11, 30.)

Killing Forbidden.

Thou shalt not kill. (Ex. 20: 13.)

No murderer hath eternal life abiding in him. (1 John 3: 15.)

The Blood-Shedder Must Die.

At the hand of every man's brother will I require the life of man. Whoso shedeth man's blood, by man shall his blood be shed. (Gen. 9: 5, 6.)

The Blood-Shedder Must Not Die.

And the Lord set a mark upon Cain, lest any finding him should kill him. (Gen. 4: 15.)

The Making of Images Forbidden.

Thou shalt not make unto thee any graven image, or any likeness of anything that is in heaven above, or that is in the earth beneath. (Ex. 20: 4.)

The Making of Images Commanded.

Thou shalt make two cherubims of gold. . . . And the cherubims shall stretch forth their wings on high, covering the mercy seat with their wings, and their faces shall look one to another. (Ex. 25: 18, 20.)

Slavery and Oppression Ordained.

Cursed be Canaan; a servant of servants shall he be unto his brethren. (Gen. 9: 25.)

Of the children of the strangers that do sojourn among you, of them shall ye buy. . . . They shall be your bondmen forever; but over your brethren, the children of Israel, ye shall not rule with rigor. (Lev. 25: 45, 46.)

I will sell your sons and daughters into the hands of the children of Judah, and they shall sell them to the Sabeans, to a people afar off; for the Lord hath spoken it. (Joel 3: 8.)

Slavery and Oppression Forbidden.

Undo the heavy burdens. . . . Let the oppressed go free, . . . break every yoke. (Is. 58: 6.)

Thou shalt neither vex a stranger, nor oppress him. (Ex. 22: 21.)

He that stealeth a man, and selleth him, or if he be found in his hand, he shall surely be put to death. (Ex. 21: 16.)

Neither be ye called masters. (Mat. 23: 10.)

Improvidence Enjoined.

Consider the lilies of the field, how they grow; they toil not, neither do they spin. . . . If God so clothe the grass of the field . . . shall he not much more clothe you? . . . Therefore, take no thought, saying, What shall we eat? or what shall we drink? or wherewithal shall we be clothed? . . . Take, therefore, no thought for the morrow. (Mat. 6: 28, 30, 31, 34.)

Give to every man that asketh of thee, and of him that taketh away thy goods, ask them not again. . . . And lend, hoping for nothing again, and your reward shall be great. (Luke 6: 30, 35.)

Sell that ye have and give alms. (Luke 12: 33.)

Improvidence Condemned.

But if any provide not for his own, especially for those of his own house, he hath denied the faith, and is worse than an infidel. (1 Tim. 5: 8.)

A good man leaveth an inheritance to his children's children. (Prov. 13: 22.)

Anger Approved.

Be ye angry and sin not. (Eph. 4: 26.)

And he [Elisha] turned back and looked on them and cursed them in the name of the Lord. And there came forth two she-bears out of the wood and tare forty and two children of them. (2 Kings 2: 24.)

And when he had looked round about on them with anger, . . . he saith unto the man, Stretch forth thy hand. (Mark 3: 5.)

Anger Disapproved.

Be not hasty in thy spirit to be angry; for anger resteth in the bosom of fools. (Eccl. 7: 9.)

Make no friendship with an angry man. (Prov. 22: 24.)

The wrath of man worketh not the righteousness of God. (James 1: 20.)

Good Works to be Seen of Men.

Let your light so shine before men, that they may see your good works. (Mat. 5: 16.)

Good Works Not to be Seen of Men.

Take heed that ye do not your alms before men, to be seen of them. (Mat. 6: 1.)

Judging of Others Forbidden.

Judge not, that ye be not judged. For with what judgment ye judge, ye shall be judged. (Mat. 7: 1, 2.)

Judging of Others Approved.

Do ye not know that the saints shall judge the world? And if the world shall be judged by you, are ye unworthy to judge the smallest matters? Know ye not that we shall judge angels? How much more things that pertain to this life? If, then, ye have judgments of things pertaining to this life, set them to judge who are least esteemed in the church. (1 Cor. 6: 2, 3, 4.)

Do not ye judge them that are within? (1 Cor. 5: 12.)

Jesus Taught Non-Resistance.

Resist not evil, but whosoever shall smite thee on the right cheek, turn him the other also. (Mat. 5: 39.)

All they that take the sword shall perish with **the sword**. (Mat. 26: 52.)

Jesus Taught and Practiced Physical Resistance.

He that hath no sword, let him sell **his garment and** buy one. (Luke 22: 36.)

And when he had made a scourge of small cords, **he drove** them all out of the temple. (John 2: 15.)

Jesus Warned his Followers Not to Fear Being Killed.

Be not afraid of them that kill the body. (Luke 12: 4.)

Jesus Himself Avoided the Jews for Fear of Being killed.

After these things Jesus walked in Galilee; for he would not walk in Jewry, because the Jews sought to kill him. (John 7: 1.)

Public Prayer Sanctioned.

And Solomon stood before the altar of the Lord, in the presence of all the congregation of Israel, and spread forth his hands toward heaven. [Then follows the prayer.] And it was so, that when Solomon had made an end of praying all his prayer and supplication unto the Lord, he arose from before the altar of the Lord, from kneeling on his knees, with his hands spread up to heaven. . . . And the Lord said unto him, I have heard thy prayer and thy supplication that thou hast made before me. (1 Kings 8: 22, 54, and 9: 3.)

Public Prayer Disapproved.

When thou prayest, thou shalt not be as the hypocrites are; for they love to pray standing in the synagogues, **and** in the corners of the streets, that they may be seen **of men**. . . . But thou, when thou prayest, enter into thy closet, and when thou hast shut thy door; pray to thy Father which is in secret. (Mat. 6: 5, 6.)

Importunity in Prayer Commended.

Because this widow troubleth me, I will avenge her, lest by her continual coming she weary me. . And shall not God avenge his own elect, which cry day and night unto him? (Luke 18: 5, 7.)

Because of his importunity he will rise, and give him as many as he needeth. (Luke 11: 8.)

Importunity in Prayer Condemned.

But when ye pray, use not vain repetitions, as the heathen do; for they think that they shall be heard for their much speaking. Be ye not therefore like unto them; for your Father knoweth what things ye have need of before ye ask him. (Mat. 6: 7, 8.)

The Wearing of Long Hair by Men Sanctioned.

And no razor shall come on his head; for the child shall be a Nazarite unto God from the womb. (Judges 13: 5.)

All the days of the vow of his separation there shall no razor come upon his head; until the days be fulfilled in the which he separateth himself unto the Lord, he shall be holy, and shall let the locks of the hair of his head grow. (Num. 6: 5.)

The Wearing of Long Hair by Men Condemned.

Doth not even nature itself teach you, that if a man have long hair, it is a shame unto him? (1 Cor. 11: 14.)

Circumcision Instituted.

This is my covenant which ye shall keep between me and you and thy seed after thee: Every man child among you shall be circumcised. (Gen. 17: 10.)

Circumcision Condemned.

Behold, I, Paul, say unto you, that if ye be circumcised, Christ shall profit you nothing. (Gal. 5: 2.)

The Sabbath Instituted.

And God blessed the seventh day, and sanctified it. (Gen. 2: 3.)

Remember the Sabbath day to keep it holy. (Ex. 20: 8.)

The Sabbath Repudiated.

The new moons and sabbaths, the calling of assemblies, I cannot away with; it is iniquity. (Is. 1: 13.)

One man esteemeth one day above another; another esteemeth every day alike. Let every man be fully persuaded in his own mind. (Rom. 14: 5.)

Let no man therefore judge you in meat, or in drink, or in respect of a holy day, or of the new moon; or of the sabbath days. (Col. 2: 16.)

The Sabbath Instituted because God Rested the Seventh Day.

For in six days the Lord made heaven and earth, the sea, and all that in them is, and rested the seventh day; wherefore the Lord blessed the Sabbath day, and hallowed it. (Ex. 20: 11.)

The Sabbath Instituted for a Very Different Reason.

And remember that thou wast a servant in the land of Egypt, and that the Lord thy God brought thee out thence through a mighty hand and by a stretched-out arm; *therefore* the Lord thy God commanded thee to keep the Sabbath day. (Deut. 5: 15.)

No Work to be Done on the Sabbath under Penalty of Death.

Whosoever doeth any work in the Sabbath day, he shall surely be put to death. (Ex. 31: 15.)

They found a man that gathered sticks upon the Sabbath day. . . . And all the congregation brought him without the camp and stoned him with stones, and he died; as the Lord commanded Moses. (Num. 15: 32, 36.)

Jesus Broke the Sabbath and Justified the Act.

Therefore did the Jews persecute Jesus, and sought to slay him because he had done these things on the Sabbath day. (John 5: 16.)

At that time Jesus went on the Sabbath day through the corn; and his disciples were a hungered, and began to pluck the ears of corn, and to eat. But when the Pharisees saw it they said unto him, Behold, thy disciples do that which is not lawful to do upon the Sabbath day. But he said unto them, . . . Have ye not read in the law, how that on the Sabbath days the priests in the temple profane the Sabbath, and are blameless? (Mat. 12: 1, 2, 3, 5.)

Baptism Commanded

Go ye therefore and teach all nations, baptizing them in the name of the Father, and of the Son, and of the Holy Ghost. (Mat. 28: 19.)

Baptism Not Commanded.

For Christ sent me not to baptize, but to preach the gospel. . . . I thank God that I baptized none of you but Crispus and Gaius. (1 Cor. 1: 17, 14.)

Every Kind of Animal Allowed for Food.

Every moving thing that liveth shall be meat for you. (Gen. 9: 3.)

Whatsoever is sold in the shambles that eat. (1 Cor. 10: 25.)

There is nothing unclean of itself. (Rom. 14: 14.)

Certain Kinds of Animals Prohibited for Food.

Nevertheless, these shall ye not eat, of them that chew the cud or of them that divide the cloven hoof; as the camel and the hare, and the coney; for they chew the cud, but divide not the hoof; therefore, they are unclean unto you. And the swine, because it divideth the hoof, yet cheweth not the cud, it is unclean unto you; ye shall not eat of their flesh, nor touch their dead carcass. (Deut. 14: 7, 8.)

The Taking of Oaths Sanctioned.

If a man vow a vow unto the Lord, or swear an oath to bind his soul with a bond, he shall not break his word; he shall do according to all that proceedeth out of his mouth. (Num. 30: 2.)

He that sweareth in the earth shall swear by the God of truth. (Is. 65: 16.)

Now, therefore, swear unto me here by God. . . . And Abraham said, I will swear. . . . There they sware both of them. (Gen. 21: 23, 24, 31.)

Because he [God] could swear by no greater, he sware by himself. (Heb. 6: 13.)

And I . . . made them swear by God. (Neh. 13: 25.)

The Taking of Oaths Forbidden.

But I say unto you, swear not at all; neither by heaven for it is God's throne; nor by the earth for it is his footstool. (Mat. 5: 34.)

Marriage Approved and Sanctioned.

And the Lord said, It is not good that the man should be alone: I will make him a help-meet for him. (Gen. 2: 18.)

And God said unto them, Be fruitful and multiply, and replenish the earth. (Gen. 1: 28.)

For this cause shall a man leave father and mother and shall cleave to his wife. (Mat. 19: 5.)

Marriage is honorable in all. (Heb. 13: 4.)

Marriage Disapproved.

It is good for a man not to touch a woman. . . . For I [Paul] would that all men were even as I myself. . . . It is good for them if they abide even as I. (1 Cor. 7: 1, 7, 8.)

Freedom of Divorce Permitted.

When a man hath taken a wife and married her, and it come to pass that she find no favor in his eyes, . . . then let him write her a bill of divorcement, and give it in her hand, and send her out of his house. (Deut. 24: 1.)

When thou goest out to war against thine enemies, and the Lord thy God hath delivered them into thy hands, and thou hast taken them captive, and seest among the captives a beautiful woman and hast a desire unto her, . . . then thou shalt bring her home to thy house; . . . and after that thou shalt go in unto her and be her husband, and she shall be thy wife. And it shall be, if thou have no delight in her, then thou shalt let her go whither she will; but thou shalt not sell her at all for money; thou shalt not make merchandize of her. (Deut. 21: 10–14.)

Divorce Restricted.

But I say unto you, that whosoever shall put away his wife, saving for the cause of fornication, causeth her to commit adultery. (Mat. 5: 32.)

Adultery Sanctioned.

But all the women children that have not known a man by lying with him, keep alive for yourselves. (Num. 31: 18.)

And the Lord said unto Hosea, Go, take thee a wife of whoredoms. . . . Then said the Lord to me, Go yet, love a woman, beloved of her friend, yet an adulteress. . . . So I bought her; . . . and I said unto her, Thou shalt abide for me many days; thou shalt not play the harlot, and thou shalt not be for another man; so will I also be for thee. (Hosea 1: 2, and 3: 1, 2, 3.)

Adultery Forbidden.

Thou shalt not commit adultery. (Ex. 20: 14.)

Whoremongers and adulterers God will judge. (Heb. 13: 4.)

Marriage or Cohabitation with a Sister Denounced.

Cursed is he that lieth with his sister, the daughter of his father, or the daughter of his mother. (Deut. 27: 22.)

And if a man shall take his sister, his father's daughter, or his mother's daughter, . . . it is a wicked thing. (Lev. 20: 17.)

Abraham Married his Sister, and God Blessed the Union.

And Abraham said, . . . She is my sister; she is the daughter of my father, but not the daughter of my mother; and she became my wife. (Gen. 20: 11, 12.)

And God said unto Abraham, As for Sarah, thy wife, . . . I will bless her, and give thee a son also of her. (Gen. 17: 15, 16.)

A Man May Marry His Brother's Widow.

If brethren dwell together, and one of them die and have no child the wife of the dead shall not marry without unto a stranger; her husband's brother shall go in unto her, and take her to him to wife. (Deut. 25: 5.)

A Man May Not Marry his Brother's Widow.

If a man shall take his brother's wife, it is an unclean thing; . . they shall be childless. (Lev. 20: 21.)

Hatred to Kindred Enjoined.

If any man come unto me, and hate not his father, and mother, and wife, and children, and brethren, and sisters, yea, and his own life also, he cannot be my disciple. (Luke 14: 26.)

Hatred to Kindred Condemned.

Honor thy father and mother. (Eph. 6: 2.)

Husbands, love your wives. . . . For no man ever yet hated his own flesh. (Eph. 5: 25, 29.)

Whosoever hateth his brother is a murderer. (1 John 3: 15.)

Intoxicating Beverages Recommended.

Give strong drink unto him that is ready to perish, and wine to those that be of heavy hearts. Let him drink and forget his poverty, and remember his misery no more. (Prov. 31: 6, 7.)

And thou shalt bestow that money for whatsoever thy soul lusteth after, for oxen, or for sheep, or for wine, or for strong drink. (Deut. 14: 26.)

Drink no longer water, but use a little wine for thy stomach's sake, and thine often infirmities. (1 Tim. 5: 23.)

Wine that maketh glad the heart of man. (Ps. 104: 15.)

Wine which cheereth God and man. (Judges 9: 13.)

Intoxicating Beverages Discountenanced.

Wine is a mocker, strong drink is raging, and whosoever is deceived thereby is not wise. (Prov. 20: 1.)

Look not thou upon the wine when it is red; when it giveth his color in the cup. . . . At the last it biteth like a serpent and stingeth like an adder. (Prov. 23: 31, 32.)

It is Our Duty to Obey Rulers, Who are God's Ministers and Punish Evil Doers Only.

Let every soul be subject unto the higher powers. For there is no power but of God; the powers that be are ordained of God. Whosoever, therefore, resisteth the power, resisteth the ordinance of God; and they that resist shall receive to themselves damnation. For rulers are not a terror to good work, but to evil. . . . For this cause pay ye tribute also; for they are God's ministers, attending continually upon this very thing. (Rom. 13: 1, 2, 3, 6.)

The Scribes and Pharisees sit in Moses seat; all, therefore, whatsoever they bid you observe, that observe and do. (Mat. 23: 2, 3.)

Submit yourselves to every ordinance of man for the Lord's sake; whether it be to the king as supreme, or unto governors as unto them that are sent of him for the punishment of evil-doers. (1 Pet. 2: 13, 14.)

I counsel thee to keep the king's commandment. . . . Whoso keepeth the commandment shall feel no evil thing. (Eccl. 8: 2, 5.)

It is Not Our Duty Always to Obey Rulers, Who Sometimes Punish the Good, and Receive Damnation Therefor.

But the midwives feared God, and did not as the king of Egypt commanded them. . . . Therefore God dealt well with the midwives. (Ex. 1: 17, 20.)

Shadrach, Meshach, and Abednego answered and said, . . . Be it known unto thee, O king, that we will not serve thy gods, nor worship the golden image which thou hast set up. (Dan. 3: 16, 18.)

Wherefore king Darius signed the writing and the decree, . . . (that whoever shall ask a petition of any God or man for thirty days, . . . he shall be cast into the den of lions). . . . Now, when Daniel knew that the writing was signed, he went into his house and . . . kneeled upon his knees three times a day and prayed, . . . as he did aforetime. (Dan. 6: 9, 7, 10.)

And the *rulers* were gathered together against the Lord and against his Christ. For of a truth, against thy holy child Jesus, whom thou hast anointed, both *Herod* and *Pontius Pilate*, with the Gentiles, and the people of Israel, were gathered together. (Acts 4: 26, 27.)

Beware of the Scribes, which love to go in long clothing, and love salutations in the market places, and the chief seats in the synagogues. . . . These shall receive greater damnation. (Mark 12: 38, 39, 40.)

And *Herod* with his men of war set him at naught, and mocked him, and arrayed him in a gorgeous robe, and sent him again to Pilate. . . . And *Pilate* gave sentence. . . . And when they were come to the place which is called Calvary, there they crucified him. . . . And the people stood by beholding. And the *rulers* also with them derided him. (Luke 23: 11, 24, 33, 35.)

Woman's Rights Denied.

And thy desire shall be to thy husband, and he shall rule over thee. (Gen. 3: 16.)

I suffer not a woman to teach, nor to usurp authority over the man, but to be in silence. (1 Tim. 2: 12.)

They are commanded to be under obedience, as also saith the law. (1 Cor. 14: 34.)

Even as Sarah obeyed Abraham, calling him lord. (1 Peter 3: 6.)

Woman's Rights Affirmed.

And Deborah, a prophetess, . . . judged Israel at that time. . . . And Deborah said unto Barak, Up, for this is the day in which the Lord hath delivered Sisera into thy hand. . . . And the Lord discomfited Sisera, and all his chariots, and all his host, with the edge of the sword before Barak. (Judges 4: 4, 14, 15.)

The inhabitants of the villages ceased; they ceased in Israel, until that I, Deborah, arose, that I arose, a mother in Israel. (Judges 5: 7.)

And on my hand-maidens I will pour out in those days my spirit, and they shall prophesy. (Acts 2: 18.)

And the same man had four daughters, virgins, which did prophesy. (Acts 21: 9.)

Obedience to Masters Enjoined.

Servants, obey in all things your masters according to the flesh. . . . And whatsoever ye do, do it heartily as to the Lord. (Col. 3: 22, 23.)

Servants, be subject to your masters with all fear; not only to the good and gentle, but also to the froward. (1 Peter 2: 18.)

Obedience Due to God Only.

Thou shalt worship the Lord thy God, and him only shalt thou serve. (Mat. 4: 10.)

Be ye not the servants of men. (1 Cor. 7: 23.)

Neither be ye called masters; for one is your master, even Christ. (Mat. 23: 10.)

There is an Unpardonable Sin.

He that shall blaspheme against the Holy Ghost hath never forgiveness. (Mark 3: 29.)

There is No Unpardonable Sin.

And by him all that *believe* are justified from *all* things. (Acts 13: 39.)

HISTORICAL FACTS.

Man was Created After the Other Animals.

And God made the beast of the earth after his kind, and cattle after their kind. . . . And God said, Let us make man. . . . So God created man in his own image. (Gen. 1: 25, 26, 27.)

Man was Created Before the Other Animals.

And the Lord God said, It is not good that the man should be alone; I will make him a help-meet for him. And out of the ground the Lord God formed every beast of the field, and every fowl of the air, and brought them unto Adam to see what he would call them. (Gen. 2: 18, 19.)

Noah, by God's Command, Took Into the Ark Clean Beasts by Sevens.

And the Lord said unto Noah, . . . Of every clean beast thou shalt take to thee by sevens. . . . And Noah did according to all that the Lord commanded him. (Gen. 7: 1, 2, 5.)

Noah, by God's Command, Took Into the Ark Clean Beasts by Twos.

Of clean beasts . . there went in two and two unto Noah into the Ark, . . as God had commanded Noah. (Gen. 7: 8, 9.)

Seed Time and Harvest were Never to Cease.

While the earth remaineth, seed time and harvest . . shall not cease. (Gen. 8: 22.)

Seed Time and Harvest Did Cease for Seven Years.

And the seven years of dearth began to come. . . . And the famine was over all the face of the earth. (Gen. 41: 54, 56.)

For these two years hath the famine been in the land; and yet there are five years in which there shall neither be earing nor harvest. (Gen. 45: 6.)

God Hardened Pharaoh's Heart.

But I will harden his heart, that he shall not let the people go. (Ex. 4: 21.)

And the Lord hardened the heart of Pharaoh. (Ex. 9: 12.)

Pharaoh Hardened His Own Heart.

But when Pharaoh saw that there was respite, he hardened his heart, and hearkened not unto them. (Ex. 8: 15.)

All the Cattle and Horses in Egypt Died.

Behold, the hand of the Lord is upon thy cattle which is in the field, upon the horses, upon the asses, upon the camels, upon the oxen, and upon the sheep. . . . And all the cattle of Egypt died. (Ex. 9: 3, 6.)

All the Horses of Egypt did Not Die.

But the Egyptians pursued after them (all the horses and chariots of Pharaoh, and his horsemen, and his army) and overtook them encamping by the sea. (Ex. 14: 9.)

John the Baptist Recognized Jesus as the Messiah.

The next day John seeth Jesus coming unto him, and saith, Behold the Lamb of God, which taketh away the sin of the world. . . . And I saw and bare record that this is the Son of God. (John 1: 29, 34.)

John the Baptist did Not Recognize Jesus as the Messiah.
Now, when John had heard in the prison the works of Christ, he sent two of his disciples, and said unto him, Art thou he that should come, or do we look for another? (Mat. 11: 2, 3.)

John the Baptist was Elias.
This is Elias which was for to come. (Mat. 11: 14.)

John the Baptist was Not Elias.
And they asked him, What then? Art thou Elias? And he saith, I am not. (John 1: 21.)

The Father of Joseph, Mary's Husband, was Jacob.
And Jacob begat Joseph, the husband of Mary, of whom was born Jesus. (Mat. 1: 16.)

The Father of Mary's Husband was Heli.
Being . . . the son of Joseph which was the son of Heli. (Luke 3: 23.)

The Father of Salah was Arphaxad.
And Arphaxad lived five and thirty years and begat Salah. (Gen. 11: 12.)

The Father of Sala was Cainan.
Which was the son of Sala, which was the son of Cainan, which was the son of Arphaxad. (Luke 3: 35, 36.)

The Infant Jesus was Taken into Egypt.
He took the young child and his mother by night and departed into Egypt, and was there until the death of Herod. . . . But when Herod was dead . . . he arose and took the young child and his mother and came . . . and dwelt in a city called Nazareth. (Mat. 2: 14, 15, 19, 21, 23.)

The Infant Jesus was Not Taken into Egypt.
And when the days of her purification, according to the law of Moses, were accomplished, they brought him to Jerusalem, to present him to the Lord. . . . And when they

had performed all things, according to the law of the Lord, they returned . . . to their own city, Nazareth. (Luke 2: 22, 39.)

Jesus was Tempted in the Wilderness.

And *immediately* [after his baptism] the spirit driveth him into the wilderness. And he was there in the wilderness *forty days* tempted of Satan. (Mark 1: 12, 13.)

Jesus was Not Tempted in the Wilderness.

And the *third day* [after his baptism] there was a marriage in Cana of Galilee. . . . And both Jesus was called and his disciples to the marriage. (John 2: 1, 2.)

Jesus Preached his First Sermon Sitting on the Mount.

And, seeing the multitude, he went up into a *mountain*, and when he was *set* his disciples came unto him. And he opened his mouth and taught them, saying. (Mat. 5: 1, 2.)

He Preached his First Sermon Standing in the Plain.

And he came down with them and *stood* in the *plain*; and the company of his disciples and a great multitude of people . . . came to hear him. . . . And he lifted up his eyes on his disciples and said. (Luke 6: 17, 20.)

John was in Prison when Jesus went into Galilee.

Now, after that John was put in prison, Jesus came into Galilee, preaching the gospel of the kingdom of God. (Mark 1: 14.)

John was Not in Prison when Jesus went into Galilee.

The day following Jesus would go forth into Galilee. (John 1: 43.)

After these things came Jesus and his disciples into the land of Judea. . . . And John was also baptizing in Enon. . . . For John was *not yet* cast into prison. (John 3: 22, 23, 24.)

The Disciples were Commanded to Take a Staff and Sandals.

And commanded them that they should take nothing for their journey save *a staff* only; no scrip, no bread, no money in their purse; but be shod with *sandals*. (Mark 6: 8, 9.)

They were Commanded to Take Neither Staves Nor Sandals.

Provide neither gold, nor silver, nor brass in your purses; nor scrip for your journey, neither two coats, *neither shoes, nor yet staves.* (Mat. 10: 9, 10.)

Two Blind Men Besought Jesus.

And behold, two blind men sitting by the way-side, when they heard that Jesus passed by, cried out, saying, Have mercy on us, O Lord thou son of David. (Mat. 20: 30.)

Only One Blind Man Besought Him.

A certain blind man sat by the way-side begging. . . . And he cried, saying, Jesus, thou son of David, have mercy on me. (Luke 18: 35, 38.)

Two Men Coming Out of the Tombs Met Jesus.

There met him two, possessed with devils, coming out of the tombs. (Mat. 8: 28.)

Only One Man Coming Out of the Tombs Met Him.

There met him, coming out of the tombs, a man with an unclean spirit. (Mark 5: 2.)

A Centurion Besought Jesus to Heal his Servant.

There came unto him a centurion, beseeching him, and saying, Lord, my servant lieth at home sick of the palsy. (Mat. 8: 5, 6.)

Not the Centurion, but his Messengers, Besought Jesus.

He sent unto him the elders of the Jews, beseeching him that he would come and heal his servant. And when they came to Jesus, *they* besought him. (Luke 7: 3, 4.)

Jesus was Crucified at the Third Hour.

And it was the third hour, and they crucified him. (Mark 15: 25.)

He was Not Crucified Until the Sixth Hour.

And it was the preparation of the passover, and about the sixth hour; and he saith unto the Jews, Behold your king. . . . Shall I crucify your king? (John 19: 14, 15.)

The Two Thieves Reviled Jesus.

The thieves also, which were crucified with him, cast the same in his teeth. (Mat. 27: 44.)

And they that were crucified with him, reviled him. (Mark 15: 32.)

Only One of the Thieves Reviled Him.

And one of the malefactors which were hanged railed on him. . . . But the *other* answering, *rebuked him*, saying, Dost thou not fear God, seeing thou art in the same condemnation? (Luke 23: 39, 40.)

Vinegar Mingled with Gall was Offered Jesus.

They gave him vinegar to drink, mingled with gall. (Mat. 27: 34.)

Wine Mingled with Myrrh was Offered to Him.

And they gave him to drink, wine mingled with myrrh. (Mark 15: 23.)

Satan Entered into Judas while at the Supper.

And after the sop Satan entered into him. (John 13: 27.)

Satan Entered into him Before the Supper.

Then entered Satan into Judas. . . . And he went his way and communed with the chief priests and captains, how he might betray him. . . . *Then* came the day of unleavened bread when the passover must be killed. (Luke 22: 3, 4, 7.)

Judas Returned the Pieces of Silver.

Then Judas ... brought again the thirty pieces of silver to the chief priests and elders. (Mat. 27: 3.)

Judas did Not Return the Pieces of Silver.

Now, this man purchased a field with the reward of iniquity. (Acts 1: 18.)

Judas Hanged Himself.

And he cast down the pieces of silver in the temple, and departed, and went and hanged himself. (Mat. 27: 5.)

Judas did Not Hang Himself, but Died Another Way.

And falling headlong he burst asunder in the midst, and all his bowels gushed out. (Acts 1: 18.)

The Potter's Field was Purchased by Judas.

Now, this man purchased a field with the reward of iniquity. (Acts 1: 18.)

The Potter's Field was Purchased by the Chief Priests.

And the chief priests took the silver pieces ... and bought with them the potter's field. (Mat. 27: 6, 7.)

But One Woman Came to the Sepulcher.

The first day of the week cometh Mary Magdalene, early, when it was yet dark, unto the sepulcher. (John 20: 1.)

Two Women Came to the Sepulcher.

In the end of the Sabbath, as it began to dawn toward the first day of the week, came Mary Magdalene, and the *other Mary*, to see the sepulcher. (Mat. 28: 1.)

Three Women Came to the Sepulcher.

And when the Sabbath was past, Mary Magdalene, and Mary the mother of James, and Salome, had brought sweet spices, that they might come and anoint him. (Mark 16: 1.)

More than Three Women Came to the Sepulcher.

It was Mary Magdalene, and Joanna, and Mary the mother of James, and *other women* that were with them. (Luke 24: 10.)

It was at Sunrise when they Came to the Sepulcher.

And very early in the morning, the first day of the week, they came unto the sepulcher, at the rising of the sun. (Mark 16: 2.)

It was some time Before Sunrise when They came.

The first day of the week, cometh Mary Magdalene, early, while it was *yet dark*, unto the sepulcher. (John 20: 1.)

Two Angels were Seen at the Sepulcher, Standing up.

And it came to pass, as they were much perplexed thereabout, behold, two men *stood* by them in *shining garments*. (Luke 24: 4.)

But One Angel was Seen, and He was Sitting Down.

For the angel of the Lord descended from heaven, and came and rolled back the stone from the door, and sat upon it. . . . And *the angel* answered and said unto the women, Fear not. (Mat. 28: 2, 5.)

Two Angels were Seen within the Sepulcher.

And as she wept she stooped down and looked into the sepulcher, and seeth two angels in white. (John 20: 11, 12.)

But One Angel was Seen within the Sepulcher.

And entering into the sepulcher, they saw a young man sitting on the right side, clothed in a long white garment. (Mark 16: 5.)

The One Angel Seen was Without the Sepulcher.

The angel . . . rolled back the stone from the door, and sat upon it. (Mat. 28: 2.)

The Women went and Told the Disciples of Christ's Resurrection.

And they departed quickly from the sepulcher, with fear and great joy, and did run to bring his disciples word. (Mat. 28: 8.)

And returned from the sepulcher, and told all these things unto the eleven. (Luke 24: 9.)

The Women did Not Go and Tell the Disciples.

And they went out quickly and fled from the sepulcher; for they trembled and were amazed; neither said they anything to any man. (Mark 16: 8.)

The Angels Appeared After Peter and John Visited the Sepulcher.

Peter therefore went forth, and that other disciple, [whom Jesus loved,] and came to the sepulcher, . . . and went into the sepulcher, and seeth the linen clothes. . . . . Then the disciples went away again. But Mary stood without at the sepulcher, weeping; and as she wept she stooped down and looked into the sepulcher, and seeth two angels in white. (John 20: 3, 6, 10–12.)

The Angels Appeared Before Peter Alone Visited the Sepulcher.

Behold, two men stood by them [the women] in shining garments. . . . And they . . . returned from the sepulcher, and told all these things unto the eleven. . . . Then arose Peter, and ran unto the sepulcher, and stooping down he beheld the linen clothes laid by themselves, and departed wondering. (Luke 24: 4, 8, 9.)

Jesus Appeared First to Mary Magdalene Only.

Now, when Jesus was risen early, the first day of the week, he appeared first to Mary Magdalene. (Mark 16: 9.)

And when she had thus said, she turned herself back and saw Jesus standing, and knew not that it was Jesus. (John 20: 14.)

Jesus Appeared First to the Two Marys.

And as they [Mary Magdalene and the other Mary] went to tell his disciples, behold Jesus met them, saying, All hail. (Mat. 28: 9.)

He Appeared to Neither of the Marys.

(See Luke 24: 1–11.)

Jesus was to be Three Days and Three Nights in the Grave.

So shall the son of man be three days and three nights in the heart of the earth. (Mat. 12: 40.)

He was but Two Days and Two Nights in the Grave.

And it was the third hour, and they crucified him. . . . It was the preparation, that is, the *day before the Sabbath*. . . . And Pilate . . . gave the body to Joseph. And he . . . laid him in a sepulcher. . . . Now, when Jesus was risen early the *first day of the week*, he appeared first to Mary Magdalene. (Mark 15: 25, 42, 44, 45, 46; and 16: 9.)

The Holy Ghost Was Bestowed at Pentecost.

But ye shall receive power after that the Holy Ghost is come upon you. . . . Ye shall be baptized with the Holy Ghost not many days hence. (Acts 1: 8, 5.)

And when the day of Pentecost was fully come they were all of one accord in one place. . . . And they were all filled with the Holy Ghost. (Acts 2: 1, 4.)

The Holy Ghost was Bestowed Before Pentecost.

And when he said this he breathed on them, and saith unto them, Receive ye the Holy Ghost. (John 20: 22.)

The Disciples were Commanded Immediately After the Resurrection to go into Galilee.

Then said Jesus unto them, Be not afraid; go tell my brethren that they go into Galilee, and there shall they see me. (Mat. 28: 10.)

They were Commanded Immediately After the Resurrection to Tarry at Jerusalem.

But tarry ye in the city of Jerusalem until ye be endued with power from on high. (Luke 24: 49.)

Jesus First Appeared to the Eleven Disciples in a Room at Jerusalem.

And they rose up the same hour and returned to Jerusalem, and found the eleven gathered together. . . . And as they thus spake, Jesus himself stood in the midst of them. . . But they were terrified and affrighted, and supposed that they had seen a spirit. (Luke 24: 33, 36, 37.)

The same day, at evening, being the first day of the week, when the doors were shut where the disciples were assembled, . . . came Jesus and stood in the midst. (John 20: 19.)

He First Appeared to them on a Mountain in Galilee.

Then the eleven disciples went away into Galilee, into a mountain where Jesus had appointed them. And when they saw him they worshipped him, but some doubted. (Mat. 28: 16, 17.)

Jesus Ascended from Mount Olivet.

And when he had spoken these things, while they beheld, he was taken up, and a cloud received him out of their sight. . . . Then returned they unto Jerusalem, from the mount called Olivet. (Acts 1: 9, 12.)

He Ascended from Bethany.

And he led them out as far as to Bethany; and he lifted up his hands and blessed them. And it came to pass while he blessed them, he was parted from them, and carried up into heaven. (Luke 24: 50, 51.)

Did he Ascend from Either Place?

Afterward he appeared unto the eleven as they *sat at meat*, and upbraided them with their unbelief. . . . So then, after the Lord had spoken unto them, he was received up into heaven. (Mark 16: 14, 19.)

Paul's Attendants Heard the Voice, and Stood Speechless.

And the men which journeyed with him [Paul] *stood speechless, hearing* a voice but seeing no man. (Acts 9: 7.)

His Attendants Heard Not the Voice, and were Prostrate.

And they that were with me saw indeed the light and were afraid; but they *heard not* the voice of him that spake to me. (Acts 22: 9.)

And when we were *all fallen to the earth*, I heard a voice. (Acts 26: 14.)

Abraham Departed to go into Canaan.

And Abram took Sarah, his wife, and Lot, his brother's son, . . and they went forth to go into the land of Canaan, and into the land of Canaan they came. (Gen. 12: 5.)

Abraham Went not Knowing Where.

By faith Abraham, when he was called to go out into a place which he should after receive for an inheritance, obeyed; and he went out, not knowing whither he went. (Heb. 11: 8.)

Abraham had Two Sons.

Abraham had two sons; one by a bond-maid, the other by a free woman. (Gal. 4: 22.)

Abraham had but One Son.

By faith, Abraham when he was tried offered up Isaac, . . . his only begotten son. (Heb. 11: 17.)

Keturah was Abraham's Wife.

Then again Abraham took a wife, and her name was Keturah. (Gen. 25: 1.)

Keturah was Abraham's Concubine.

The sons of Keturah, Abraham's concubine. (1 Chron. 1: 32.)

Abraham Begat a Son when he was a Hundred Years Old, by the Interposition of Providence.

Sarah conceived and bare Abraham a son in his old age, at the set time of which God had spoken to him. (Gen. 21: 2.)

And being not weak in the faith, he considered not his own body, now dead, when he was about a hundred years old. (Rom. 4: 19.)

Therefore sprang there from one, and him as good as dead, so many as the stars of the sky. (Heb. 11: 12.)

Abraham Begat Six Children More After he was a Hundred Years Old, Without any Interposition of Providence.

Then again Abraham took a wife, and her name was Keturah; and she bare him Zimram, and Jockshan, and Medan, and Midian, and Ishbak, and Shuah. (Gen. 25: 1, 2.)

Jacob Bought a Sepulcher of the Sons of Hamor.

And the bones of Joseph . . . buried they in Shechem, in a parcel of ground which Jacob bought of the sons of Hamor, the father of Shechem. (Josh. 24: 32.)

Abraham Bought it of the Sons of Emmor.

In the sepulcher that Abraham bought for a sum of money of the sons of Emmor, the father of Sychem. (Acts 7: 16.)

God Promised the Land of Canaan to Abraham and his Seed.

And the Lord said unto Abraham, . . . All the land which thou seest, to thee will I give it, and to thy seed forever. . . . Unto thee and to thy seed after thee. (Gen. 13: 14, 15, and 17: 8.)

Abraham and his Seed Never Received the Promised Land.

And he gave him [Abraham] none inheritance in it, no, not so much as to set his foot on. (Acts 7: 5.)

By faith he sojourned in the land of promise as in a strange country, dwelling in tabernacles with Isaac and Jacob, the heirs with him of the same promise. . . . These all died in faith, *not having received the promises*. (Heb. 11: 9, 13.)

Baasha Died in the Twenty-sixth Year of Asa.

So Baasha slept with his fathers, . . . and Elah, his son, reigned in his stead. . . . In the twenty and sixth year of Asa, king of Judah, began Elah to reign over Israel. (1 Kings 16: 6, 8.)

Baasha did Not Die in the Twenty-sixth Year of Asa.

In the *six and thirtieth* year of the reign of Asa, Baasha, king of Israel, came up against Judah. (2 Chron. 16: 1.)

Ahaziah was the Youngest Son of Jehoram.

And the inhabitants of Jerusalem made Ahaziah, his [Jehoram's] youngest son, king in his stead; for the band of men that came with the Arabians to the camp had slain all the eldest. (2 Chron. 22: 1.)

Ahaziah was Not the Youngest Son of Jehoram.

The Lord stirred up against Jehoram the spirit of the Philistines, and of the Arabians, . . . and they came up into Judah . . . and carried away all the substance that was found in the king's house, and sons also, and his wives; so that there was never a son left him, save *Jehoahaz*, the *youngest* of his sons. (2 Chron. 21: 16, 17.)

Ahaziah was Twenty-two Years Old when he Began to Reign, being Eighteen Years Younger than his Father.

Thirty and two years old was he [Jehoram] when he began to reign; and he reigned *eight* years in Jerusalem. . . . And Ahaziah reigned in his stead. . . . *Two and twenty* years old was Ahaziah when he began to reign. (2 Kings 8: 17, 24, 26.)

Ahaziah was Forty-two Years Old when he Began to Reign, being Two Years Older than his Father.

Thirty and two years old was he [Jehoram] when he began to reign, and he reigned in Jerusalem *eight* years. And the inhabitants of Jerusalem made Ahaziah his youngest son, king in his stead. *Forty and two* years old was Ahaziah when he began to reign. (2 Chron. 21: 20, and 22: 1, 2.)

Michal had No Child.

Therefore Michal, the daughter of Saul, had no child unto the day of her death. (2 Sam. 6: 23.)

Michal had Five Children.

The five sons of Michal, the daughter of Saul. (2 Sam. 21: 8.)

David was Tempted by the Lord to Number the People.

And the anger of the Lord was kindled against Israel, and he moved David against them to say, Go, number Israel and Judah. (2 Sam. 24: 1.)

David was Tempted by Satan to Number the People.

And Satan stood up against Israel, and provoked David to number Israel. (1 Chron. 21: 1.)

SELF-CONTRADICTIONS OF THE BIBLE. 185

There were 800,000 Warriors of Israel and 500,000 of Judah.

And Joab gave up the sum of the number of the people unto the king; and there were in Israel eight hundred thousand valiant men that drew the sword; and the men of Judah five hundred thousand men. (2 Sam. 24: 9.)

There were 1,100,000 of Israel and 470,000 of Judah.

And Joab gave the sum of the number of the people unto David. And all they of Israel were a thousand thousand and a hundred thousand [1,100,000] men that drew the sword; and Judah was four hundred three score and ten thousand [470,000] men that drew the sword. (1 Chron. 21: 5.)

David Sinned in Numbering the People.

And David's heart smote him after that he had numbered the people. And David said unto the Lord, I have sinned greatly in that I have done. (2 Sam. 24: 10.)

David Never Sinned except in the Matter of Uriah.

David did that which was right in the eyes of the Lord, and turned not aside from anything that he commanded him all the days of his life, save only in the matter of Uriah the Hittite. (1 Kings 15: 5.)

David Slew 700 Syrian Charioteers and 40,000 Horsemen.

And David slew the men of the seven hundred chariots of the Syrians, and forty thousand horsemen. (2 Sam. 10: 18.)

David Slew 7,000 Syrian Charioteers and 40,000 Footmen.

And David slew of the Syrians seven thousand men which fought in chariots, and forty thousand footmen. (1 Chron. 19: 18.)

David Paid for a Threshing Floor Fifty Shekels of Silver.

So David bought the threshing floor and the oxen for fifty shekels of silver. (2 Sam. 24: 24.)

David Paid for it Six Hundred Shekels of Gold.

So David gave to Ornan for the place six hundred shekels of gold. (1 Chron. 21: 25.)

Goliath was Slain by David.

And there went out a champion out of the camp of the Philistines, named Goliath of Gath. . . . So David . . . smote the Philistine and slew him. (1 Sam. 17: 4, 50.)

Goliath was Slain by Elhanan.

Elhanan, the son of Jaare-origim, a Bethlehemite, slew ["the brother of," supplied by the translators] Goliath the Gittite. (2 Sam. 21: 19.)

SPECULATIVE DOCTRINES.

Christ is Equal with God.

I and my Father are one. (John 10: 30.)

Who, being in the form of God, thought it not robbery to be equal with God. (Phil. 2: 6.)

Christ is Not Equal with God.

My Father is greater than I. (John 14: 28.)

Of that day and hour knoweth no man, no, not the angels of heaven, but my Father only. (Mat. 24: 36.)

Christ Judged Men.

The Father judgeth no man, but hath committed all judgment to the Son. . . . As I hear I judge. (John 5: 22, 30.)

Christ Judged No Man.

I judge no man. (John 8: 15.)

If any man hear my words and believe not, I judge him not; for I came not to judge the world, but to save the world. (John 12: 47.)

Jesus was All Powerful.

All power is given unto me in heaven and in earth. (Mat. 28: 18.)

The Father loveth the son, and hath given all things into his hand. (John 3: 35.)

Jesus was Not All Powerful.

And he could there do no mighty work, save that he laid his hands on a few sick folk and healed them. (Mark 6: 5.)

The Law was Superceded by the Christian Dispensation.

The law and the prophets were until John; since that time the kingdom of God is preached. (Luke 16: 16.)

Having abolished in the flesh the enmity, even the law of commandments contained in ordinances. (Eph. 2: 15.)

But now we are delivered from the law. (Rom. 7: 6.)

The Law was Not Superceded by the Christian Dispensation.

I come not to destroy but to fulfill. For verily I say unto you, till heaven and earth pass, one jot or one title shall in no wise pass from the law till all be fulfilled. Whosoever therefore shall break one of these least commandments and shall teach men so, he shall be called the least in the kingdom of heaven. (Mat. 5: 17, 18, 19.)

Christ's Mission was Peace.

And suddenly there was with the angel a multitude of the heavenly host praising God and saying, Glory to God in the highest, and on earth peace, good will toward men. (Luke 2: 13, 14.)

And thou, child, shall be called the Prophet of the Highest. . . . To guide our feet into the way of peace. (Luke 1: 76, 79.)

And his name shall be called . . . The Prince of Peace. (Is. 9: 6.)

Christ's Mission was Not Peace.

Think not that I am come to send peace on earth; I came not to send peace, but a sword. (Mat. 10: 34.)

I am come to send fire on the earth. (Luke 12: 49.)

Christ Received not Testimony from Man.

Ye sent unto John and he bare witness unto the truth. But I receive not testimony from man. (John 5: 33, 34.)

Christ Did Receive Testimony from Man.

And ye also shall *bear witness*, because ye have been with me from the beginning. (John 15: 27.)

Christ's Witness of Himself is True.

I am one that bear witness of myself. . . . Though I bear record of myself, yet my record is true. (John 8: 18, 14.)

Christ's Witness of Himself is Not True.

If I bear witness of myself, my witness is not true. (John 5: 31.)

It was Lawful for the Jews to Put Jesus to Death.

The Jews answered him, We have a law, and by our law he ought to die. (John 19: 7.)

It was Not Lawful for the Jews to Put him to Death.

The Jews therefore said unto him, It is not lawful for us to put any man to death. (John 18: 31.)

Children are Punished for the Sins of their Parents.

I, the Lord thy God, am a jealous God, visiting the iniquities of the fathers upon the children. (Ex. 20: 5.)

Because by this deed thou hast given great occasion to the enemies of the Lord to blaspheme, the child also that is born unto thee shall surely die. (2 Sam. 12: 14.)

Children are Not Punished for the Sins of their Parents.

The son shall not bear the iniquity of the father. (Ezek. 18: 20.)

Neither shall the children be put to death for the fathers. (Deut. 24: 16.)

Man is Justified by Faith Alone.

By the deeds of the law there shall no flesh be justified. (Rom. 3: 20.)

Knowing that a man is not justified by the works of the law, but by the faith of Jesus Christ. (Gal. 2: 16.)

The just shall live by faith. And the law is not of faith. (Gal. 3: 11, 12.)

For if Abraham were justified by works, he hath whereof to glory. (Rom. 4: 2.)

Man is Not Justified by Faith Alone.

Was not Abraham our father justified by works? . . . Ye see then how that by works a man is justified, and not by faith only. (James 2: 21, 24.)

The doers of the law shall be justified. (Rom. 2: 13.)

It is Impossible to Fall from Grace.

And I give unto them eternal life, and they shall never perish, neither shall any pluck them out of my hand. (John 10: 28.)

Neither death, nor life, nor angels, nor principalities, nor powers, nor things present, nor things to come, nor hight nor depth, nor any other creature, shall be able to separate us from the love of God which is in Christ Jesus our Lord. (Rom. 8: 38, 39.)

It is Possible to Fall from Grace.

But when the righteous turneth away from his righteousness, and committeth iniquity, and doeth according to all the abominations that the wicked man doeth, shall he live? All his righteousness that he hath done shall not be mentioned; in his trespass that he hath trespassed, and in his sin that he hath sinned, in them shall he die. (Ezek. 18: 24.)

For it is impossible for those who were once enlightened, and have tasted of the heavenly gift, and were made partakers of the Holy Ghost, and have tasted the good word of God, and the powers of the world to come, if they shall fall away, to renew them again unto repentance. (Heb. 6: 4, 5, 6.)

For if, after they have escaped the pollutions of the world through the knowledge of the Lord and Savior Jesus Christ, they are again entangled therein and overcome, the latter end is worse with them than the beginning. For it had been better for them not to have known the way of righteousness than, after they have known it, to turn from the holy commandment delivered unto them. (2 Peter 2: 20, 21.)

No Man is Without Sin.

For there is no man that sinneth not. (1 Kings 8: 46.)

Who can say, I have made my heart clean; I am pure from my sin? (Prov. 20: 9.)

For there is not a just man upon earth, that doeth good and sinneth not. (Eccl. 7: 20.)

There is none righteous, no, not one. (Rom. 3: 10.)

Christians are Sinless.

Whosoever is born of God doth not commit sin; . . . he cannot sin, because he is born of God. . . . Whosoever abideth in him sinneth not. . . . He that committeth sin is of the devil. (1 John 3: 9, 6, 8.)

There is to be a Resurrection of the Dead.

The trumpet shall sound and the dead shall be raised. (1 Cor. 15: 52.)

And I saw the dead, small and great, stand before God; . . . and they were judged, every man according to their works. (Rev. 20: 12, 13.)

The hour is coming in the which all that are in the graves shall hear his voice, and shall come forth. (John 5: 28, 29.)

For if the dead rise not, then is not Christ raised. (1 Cor. 15: 16.)

There is to be no Resurrection of the Dead.

As the cloud is consumed and vanisheth away, so he that goeth down to the grave shall come up no more. (Job. 7: 9.)

The dead know not anything, neither have they any more a reward. (Eccl. 9: 5.)

They are dead, they shall not live; they are deceased, they shall not rise. (Is. 26: 14.)

Reward and Punishment to be Bestowed in this World.

Behold the righteous shall be recompensed in the earth, much more the wicked and the sinner. (Prov. 11: 31.)

Reward and Punishment to be Bestowed in the Next World.

And the dead were judged out of those things which were written in the books, according to their works. (Rev. 20: 12.)

Then he shall reward every man according to his works. (Mat. 16: 27.)

According to that he hath done, whether it be good or bad. (2 Cor. 5: 10.)

Annihilation the Portion of all Mankind.

Why died not I from the womb? Why did I not give up the ghost when I came out of the belly? . . . For now should I have lain still and been quiet; I should have slept; then had I been at rest, with kings and counselors of the earth, which built desolate places for themselves; or with princes that had gold, who filled their houses with silver; or as a hidden, untimely birth I had not been; as infants which never saw the light. *There* the wicked cease from troubling, and there the weary be at rest. . . . The small and great are there, and the servant is free from his master. Wherefore is light given to him that is in misery, and life unto the bitter in soul, which long for death, but it cometh not, . . . which rejoice exceedingly and are glad, when they can find the grave? (Job. 3: 11, 13-17, 19-22.)

The dead know not anything. . . . For there is no work, nor device, nor knowledge, nor wisdom in the grave whither thou goest. (Eccl. 9: 5, 10.)

For that which befalleth the sons of men befalleth the beasts, even one thing befalleth them; as the one dieth, so dieth the other; yea, they have all one breath; so that a man hath no pre-eminence above a beast. . . . All go unto one place. (Eccl. 3: 19, 20.)

Endless Misery the Portion of a Part of Mankind.

These shall go away into everlasting punishment. (Mat. 25: 46.)

And the devil that deceived them was cast into the lake of fire and brimstone, where the beast and the false prophet are, and shall be tormented day and night for ever and ever. . . . And whosoever was not found written in the book of life was cast into the lake of fire. (Rev. 20: 10, 15.)

And the smoke of their torment ascendeth up forever and ever. (Rev. 14: 11.)

And many of them that sleep in the dust shall awake, some to everlasting life, and some to shame and everlasting contempt. (Dan. 12: 2.)

The Earth is to be Destroyed.

The earth also and the works that are therein shall be burned up. (2 Peter 3: 10.)

They shall perish, but thou remainest. (Heb. 1: 11.)

And I saw a great white throne, and him that sat on it, from whose face the earth and the heaven fled away, and there was no place found for them. (Rev. 20: 11.)

The Earth is Never to be Destroyed.

Who laid the foundations of the earth that it should not be removed forever. (Ps. 104: 5.)

But the earth abideth forever. (Eccl. 1: 4.)

No Evil Shall Happen to the Godly.

There shall no evil happen to the just. (Prov. 12: 21.)

Who is he that will harm you, if ye be followers of that which is good? (1 Peter 3: 13.)

Evil Does Happen to the Godly.

Whom the Lord loveth he chasteneth, and scourgeth every son whom he receiveth. (Heb. 12: 6.)

And the Lord said unto Satan, Hast thou considered my servant, Job, that there is none like him in the earth, a perfect and upright man? . . . So went Satan forth . . . and smote Job with sore boils from the sole of his foot unto his crown. (Job 2: 3, 7.)

Worldly Good and Prosperity the Lot of the Godly.

There shall no evil happen to the just. (Prov. 12: 21.)

For the Lord loveth judgment and forsaketh not his saints; they are preserved forever. . . . The wicked watcheth the righteous and seeketh to slay him. The Lord will not leave him in his hand, nor condemn him when he is judged. . . . Mark the perfect man, and behold the upright; for the end of that man is peace. (Ps. 37: 28, 32, 33, 37.)

Blessed is the man that walketh not in the counsel of the ungodly. . . . Whatsoever he doeth shall prosper. (Ps. 1: 1, 3.)

And the Lord was with Joseph, and he was a prosperous man. (Gen. 39: 2.)

So the Lord blessed the latter end of Job more than his beginning. (Job 42: 12.)

Worldly Misery and Destitution the Lot of the Godly.

They were stoned, they were sawn asunder, were tempted, were slain with the sword; they wandered about in sheep-skins and goat-skins; being destitute, afflicted, tormented; . . . they wandered in deserts, and in mountains, and in dens and caves of the earth. (Heb. 11: 37, 38.)

These are they which came out of great tribulation. (Rev. 7: 14.)

Yea, and all that will live godly in Christ Jesus shall suffer persecution. (2 Tim. 3: 12.)

And ye shall be hated of all men for my name's sake. (Luke 21: 17.)

Worldly Prosperity a Blessing and a Reward of Righteousness.

There is no man that hath left house or brethren, or sisters, or father, or mother, or wife, or children, or lands, for my sake and the gospel's, but he shall receive a hundred-fold now in this time, houses, and brethren, and sisters, and mothers, and children, and lands. (Mark 10: 29, 30.)

I have been young, and now am old; yet have I not seen the righteous forsaken nor his seed begging bread. (Ps. 37: 25.)

Blessed is the man that feareth the Lord. . . . Wealth and riches shall be in his house. (Ps. 112: 1, 3.)

If thou return unto the Almighty, thou shalt be built up. . . . Then thou shalt lay up gold as dust. (Job 22: 23, 24.)

In the house of the righteous is much treasure. (Prov. 15, 6.)

Worldly Prosperity a Curse and a Bar to Future Reward.

Blessed be ye poor. (Luke 6: 20.)

Lay not up for yourselves treasures upon earth. . . . For where your treasure is there will your heart be also. (Mat. 6: 19, 21.)

And it came to pass that the *beggar* died, and was carried by the angels into Abraham's bosom. (Luke 16: 22.)

It is easier for a camel to go through the eye of a needle than for a rich man to enter into the kingdom of God. (Mat. 19: 24.)

Wo unto you that are rich! for ye have received your consolation. (Luke 6: 24.)

The Christian Yoke is Easy.

Come unto me all ye that labor and are heavy laden, and I will give you rest. Take my yoke upon you. . . . For my yoke is easy and my burden is light. (Mat. 11: 28–30.)

Who is he that will harm you, if ye be followers of that which is good? (1 Peter 3: 13.)

The Christian Yoke is Not Easy.

In the world ye shall have tribulation. (John 16: 33.)

Yea, and all that will live godly in Christ Jesus shall suffer persecution. (2 Tim. 3: 12.)

Whom the Lord loveth he chasteneth, and scourgeth every son whom he receiveth. . . . But if ye be without chastisement, whereof all are partakers, then are ye bastards and not sons. (Heb. 12: 6, 8.)

The Fruit of God's Spirit is Love and Gentleness.

The fruit of the spirit is love, joy, peace, long-suffering, gentleness, goodness. (Gal. 5: 22.)

The Fruit of God's Spirit is Vengeance and Fury.

And the spirit of the Lord came mightily upon him. . . . And he . . . slew a thousand men. (Judges 15: 14, 15.)

And it came to pass on the morrow that the evil spirit from God came upon Saul, . . . and there was a javelin in Saul's hand. And Saul cast the javelin; for he said, I will smite David even to the wall with it. (1 Sam. 18: 10, 11.)

Prosperity and Longevity Enjoyed by the Wicked.

Wherefore do the wicked live, become old, yea, are mighty in power? Their seed is established in their sight with them, and their offspring before their eyes. Their houses are safe from fear. (Job 21: 7, 8, 9.)

They [men of the world] are full of children and leave the rest of their substance to their babes. (Ps. 17: 14.)

I was envious at the foolish when I saw the prosperity of the wicked. . . . They are not in trouble as other men. . . . Behold, these are the ungodly who prosper in the world; they increase in riches. (Ps. 73: 3, 5, 12.)

There is a wicked man that prolongeth his life in his wickedness. (Eccl. 7: 15.)

Wherefore doth the way of the wicked prosper? Wherefore are all they happy that deal very treacherously? (Jer. 12: 1.)

Prosperity and Longevity Denied to the Wicked.

The light of the wicked shall be put out. . . . Terrors shall make him afraid on every side. . . . He shall be driven from light into darkness, and chased out of the world. He shall neither have son nor nephew among his people, nor any remaining in his dwellings. (Job. 18: 5, 12, 18, 19.)

But it shall not be well with the wicked, neither shall he prolong his days. (Eccl. 8: 23.)

Bloody and deceitful men shall not live out half their days. (Ps. 55: 23.)

The years of the wicked shall be shortened. (Prov. 10: 27.)

They [the hypocrites] die in youth. (Job. 36: 14.)

Be not over much wicked, neither be foolish; why shouldst thou die before they time? (Eccl. 7: 17.)

Poverty is a Blessing.

Blessed be ye poor. . . . Woe unto you that are rich! (Luke 6: 20, 24.)

Hath not God chosen the poor of this world, rich in faith, and heirs of the kingdom? (James 2: 5.)

Riches a Blessing.

The rich man's wealth is his strong tower, but the destruction of the poor is their poverty. (Prov. 10: 15.)

If thou return unto the Almighty then thou shalt be built up. . . . Thou shalt then lay up gold as dust. (Job 22: 23, 24.)

So the Lord blessed the latter end of Job more than his beginning, for he had 14,000 sheep, and 6,000 camels and a thousand yoke of oxen, and a thousand she asses. (Job 42: 12.)

Neither Poverty nor Riches a Blessing.

Give me neither poverty nor riches; feed me with food convenient for me; lest I be full and deny thee, and say, Who is the Lord? or lest I be poor and steal, and take the name of my God in vain. (Prov. 30: 8, 9.)

Wisdom a Source of Enjoyment.

Happy is the man that findeth wisdom. . . . Her ways are ways of pleasantness, and in her paths are peace. (Prov. 3: 13, 17.)

Wisdom a Source of Vexation, Grief, and Sorrow.

And I gave my heart to know wisdom. . . . I perceived that this also is vexation of spirit. For in much wisdom is much grief, and he that increaseth knowledge increaseth sorrow. (Eccl. 1: 17, 18.)

A Good Name a Blessing.

A good name is better than precious ointment. (Eccl. 7: 1.).

A good name is rather to be chosen than great riches. (Prov. 22: 1.)

A Good Name is a Curse.

Woe unto you when all men shall speak well of you. (Luke 6: 26.)

Laughter Commended.

To everything there is a season, and a time. . . . A time to weep and a time to laugh. (Eccl. 3: 1, 4.)

Then I commended mirth, because a man hath no better thing under the sun than to eat and to drink, and to be merry. (Eccl. 8: 15.)

A merry heart doeth good, like a medicine. (Prov. 17: 22.)

Laughter Condemned.

Woe unto you that laugh now. (Luke 6: 25.)

Sorrow is better than laughter; for by the sadness of the countenance the heart is made better. The heart of the wise is in the house of mourning; but the heart of fools is in the house of mirth. (Eccl. 7: 3, 4.)

The Rod of Correction a Remedy for Foolishness.

Foolishness is bound in the heart of a child, but the rod of correction shall drive it far from him. (Prov. 22: 15.)

There is No Remedy for Foolishness.

Though thou shouldst bray a fool in mortar, . . . yet will not his foolishness depart from him. (Prov. 27: 22.)

Temptation to be Desired.

Count it all joy when ye fall into divers temptations. (James 1: 2.)

Temptation Not to be Desired.

Lead us not into temptation. (Mat. 6: 13.)

Prophecy is Sure.

We have also a more sure word of prophecy, whereunto ye do well that ye take heed, as unto a light that shineth in a dark place. (2 Peter 1: 19.)

Prophecy is Not Sure.

At what instant I shall speak concerning a nation, and concerning a kingdom, to pluck up, and to pull down, and to destroy it; if that nation against whom I have pronounced, turn from their evil, I will repent of the evil that I thought to do unto them. And at what instant I shall speak concerning a nation and concerning a kingdom, to build and to plant it; if it do evil in my sight, that it obey not my voice, then I will repent of the good wherewith I said I would benefit them. (Jer. 18: 7–10.)

The prophets prophesy falsely, and the priests bear rule by their means. . . . From the prophet even unto the priest every one dealeth falsely. (Jer. 5: 31, and 6: 13.)

Man's Life was to be One Hundred and Twenty Years.

His days shall be a hundred and twenty years. (Gen. 6: 3.)

Man's Life is but Seventy Years.

The days of our years are three score years and ten. (Ps. 90: 10.)

Miracles a Proof of Divine Mission.

Now, when John had heard in the prison the works of Christ, he sent two of his disciples, and said unto him, Art thou he that should come, or do we look for another? Jesus answered and said unto them, Go and show John again those things which ye do hear and see; the blind receive their sight, and the lame walk, the lepers are cleansed, and the deaf hear, the dead are raised. (Mat. 11: 2–5.)

Rabbi, we know that thou art a teacher come from God; for no man can do these miracles that thou doest, except God be with him. (John 3: 2.)

And Israel saw that great work which the Lord did upon the Egyptians; and the people feared the Lord and believed the Lord and his servant Moses. (Ex. 14: 31.)

Miracles Not a Proof of Divine Mission.

And Aaron cast down his rod before Pharaoh, and before his servants and it became a serpent. Then Pharaoh also called the wise men and the sorcerers. Now, the magicians of Egypt, they also did in like manner with their enchantments, for they cast down every man his rod, and they became serpents. (Ex. 7: 10–12.)

If there arise among you a prophet, or a dreamer of dreams, and giveth thee a sign or a wonder, and the sign or the wonder come to pass whereof he spake unto thee, saying, Let us go after other gods which thou hast not known, and let us serve them, thou shalt not hearken unto the words of that prophet or that dreamer of dreams. (Deut. 13: 1–3.)

If I by Beelzebub cast out devils, by whom do our sons cast them out? (Luke 11: 19.)

Moses was a Very Meek Man.

Now, the man Moses was very meek, above all the men which were upon the face of the earth. (Num. 12: 3.)

Moses was a Very Cruel Man.

And Moses said unto them, Have ye saved all the women alive? . . . Now, therefore, kill every male among the little ones, and kill every woman that hath known man. (Num. 31: 15, 17.)

Elijah Went up to Heaven.

And Elijah went up by a whirlwind into heaven. (2 Kings 2: 11.)

None but Christ Ever Ascended into Heaven

No man hath ascended up to heaven, but he that came down from heaven, even the Son of Man. (John 3: 13.)

All Scripture is Inspired.

All scripture is given by inspiration of God. (2 Tim. 3: 16.)

Some Scripture is Not Inspired.

But I speak this by permission and not by commandment. . . . But to the rest speak I, not the Lord. (1 Cor. 7: 6, and 5: 12.)

That which I speak, I speak it not after the Lord. (2 Cor. 11: 17.)

THE DEVIL.

I have nothing new to offer on this old subject, and I therefore warn the reader not to expect any wonderful revelations. The Devil is not an object of recent discovery. He is as old as the hills. Everybody seems to know him, and he seems to know everybody. It would therefore be in vain for me to attempt to give any information respecting this old friend. However, as there are some thoughts which persist in bolting into my mind regarding old Nick, I have concluded to jot them down for those who have a taste for devilish reading.

It was always a question that greatly perplexed me, when a boy, why God should create the Devil. I never could see it in any other light than that of an egregious blunder. Why should an infinitely good being create an infinitely bad being? Why did not the Creator make all of his creatures perfect? Why did he not save them from being lost? Why did he form man to place him in the garden to be tempted and ruined when it was in the Creator's power to prevent his fall? Why did he not create him so good and so strong that it would be impossible for him to do wrong? Why was the Serpent (the Devil) made so much stronger and wiser than man? If Adam had only been made a great deal stronger, and the Serpent less seductive, the human race might have had a glorious and brilliant career. But as it was a powerful serpent-devil on the one hand, and on the other, a weak-headed know-nothing man, is it not clear that better results could not have been expected?

Why did not the author of the red man (Adam) tell him that he was going to have a severe temptation?—that he was soon to meet his great adversary? It is highly probable that Adam could have made a better showing if he had only been advised of the situation in time. But as it was he did not have a fair chance. It would have been no more than justice to have told Adam and Eve all about the Serpent-devil which was hid away somewhere in the garden like a snake in the grass. It would have been only fair to have posted on all the fences and walls about the garden, this sign, "Adam and Eve, Beware of Snakes!" This would have given them a chance for their lives. Poor Adam and Eve! They were not a bad lot, but were transplanted too early, and were nipped in the bud by the great original Serpent, who was acting according to his nature and circumstances, and therefore we cannot find it in our hearts to be too severe on his Satanic Majesty. If Satan was great, it was not won by his own powers, he had greatness thrust upon him. Let us be just; let us give the Devil his due. I have no doubt but he has grievances, if there were any court where he could offer his complaints.

The Creator made both man and Serpent-devil, knowing just what would and must come to pass, and he did it all for his own glory. He also made hell for his own glory. Surely the Lord's ways are not our ways. For no Modoc Indian would entertain such a design toward his children, no matter how bad they might be, or how vicious his own nature.

We cannot think of a creator without seeing that he as the author of all things, is responsible for *good* and *evil*, for *right* and *wrong*, for *ignorance* and *knowledge*, for *truth* and *error*. Man is therefore, no more responsible for his nature than a steam engine is responsible for its defects. The defects must be attributed to the maker in both cases.

Adam knew good and evil without eating of the tree of knowledge. He had a brain, and his thoughts were imperfect; sometimes they were relatively correct, and then **again** they were wholly wrong or in error. This was knowing good and evil, therefore he knew good and evil without eating of the prohibited fruit, just as surely as he had a brain. The tree of knowledge is a very childish story. Knowledge does not grow on trees, nor does much of it exist in heads which entertain such fables as a divine revelation.

Man was created with a brain to do his thinking and knowing, and by its very nature of knowing he must know good and evil, and yet he is cursed for knowing good and evil. As well might the Creator give the bird wings, toss it in the air and then damn it for flying. But even supposing the story to be true, namely, that the fruit of the tree made one to know good and evil, why should such desirable fruit be forbidden? What would the world be without the knowledge of good and evil? Man cannot know *good* without also knowing *evil*. They are inseparable. God himself knows good and evil, and if it is good for him to have such knowledge, then it surely must be good for you and me. The love of knowledge is the fountain of life. Man must have knowledge or his life is a mere cipher. All hail then to Mother Eve, who first tasted of the tree of knowledge, who first quenched her thirst at this fountain from which the whole race of thirsty souls have delighted to drink. Mythology abounds in stories about the gods; about their imperfections and weaknesses, but this account of the Serpent-devil and the tree of knowledge is the silliest fable of all, and has entailed indescribable misery upon the human race. The prohibition of knowledge has left an inherited twist in human nature. Even now in the afternoon of the nineteenth century mankind does not know much—and it is largely due to this first commandment not to partake of the fruit of the tree of knowledge. Has not the church always prohibited knowledge? Has she not stood in the way of every great reform? Knowledge is not important. Only believe. Believe in the Bible, but believe it only as the priest explains it.

It seems that the Serpent-devil knew more about the nature of man, and what would result from his eating the fruit of the tree of knowledge than God did. Jehovah told Adam in plain terms, that if he ate of the fruit of that tree he would die that very day. But the Serpent-devil told Eve (in French I suppose) that she and her "hubby" would do no such a thing, but on the contrary it would be a great blessing to them, and that they would become as gods (there were lots of gods in those days and many of them "no great shakes"), knowing good and evil. It turned out just as the Serpent-devil had told Mother Eve; they did not die. And when God saw what Adam and Eve had done he called a conclave of gods, and after due deliberation voted to drive them out of the garden penniless, to live upon the cold charities of an unfriendly world. And this is the same God who commands us to *forgive* and to *love* our enemies. That would not be god-like, and therefore I hold the commandment invalid.

In this august assemblage of the celestial hosts, one of their number assigns the reasons for expelling Adam and Eve from the garden in these words: "Behold the man (and woman) has become as one of us to know good and evil." (Gen. 3: 22.) Here we see it is a surprise to the gods that man had become as one of them, knowing good and evil. Yet these gods are supposed to *know all things* from all eternity to all eternity. Do the gods forget things as we poor mortals do?

The Serpent had told Eve just what would happen, and God told Adam just that which did not happen. The Serpent said: "For God doth know that in the day ye eat thereof, then your eyes shall be opened, and ye shall be as gods, knowing good and evil. Ye shall not surely die." (Gen. 3: 5, 4.) The Serpent gave it straight, and God made a mistake to say the least. In all this story about the fall of man, the Devil appears to be a better friend of man than his Creator.

The Serpent was in reality not the enemy, but the friend of man. He spoke words of truth and encouragement to Adam at a time when he needed good counsel. It is not to be forgotten that he spoke the truth. The poisonous tongue of malice has called him the father of lies, but this saying is a lie itself—and a bald-headed lie of sufficient antiquity to be itself most appropriately called the father of lies. The Devil, Lucifer, is the light-bearer, the truth revealer; but the world at large has an impression that there is a screw loose somewhere, and have unwittingly ascribed the evil to the Devil, when a very slight study of his character and deeds will show that "the Devil is not half as black as he is painted."

The next account we have of him is in the book of Job (not a Hebrew writing), where he appears under the title of Satan. It is to be borne in mind that he has many names. In the book of Genesis we left him a serpent with a curse pronounced upon him: "Because thou hast done this thou art cursed above all cattle [what kind of cattle is a snake?] and above every beast of the field; upon thy belly thou shalt go, and dust shalt thou eat all the days of thy life." (Gen. 3:14.) Prior to the great fall of Adam and Eve, when they fell upward and became as the gods, it seems the Serpent had always hopped along erect, on the tip end of his tail, but because he had divulged some court secrets, he was condemned to crawl upon his belly the rest of his natural life (which is, I should remark, uncommonly long); but in the book of Job he says of himself that he has been "walking up and down in the earth." Who told him to get up? Was he not cursed to go on his belly for all time to come? How could he walk? A snake has no legs. When, where, how, and by whom was this transformation of a hideous serpent into a prince-like man, accomplished? I don't know. Perhaps it is a sort of Santa Claus story, coming down to us from the childhood of the race. All peoples have similar traditions which spring from early myths. Our Devil story will have to get in line and march in the procession of fables. There are many people, and people of the very best kind, who do not have any Devil. He has left them and gone on a permanent vacation. On the other hand, there are folks who could not feel happy if they thought there were no

Devil. To all such, who may read this, I would ask a few questions which if they will intelligently answer, I shall be greatly obliged.

Did the Serpent talk? How could he speak without having the vocal organs necessary to human speech? Who taught him the use of language? What language did he speak? Was it French? I merely suggest the French, as Adam and Eve took French leave of the garden. Did the Serpent reason like a man? How could he with such a small head and not even a spoonful of brains, know so much more than Adam and Eve? Yea, he even knew more than God himself—for God did not know, or else he fibbed, that man would not die if he ate the forbidden fruit. He did not seem to know that man would become as the gods by partaking of this tree, but the Serpent knew all this and possibly much more; but how could so much superior knowledge be crowded into so small a head? Some of our congressmen with domes of unusual dimensions do not know as much as this inexperienced Serpent did. How are we to account for this? Let some devilishly wise man explain to a benighted world why Satan has been so wickedly traduced.

In the book of Job we have a second account of the Devil: "Now there was a day when the sons of God came to present themselves before the Lord, and Satan came also among them. And the Lord said unto Satan, Whence comest thou? Then Satan answered the Lord and said, From going to and fro in the earth, and from walking up and down in it. And the Lord said unto Satan, Hast thou considered my servant Job, that there is none like him in the earth, a perfect and upright man, one that feareth God and escheweth evil? Then Satan answered the Lord and said, Doth Job fear God for naught? Hast not thou made a hedge about him, and about his house, and about all that he hath on every side? Thou hast blest the work of his hands and his substance is increased in the land. But put forth thine hand now and touch all that he hath, and he will curse thee to thy face. And the Lord said unto Satan,

Behold all that he hath is in thy power; only upon himself put not forth thy hand. So Satan went from the presence of the Lord." (Job 1: 6-12.) Then follows an account of the destruction of the cattle and children of Job, and yet he would not curse God. Satan then suggested that to afflict him in person would bring out his weakness and deeply hidden wickedness. Job was tormented with boils, and three gratuitous advisors, and did not curse God, but came very nearly giving his counselors a cuss word or two. They exasperated him beyond measure.

Now while it must be admitted that the Devil does not show up to as great advantage in this fable as he does in that relating to the tree of knowledge, yet we should not jump to our conclusions. Let us review this Job story.

We are surprised at the dignified manners of Satan. He walks in with lordly airs among the sons of God. No one present said to him, "Get out of here." He struts around in the gay company as one of them. We hardly know how to understand such familiarity possible between the sons of God and Satan. If, however, the sons of God in those days were no better than the sons of God are in these, it is not in the least surprising that Satan should conduct himself as well as the best of them. But why did God permit him to do these cruel things to Job? In a certain book by God, we are told to "resist the Devil and he will flee from thee." This would have been splendid medicine for the doctors who prescribed it. Satan did not come there so far as we see to work any temptation. It was God who set up the temptation before Satan. He began by asking Satan what he thought of Job. What mattered it what his opinion of Job might be? Why should his opinion be asked? Was it not showing respect to him? God should have said, "Get behind me Satan."

Satan had seen many men who could not stand in the hour of trial, and not knowing Job he took him for a man of that kind; God, however, knew Job to be a "perfect" man and ought to have protected him from all evil. Yet he did nothing of the kind, but on the contrary, clothed Satan with power of destroying his cattle and children, and afflicting him with tormenting boils. We see then that it is not Satan who is responsible for the sufferings of the patient man, but God himself, who first shows respect to Satan's presence and his opinions, then gives him power by which he does a monstrous wrong to a good man and his family. But if Satan's part is bad God's is worse. He is the author of all of Job's miseries. If God had been just, he would not have led off to his Satanic Majesty with such a temptation as to ask him his opinion of Job. It was immaterial what his opinion was; but it was all important that if there were a God in Israel that he should protect and honor the "perfect" man, Job.

But aside from the barbarities of this myth, look at its childish absurdities. How could the omniscient, whose eyes are in every place, beholding the evil and the good, need to ask Satan where he came from! Was not God, the omnipresent, everywhere on earth? If Satan had been going up and down the country would He not of necessity have met God again and again? Obviously these great opponents must have often met. Again, it was useless for God to ask Satan what his opinion of Job was, or would be after he tested him, as he knows all things past, present, and to come, in heaven, earth and hell (I mean hades). It is evident that Satan's opinion is not needed or cared for, because after all the trials Job suffered were ended, there is not one word given as to what Satan's opinion of Job was, and yet in the beginning of the story this seems to be its sole object. After Job suffers a long time from bodily sores and "miserable comforters" Satan vanishes from the scene in a very obscure way, and God blesses Job with twice as much as he had before. He had more sheep, more camels, more oxen, and more asses. He became father of seven sons and three daughters, the same number of sons and daughters that were slain by Satan, instigated by God. Why were these ten innocent persons murdered? Had they no rights that a just God was bound to respect? Shall not the judge of all the earth do right? Certainly he ought to. But in this case the judge pleads guilty of this crime. In reply to Satan God says: "Although thou movedst me against him to destroy him *without cause.*" (Job 2: 3.) Here is an unqualified confession of wronging Job and his children without a show of justice; and even the cattle, I imagine, would protest against the outrageous slaughter perpetrated on them. If these asses were like Balaam's, I am sure they would enter suit for damages.

"So the Lord blessed the latter end of Job more than his beginning, for he had fourteen thousand sheep, and six thousand camels, and a thousand yoke of oxen, and a thousand she asses. He had also seven sons and three daughters." (Job 42: 12, 13.) It is clear that the Lord had nothing to do whatever with these blessings. Job had had sheep, camels, oxen, asses, and children before, without any assistance from the Lord; and if he secured a similar stock of cattle and a family of children it was by his own management and husbandry.

But supposing them a gift from God as damages sustained by Job at the hand of Satan through the instigation of God, yet they could not assuage his grief for the loved ones ruthlessly torn from his embrace. It is easy to see that this story is nothing more than an oriental tale—a myth. It is wanting not only in fact, but it teaches very bad morals. There is nothing ennobling in it. 1. God had no moral right to permit Satan to come unrebuked into the company of the sons of God. An earthly father teaches his children to avoid "evil communications," but on this occasion the heavenly father did not scorn the company of Satan, but treated him respectfully. 2. Again, the infinite being would not need to ask the Devil what his opinion of Job was, for he would know beforehand. 3. The infinitely good being would not want the Devil's opinion—nor would he value it a straw, if it were given before it was asked. 4. The infinitely just ruler of the universe would not give the great adversary of man and God such diabolical power over that "perfect and upright man" Job. Nor would he have permitted the three "miserable comforters," reeling mentally under the blind staggers of a blind theology, to have added more torment to that imposed by his Satanic Majesty. Nor would he have permitted him to murder the seven sons and three daughters, as a mere matter of experiment in testing Job's staying powers. All this is so horrible that the afterthought of more camels and asses, as a compensation is an insufficient patch to cover the unqualified wrongs done to the man of Uz. Even Job does not shine as conspicuously in all this as he should. Job ought to have protested with all his might and main against both God and Devil, that his individual rights were invaded. He should have taken a change of venue, to have a hearing before some other god, where there was a slight hope of securing more justice. But he didn't and the consequence is we are all advised, when suffering the outrageous wrongs of despotism, to "be patient like Job." It has been a great evil to the human family that Job was no "kicker;" it has opened wide the flood gates of tyranny, and transfused the cowardly blood of sheep into the veins of men. Oh, that Job had kicked and taken an appeal, what an inspiration it would be to the fold of God now, to resist the shears of the fleecers! to rebel against the rule of robbers!

Some questions to be answered by the man who pounds the Bible and claims to understand the Greek scriptures:

1. Who were the sons of God?
2. How many were there present, and were there still more of them elsewhere?
3. Where did they come from?
4. Were they any relation to the people of Nod?
5. Who were their mothers?
6. What were their occupations?
7. Where are they now?
8. Where did the Devil come from?
9. Did God create him or did he make himself?

10. If God made him then is he not responsible for all that old Nick does?

11. If he is as terribly demoniacal as orthodox theology describes him, "why in 'l don't God kill the Devil?"

12. If he cannot kill him does it not prove that the Devil is his match; and if he can, but will not, does it not prove that he sustains him and approves of his work?

13. In the light of modern theology is not the Devil almost always successful? Does he not have a larger kingdom, a larger following than God?

14. Why did the Creator inflict such a hellish punishment upon Adam and Eve, and let the Serpent off so lightly?

15. Has the punishment inflicted upon the Devil lessened his power?

16. Have the curses which God has pronounced on the world made it better?

17. Is there any place in the record, accounts of the Devil's stealing, robbing, and murdering?

18. Are there not numerous stories in the Bible recounting the robberies and murders perpetrated in the name and by the sanction of God? Some times the people of God destroyed five thousand, ten thousand, twenty thousand, fifty thousand, seventy thousand, and in one instance six hundred and seventy thousand, as in the case of Pharaoh and his hosts in the Red sea. Did Satan ever try to do anything as hellish as this?

19. Is the Devil the father of lies? When did he tell a deliberate falsehood? To Eve? Oh no, it was the other party who did that business.

20. Did he lie when he took Jesus up into an exceeding high mountain, etc., and saith unto him, "All these will I give thee," etc.? (Mat. 4: 8.) It is claimed that old Beelzebub lied on this occasion. It would hit the bull's eye in the center if we were to say that the writer of this story about Jesus being carried off bodily into an exceeding high mountain, was the boy responsible for this lie. But without resting the case there let us see how it opens out. It is

urged that "the earth is the Lord's and the fullness thereof;" but it may be urged that the Devil is called "the prince of this world," implying that he has just claims both by conquest and possession; and therefore he could have given at least a quitclaim deed.

The Devil is an expensive luxury of the church. It costs about $1,000,000,000 annually for preaching against the Devil. Even if there is less said derogatory to his Satanic Majesty now-adays, yet it costs just as much, and more too, for drawing it mild, than it did formerly, for describing the split hoof, horns, and spear-headed tail, hell, etc. Notwithstanding the fact that the people want less Devil and more bread and beef, yet they must have some Devil. Hence the church clings to its Devil-idol with which to scare the people. To give up the Devil is to break up house-keeping all around. If there be no Devil then there is no hell; and if no hell, there is no salvation; and if no salvation there is no need of preaching; and "no preach no pay." How could a fat minister with a fat salary, look such a ghost as that in the face? Yes, it would be impossible for the church to survive without the Devil. The clergy have to fall back upon him in times of revival to stir up the fears of uninformed people.

The Devil has had many hard names heaped upon him, for example: The Tempter; the Adversary or Satan; Beelzebub; the Prince of Devils; the Strong One; the Enemy, or the Hostile One; the Serpent; Lying Spirit; Lucifer; Son of the Morning; Prince of Darkness; Prince of the Power of the Air; the Accuser; Angel of the Bottomless Pit; Angel of Light; Mammon; Belial; Legion; the Foul Spirit; the Unclean Spirit; the God of this World; the Great Red Dragon; Abaddon; Apollyon, the Destroyer, etc. Besides these *sacred* titles, he is equally well known by certain house-hold names, as, Old Nick; Old Splitfoot; the Old Scratch; Old Harry; Old Horny; the Old Boy; the Deuce; the Dickens; auld Clouty; Nickie; Ben; his Satanic Majesty, etc. It must be confessed that these names do not carry much sanctity with them, nor do they leave us in love with the character they represent. But before we proceed further, it is only simple justice (that is giving the Devil his due), to call attention to the various names by which God has been known.

The early Hebrew literature speaks of *gods*, not God. We find the following names ascribed to them: El; Elohim; El Shaddai; Shaddai; Elvoh; Yahve, or Jah. The following is a personal photograph as nearly as we can draw it, of the Jewish Jehovah as described in the Bible: "There went up a smoke out of his nostrils, and fire out of his mouth devoured: coals were kindled by it." (Ps. 18: 8.) "Round about him were dark waters and thick clouds of the skies." (Ps. 18: 11.) "His head and his hairs were white like wool, as white as snow; and his eyes were as a flame of fire." (Rev. 1: 14.) "And his feet like unto fine brass, as if they burned in a furnace." (Rev. 1: 15.) "He had horns coming out of his hand." (Hab. 3: 4.) "And burning coals went forth at his feet." (Hab. 3: 5.) "In the midst of the seven candlesticks one like unto the son of man, clothed with a garment down to the foot and girt about the paps with a golden girdle." (Rev. 1: 13.) "And he had in his right hand seven stars; and out of his mouth went a sharp two-edged sword." (Rev. 1: 16.)

This God has violated all the moral laws he ever gave to man. He approved of lying, robbing, adultery, murder, war, and all the great crimes known to man.

Is it any wonder that Theodore Parker should say to the Calvinist who was trying to convert him, "The difference between us is simple,—your *God* is my *Devil*."

The reader has his choice—or he may say "good Lord good Devil," and float with the current. There is, however, no disguising the fact that between God and the Devil, as described in the Bible, the Devil sustains the better moral character of the two. He is not spotless and clean, it is true, but he has infinitely less bloodshed to answer for than Jehovah.

Where the Devil did he come from? I am reminded of this form of expression by a little incident related of a Scotch preacher, who took for his text, on one occasion, the following passage: "The Devil, as a roaring lion, walketh about seeking whom he may devour." (1 Peter 5: 8.) It must be borne in mind, in order to better understand the full force and beauty of the preacher's division of the text into three heads, that it was common in earlier times to repeat the pronoun in a sentence, for example, John Smith, his book, Mary she has come home, etc. In charming accord with this old style, the minister divided his text into three parts. He said, "My brethren, we will first inquire where the Devil he was walking to? and secondly, who the Devil he wanted to devour? and thirdly, what the Devil he was roaring about?"

Having gratuitiously thrown in this gem, we proceed to answer the question, "Where the Devil, did he come from?"

It is evident that the earlier Hebrew literature is almost wholly free from any traces of a personal Devil, and that later writings of the same people show strong outline of such a personality of evil.

While it is true that Satan is a Hebrew word, it is equally true that the word does not denote a being at all, but means anything adverse or opposing. We may cite in illustration a few passages. Second Samuel 19: 22: "David said, What have we to do with you, ye sons of Jeremiah, that ye should this day be adversaries unto me?" First Kings 11: 14: "And Jehovah stirred up an adversary unto Solomon, Hadad the Adomite." First Kings 11: 23: "And God stirred up *another* adversary, Rezon, the son of Eliadah."

In these instances, the word rendered adversary or adversaries, is Satan, and means nothing more than an opponent.

When the Jews were carried captives to Babylon, they came into immediate contact with a people, the Persians, who believed in a good being and a bad one. Ormazd was their good God, and Ahriman their Devil. The latter was as clearly defined in the duality of Zoroastrian theology, as the former. During their seventy years' captivity it could not be otherwise, than that the enslaved people should imbibe some of the customs and beliefs of their masters. If they went so far as to change the characters of their language from the original Hebrew letters to those of the Chaldas, it is easy to see that they would of course, adopt this notion of an evil principle and personality, so prevalent at that time in Chaldea. After the Babylonian exile the doctrine of a Devil became a part of the Jewish belief, and the evil spirit was termed Satan, as he was the foe or adversary of God. In First Chronicles 21: 1, there is a circumstance related in which Satan or the Devil is the principal agent. The words are: "And Satan stood up against Isreal and provoked David to number Israel." Now the book of Chronicles being written after the captivity, it was quite natural that the writer should consider and designate the enemy of God, the Devil or Satan. But the same event is mentioned in another of the Jewish books, written before the captivity, and the temptation of David is referred to entirely another being. Here the words are:

"And again the anger of the Lord was kindled against Israel, and moved David against them, to say, 'Go number Israel and Judah,' Thus in the earlier books, the affair is attributed to the Lord, but in the books written after the Jewish connection with the Chaldeans and Persians, Satan is blamed for the same act. This, beyond doubt proves the source of the Christian superstition respecting the Devil." ("The Devil," by John Watts.)

"With this dualistic system the Jews came in contact during their captivity at Babylon, and are supposed to have retained permanent traces of it in their subsequent theology. The conception of the Devil and of a lower kingdom of demons or devils is the evident illustration of this. (Ency. Brit. V. Devil.)

"The reason why there was no Devil in the early books was because none was needed then. The gods considered themselves as being quite equal to any emergency that might arise in the way of wickedness."—M. D. Conway.

In other words, the Devil is a myth coming out of the terrible darkness of remote ages. Every fear that the primitive man and men of barbarous races have had, painted devils before their minds of every description. The master mind has said:

"'Tis the eye of child-hood
That fears a painted Devil."

The thought that millions of people commonly well informed on general matters, still believe in this barbarous myth, must shock and oppress like an incubus every sensitive and well-informed mind. Such people can smile pleasantly over the homely myth of Santa Claus, but the Devil is altogether a different personage. An old lady was once told that the Devil was dead. She sat silent for a moment, and then replied, "Well, you may think so, but we hope for better things."

As the horrid doctrine of witchcraft under the light of advancing knowledge has had to retire into the background of oblivion; as the Puritan doctrine of infant damnation has been relegated to the limbo of forgetfulness; as hell's fire has burned to ashes and the ashes become cold, so too, is the doctrine of a personal Devil retreating from the minds of all sensible people.

SOUL FARRAGO.

What is, and Where is the Soul?

Until the Greek philosophy taught the world how to use and abuse abstract notions, immaterialism was not an attainable phase of thought. (Prof. Bain, "Mind and Body," p. 143.)

Thought necessarily supposes conditions. To think is to condition, and conditional limitation is the fundamental law of the possibility of thought. For, as the greyhound cannot outstrip his shadow, nor (by a more appropriate simile) the eagle out-soar the atmosphere in which he floats, and by which alone he may be supported; so the mind cannot transcend the sphere of limitation, within and through which exclusively the possibility of thought is realized. (Sir William Hamilton, "Philosophy" p. 456.)

In this paper an attempt is made to answer two very important questions, namely: What is, and where is the soul? in such fashion that everybody will be satisfied that he has a soul, and the exact spot it occupies in his mundane tabernacle. Here are a number of opinions on this subject, by the most learned men the world has ever produced. In a multitude of counsel there is wisdom. The first witness I shall put upon the stand is:

Pythagoras: (6th c. B. C.) The soul is number and a harmony. Taught the doctrine of metempsychosis. His disciples held the soul to be an aggregate of particles of great subtilty pervading the air in constant agitation.

Heraclitus: (6th c. B. C.) The soul is a spark of the stellar essence: "Scintilla stellaris essentia."

Pherecides: (6th c. B. C.) Souls existed from all eternity.

Anaximenes: (Ionic philosopher, 5th c. B. C.) God is air, air is a life-giving principle to man. The soul is air.

Diogenes of Appollonia: (Greek natural philosopher, 5th c. B. C.) The soul of the world and the soul of man is air.

Anaxagoras: (5th c. B. C.) The soul is an immortal, aerial spirit.

Socrates: (4th c. B. C.) The soul is corporeal and eternal.

Epicurus: (4th c. B. C.) The soul is a bodily substance, composed of subtile particles, disseminated through the whole frame, and having a great resemblance to spirit or breath.

Empedocles: (Sicilian philosopher and poet, 5th c. B. C.) Declared himself to have been "a boy, a girl, a bush, a bird, a fish;" that the soul inhabits every form of animal and plant.

Aristotle: (4th c. B. C.) Plants have souls without consciousness. Animals have souls, but inseparable from body. The human body is inseparable from mind, but the human mind is divided into active and passive intellect. The active intellect is pure form, detached from matter, and immortal.

Josephus: (1st c.) There were three sects among the Jews—the Pharisees, Sadduces, and the Essenes. The Pharisees believed in metempsychosis; the Sadduces believed that the soul perished with the body; the Essenes held that the soul was immortal. The soul descended in an aerial form into the body, from the highest region of the air, whither they were carried back again by a violent attraction, and after death those which had belonged to the good dwelled beyond the ocean in a country where there was neither heat nor cold, nor wind nor rain.

Pliny: (2d c.) The body and the soul have, from the moment of death, as little sensation as before birth.

Justin Martyr: (2d c.) It is heresy to say that the soul is taken up into heaven, men rise with the same bodies.

Tatian: (2d c.) There are two spirits conjoined in the human body. A material and an immaterial spirit.

Athenagoras: (2d c.) The soul is spiritual, but with a spirituality subject to material tendencies.

Origen: (3d c.) The soul is neither spirit nor matter.

Augustine: (4th c.) The soul has neither length, breadth, nor thickness. It acts on the body through the corporeal substances of light and air, which substances are mingled through the denser parts of the body. The commands of the soul are first communicated to this subtle matter, and by it immediately conveyed to the heavier elements.

Tertullian: (Latin father, about 160.) The soul has the human form, the same as its body, only it is delicate, clear, and ethereal. Unless it were corporeal, how could it be effected by the body, be able to suffer, or be nourished within the body?

St. Ambrose: (4th c.) We know nothing but what is material, excepting only the ever venerable Trinity.

St. Hilary: (5th c.) There is nothing created which is not corporeal, neither in heaven nor in earth, neither visible nor invisible; all is formed of elements; and souls, whether they inhabit a body, or are without a body, have always a corporeal substance.

Gregory Nazianzen: (4th c.) Soul, or spirit, is composed of two properties—motion and diffusion.

Bishop Nemesius: (5th c.) The soul is an immaterial substance. It is involved, as Plato taught, in eternal, self-produced motion, from which the motion of the body is derived. The pre-existence of the soul proves its suprasensible character, and its immortality.

Faustus: (Bishop of Regium, in Gaul, A. D. 470.) All created things are matter; the soul being composed of air, God alone is incorporeal.

Mamertus: (In reply to the bishop.) Man was made in the image of God. Now, as there can be no likeness to God in matter, therefore it must be found in the soul, therefore the soul is immaterial. The soul is present in every part of the body as well as in the whole, just as God is present in the whole universe, otherwise a part of it would be lost when any portion of the body is cut off. The soul is not contained in the body, but in reality contains it. Hence, it must be immaterial, for no material substance can at once contain the body and be within it as its animating principle.

Thomas Aquinas: (13th c.) The soul is the Actuality of body, as heat, which is the source whence bodies are made hot, is not body, but a sort of actuality of body. The soul of man is an independent substance.

Duns Scotus: (13th c. British philosopher.) The soul is a created something, the basis of all finite existence, including corporeal matter itself.

Albert Magnus: (13th c.) Held that the active intellect is a part of the soul, and is immortal by virtue of its community with God.

Gassendi: (French philosopher, 17th c.) There is no evidence of the spirituality of the soul.

Malebranche: (Priest and philosopher, 17th c.) We see all in God, who is in fact our soul.

Locke: (17th c.) Matter may think, and God may communicate thought to matter.

Paracelsus: (15th c.) Taught there were four souls—vegetal, sensitive, rational, and spiritual. Campanella demonstrates this last by the fact that carcasses bleed at the sight of the murderer.

Mansel: ("Philosophy of Consciousness," p. 327.) We are not authorized to say that we know the soul to be simple, and that, therefore, it is indestructible; but only that we do not know the soul to be compound, and, therefore, that we cannot infer its mortality from the analogy of bodily dissolution.

"Buck's Theo. Dic." defines soul: That vital, immaterial, active substance, or principle in man, whereby he perceives, remembers, reasons, and wills. It is rather to be described as to its operations than to be defined as to its essence. Various, indeed, have been the opinions of philosophers concerning its substance.

Parkhurst: (A distinguished Hebrew lexicographer.) As a noun, *nephesh* hath been supposed to signify the spiritual part of man, or what we commonly call the soul. I must, for myself, confess that I can find no passage where it hath undoubtedly this meaning.

Hobbes: Spirit is synonymous with ghost—a mere phantom of the imagination.

Locke: ("Understanding," p. 419.) We can no more know that there are finite spirits really existing, by the idea we have of such things in our minds, than by the ideas any one has of fairies, or centaurs; he can come to know that things answering those ideas do really exist.

Voltaire: The Greeks distinguish three sorts of souls—*Psyche*, signifying the sensitive soul—the soul of the senses; hence it was that Love, the son of Aphrodite, had so much passion for Psyche, and that she loved him so tenderly. *Pneuma*, the breath which gave life and motion to the whole machine, and which we have rendered by *spiritus*—spirit—a vague term which has received a thousand different acceptations. And lastly, *Nous*, intelligence. Thus we possess three souls, without having the slightest notion of any of them. . . . What are we to think of a child with two heads, which is otherwise well formed? Some say that it has two souls, because it is furnished with two pineal glands, with two callous substances, with two *sensoria communia*. Others answer, that there cannot be two souls with but one breast and one navel. . . . The word soul is one of those which everyone pronounces without understanding it. We understand those things of which we have an idea, but we have no idea of soul—spirit; therefore, we do not understand it.

John Calvin: The soul is an immortal essence, the nobler part of man. It is a creation out of nothing, not an emanation; it is essence without motion, not motion without essence. It is not properly bounded by space, still it occupies the body as a habitation, animating its parts and endowing its organs for their several functions.

Dugald Stewart: Although we have the strongest evidence that there is a thinking and sentient principle within us, essentially distinct from matter, yet we have no direct evidence of the possibility of this principle exercising its various powers in a separate state from the body. On the contrary, the union of the two, while it subsists, is evidently of the most intimate nature.

Joseph Priestly: It being a rigid canon of the Newtonian logic not to multiply causes without necessity, we should adhere to a single substance until it be shown, which cannot be, that the properties of mind are incompatible with the properties of matter. He was opposed to protecting and perpetuating absurdity by dodging behind mystery. That there is no difference between spiritual substance and nothing at all. That the doctrine of a separate soul embarrasses the whole system of Christianity.

McBeth: The times have been that when the brains were out the man would die, and there an end.

Buchner: Experience and daily occupation teach us that the spirit perishes with the material substratum—that man dies. ("Matter and Force.")

Burmeister: That the soul of a deceased person does not re-appear after death, is not contested by rational people. Spirits and ghosts are only seen by diseased or superstitious individuals.

Vogt: Physiology decides definitely and categorically against individual immortality, as against any special existence of the soul. The soul does not enter the fœtus like the evil spirit into persons possessed, but is a product of the development of the brain, just as muscular activity is a product of muscular development. So soon as the substances composing the brain are aggregated in a similar form, will they exhibit the same functions. We have seen that we can destroy mental activity by injuring the brain. By observing the development of the child we also arrive at the conviction that the activity of the soul progresses in proportion as the brain is gradually developed. The fœtus manifests no mental activity, which only shows itself after birth when the brain acquires the necessary material condition. Mental activity changes with the period of life, and ceases altogether at death.

Lecky: ("Rat. in Europe," p. 341, v. I.) Not one of the early fathers entertained the same opinion as the majority of Christians do of the present day, that the soul is perfectly simple, and entirely destitute of all body, figure, form, and extension. On the contrary, they all acknowledged it to contain something corporeal, although of a different kind and nature from the bodies of this mortal sphere. . . . Tertullian mentions a woman who had seen a soul, which she described as "a transparent and lucid figure, in the perfect form of a man." St. Anthony saw the soul of Ammon carried up to heaven. The soul of a Libyan hermit named Marc was borne to heaven in a napkin. Angels also were not unfrequently seen, and were universally believed to have cohabited with the daughters of the antediluvians. . . . Sometimes the soul was portrayed as a sexless child, rising out of the mouth of the corpse.

John Meslier: ("Testimony of a Dying Priest.") The barbarians, like all ignorant men, attribute to spirits all the effects of which their inexperience prevents them from discovering the true causes. Ask a barbarian what causes your watch to move, he will answer, "A spirit." Ask our philosophers what moves the universe, they will tell you, "It is a spirit." Ask a theologian what he means by a spirit. He will answer that it is an unknown substance, which is perfectly simple, which has nothing tangible, nothing in common with matter. In good faith, is there any mortal who can form the least idea of such a substance.

James F. Ferrier: (Institutes of Metaphysics.) In vain does the Spiritualist found an argument for the existence of a separate immaterial substance on the alleged incompatibility of the intellectual and physical phenomena to co-inhere in the same sub-stratum. Materiality may very well stand the brunt of that unshotted broadside. This mild artifice can scarcely expect to be treated as a serious observation. Such a hypothesis cannot be meant to be in earnest. Who is to dictate to nature what phenomena, or what qualities inhere in what substances; what effects may result from what causes? Matter is already in the field as an acknowledged entity—this both parties admit. Mind, considered as an independent entity, is not so unmistakably in the field. Therefore as entities are not to be multiplied without necessity, we are not entitled to postulate a new cause, so long as it is possible to account for the phenomena by a cause already in existence; which possibility has never yet been disproved.

Draper: (John William.) Chemistry furnishes us with a striking example of the doctrine of Diogenes of Apollonia, that the air is actually a spiritual being; for, on the discovery of several of the gases by the early experimenters, they were not only regarded as of a spiritual nature, but actually received the name under which they pass to this day, *gheist* or gas, from a belief that they were ghosts. ("Int. Dev.," p. 103, v. 1.)

W. R. Grove: ("Correlation and Conservation of Forces," p. 103.) The ancients when they witnessed natural phenomenon, removed from ordinary analogies, and unexplained by any mechanical action known to them, referred it to a soul, a spiritual or preternatural power: thus amber and the magnet were supposed by Thales to have a soul; the functions of digestion, assimilation, etc., were supposed by Paracelsus to be effected by a spirit (the Archæus). Air and gases were also at first deemed spiritual, but subsequently became invested with a more material character, and the word gas, from geist, a ghost or spirit, affords us an instance of the gradual transmission of a spiritual into a physical conception.

Buchner: Now, in the same manner as the steam engine produces motion, so does the organic complication of force-endowed materials produce in the animal body a sum of effects, so interwoven as to become a unit, and is then by us called spirit, soul, thought.

Taylor: Mr. Darwin saw two Malay women in Keeling Island, who had a wooden spoon dressed in clothes like a doll. This spoon had been carried to the grave of a dead man, and becoming inspired at full moon, in fact lunatic, it danced about convulsively like a table or a hat at a modern spirit-*seance*. ("Early History of Mankind," p. 139, v. 2.) Savages believe that their pots, kettles, pans, etc., have souls. His knives, tobacco-pipes, the winds, water, fire, storm, etc., have souls.

Samuel Johnson: ("Oriental Religions," p. 543.) Various North-American tribes believe that the soul of a dying person may be drawn into the bosom of a sterile woman, or blown by the breath into that of the nearest relative, and so come again to birth in the way that the receiver desires.

Theodore Parker, John Wesley, Jeremy Taylor, Coleridge, Lamartine, Agassiz, and hosts of other men well known to fame, taught that animals as well as men, had immortal souls.

Brodie: (President of the Royal Society, 1858.) The mind of animals is essentially the same as that of man. Every one familiar with the dog will admit that that creature knows right from wrong, and is conscious when he has committed a fault.

Du Bois-Reymond: With awe and wonder must the student of nature regard that microscopic molecule of nervous substance which is the seat of the laborious, constructive, orderly, loyal, dauntless soul of the ant. It has developed itself to its present state through a countless series of generations.

John Fiske: But the propriety of identifying soul and breath, which really quits the body at its decease, has furnished the chief name for the soul, not only to the Hebrew, the Sanskrit, and the classic tongues; not only to German and English, where *geist*, and *ghost*, according to Max Muller, have the meaning of "breath," and are akin to such words as *gas*, *gust*, and *geyser;* but also to numerous barbaric languages. ("Myths and Myth-Makers," p. 225.) The belief in wraiths was survived into modern times, and now and then appears in that remnant of primeval philosophy known as "Spiritualism," as for example, in the case of the lady who "thought she saw her own father look in at the church window at the moment he was dying at his own house." (Ib., p. 229.) The Kamtchadales expressly declare that all animals, even flies and bugs, will live after death,—a belief, which, in our day, has been indorsed on philosophical grounds by an eminent living naturalist. (Ib., 230.) [Mr. Fiske refers to Agassiz.]

M. Figuier: Human souls are for the most part the surviving souls of deceased animals; in general, the souls of precocious children like Mozart come from nightingales, while the souls of great architects have passed into them from beavers, and etc., etc. ("The To-morrow of Death," p. 247.)

W. Lauder Lindsay: By no kind of scientific evidence can it be proved that soul exists, whether in man or other animals. . . Nor should it be forgotten that, according to many writers, the word or term "soul" is regarded as synonymous with "mind," in which case there can be no question as to its possession by the higher animals. While the term "soul" has also been applied—in figurative senses no doubt—even to plants. ("Mind in the Lower Animals," v. 1, p. 101.) It obviously lies with those who assert dogmatically that all men have immortal souls, while no animals possess them, to reconcile with such a conviction the provable fact that many animals are superior to many men, not only in general intelligence, but also as regards moral sense and religious feeling. (Ib.) Ideas of justice or right, feelings of decency or shame, that combination or essence of moral qualities known as conscience, are as certainly present in some animals as they appear to be absent in countless numbers of men. (Ib., p. 103.)

Ernst Haeckel: The final result of this comparison is this: That between the most highly developed animal souls, and the lowest developed human souls there exists only a small quantitative, but no qualitative difference, and this difference is much less than the difference between the lowest and the highest human souls, or than the difference between the lowest and the highest animal souls. ("Hist. of Creation," v. 2, p. 362.) Some of the wildest tribes, of men, in Southern Asia and Eastern Africa have no trace whatever of the first foundations of all human civilization of family life, and marriage. They live together, in herds, like apes, generally climbing on trees and eating fruits; they do not know of fire, and use stones and clubs as weapons, just like the higher apes. (Ib., p. 363.)

Descartes: (17 c.) Matter, whose essence is extension, is known by the senses; mind, whose essence is thinking, can be known only by self-consciousness. The thinking principle is immaterial.

Origen: The nature of the soul is such as to make her capable of existing eternally, backward as well as forward, because her spiritual essence, as such, makes it impossible that she should, either through age or violence, be dissolved.

Rev. Joseph Baylee, D. D.: (Principal of St. Aidan's College, Birkenhead, England.) Man is eternal. He was in existence before he was born; sinned before he was born, and if he had never been born would have suffered eternal damnation for that sin. (Dis. on God and the Bible between Dr. Baylee and Mr. Bradlaugh.)

Draper: ("Conflict," p. 127.) Moreover, to many devout persons there is something very revolting in the suggestion that the Almighty is a servitor to the caprices and lusts of men, and that at a certain term after its origin, it is necessary for him to create for the embryo a soul.

Vedic Theology: The soul is a particle of that all-pervading principle, the Universal Intellect, or Soul of the World, detached for a while from its primitive source; and placed in connection with the bodily frame, but destined, by an inevitably as rivers run back to be lost in the ocean from whence they arose.

The Bible: As the cloud is consumed and vanisheth away, so he that goeth down to the grave shall come up no more. (Job 7: 9.) They are dead, they shall not live; they are deceased, they shall not rise; therefore hast thou visited and destroyed them, and made all their memory to perish. (Isa. 26: 14.) For the living know that they shall die, but the dead know not anything, neither have they any more a reward, for the memory of them is forgotten. Whatsoever thy hand findeth to do, do it with thy might, for there is no work, nor device, nor knowledge, nor wisdom in the grave whither thou goest. (Eccl. 9: 5, 10.) For that which befalleth the sons of men befalleth beasts, even one thing befalleth them: as the one dieth, so dieth the other; yea, they have all one breath; so that a man hath no pre-eminence above a beast; for all is vanity. All go unto one place, all are of the dust and all turn to dust again. Who knoweth the spirit of man that goeth upward; and the spirit of the beast that goeth downward to the earth? (Eccl. 3: 19–22.) There (the grave) the wicked cease from troubling; and there the weary be at rest. (Vide Job 3: 11–22.)

Having thus successfully responded to the interrogatory, What is the soul? that is to say, the constituent thereof, let us now very briefly settle the *locus in quo:*

Plato: The soul is located in the brain.

Aristotle: The soul is located in the heart.

Heraclitus: The soul is located in the blood.

Epicurus: The soul is located in the chest.

Critios: The soul is located in the blood.

Sommering: The soul is located in the ventricles.

Kant: The soul is located in the water contained in the ventricles.

Plotinus: The body is located in the soul, and not the soul in the body.

Ennemoser: The whole body is the seat of the soul.

Fischer: The soul is located in the nervous system.

Ficinus: The soul is located in the heart.

Descartes: The soul is located in the pineal gland.

Boutekoe: The soul is located in the *corpus callosum*.

Willis: The soul is located in the *corpora striata*.

Vieussens: The soul is located in the *centrum ovale*.

Boerhaave: The soul is located on the boundary line of the gray and white substance.

Mayer: The soul is located in the *medulla oblongata*.

Camper: The soul is located in the pineal gland, *nates* and *testes*.

Dohoney: Scientifically speaking, man is a threefold being: body, soul, and spirit. The home of the spirit is the *cerebrum*, while the seat of the soul is the *cerebellum*. ("Man," p. 118.)

La Pieronie: The dwelling place of the soul is in the callous body.

Buchner: Some authors imagine that the soul, under certain circumstances, leaves the brain for a short time and occupies another part of the nervous system. The solar plexus, a concatenation of sympathetic nerves, situated in the abdomen, was especially pointed out as the favored spot. ("Force and Matter," p. 195.)

Prochaska: Assumed that the *cerebrum* and the *cerebellum* were the seat of "soul sensations," and the *sensorium commune* the seat of "body sensations."

Whytt: As the schoolmen supposed the Deity to exist in every *ubi* but not in any place, which is to say in Latin that he exists everywhere, but in English nowhere, so they imagined the soul of man not to occupy space, but to exist in an indivisible point.

Prof. Erdmann: The theory that the soul has its seat in the brain, must lead to the result that when the body is separated from the head, the soul should continue to exist.

Fortlage: There are certain errors in the human mind. The error of the seat of the soul in the brain is one of them.

McCulloch says, in his able work on the "Credibility of the Scriptures": There is no word in the Hebrew language that signifies either soul or spirit, in the technical sense in which we use the terms, as implying something distinct from the body. ("Credibility of Scriptures," p. 491, v. 2.)

Kitto, in his "Cyclopedia of Biblical Literature," renders Genesis 2: 7, as follows: "And Jehovah God formed the man [Heb. the Adam] of dust from the ground, and blew into his nostrils the breath of life: and *the man* became a *living animal.*

Bishop Tilotson says: The immortality of the soul is rather *supposed*, or taken for granted, than expressly revealed in the Bible.

The Egyptian doctrine of the soul is one of the most important, as it is the most ancient, for this nation seems to have been the first to declare that the soul was immortal. (Chambers' Encyclopedia.) R. PETERSON.

IMMORTALITY.

There is still another question. Why should God, a being of infinite tenderness, leave the question of immortality in doubt? How is it that there is nothing in the Old Testament on this subject? Why is it that he who made all the constellations did not put in his heaven the star of hope? How do you account for the fact that you do not find in the Old Testament, from the first mistake in Genesis to the last curse in Malachi, a funeral service? Is it not strange that some one in the Old Testament did not stand by an open grave of father or mother and say, "We shall meet again"? Was it because the divinely inspired men did not know? You taunt me by saying that I know no more of the immortality of the soul than Cicero knew. I admit it. I know no more than the lowest savage, no more than a doctor of divinity, that is to say, nothing.—Ingersoll, Ingersoll-Field Discussion.

Some urge that the soul is life. What is life? Is it not the word by which we express the aggregate normal functional activity of vegetable and animal organisms, necessarily differing in degree, if not in kind, with each different organization? To talk of immortal life, and yet to admit the decay and destruction of the organization, is much the same as to talk of a square circle. You link together two words which contradict each other. The solution of the soul problem is not so difficult as many imagine. The greatest difficulty is, that we have been trained to use certain words as "God," "matter," "mind," "spirit," "soul," "intelligence," and we have been further trained to take these words as representatives of realities, which in fact, they do not represent. We have to unlearn much of our school lore. We have specially to carefully examine the meaning of each word we use. I am told that the mind and the body are separate from one another. Are the brightness and steel of the knife separate? Is not brightness the quality attaching to a certain modification of existence—steel? Is not intelligence a quality attaching to a certain modification of existence—man? The word brightness has no meaning, except as relating to some bright thing. The word intelligence, no meaning, except as relating to some intelligent thing. I take some water and drop it upon the steel, in due course the process of oxidation takes place, and the brightness is gone. I drop into a man's brain a bullet; the process of the destruction of life takes place, and his intelligence is gone. By changing the state of the steel we destroy its brightness, and by disorganizing the man destroy his intelligence. Is mind an entity or result? an existence or a condition? Surely it is but the result of organic activity, a phenomenon of animal life. ("Has Man a Soul?" Charles Bradlaugh.)

The idea of immortality, like the great sea, has ebbed and flowed in the human heart, beating its countless waves of hope and joy against the shores of time, and was not born of an book, nor of any religion, nor of any creed; it was born of human affection, and will continue to ebb and flow beneath the clouds and mists of doubt and darkness as long as love kisses the lips of death. It is the rainbow of hope shining upon the tears of grief. We love, therefore we wish to live, and the foundation of the idea of immortality is human affection and human love, and I have a thousand times more confidence in the affections of the human heart, in the deep and splendid feelings of the human soul than I have in any book that ever was or ever can be written by mortal man.—Ingersoll.

Is This Life the "Be-all and End-all?"

To answer that question, or to give my views on the subject as to whether man lives after death or is extinguished as a living being by death, would ordinarily involve a long preliminary discourse; but I think I can give you my views, such as they are, in a few words. Life is sensation, sensibility, the power of feeling. Without sensation there is no life. We feel with our nerves; we see with our eyes; we hear with our ears. Without nerves there would be no feeling, without eyes no seeing, without ears no hearing. These senses, therefore, of feeling, seeing, hearing, exist in combination with certain forms of matter, and cannot exist without such combination. So the mind exists in combination with the matter, brain. Without the brain there can be no mental phenomena, no thinking, no perceiving. These things are palpable; they are truths which may not be disputed. Therefore, if death destroys our nerves, it destroys our power of feeling; if it destroys our eyes, it destroys our power of seeing; if it destroys our ears, it destroys our power of hearing; if it destroys our brain, it destroys our power of thinking and perceiving. The man lies down, feeling nothing, seeing nothing, knowing nothing; he is a corpse. Separated from the brain, the mind cannot act, cannot think, cannot conceive; therefore, if it exists at all, it is the same as if it were dead. In that condition, the mind can no more think or perceive than the dust into which the decomposed nerves have fallen can feel. What follows then? That the man has come to an end, entirely; he is extinguished.—Selected.

So you must equally bear with the comparatively small number of scientists who, within the last three hundred years, have worked out the hypothesis that the soul is not matter, substance, or entity, at all, but simply the continuous action or process of the nervous systems of animals, and especially of the brain of man, in answer to their environment. In a word, the life, soul, spirit, mind, thought, feeling, and consciousness are but varying tones of the music which our nervous systems give out when the world plays upon them—much as the piano answers to the touch of our hands. The music was not in, nor the property of the piano, nor of the hand, but it arises and exists only by reason of the playing-contact of the two. Thus the life or soul is not a property of brain-matter, or of our nerves, nor of the world or its impinging force; but when those world forces by touch, heat, light, electricity and foods do reach so as to act upon the nerves and brain, then comes their reaction, and we call that reaction feeling, life, soul, thought, reason, etc., through all of the varying music of consciousness, whether exhibited by a child, a savage, a Newton or a Goethe.—Anon.

Materialism--Prof. Tyndall.

If Materialism is confounded, science is rendered dumb. . . . Materialism, therefore, is not a thing to be mourned over, but to be honestly considered; accepted if wholly true, rejected if false. ("Fragments of Science," p. 221.) It ought to be known and avowed that the physical philosopher, as such, must be a pure Materialist. His inquiries deal with matter and force, and with them alone. (Ib., p. 72.) As regards knowledge, physical science is polar. (Ib., p. 52.) It is the advance of [this] knowledge that has given a materialistic color to the philosophy of our age. (Ib., p. 222.) We may fear and scorn Materialism; but he who knew all about it, and could apply his knowledge, might become the preacher of a new gospel. (Ib., p. 221.)

Through our neglect of the monitions of a reasonable Materialism, we sin and suffer daily. (Ib., p. 224.) The practical monitions are plain enough which declare that on our dealings with matter depend our weal or woe, physical and moral. (Ib., p. 222.) It is our duty not to shirk—it ought rather to be our privilege to accept, the established results of physical inquiries; for here, assuredly, our ultimate weal depends upon our loyalty to truth. Is mind degraded by this recognition of its dependence [on matter]? Assuredly not. Matter, on the contrary, is raised to the level it ought to occupy, and from which timid ignorance would remove it. (Ib., p. 221.)

Matter is not that empty capacity which philosophers and theologians have pictured it, but the universal mother, who brings forth all things as the fruit of her own womb. Nature is seen to do all things spontaneously, without the meddling of the gods. (Ib., p. 193.) Matter I define as that mysterious thing by which all that is, is accomplished. How it came to have the power which it possesses is a question on which I never ventured an opinion. (Ib., p. 193.) I discern in matter the promise and potency of all terrestrial life. (Ib., p. 251.)

Does life belong to what we call matter, or is it an independent principle infused into matter at some suitable epoch? (Ib., p. 131.) There does not exist a barrier, possessing the strength of a cobweb, in opposition to the hypothesis which ascribes the appearance of life to that "potency of matter" which finds its expression in natural evolution. . . . Divorced from matter, where is life? (Ib., p. 192.) To man, as we know him, matter is necessary to consciousness. (Ib., p. 192.) Every meal we eat, and every cup we drink, illustrates the mysterious control of mind by matter. (Ib., p. 50.)

If these statements startle, it is because matter has been defined and maligned by philosophers and theologians, who were ignorant alike of its mystical and transcendental powers. (Ib., p. 51.) Two courses, and two only, are possible: either let us open our doors freely to the conception of creative acts, or, abandoning them let us radically change our notions of matter. (Ib., p. 191.) Without this total revolution of the notions now prevalent, the evolution hypothesis must stand condemned. (Ib., p. 133.)

If we look at matter as defined by our scientific text-books, the notion of conscious life coming out of it cannot be formed by the mind. (Ib., p. 191.) Spirit and matter have ever been present to us in the rudest contrast: the one as all noble, the other as all vile. But is this correct? Upon the answer to this question, all depends. (Ib., p. 133.)

Physiology proves Materialism to be true, and the following testimony to that fact by eminent scientific men is only a small part of what might be quoted of similar tenor:

Bain tells us: The most careful and studied observations of physiologists have shown *beyond question*, that the brain as a whole is indispensible to thought, feeling, and volition.

Dr. Ferrier says: The brain is the organ of mind, and that mental operations are possible only in and through it. This fact is so well established that we may start from it as we should from any ultimate fact.

Prof. Virchow, of Berlin, says: Every one must admit that without a brain, nay, more, without a good and well developed brain, the human mind has *no* existence.—Man has a mind and rational *will* only in as much and in so far as he possesses a brain.

Huxley says: What we call the operations of the mind are *functions* of the *brain*, and the materials of consciousness are products of *cerebral activity*. Sensations are products of the inherent *properties* of the thinking organ.

Tyndall says: We believe that every thought and every feeling has its definite mechanical correlative in the nervous system; that it is accompanied by a certain separation and remarshalling of the atoms of the brain.

Dr. Maudsley says: I do not go beyond what facts warrant, when I say that, when a thought occurs in the mind, there *necessarily* occurs a correlative change in the gray matter of the brain. Without it, the thought could not arise; with it, it can not fail to rise.

What is matter! I take a handful of earth in my hands, and into that dust I put seeds, and arrows from the eternal quiver of the sun smite it, and the seeds grow and bud and blossom, and fill the air with perfume in my sight. Do you understand that? Do you understand how this dust and these seeds and that light and this moisture produced that bud and that flower and that perfume? Do you understand that any better than you do the production of thought? Do you understand that any better than you do a dream? Do you understand that any better than you do the thoughts of love that you see in the eyes of the one you adore? Can you explain it? Can you tell what matter is? Have you the slightest conception? Yet you talk about matter as though you were acquainted with its origin; as though you had compelled, with clenched hands, the very rocks to give up the secret of existence. Do you know what force is? Can you account for molecular action? Are you familiar with chemistry? Can you account for the loves and hatreds of the atoms? Is there not something in matter that forever eludes you? Can you tell what matter really is? Before you cry Materialism, you had better find what matter is. Can you tell of anything without a material basis? Is it possible to imagine the annihilation of a single atom? Is it possible for you to conceive of the creation of a single atom? Can you have a thought that is not suggested to you by what you call matter? Did any man or woman or child ever have a solitary thought, dream or conception, that was not suggested to them by something they had seen in nature?—Ingersoll.

The Origin of Belief in the Soul.

* * * I had waited at some distance, and as the day grew stronger, saw that this new grave was not the only one upon that lonely height.

On my right was a mound on which lay the betel-box, the pipe, the haversack, and "dah" (or chopper-knife) that in life had been his who lay beneath. I turned to rest on the trunk of a fallen tree, when I heard the sound of footsteps. The childless man and woman were passing. I knew the man, and I spoke to him. He had often been my guide in former visits to his village. He stopped. His wife passed on. I asked, tenderly I hope, as to his child. What was the cause of death?

"Fever." Then he squatted down, drew out his pipe, filled and lit it.

"Whose grave is that?" I asked, pointing to the mound with the betel-box and "dah."

"One of the men of my village," he replied; "he died some months ago."

"Why do you leave his betel-box, haversack, and 'dah' on the grave? What use can it be to him?"

"It is our custom."

"But why?"

"His 'lah' (spirit) will require them."

"But you see his 'lah' has not taken them. They are still there, and they are rotting away."

"Oh, no!" Very promptly. "What you see are only the forms of the things. Their 'lahs' have gone away and are with the man's 'lah.'"

"Where?"

"In another world below this."

"And so people's 'lahs' after death go to another world and work as in this?"

"Yes; and if they had no haversack, and no betel-box, and no 'dah' how would they get on? How could they cut down forest and cultivate rice for food if they had no 'dah'?"

He added after a pause:

"So our people say, but I don't know. I am ignorant. I am only a poor jungle fowl."

"But," I persisted, "how do your people know that it is true—that the betel-box, the haversack, the knife, and other things have 'lahs,' or even that the man has a 'lah'?"

The Karen was silent for a while. Then he said—

"My child is dead—his body is buried there. It can not move and go about; yet I know that in my sleep he will come to me. He will speak, and I shall speak to him. It is not his body but his 'lah' that will come. So also I lost an ax long ago. It fell in the forest somewhere. I could not find it, but in my sleep I have seen its 'lah' and have held it in my hand." He paused, and went on: "It must have a 'lah,' for iron and handle have rotted away long ago, yet I held them last night in my hand."

"Then the 'lah' lives independently of the body?"

"Yes. Our people say so."

I was silent. Here among these savages I saw how the germs of belief in a future life are laid, from what delusion they spring.

Then looking back to the far-off times, when the ancestors of our own now civilized race were savages with minds as undeveloped as that of the savage before me, I saw how from the mystery of dream-appearances rose the belief in the dual nature of things. I saw how this belief, extending first to all things animate and inanimate, came in the slow evolution of man's intellect, by the elimination of the grosser and cruder portion of his thought to hold at length only of living things.

No profound thought—no deep insight into human nature is needed to trace along general lines its further development.

Man in his selfish egoism making himself the center of all nature, has deemed that he alone is thus favored and raised above the rest of the universe.

Moreover it is a belief that with all its uncertainties has an intrinsic attractive beauty in the hope it gives to man, that love and happiness will last beyond the grave.

Above all—fatalest of all, it is a belief that offers to the craft of the priest, power over his fellow man.

Thus, flattering to man's self-love, useful as an engine of power, affording an easy explanation of mysteries in life and death, this belief in a soul really rising in "the mists and shadows of sleep," has come down to us as god-revealed from on high.—C. T. Bingham, in "Progress," London, England.

"When a Man Dies what Becomes of his Soul?"

A friend of mine meeting me in the streets of Chicago one day, without much ceremony propounded the above question; "Say, Brother Bell," he began, "I would like to have you tell me what becomes of a man's soul when he dies?" In reply I said, "Do you see that man walking on the other side of the street?" "Yes," he said, "that is old Johnson." I then called his attention to the peculiar movement of the old gentleman. "See what a peculiar gait he has." He assented that our friend's gait was peculiar. As we were contemplating him, he stopped to look in a store window. When he halted I turned to my questioner and asked, "Where has Mr. Johnson's gait gone since he stopped walking?" He very candidly acknowledged that a man's gait was not a thing, not an entity, but a mode of motion, and that when the body ceased to move, there was no gait. I asked him if thinking (the soul) was not a motion or activity of the brain, and that when it ceased to act, if there was any soul or thinking left. I have a very distinct remembrance that he talked a long time and said nothing.

Some Soul Questions.

1. Where does the soul come from?
2. Is the soul an entity or nonentity?
3. Of what is the soul composed?
4. When does the soul enter the body, before or after birth?
5. In what part of the body is the soul located?
6. If the soul is located in all parts of the body what becomes of that part of the soul contained in an amputated part of a living body?
7. Is the soul an organization independent of the body?
8. Does the soul develop as the body develops?
9. Is the soul of an infant of the same size and weight as the soul of an adult?
10. Is the soul of a negro of the same color as the soul of a caucasian?
11. Is the soul of an idiot as well developed as the soul of an intelligent person?
12. When does the soul leave the body, at death or at the resurrection day?
13. If the soul leaves the body at death, where does it sojourn while waiting for the resurrection morn?
14. If a living person was placed in an air-tight jar, and the jar sealed hermetically, at death how would the soul make its exit?

15. After leaving the body what direction does the soul pursue to reach its final destination?

16. What length of time does it require for the soul to reach its final destination?

17. Where and at what distance from the earth is the soul land located?

18. Has the soul the physical organs indispensible to mental action and consciousness?

19. If not, of what use would the soul be?

20. Is the soul sensible or insensible to pain?

21. Of what shape is the soul?

22. Of what color is the soul?

23. Does the soul retain its sex?

24. When and where are the souls made, or did they always exist?

25. We have five infallible witnesses to prove the existence of matter, namely, hearing, seeing, tasting, smelling, and feeling. By these five witnesses we prove the existence and the component parts of matter. Can you by the aid of these five senses prove the existence of souls?—W. C. Clow.

DESIGN ARGUMENT.

Nothing could have come by chance, it is said, and therefore it is inferred that this universe must have been created by a God.

Let us view this famous argument for a moment. God is something or nothing. To say he is nothing is to say there is no God. If he is something, he is not merely a property or quality, but an existence *per se*—an entity, a substance, whether material or immaterial is unimportant. If he is a substance, a material, or spiritual being, there must be order, harmony, and adaptation, or fitness, in his divine nature, to enable him to perceive, reflect, design, and execute his plans. If Deity does not reason, does not cogitate, but perceives truth without the labor of investigation and contrivance, he must still possess an adaptation or fitness thus to perceive, as well as to execute his design.

To say God is without order, harmony, and adaptation, or fitness, is to say he is a mere chaos—worse than that imaginary chaos that theologians tell us would result if divine agency were withdrawn from the universe. If a being without order, harmony, and adaptation, or a divine chaos, can create an orderly universe then there is no consistency in saying that unintelligent matter could not have produced the objects that we behold. If order, harmony, and adaptation do exist in the divine mind (or in the substance which produces thought, power, and purpose in the divine mind) they must be eternal, for that which constitutes the essential nature of a God must be the eternal basis of his being. If the order, harmony, and adaptation in God are co-existent with him, are eternal, they must be independent of design, for that which never began to exist could not have been produced, and does not therefore admit of design. If order, harmony, and adaptation are independent of design in the divine mind, it is certain that order, harmony, and adaptation exist, and are not evidence of a pre-existent, designing intelligence.

If order, harmony, and adaptation exist, which were not produced by design, which are therefore no evidence of design, it is unreasonable and illogical to infer designing intelligence from the fact alone that order, harmony, and adaptation exist in nature. Therefore an intelligent Deity cannot be inferred from the order, harmony, and adaptation in nature. If the order, harmony, and adaptation in Deity, to produce his thoughts, and to execute his plans, are eternal, why may not the formation of matter into worlds, and the evolutions of the various forms of vegetable and animal life on this globe be the result of the ceaseless action of self-existent matter in accordance with an inherent eternal principle of adaptation? Is it more reasonable to suppose the universe was created, or constructed by a being in whom exists the most wonderful order and harmony, and the most admirable adaptation to construct a universe (which order, harmony, and adaptation could have had no designing cause), than to suppose that the universe itself in its entirety is eternal, and the self-producing cause of all the manifestations we behold?

Is a God uncaused, and who made everything from nothing, more easy of belief than a universe uncaused and existing according to its own inherent nature? Is it wonderful that matter should be self-existent; that it should possess the power to form suns, planets, and construct that beautiful ladder of life that reaches from the lowest forms of the vegetable kingdom up to man? How much more wonderful that a great being should exist, without any cause, who had no beginning, and who is infinitely more admirable than the universe itself.

Again, the plan of a work is as much evidence of intelligence and design as the work which embodies the plan. The plan of a steam engine in the mind of Fitch—the plan of the locomotive in the mind of Stephenson—was as much evidence of design as the piece of machinery after its mechanical construction. If God be an omniscient being—a being who knows everything; to whose knowledge no addition can be made— his plans must be eternal—without beginning, and therefore uncaused. If God's plans are not eternal; if from time to time new plans originate in his mind, there must be an addition to his knowledge, and if his knowledge admits of addition, it must be finite. But if his plans had no beginning; if, like himself, they are eternal, they must, like him, be independent of design. Now, the plan of a thing, we have already seen, is as much evidence of design as the object which embodies the plan. Since the plans of Deity are no proof of design that produced them (for they are supposed to be eternal), the plan of this universe, of course, was no evidence of a designing intelligence that produced it. But since the plan of the universe is as much evidence of design as the universe itself, and since the former is no evidence of design, it follows that design cannot be inferred from the existence of the universe.

The absurdity of the *a posteriori* argument of a God consists in the assumption that what we call order and adaptation in nature are evidence of design, when it is evident that whether there be a God or not, order and adaptation must have existed from eternity, and are not therefore necessarily proof of a designing cause. The reasoning of the theologian is like that of the Hindoo in accounting for the position of the earth. "Whatever exists must have some support," said he. The earth exists, and is therefore supported. He imagined it resting on the back of an elephant. The elephant needing some support, he supposed rested on the back of a huge tortoise. He forgot that according to his own premise that whatever exists must have some support, that the tortoise should rest on something. The inconclusiveness of his reasoning is apparent to a child. Whatever exists is supported. The earth exists. Therefore, the earth is supported; it rests on an elephant; the elephant rests on a tortoise; the tortoise exists, but nothing is said about its support.

The theologian says order, harmony, and adaptation are evidence of a designing intelligence that produced them. The earth and its productions show order, harmony, and adaptation. Therefore, the earth and its productions have been produced by an intelligent designer. Just as the Hindoo stopped reasoning when he imagined the earth on an elephant, and the elephant on a tortoise, so the theologian stops reasoning when he says, God made the world. But as surely as from the premise that whatever exists must have some support, follows the conclusion that the tortoise rests on something, as rests on it the elephant, does it follow from the proposition that order, harmony, and adaptation are proof of an intelligent designer, that the order, harmony, and adaptation in the Deity to produce the effects ascribed to him are evidence of an intelligent designer who made him, as the various parts of nature, adapted to one another, are evidence of an intelligent designer that produced them. This reasoning leads to the conclusion that there has been an infinite succession of creative and created Gods, which is inconsistent with the idea of a First Cause, the creator of the universe. Then why attempt to explain the mysteries of the universe by imagining a God who produced everything but himself, and why argue from the order and fitness in the world the existence of a designer. It reminds me of the ostrich, that having buried its head in the sand, so as to render invisible its pursuers, fancies there is no further need of exertion to escape from the dangers and difficulties which surround it.

"Design represented as a search after final cause, until we come to a first cause, and then stop," says F. N. Newman, "is an argument I confess which in itself brings me no satisfaction." "The attempt," says Buckle, "which Paley and others have made to solve this mystery by rising from the laws to the cause are evidently futile, because to the eye of reason the solution is as incomprehensible as the problem, and the arguments of the natural theologian, in so far as they are arguments, must depend on reason."

Design implies the use of means for the attainment of ends. Man designs, plans, contrives and uses secondary agencies to accomplish his purposes, because unable to attain his ends directly. But how absurd to speak of contrivance and design in a being of infinite power and knowledge. Man, to build steamships has to fell trees and hew them into various shapes, get iron from the earth and smelt it in furnaces, and work it into bolts, braces, nails, etc., hundreds of workmen, carpenters, joiners, blacksmiths, cabinet-makers, painters, caulkers, riggers, etc., labor for months before the vessel can be launched. If man possessed the power to speak into existence a steamship, would he contrive, plan and use means to construct it? On the contrary, would it not come instantly into existence as a complete, perfect whole?

But the existence of a steamer, since it is only a means to an end, would be inconsistent with unlimited power in man. If he were able to effect his purposes why should he construct a vessel with which to visit far off lands? Infinite power would enable him to cross the ocean by the mere exercise of his will. It is evident at a glance that the use of means is incompatible with infinite knowledge and infinite power. This argument . . . in proving too much proves nothing, and demonstrates its own worthlessness, and therefore we cast it aside. Design implies finiteness; man designs and has to calculate and use means to accomplish his end. If he were all powerful would he use that power to construct ships to cross the ocean, or armies to win battles, when he could accomplish his end without, and by those means demonstrate that he is infinite in power? An infinite being would not have to employ means to complete his works; he would not have to doubt and cogitate before he accomplished his design; that would be the method of man. It is absurd to suppose that a God did all those things. We supposed God infinite in everything, in his power, in his love and kindness. He has power to do everything. And yet the world is so constructed that at every step we take we crush to death creatures as minutely and curiously formed as ourselves. They kill one another in numerous struggles, and life has been such a series of bloody battles, resulting in destruction of life, that the Waterloos and Solferinos of history are nothing in comparison. Where is the design in the volcano that belches forth its fiery billows and buries in ruins a Pompeii and a Herculaneum? Where is the design in the tornado that sends a fleet with its precious freight of humanity beneath the remorseless waves? Where is the design in the suffering and torture that thousands feel this very moment in the chambers of sickness, and in the hospitals full of diseases? Where is the evidence of a great being who has the power to make men happy, and yet allows the world to go on in all its misery—such misery as it makes one's heart ache to see, and which we, imperfect creatures as we are, would gladly stop if we could?

And where is the design in the thousands of facts which science has brought to light, showing that there are organs and parts that serve no purpose at all, but on the contrary, are injurious to their possessors? Why do some animals, like the dugong, have tusks that never cut through the gums? Why has the guinea pig teeth that are shed before it is born? Science tells us these rudimentary structures are the remnants of a former state, in which these parts were of service; but theology, which requires us to believe that a God made all these animals as we now see them, cannot possibly reconcile these facts with infinite wisdom and goodness.

Adaptation in organisms instead of having been produced by a Deity, we hold is largely the result of natural selection. Adaptation must exist as the adjustment of objects to their environments. If a flock of sheep be exposed to the weather of a severe climate, those of them having the thinnest wool, affording the least protection from the cold, will perish. Those with the thickest wool and hardiest nature will survive every year, and by the law of heredity, transmit their favorable variations. By this process those best adapted to the climate live, and the others perish. Thus in the struggle for life we have the "survival of the fittest," without any design whatever. But the theologian comes along and looking at the sheep, says: "See how God has adapted these sheep to the climate." He forgets the thousands that have shivered and perished in winter's cold as the condition of this adaptation. So animals change the color of their coverings in accordance with their environments. The bears among the icebergs of the North are white, because in the struggle for life every light variation has been favorable to the animal—has facilitated its escape from the hunter and its preying upon the living things upon which it subsists. Those with darker coverings have gradually become extinct, leaving in undisputed possession of the snow banks and icebergs this species, which in color resembles the general aspect of its surroundings. Look at the rabbits. Some change their color every year; some are brown in the summer and white like the snow in winter. Those with this tendency to change their color during the year, having the most favorable variation, have persisted, and this tendency, by heredity, has been accumulated, until it has become a part of the nature of the animal.

These are but illustrations of a principle discovered by Darwin and Wallace, which explains largely how, not only color and thickness of coverings, but speed, strength and suppleness of body, keenness of sight and hearing, and all other parts and powers of organism have been developed in adaptation to their environment, without any special design whatever.

It is said we have no evidence of the eternal existence of the universe, because we have no personal observation of it. But is there any personal observation to prove the existence of an eternal God? Yet it is believed in by our opponents. We believe the universe always has existed in the past, because we see no trace of a beginning; we believe it will always exist in the future, because we see no prospect or possibility of an end. Worlds have their formation and dissolution; but the substance is neither augmented nor diminished. Matter is indestructible and eternal. We are not, therefore, in need of a creator. B. F. UNDERWOOD.

Do the natural affairs of this world show a designer? Is there a conscious intelligence at work guiding all the affairs of this world! We see no evidence of a wise and benevolent design in the creation of wild, ravenous birds and beasts of prey. We fail to see anything like a kind providence in earthquakes, volcanoes, floods, tidal-waves, storms at sea, drouth, famine, and pestilence. Is there a supreme intelligence which causes monstrosities, sends epidemics, horrid diseases, plants parasites upon the human body? Are lice, tape-worms, bed-bugs, fleas, flies, grasshoppers, and mosquitoes "blessings in disguise?" Are abject poverty and misery divine blessings? Is ignorance a gracious boon in mercy sent? Pain and misery are not exceptional features of man's life on earth, but they are chief characteristics of it. Are some unconscious of their degradation? Shall we infer therefrom that ignorance is bliss? If this unconsciousness of degradation on the part of some shall be considered as evidence of a benevolent designer, then what shall we say in the case of those who are conscious of their degradation?

"If," says Haeckel, "we contemplate the common life and mutual relations between plants and animals (man included) we shall find everywhere and at all times, the very opposite of that kindly and peaceful social life which the goodness of the creator ought to have prepared for his creatures: we shall rather find everywhere a pitiless, most embittered struggle of all against all." Large fish eat small ones, large birds devour the smaller, and the ferocious beasts of prey live upon the weaker and less fleet animals. In this struggle for existence there is one perpetual battle; the smaller, weaker and less fleet are captured and devoured by the stronger, and man destroys and eats any of them at his pleasure.

Is there a display of intelligence and benevolent design in creating man with strength and wisdom to slaughter his prey at will? Then where is the benevolence of design in creating the animals to be thus slaughtered?

The universe, we shall find, does not exhibit evidence of a conscious intelligent design. Says Shelley: "We must prove design before we can infer a designer."

Mr. Talmage insists that it takes no especial brain to reason out a "design" in nature, and in a moment afterward says: "When the world slew Jesus, it showed what it would do with the eternal God if once it could get its hands upon him." Why should a God of infinite wisdom create people who would gladly murder their creator? Was there any particular "design" in that? Does the existence of such people conclusively prove the existence of a good designer? ("Ingersoll's Interviews," p. 46.)

Providence.

Religious people see Providence in everything. Strange it is, too, that the most marked displays of Providence are seen in shipwrecks, railroad collisions, or in all devastating fires, floods, and plagues. In such appalling calamities as lead most sensible men to say with Æneas, "If there be gods, they certainly take no interest in the affairs of men," the Christian sees proof of a good guardian, a saving God, where nothing but destruction and ruin mark his pathway. There is a strange fatuity manifested by believers in this doctrine. Not long since a young man died very suddenly in Boston. There was a post-mortem examination by regular physicians, and a coroner's jury, who mutually deliberated over the body as to the cause of its death. The doctors found the young man's stomach somewhat irritated. On close inspection the contents of the stomach were found to be a mixture of bread and butter, mince pie and coffee, ham and eggs, buckwheat cakes, oyster stew, plum pudding, pound cake, corned beef, ice cream, more mince pie, and baked beans.

The jury gave the case most grave and deliberate consideration, and in accordance therewith returned the verdict: "Came to his death by a mysterious dispensation of the afflictive hand of Providence." Just so! Anything, however evil, unjust or foolish may be attributed to Providence; yet he remains both wise and good.

Why, if this world is created and controlled by infinite wisdom and benevolence, are not all things beautiful? One of man's noblest endeavors is to beautify. But we see many flowers and plants which are not beautiful.

Many parts of the earth are inhospitable and forbidding. What beauties on the other hand lie buried at the bottom of the ocean, its flora, shells, and corals! But no human eye ever sees them. Wherein is the evidence of design? Where is the evidence of design in the horrid monsters which once filled the oceans? Where is the design in creating such monstrosities as we see among animals?

Did the designer intend that parasites should infest the human body? The creator made the parasites (lice) and their proper dwelling-place seems to be the human body. The human body gives them their proper food. They are so constituted as to reproduce themselves rapidly and thus persist in feeding upon man.

The question is immediately raised: "Were the lice made for man, or man for the lice?" When did it ever occur to a sane mind that bed-bugs and mosquitoes and fleas were created with a benevolent design?

These facts are irreconcileable with the notion of a supreme and beneficent Providence.

Where is the evidence of benevolent design in earthquakes, floods, volcanoes, drouth, famine, and ten thousand ills which flesh is heir to? Where is the moral purpose? Where is the benevolence in peopling the earth with millions of human beings who live lives of poverty and misery?

But it is argued that we cannot see it all now, but by and by it will be made plain to us, that is, when we get into the other world. This is begging the question. The Christian says creation shows a creator, who first created the universe and now presides over it. But when we bring the facts of this world, its abounding evils and human miseries, to show the absence of any benevolent superintendence, he promises to make good his argument in the next world. This is asking a fellow to wait too long. Again, it is argued by the Christian that God ordained pain to work out good; but how comes it that this ordination of working good out of evil does not take place? Sometimes one man is made better by it, and another is brutalized by it. How does this come to pass if pain was ordained to work good? Has the plan of the designer failed? "The evils of this world are ordained for the purpose of developing our souls; only by pain and suffering can we be prepared for heaven." Little children who die, according to this dogma, can never be developed.

Are not two sparrows sold for a farthing? and one of them shall not fall to the ground without your Father? (Mat. 10: 29.)

But sparrows do fall to the ground nevertheless. And if some do not fall to the ground that wicked bird the sparrow-hawk, devours them sometimes before they have an opportunity to fall. It is the same wise and kind Providence who makes the sparrow and the sparrow-hawk, but perhaps the poor sparrow does not recognize the wisdom and mercy of having a destroyer. But our good Christian friends will have it that all things come to pass by the direct control of an all-wise and all-good Providence. The Chicago fire, the Boston fire, and others are all dispensations of Providence, if we may believe the ministers, and they are the only ones who pretend to have positive information of the facts. The bursting of a mill-dam, or a tidal-wave, or anything and everything else that carries the besom of destruction to thousands is to them a well-known intervention of the hand of a wise and merciful Providence. It is the same, with good fortune; if we as a people have great prosperity, large harvests and abundance of trade, it is because of this "All-wise Providence." He brings the evil and the good, miseries and joys, sins and salvation.

How do we know there is a kind Providence watching over this world? "Oh!" says our Christian friend, "we see this manifested in the kindly adaptations of nature to man's conditions, everything seems to have been made for man's comfort." But, this general adaptation of man to nature and of nature to man, proves nothing of a conscious intelligence ruling over the universe. The maggot in the cheese might look around him and say, if he could talk: "All this cheese was made for me, because it's perfectly adapted to my wants and conditions." Man and maggot are adapted to their surroundings, because their surroundings have made them what they are.

After attempting to prove the existence of a special Providence, and failing, the Christian then craw-fishes into absurd talk of a *mysterious* Providence, a *dark dispensation* of Providence, an *inscrutible* Providence, an *inexplicable* Providence. And when driven from this refuge, he at last exclaims: "Well, if it all seems dark and hidden from our understanding here, it will *all* be made clear when we pass over to the other side." Yes, but you admit by this statement that you know now positively nothing of a conscious intelligence ruling the universe, why not say so?

The fundamental idea of a special Providence, is that he prevents accidents; but in spite of special Providence, accidents do occur. And even these mishaps, which show that no such thing as Providence exists, are claimed by the superstitious as proof of a *mysterious* Providence.

Francis Bacon says: We shall do well to bear in mind the ancient story of one who in Pagan times was shown a temple with a picture of all the persons who had been saved from shipwreck, after paying their vows. When asked whether he did acknowledge the power of the gods, "Aye," he answered, "but where are they painted who were drowned after their vows?" (Jevon's "Principles of Science," part 2, p. 5.)

We learn from the little care which nature takes of *single* individuals. Thousands of them are sacrificed without hesitation or repentance in the plenty of nature. Even with regard to man we make the same experience. Not one half of the human race reach the second year of their age, but die almost without having known that they ever lived. We learn this very thing also from the misfortunes and mishaps of all men, the good as well as the bad, which cannot well be made to agree with the special preservation or co-operation of the creator. (Feuerbach's "Essence of Religion.")

But with the conception of a supreme beneficience this gratuitous infliction of misery, in common with other terrestrial creatures capable of feeling, is also absolutely incompatible.—Spencer.

In short, there can be no hypothesis of a "moral government" of the world which does not implicitly assert an "immoral government." (Fisk's "Cosmic Philosophy," vol. 2, p. 407.)

But the believer in the inspiration of the Bible is compelled to declare that there was a time when slavery was right—when men could buy, and women could sell, their babes. He is compelled to insist that there was a time when Polygamy was the highest form of virtue; when wars of extermination were waged with the sword of mercy; when religious toleration was a crime, and when death was the just penalty for having expressed an honest thought. He must maintain that Jehovah is just as bad now as he was four thousand years ago, or that he was just as good then as he is now, but that human conditions have so changed that slavery, polygamy, religious persecutions, and wars of conquest are now perfectly devilish. Once they were right—once they were commanded by God himself; now, they are prohibited. There has been such a change in the conditions of man that, at the present time, the Devil is in favor of slavery, polygamy, religious persecution, and wars of conquest. That is to say, the Devil entertains the same opinion to-day that Jehovah held four thousand years ago, but in the meantime Jehovah has remained exactly the same —changeless and incapable of change. . . . A very curious thing about these commandments is that their supposed author violated nearly every one. From Sinai, according to the account, he said: "Thou shalt not kill," and yet he ordered the murder of millions; "Thou shalt not commit adultery," and yet he gave captured maidens to gratify the lust of captors; "Thou shalt not steal," and yet he gave to Jewish marauders the flocks and herds of others; "Thou shalt not covet thy neighbor's house, nor his wife," and yet he allowed his chosen people to destroy the homes of neighbors and to steal their wives; "Honor thy father and thy mother," and yet this same God had thousands of fathers butchered, and with the sword of war killed children yet unborn; "Thou shalt not bear false witness against thy neighbor," and yet he sent abroad "lying spirits" to deceive his own prophets, and in a hundred ways paid tribute to deceit. So far as we know, Jehovah kept only one of these commandments—he worshipped no other God. ("Ingersoll's Reply to Black.")

It is said of Christ that he was infinitely kind and generous, infinitely merciful because when on earth he cured the sick, the lame, and the blind. Has he not as much power now as he had then? If he has and is the God of all worlds, why does he not now give back to the widow her son? Why does he withhold light from the blind, and why does one who had the power miraculously to feed thousands allow millions to die for want of food? Where is he now? ("Ingersoll's Interviews.")

First Cause.

Assuming then, the existence of a First Cause, let us inquire for a moment into its nature. The First Cause must be *infinite*. For if we regard it as finite, we regard it as bounded or limited, and are thus compelled to think of a region beyond its limits, which region is uncaused. And if we admit this, we virtually abandon the doctrine of causation altogether. We, therefore, have no alternative but to regard the First Cause as infinite.

We are no less irresistibly compelled to regard the First Cause as independent. For if it be dependent, that on which it depends must be the First Cause. The First Cause can therefore have no necessary relation to any other form of being; since if the presence of any other form of existence is necessary to its completeness, it is partially dependent upon such other form of existence, and cannot be the First Cause. Thus the First Cause, besides being infinite, must be complete in itself, existing independently of all relations,—that is, it must be *absolute*.

To such conclusions, following the most refined metaphysical philosophy of the day, are we easily led. By the very limitations of our faculties, we are compelled to think of a First Cause of all phenomena; and we are compelled to think of it as both infinite and absolute.

Nevertheless, it will not be difficult to show that such a conclusion is utterly illusive; and that in joining together, the three conceptions of Cause, of Infinite, and of Absolute, we have woven for ourselves a net-work of contradictions, more formidable, more disheartening than any that we have yet been required to contemplate. For, in the first place, that which is a cause cannot at the same time be absolute. For the definition of the Absolute is that which exists out of all relations; whereas a cause not only sustains some definite relation to its effect, but it exists as a cause only by virtue of such relation. Suppress the effect, and the cause has ceased to be a cause. The phrase "absolute cause," therefore, which is equivalent to "non-relative cause," is like the phrase "circular triangle." The two words stand for conceptions which cannot be made to unite. "We attempt," says Mr. Mansel, "to escape from this apparent contradiction by introducing the idea of succession in time. The Absolute exists first by itself, and afterwards becomes a cause. But here, we are checkmated by the third conception, that of the Infinite. How can the Infinite become that which it was not from the first? If causation is a possible mode of existence, that which exists without causing is not infinite; that which becomes a cause has passed beyond its former limits.

"But supposing all these obstacles overcome, so that we might frame a valid conception of a cause which is also absolute and infinite: have we then explained the origin of the universe? Have we advanced one step toward explaining how the Absolute can be the source of the Relative, or how the Infinite can give rise to the Finite?" To continue with Mr. Mansel, "if the condition of causual activity is a higher state than that of quiesence, the Absolute . . . has passed from a condition of comparative imperfection to one of comparative perfection; and therefore was not originally perfect. If the state of activity is an inferior state to that of quiesence, the Absolute in becoming a cause has lost its original perfection. There remains only the supposition that the two states are equal, and the act of creation one of complete indifference. But this supposition annihilates the unity of the Absolute." (John Fiske, "Cosmic Philosophy.")

THE SUNDAY QUESTION.

It is related that once upon a time, a number of grave and reverend rabbins earnestly disputed among themselves, whether it was lawful or not to eat an egg that was laid upon the Sabbath day. In the minds of some of these grave and wise masters it was held to be a prohibited egg, but in the stomachs of others of their number such eggs were held as too good to be despised.

In the Blue Laws of Connecticut by Rev. Sam Peters, we have Puritan scruples put in rhyme:

"Upon the Sabbath day they'll no physick take,
Lest it should worke, and so the Sabbath breake."

There have always been great disputes over this subject which we call in general terms the "Sunday Question." Why do so many misunderstandings arise upon this matter? Simply because people do not understand the question. Millions of devout worshippers use the terms Sunday and Sabbath as if they were synonymous. Millions of superstitious persons cherish obligations to maintain better conduct on Sunday than on any other day in the week. They cannot understand that it is fit and proper to do on Sunday anything that it is fit and proper to do on any other day. The tendency to perform the duties of life correctly on Sunday leaves room and disposition not to perform them so well on the other six days of the week. Such people live cream lives on Sunday and skim-milk lives all the rest of the week. It won't do; because it tends to demoralize rather than establish the noble sentiments of morality and manhood. If we would know how to observe Sunday we must know something more about it than we have unconsciously learned from the nursery stories of our childhood. Let us begin with the names of

The Days of the Week.

We trace these names to our Saxon ancestors. By them the seven days of the week were called Son-daeg, Moon-daeg, Tuisdaeg, Woden's-daeg, Thurres-daeg or Thor's-day, Friga's-daeg, and Seterne's-daeg. These were the names of ancient deities. As seven planets and seven metals were at that time known—the sun, the moon, Mars, Mercury, Jupiter, Venus and Saturn being the planets of astrology—a due allotment was made, gold was held sacred to the sun, silver to the moon, iron to Mars, etc. Even the portions of time were in a like manner dedicated; the seven days of the week were respectively given to the seven planets of astrology. The names imposed on these days, and the order in which they occur, are obviously connected with the Ptolemaic hypothesis of astronomy, each of the planets having an hour assigned to it in its order of occurrence, and the planet ruling first the hour of each day giving its name to that day. Thus arranged, the week is a remarkable instance of the longevity of an institution adapted to the wants of man. It has survived through many changes of empire and has forced itself on the ecclesiastical system of Europe, which, unable to change its idolatrous aspect, has encouraged the vulgar error that it owes its authenticity to the holy scriptures; an error too plainly betrayed by the Pagan names that the days bear, and also by their order of occurrence. ("Intellectual Development of Europe," by John W. Draper, vol. 1, p. 403.)

It is remarkable that every day of the week is by different nations devoted to the public celebration of religious services:—Sunday by the Christians, Monday by the Greeks, Tuesday by the Persians, Wednesday by the Assyrians, Thursday by the Egyptians, Friday by the Turks, Saturday by the Jews.

From a passage in Genesis, in which the first reference to a Sabbath occurs, the inference has been drawn (an inference not warranted by the text) that the first parents of the human race were taught by God himself to divide time into weeks, and to set apart a portion as a day of rest, and for religious purposes. If so, it would of course follow that this institution, or some traces of it, would be found among all nations; and the impression, therefore, on the mind of a very large class of persons, is a very natural one, that however much a Sabbath may have fallen into disuse, or be now disregarded, the week of seven days has been kept by all generations of mankind from the days of creation, and continues to be observed in every part of the world. ("Westminster Review," October 1850, p. 134.)

It is, however, true that observance of one day in seven as a day of rest, recreation, and pleasure obtains in many countries. How then did it come about if it was not revealed to man, that we keep in a special manner

One Day in Seven?

The observance of a seventh part of the week is no more a revelation than the multiplication table is. It was natural for man to measure the spaces of time. The revolution of the earth, or from sun to sun was a day, and from new moon to new moon was a month of twenty-eight days. It was a most natural thing to have feasts at the full of the moon and at new moon; between these times were the "horned moon," and this marked another division of time. It was easy to divide the full moon into four periods, each of seven days. Hence originated the observance of one day in seven. After the moon time had been divided into four parts each of seven days and the days specifically named, then the old phraseology of "new moon days" was dropped as it was no longer needed.

There are two different reasons given for observing the Sabbath:

For in six days the Lord made heaven and earth, the sea and all that in them is, and rested the seventh day; wherefore the Lord blessed the Sabbath day and hallowed it. (Exodus 20: 11.)

And remember that thou wast a servant in the land of Egypt, and that the Lord thy God brought thee out thence through a mighty hand and by a stretched-out arm; *therefore* the Lord thy

God commanded thee to keep the Sabbath day. (Deuteronomy 5: 15.)

Here are two distinct and contradictory accounts given of the origin of the Sabbath. According to the first, God instituted the Sabbath on the seventh day of time, immediately after his six days of creation. But if we are to believe the writer of Deuteronomy the Sabbath was set up as a memorial day of the Jews' escape from Egyptian bondage; an occurrence that took place something like two thousand five hundred years after the year one, of creation. Both of these statements cannot be correct, as one excludes the other. And in view of the fact that man naturally learned to divide time into days, moons, and quarter moons we are strongly inclined to think that both of these ancient accounts are mythical.

"Remember the Sabbath day to keep it holy."

The word *holy* has lost its original signification. The Hebrew word *kadosh* means "to set apart." Parkhurst renders it, "to separate, to set apart from its common and ordinary to some higher use or purpose." It is used in this sense in Genesis 4: "And God *divided* [i.e. separated] the light from the darkness."

The vessels of the sanctuary were to be "Holy unto the Lord;" that is, they were to be kept strictly separate from other vessels, for the sanctuary.

The saba or Sabbath was a day of *rest*, and the command to keep it holy did not mean that it should be observed with solemnity, or kept by offering sacrifices or in the performance of other religious ceremonies. Other days were working days, but the Sabbath was to be a day of rest.

"The word *holy*," says a modern writer on the Sabbath, "has now become so associated in our minds with Puritanical ideas of self-mortification and with modern religious forms of worship, that we are naturally misled by it from the meaning of the original. Many pious persons suppose that the command to keep the Sabbath day *holy* was equivalent to an injunction to attend a parish church, hear two or more sermons in the course of the Sunday and during the rest of the day to keep in-doors and read the Bible. The Jews, however, did not do this, for the Bible was not written, and sermons in its exposition (which would have wanted texts) could not well be preached. Nor does it appear from any passage in the books of Moses, that religious admonitions or discourses of any kind, formed a part of the tabernacle service."

The Jewish Sabbath was emphatically a day of rest. Work, therefore, was strictly prohibited; for "Whosoever doeth any work in the Sabbath day, he shall surely be put to death." (Exodus 31: 15.)

This law was not so literal as subsequent interpreters have made it. We have an account of only *one* person being put to death for this crime. It is recorded in Numbers, 15: 32–36 that "while the children of Israel were in the wilderness they found a man that gathered sticks upon the Sabbath day."

And they that found him gathering sticks brought him unto Moses and Aaron, and unto all the congregation.

And they put him in ward, because it was not declared what should be done to him.

And the Lord said unto Moses, The man shall be surely put to death; all the congregation shall stone him with stones without the camp.

And all the congregation brought him without the camp, and stoned him with stones, and he died; as the Lord commanded Moses.

This was the only case in all the Hebrew writings, of stoning a man for gathering sticks on the Sabbath. But this single instance has engendered an infinite amount of bitter persecution in the hearts of the over-righteous, who keep the Sabbath holy and try also to make their neighbors observe it in a like manner.

Sir Humphrey Davy relates in his "Salmonia," page 1,345, that he "was walking on Arthur's Seat with some of the most distinguished professors of Edinburgh attached to the geological opinions of the late Dr. Hutton, a discussion took place upon the phenomena presented by the rocks under our feet, and to exemplify a principle, Professor Playfair broke some stones, in which I assisted the venerable and amiable philosopher.

"We had hardly examined the fragments, when a man from the crowd, who had been assisting at field-preaching, came up and warned us off, saying, 'Ye think ye are only stane-breakers; but I ken ye are Sabbath breakers, and ye deserve to be staned with your ain stanes.'"

Accidents which take place on Sunday are looked upon by some people as "Judgments of God."

In Scotland on January 16th, 1603 the citizens were dreadfully alarmed by an earthquake, on account of which a day of fasting and humiliation was appointed by the magistrates and clergy. The particular sin for which this scourge was thought to be sent, was the custom of salmon-fishing on Sunday.

But this rigid feature of the Jewish Sabbath was of a negative character, as the day was observed as a day of feasting and joy—a day something like our Thanksgiving.

A variety of minor regulations referring to bodily indulgences on that day, abundantly prove, if further proof were needed, its recognized character as a "feast-day" in the natural and general sense of the term, in Judaism. It was to be honored by the wearing of finer garments, by three special meals of the best cheer the house could afford; and it was considered a particularly meritorious thing on the part of the master of the house to busy himself personally as much as possible with the furnishing of the viands, nay, the fetching of the very wood for the cooking, so as to do as much honor to the "bride-sabbath" as in him lay.

Fasting, mourning, mortification of all and every kind, even special supplicatory prayers are strictly prohibited. (Chamber's Encyclopedia.)

If Sunday takes the place of the Sabbath, then the New Testament would clearly reveal the fact; but it does nothing of the kind. If the new religion was designed to take the place of the old, then we should expect to find Jesus plainly teaching that after his death Sunday should be observed in place of and as the Sabbath. But far from this, we find him repudiating the Jewish Sabbath, and saying nothing at all about a new day of ceremonies and worship.

We give a number of instances where Jesus intentionally repudiates and violates the common usages respecting the Sabbath:

The impotent man answered him, Sir, I have no man, when the water is troubled to put me into the pool; but while I am coming, another steppeth down before me.

Jesus saith unto him, Rise, take up thy bed, and walk.

And immediately the man was made whole, and took up his bed and walked: and on the same day was the Sabbath.

The Jews therefore said unto him that was cured, It is the Sabbath day: it is not lawful for thee to carry thy bed.

And therefore did the Jews persecute Jesus, and sought to slay him, *because* he had done these things on the *Sabbath* day. (John 5: 7, 8, 9, 10 and 16.)

The Jewish law regarding the Sabbath was strict. It was not lawful to carry burdens on that day.

Thus saith the Lord, Take heed to yourselves, and bear no burden on the Sabbath day, nor bring it in by the gates of Jerusalem. (Jeremiah 17: 21.)

And it came to pass that he went through the corn fields on the Sabbath day; and his disciples began as they went to pluck the ears of corn.

And the Pharisees said unto him, Behold, why do they on the Sabbath day that which is not lawful? And he said unto them, Have ye never read what David did, when he had need, and was a hungered, he and they that were with him?

How he went into the house of God in the days of Abiathar the high priest, and did eat the shew-bread, which is not lawful to eat, but for the priests, and gave also to them that were with him?

And he said unto them, The Sabbath was *made* for *man* and *not* man for the Sabbath. (Mark 2: 23-27.)

Jesus had repeated conflicts with the Jews on this question. He would not honor the Jewish Sabbath, and consequently the Jews made war upon him, threatening to take his life.

And the scribes and Pharisees watched him, whether he would heal on the Sabbath day; that they might find an accusation against him. But he knew their thoughts, and said to the man which had the withered hand, Rise up, and stand forth in the midst. And he arose and stood forth.

Then said Jesus unto them, I will ask you one thing: Is it lawful on the Sabbath days to do good or to do evil? to save life or to destroy it?

And looking round about upon them all, he said unto the man, Stretch forth thy hand. And he did so; and his hand was restored whole as the other. (Luke 6: 7-11.)

And they were filled with madness; and communed one with another what they might do to Jesus. (Luke 6: 11.)

We read in Luke 13: 11–14, that "there was a woman which had a spirit of infirmity eighteen years, and was bowed together, and could in no wise lift up herself."

And when Jesus saw her, he called her to him, and said unto her, Woman, thou art loosed from thine infirmity.

And he laid his hands upon her; and immediately she was made straight, and glorified God.

And the ruler of the synagogue answered with indignation, because that Jesus had *healed* on the *Sabbath* day, and said unto the people, There are six days in which man ought to work; in them therefore come and be healed, and not on the Sabbath day.

With the commandment before his eyes, saying: "Take heed to yourselves and bear no burdens on the Sabbath day as I commanded your fathers," (Jeremiah 18: 21), Jesus deliberately bade the cripple take up his bed and walk, *on* the Sabbath day.

It is remarkable that those people who love to sabbatize so much, and to *make* others do so too, do not see that while Jesus violated intentionally the Jewish Sabbath, that he never gave his disciples the slightest hint that they should observe Sunday in any manner whatever.

Paul, the *founder* of the Christian church, *rejects* the Sabbath.

Let no man, therefore, judge you in meat, or in drink, or in respect of any holy day, or of the new moon, or of the Sabbath days. (Colossians 2: 16.)

One man esteemeth one day above another: another esteemeth every day alike. Let every man be fully persuaded in his own mind.

He that regardeth the day regardeth it unto the Lord; and he that regardeth not the day, to the Lord he doth not regard it. (Romans 14: 5, 6.)

But now, after that ye have known God, or rather are known of God, how turn ye again to the weak and beggarly elements, whereunto ye desire again to be in bondage? Ye observe *days* and months and times and years. (Galatians 4: 9, 10.)

Bear in mind, reader, that there is not so much as a dot in the New Testament in favor of substituting Saturday for the Jewish Sabbath, or for observing it as a Sabbath day. Jesus and Paul both repudiate it. The *history* of the *church* is *against* the use of Sunday as the Sabbath.

St. Cyril, bishop of Jerusalem, in the year 345, says: "Turn thou not out of the way into Samaritanism or Judaism, for Jesus Christ hath redeemed thee; henceforth reject all observance of Sabbaths, and call not meats, which are really matters of indifference, common or unclean."

St. Jerome, in the year 392, says: "On the Lord's day they went to church, and returning from church they would apply themselves to their allotted works and make garments for themselves and others. The day is not a day of fasting, but a day of joy; the church has always considered it a day of joy, and none but heretics have thought otherwise."

Sir William Danville, in his "Six Texts," p. 241, says: "Centuries of the Christian era passed away before the Sunday was observed by the Christian church as a Sabbath. History does not furnish us with a single proof or indication that it was at any time so observed previous to the sabbatical edict of Constantine in A. D. 321.

The Edict of Constantine.

In the code of Justinian lib. 3, title 12, sec. 2 and 3, we find the first legal edict regulating the Sabbath:

Let all the judges and town people, and the occupation of all trades, rest on the venerable day of the sun; but let those who are situated in the country, freely and at full liberty attend to the business of agriculture, because it often happens that no other day is so fit for sowing corn and planting vines; lest the critical moment being let slip, men should lose the commodities granted by Heaven.

By a multitude of religious teachers of the present day, this decree of Constantine is recognized as the foundation of all "Sabbath" or "Lord's day" legislation; as the first recognition by the "body politic" of the usages or institutions of Christianity. But nothing can be more easily shown than that this decree was not made in the interest of Christianity; that it did not respect the Sabbath or Lord's day; and that it was not issued by a Christian ruler.

The reader will notice that the decree was partial; that it related only to certain classes, leaving other classes to still pursue their usual avocations; and that it was respecting "the venerable day of the sun." Now we appeal with confidence to every student and reader of the Bible, that in all the scriptures there is no such a day or institution known as "the venerable day of the sun." And we affirm that, in this decree, Constantine not only did not *mention* any Christian institution, but he had no *reference* to any Christian institution.

On this point let such a reputable writer as Dr. Schaff testify:

He enjoined the civil observance of Sunday, though not as *dies Domini* [Lord's day], but as *dies solis* [day of the sun], in *conformity* to his worship of *Apollo*, and in company with an ordinance for the regular consulting of the *haruspex* (321). ("History of the Christian Church," vol. 2.)

The edict of the sun's day was issued March 7; that for consulting the haruspex was issued the day following, March 8. This edict of March 8 concerned the inspection of the entrails of beasts as a means of foretelling future events. It was a heathen practice, and the decree was a heathen edict, made by a heathen ruler. This of itself is sufficient to show in what light we must regard his edict for honoring "the venerable day of the sun."

Dr. Schaff says that Constantine issued his sun's day decree "in conformity to his worship of Apollo." Who was Apollo, and what relation did his worship bear to reverencing "the day of the sun?" Webster says: "A deity among the Greeks and Romans, and worshiped under the name of *Phœbus,* the sun."

Noted Men who have Rejected the Observance of Sunday as the Sabbath.

For if there was no need of circumcision before Abraham, or of the observance of Sabbaths, feasts, and sacrifices, before Moses, no more need is there of them now, after that, according to the will of God, Jesus Christ, the Son of God, has been born without sin.—Justin Martyr.

They (the patriarchs) did not therefore regard circumcision nor observe the Sabbath, neither do we; neither do we abstain from certain foods, nor regard other injunctions which Moses subsequently delivered to be observed in types and symbols, because such things as these do not belong to Christians.—Eusebius.

As regards the Sabbath or Sunday, there is no necessity for keeping it; but if we do, it ought not to be on account of Moses's commandment, but because nature teaches us from time to time to take a day of rest. . . . If anywhere the day is made holy for the mere day's sake, then I order you to work on it, to dance on it, to do anything that will reprove this encroachment on Christian spirit and liberty.—Martin Luther.

The law of the Sabbath being thus repealed, that no particular day of worship has been appointed in its place is evident.—Milton.

They who think that by the authority of the church, the observance of the Lord's day was appointed instead of the Sabbath, as if necessary, are greatly deceived.—Melancthon.

And truly we see what such a doctrine has profited; for those who adopt it far exceed the Jews in a gross, carnal, and superstitious observance of the Sabbath.—John Calvin.

These things refute those who suppose that the first day of the week (that is, the Lord's day) was substituted in place of the Sabbath, for no mention is made of such a thing by Christ or his Apostles.—Grotius.

It will be plainly seen that Jesus did decidedly and avowedly *violate* the Sabbath. The dogma of the assembly of divines at Westminster, that the observance of the Sabbath is a part of the moral law, is to me utterly unintelligible.—Archbishop Whately.

As for the Sabbath, we be lords over the Sabbath, and may yet change it into Monday, or into any other day as we see need, or make every tenth day a holy day only, if we see cause why. We may make two every week, if it were expedient, and not one enough to teach the people. Neither was there any cause to change it from Saturday than to put difference between us and the Jews, and lest we should become servants unto the day, after their superstition. Neither need we any holy day at all if the people might be taught without it.—William Tyndall.

The effect of which consideration is, that the Lord's day did not succeed in the place of the Sabbath, but the Sabbath was wholly abrogated, and the Lord's day was merely an ecclesiastical institution.—Jeremy Taylor.

The festival of Sunday, like all other festivals, was always a human ordinance, and it was far from the intention of the Apostles to establish a divine command in this respect; far from them and the early Apostolic church to transfer the laws of the Sabbath to Sunday. Perhaps at the end of the second century a false application of this kind had begun to take place, for men appear by that time to have considered laboring on Sunday as a sin.—Neander.

Dr. McNight says: The whole law of Moses being abrogated by Christ, Christians are under no obligation to observe any of the Jewish holidays—not even the Sabbath. (Com. on Epistles, Col.)

Sabbath Engenders Cruelty.

The history of the Sabbatarians proves them to be both ignorant and cruel. We have only to make a few quotations from standard authors to prove the charge.

At the same time that James shocked in so violent a manner, the religious principles of his Scottish subjects, he acted in opposition to those of his English. He had observed, in his progress through England, that a Judaical observance of the Sunday, chiefly by means of the Puritans, was every day gaining ground throughout the kingdom; and that the people under color of religion, were contrary to former practice, debarred such sports and recreations as contributed both to their health and amusement.

Festivals which in other nations and ages are partly dedicated to public worship, partly to mirth and society, were here totally appropriated to the offices of religion and served to nourish those sullen and gloomy contemplations, to which the people were of themselves so unfortunately subject. The king imagined that it would be easy to infuse cheerfulness into the dark spirit of devotion. He issued a proclamation to allow and encourage, after divine service, all kinds of lawful games and exercises; and by his authority he endeavored to give sanction to a practice which his subjects regarded as the utmost instance of profaneness and impiety. ("Hume's History of England," vol. 4, p. 447.)

Hume, speaking of the Puritans, remarks:

They [the house of commons] also enacted laws for the strict observance of Sunday which the Puritans affected to call the Sabbath, and which they sanctified by most melancholy indolence. (Vol. 5, p. 10.)

Besides this, it is important to remark that the Puritans were more fanatical than superstitious. They were so ignorant of the real principles of government, as to direct penal laws against private vices. ("Buckle's History of Civilization in England," vol. 1, p. 261.)

The same spirit is rampant now in our prohibition laws, Sunday laws, profane swearing laws, etc. Repressing vices does not extinguish them but causes them to become more deep-seated and wide-spread. Moral natures can be made more moral only by the use of moral means.

The Puritans.

Not dancers go to heaven, but mourners; not laughers but weepers; whose tune is Lachrymae, whose music sighs for sin; who know no other cinquepace but this to heaven, to go mourning all the day long for their iniquities; to mourn in secret like doves, to chatter like cranes for their own and others' sins. Fastings, prayers, mourning, tears, tribulations, martyrdom were the only sounds that led all the saints to heaven. ("Bayne's Chief Actors in the Puritan Revolution," p. 112.)

Presbyterianism in Scotland was the twin of English Puritanism; Presbyterianism prohibited all sorts of pleasure as being sinful and of the Devil.

The following extracts are copied from Buckle's **History of Civilization in England**, volume 2, page 304:

Smiling, provided it stopped short of laughter, might occasionally be allowed; still, being a carnal pastime it was a sin to smile on Sunday. It was wrong to take pleasure in beautiful scenery; for a pious man had no concern with such matters which were beneath him, and which should be left to the unconverted.

The unregenerate might delight in these vanities, but they who were properly instructed saw nature as she really was, and knew that she, for about five thousand years, had been constantly on the move, her vigor was well nigh spent, and her pristine energy had departed. To the eye of ignorance she still seemed fair and fresh; the fact, however, was that she was worn out and decrepit; she was suffering from extreme old age; her frame no longer elastic, was leaning on one side, and she soon would perish.

Owing to the sin of man all things were getting worse, and nature was degenerating so fast that already the lilies were losing their whiteness and the roses their smell.

On this account, it was improper to care for beauty of any kind; or to speak more accurately, there was no real beauty. The world afforded nothing worth looking at save and except the Scotch Kirk, which was incomparably the most beautiful thing under heaven. To look at that was a lawful enjoyment but every other pleasure was sinful. To write poetry, for instance, was a grievous offense, and worthy of special condemnation. To listen to music was equally wrong; for men had no right to disport themselves in such idle recreation. Hence the clergy forbade music to be introduced even during the festivities of a marriage.

Dancing was so extremely sinful that an edict expressly prohibiting it was enacted by the General Assembly, and read in every church in Edinburgh.

It was a sin for any Scotch town to hold a market either on Saturday or Monday, because both days were near Sunday. It was a sin to go from one town to another on Sunday, however pressing the business might be. It was a sin to visit your friend on Sunday; it was likewise sinful either to have your garden watered or your beard shaved.

No one, on Sunday, should pay attention to his health or think of his body at all. On that day horse exercise was sinful; so was walking in the fields or in the meadows, or in the streets, or enjoying the fine weather by sitting at the door of your own house. To go to sleep on Sunday before the duties of the day were over was also sinful and deserved church censure. Bathing, being pleasant as well as wholesome, was a particularly grievous offense; and no man could be allowed to swim on Sunday.

It mattered not what man liked; the mere fact of his liking it made it sinful. Whatever was natural was wrong. The clergy deprived the people of their holidays, their amusements, their shows, their games, and their sports; they repressed every appearance of joy, they forbade all merriment, they stopped all festivities, they choked up every avenue by which pleasure could enter, and spread over the country an universal gloom.

On Sunday, in particular, he must never think of benefitting others; and the Scotch clergy did not hesitate to teach the people that on that day it was sinful to serve a vessel in distress, and that it was a proof of religion to let ship and crew perish. They might go; none but their wives, and children would suffer, and that was nothing in comparison with breaking the Sabbath. So, too, did the clergy teach, that on no occasion must food or shelter be given to a starving man, unless his opinions were orthodox.

Sunday Should be Regarded as a day of Rest and Recreation.

But every one should be protected in his individual liberty of choosing how he shall rest and enjoy himself. My neighbors certainly have no right to say how I shall conduct myself on Sunday, nor would they have if they were elected to the state or national legislature. My right to freedom of conscience is inalienable. It is true that I may be robbed of my liberty by those in power. The Sunday laws are the spoliation of the weak by the strong. A most remarkable trait of this nation is that it is constituted more than any other people that the sun ever shone upon of law *makers* and law *breakers*. It forebodes national decay. The people who indulge in this spirit are lacking in moral sentiment, and the current history of the politics and religion of this country furnish a lamentable proof of the fact.

Unconstitutionality of Sunday Laws.

There is no provision in the constitution requiring the citizens of the United States to observe Sunday in a religious manner; but there are on the contrary, distinct and unqualified guarantees made to secure the religious liberty of every one. Sunday is a day of rest in the eyes of the Constitution but not a day of religious worship. Constitutionally it is every one's privilege to spend Sunday as he chooses. He may, if he wishes, go to Sunday-school, class-meeting, preaching, prayer-meeting, and preaching again, and thus employ all his time on Sunday in religious exercises; or if he prefers, he need go only once to service and fall asleep as soon as it begins. Others who desire it may visit the parks, green fields, ride upon the cool waters or visit the libraries, museums, picture galleries, zoological gardens and such other places of amusement and instruction as they see fit. It is the right of every American citizen to decide in what way he should pursue his own happiness.

We read in Article 6 of the Constitution, that "no *religious* test shall be required as a qualification to any office or public trust under the United States." This foundation principle was supplemented by a provision in the first amendment, which says: "Congress shall make *no* laws respecting an establishment of *religion* or prohibiting the *free* exercise thereof."

What could be clearer than this, that the framers of the Constitution intended to exclude all religious questions from the charter of liberty? The Constitution recognizes the beliefs of neither Jew nor Gentile—neither Christian nor Infidel.

The one special object of the framers of the Constitution was to establish a free government, and especially did they aim to secure to the people their individual rights, and no right was so greatly in demand by the people as the right of a free conscience; the right to exercise their own judgment upon questions of religion.

"We, the people of the United States, in order to form a more perfect union, establish justice, insure domestic tranquility, provide for the common defense, promote the general welfare and *secure* the *blessings of liberty* to *ourselves* and our *posterity*, do ordain and establish this Constitution of the United States of America."

The Declaration of Independence shows us that this question of *liberty* was that which the framers of the Constitution were seeking to establish: "We hold these truths to be self-evident, that all men are created equal; that they are endowed by their creator with certain *inalienable* rights; that among these are life, liberty and the *pursuit* of happiness."

With these words of the Declaration of Independence before us and the provision in Article 6 of the Constitution, namely, thus, "no *religious test* shall ever be required as a qualification to any public trust under the United States," and the further guarantee in the first amendment, that "congress shall make *no* law respecting an establishment of *religion* or prohibiting the *free* exercise thereof;"—it is as clear as a sunbeam that all laws seeking to enforce a religious observance of Sunday are unconstitutional, and should not be executed; and where attempts are made to bind religious observance of the day upon Liberal people they should resist it as an intolerable despotism.

The different states of the Union have numerous Sunday laws, which in most cases are a dead letter. Take for instance Massachusetts. In its history seventy-five cases have been decided mostly in favor of a rigid enforcement of its Sunday laws. But both laws and decisions are powerless in controlling the people to observe Sunday as Sabbath.

The present laws of Massachusetts prohibit games, sports, concerts, plays, work, travel, idling, fishing, hunting, buying and selling, but no one feels bound to obey them. Occasionally some new society springs up calling itself "The Society of Law and Order," and goes to work to set the world right. The first thing to be done is to enforce the Sunday laws, preventing barbers from shaving, milkmen from distributing milk, newsdealers from selling papers, flower girls from selling flowers, cigar stores from selling cigars, croquet players from enjoying on their own premises an hour's exercise and amusement, steamboats from carrying excursions from the city, ball players from practicing their games, the angler from taking a few trout, and many others from finding rest and recreation in other ways. But these good people who think that the world is out of joint and they are called to set it right, find it a greater task than they had bargained for, and so they soon tire, and the old world wags along as it did before the "Law and Order" society came into existence.

Sunday laws are a solemn farce, and a burning shame. They are a warfare upon the rights of man, in the interest of ancient traditions and modern despotism.

As for travel on the Lord's day, lo! how the people go their journeys, take their pleasure rides, rattle over the streets with their horse-cars, thunder through the villages past churches with their locomotives, and plow the bogs and coastways with their yachts and excursion steamers. Who questions the right? In the line of sport and diversion, how common such things as boating and fishing and hunting and ball playing and roving over pastures, through woods, picking berries and gathering nuts, and attending many a public entertainment to which an admittance fee is charged and taken for purposes of gain, but whose character, however sacred in name, is as secular as a banjo concert or a play of the drama. No complaint. As regards traffic, do not livery stable keepers let their horses as freely on Sundays as on week days? Do not druggists sell as freely what they possess, whether cigars or whisky, hairbrushes or perfumery? Do not hotels ply their business as freely, always at the tobacco stand and often at the bar? Do not newsboys run as loose with their shouts of "Herald and Gazette?" While if you sail down of a Lord's day to Martha's Vineyard, where "religion is the chief concern," shall you not see cigar stores, fruit stores, toy stores, souvenir stores, etc., undisguisedly open for business, and pedlars hawking canes and gim-cracks unchallenged by any deacon or dignitary? When, therefore, the legislature (of Massachusetts) enacted as late as 1863 that whoever does any manner of work or business on the Lord's day shall be punished by a fine not exceeding fifty dollars, instead of a fine not exceeding ten dollars, the former penalty, it would seem that the intention must have been to provide a penalty commensurate with the gravest breaches of the statute. What are these, if they be not the running of passenger and freight railway trains, whose mercenary noise makes havoc of all Sunday calm and quiet; the repairing of railway tracks and bridges, the gangs of workmen oft so large and belligerent enough to take a city; the repairing of machinery in shops and mills; the racket of the press turning out Sunday editions of newspapers secular as politics and earthly as a quack medicine advertisement? These truly are open and most gross violations of the law, but against them what murmur has been heard taking the form of prosecution? Nay, the breaches of the law that are prosecuted and have been are for the most part the petty breaches, while the more flagrant offenders, as a rule, have offended with impunity and still so offend.

Considering, therefore, the sturdiness with which the people of the commonwealth resist the law's repeal, and the indifference with which they treat its violations, it must be confessed that Artemus Ward's sarcasm, as applied to "prohibition," applies here with peculiar force—in *favor* of the *law*, but *against* its *enforcement*. ("The Sunday Law of Massachusetts," by a member of the Massachusetts bar, p. 29.)

Puck, in its history of the United States, says: "The Puritans instituted many beautiful customs, and they had some very remarkable laws. They provided strict penalties against Sabbath breaking. On Sunday, they decreed that every able-bodied man, woman, and child in the country should go to church three times a day. They forbade reading anything except the Bible, forbade walking in the fields, and generally shut down on amusements. Then they called it the Lord's day, and thus strove to make the Lord unpopular."

Ben. Franklin on Connecticut Sundays.

The following is an extract from a letter written by Dr. Franklin to Jared Ingersoll of New Haven. The original is in the possession of the New Haven Colony Historical Society:

Philadelphia, Dec. 11, 1762.

I should be glad to know what it is that distinguishes Connecticut Religion from common Religion:—communicate, if you please, some of these particulars that you think will amuse me as a virtuoso. When I travelled in Flanders I thought of your excessively strict observation of Sunday; and that a man could hardly travel on that day among you upon this lawful occasion, without Hazard of Punishment, while where I was every one travelled, if he pleased, or diverted himself in any other way; and in the afternoon both high and low went to the Play or to the Opera, where there was plenty of Singing, Fiddling and Dancing. I looked round for God's Judgments, but saw no signs of them. The Cities were well built and full of Inhabitants, the Markets filled with plenty, the People well favored and well clothed; the Fields well tilled; the Cattle fat and strong; the Fences, Houses and Windows all in Repair; and no *Old Tenor* anywhere in the Country:—which would almost make one suspect that the Deity is not so angry at that offence as a New England Justice.   B. FRANKLIN.

If you have any inalienable rights your freedom of conscience must be one of the most fundamental. That is, it is for you to say how you will deport yourself on matters of religion. It is nothing less than despotism for your neighbor to step up to you and say: "Brother Jones, I want to see you at church to-day, and if you are not there I will see to it that there is a law passed which will make you attend church." This is what the Puritans actually did. They did it all for the glory of God, but our modern Puritans, the orthodox, seek to stop milk wagons from delivering milk on Sunday morning, flower girls from selling flowers on the streets of New York, all because of the welfare and purity of society. In several cities in Texas the sale of cigars on Sunday is a violation of the law.

But where do these members of the state and national legislatures get their power from? Do they have any except that which is delegated to them by the people? They do not get the power from the people to usurp their inalienable rights. But here is a legislature passing laws upon the religious observance of Sunday, who have never been instructed to secure the enactment of such laws. And even if ninety-nine out of a hundred should so instruct their representative, the law could not be binding upon the one hundredth person who did not so instruct his (mis)representative in congress. He can be made to obey by their brute force. And this is what legislation amounts to generally. The people are not represented by the law makers, but their interests and rights are invaded one after another until the poor people are subjugated. Among the rights of man perhaps there is none which is more generally recognized abstractly, and more frequently violated practically, than his right to freedom of conscience, or, in other words, his religious liberty. How does this come about? One of the principal reasons for this anomally is that most people think that we ought to obey without question the will of the majority. They seem to think that an enactment by congress settles the question, whatever it may be.

Here is the secret of the Sunday legislation. The church is a spiritual despotism always seeking to materialize. It is in the nature of power of all kinds to seek for more power. As a spiritual despotism the church is not a success. The nineteenth century has said to this mental and moral Lazarus, "Take up thy bed and walk." But it has no place to walk to, and hence it refuses to obey the voice of humanity. It is slowly, however, undergoing the transformation of a dissolving view.

A Common Sense View of the Sunday Question.

Jesus said that the Sabbath was made for man, and not man for the Sabbath. Now, at first sight, this seems a true and wise saying, but upon reflection we are forced to modify our estimate of it. In the first place there is no evidence that the Sabbath was ever *made* at all. It is the result of many things. The causes assigned for the institution of this day are conflicting. One reason assigned is because the Lord rested on the seventh day and was refreshed. It is a very empty noddle that can believe that statement. Such a childish view of creation would remind us of some one who had carried a heavy load up six flights of stairs, and then sat down puffing and blowing until he was *rested* and *refreshed*. Fancy an omnipotent being tired, hungry, and sleepy. A common sense view of the creation story leads us to reject it all as a myth.

Another reason assigned for the origin of the Sabbath is that it was instituted in commemoration of God's deliverance of the Hebrews out of Egypt. But this is a flat contradiction of the previous reason given for observing the Sabbath. This contradiction is enough to invalidate the evidence of both these testimonies; but that is not all—the first story about God Almighty being tired after a week's hard work, and his *resting* and being *refreshed* on the seventh day, is so evidently a myth as to need no argument. It is on a par with all stories about the man in the moon, and the bit of legend recounting the escape of the Hebrews from Egypt is full of contradictions and impossibilities which renders the story absolutely useless as a piece of evidence.

No one knows when or where the observance of the seventh day as a day of rest and recreation began. It doubtless had small beginnings in different countries and different times, and has been subject to the law of evolution. The Sabbath was not a *man*-made product, but grew in character and importance as time rolled on. Therefore it is not true to say the Sabbath was *made for man*. All the making we see in history is what the priests have done in this direction. While it is not true that the priests originated the Sabbath, yet it is true so far as we can trace the existence of the priesthood that we find them continually making the day a day for themselves. Sunday is priests' day. Everybody must go to church to listen to an ignorant man talk, scold, misrepresent, and abuse everyone who does not believe as he does. And this is called *Divine Service*. When the priest rests temporarily from his labors upon the sinner and the skeptic, he trains his guns upon some of those who profess as strongly as himself to be true blue Christians. Take the extremes; the Salvation Army saint and a fashionable member of the fashionable Episcopal church. The latter looks down upon the former and calls them "trash, rubbish," and other classical names, while the soldier of the temporal army returns the compliment by styling his brethren of the Episcopal persuasion as "the Devil's dudes." Behold! how these Christians love—to go for one another.

We have seen that there is no history for the institution of the Sabbath. We have learned also that to keep this day holy did not mean to attend preaching or prayer-meetings, or special religious services of any kind.

We have discovered that the Jewish Sabbath was not incorporated into the early Christian church. We have seen also that Jesus repudiated the Jewish Sabbath. That Paul, the founder of the church, also rejects the Sabbath; and that the early fathers did not observe it. That the great men of the middle ages repudiated it. It was left for the Puritans and Scotch Presbyterians to bewilder the undeveloped mind and poison the susceptible hearts of the people, by teaching the gloomy doctrines of Puritanism and Presbyterianism. Puritanism and Presbyterianism die hard. They still live. Their spirit is hostile to freedom. Talk to them of liberty and you will readily wake the remark, "Oh yes, we believe in liberty, but not in *license.*" Now what does license mean with such people? Why it means that you shall conform to their religious notions and practices.

Especially must you remember the Sabbath to keep it holy; that is, you are at liberty to do just as you please, if you please to do as pleases them.

Protestants all agree upon the right of free conscience, the right to believe as one chooses (which however he never can do, because he must believe according to evidence).

It is the great boast of Protestantism that the individual has a free will (another error), and that he must search the scriptures, and decide for himself. They say every man has an open Bible put before him, and he must make up his own mind on the "truth of God." When he has made up his mind, and seeks to enter a church which is full of liberty, what do the officers of the church say to him? Do they tell him that his conscience is free and the Bible is an open book for him to read and interpret as he can? Oh, no! There is no free conscience, or open Bible business when one is getting into a church. On such occasions the candidate is taken by the proper officers into an ante room, and placed upon a Procrustean bed usually called a creed, and if he is the proper length, all right, but if not he must either be stretched or sawed off to the proper dimensions. And these are the people who have such a holy horror of *license*.

A friend of mine went once to buy a pup. The price was five dollars; but as there were three pups in the basket my friend said he would give five dollars for one if he could have his choice. "Oh yes, you can have your choice," said the owner, "if ye'll choose this pup" [pointing to the most inferior one in the basket]. So it is with the church; you can have all the liberty in the world to believe, if you believe the doctrines of this or that sect. You can have your own choice, if you choose to obey the priesthood. You can have all the liberty to think as freely as you can on all subjects, if you will never mention your thoughts. Here is what M. Guizot, an eminent Christian writer has to say about the liberty granted by the church:

When the question of political securities came into debate between power and liberty; when any step was taken to establish a system of permanent institutions, which might effectually protect liberty from the invasions of power in general; the church *always* ranged herself on the side of *despotism*. ("Guizot's History of Civilization," p. 130.)

With some people almost every act, if it be not strictly religious, is a desecration of the Lord's day. It is a solemn day, and for one to smile is a desecration of the holy day, while laughing is gross wickedness. To entertain one's friends on Sunday or to enjoy music, is carnal and therefore a desecration of the Lord's day. To love flowers is evidence of depravity; to admire the beauties of nature, as a golden sunset, or a summer's sunrise, are palpable evidences of being a "man of sin." To do anything but attend church, look solemn, mourn and pray, weep and read the Bible, is of the Devil.

What a spectacle that man presents to the world who is struggling for perfection through religious beliefs and exercises. He never gets exactly there, but confidently and complacently thinks himself there or thereabouts. His next great work is to call upon others in life's highway to follow in his footsteps. He gets some followers who join with him in thanking God that they are not as other men are. Their self-righteousness becomes intense, and they become filled with the spirit of the Lord and preach believe (as we do) or be damned. Then begins persecution and torture. It is always your "dead-in-earnest" man that gets up persecutions. He is trying to gain perfection, and the natural ripe fruit of religious perfection is bigotry, intolerance, and despotism. Beware, oh! reader, of him who is seeking perfection, for you are nothing better than a worm under his heel, and if he does not crush you, it is because he is better than his God. God will crush you in the next world for not agonizing for perfection in this.

Everybody's Sunday.

I quote the following from "The Sabbath Question," a very able pamphlet by my esteemed friend, Alfred E. Giles:

We prize Sunday as a Sabbath or rest day. But it is a physiological fact that the cessation from action that refreshes or rests some persons on that day, does not so operate on everybody. We would that Sunday should be a joy, a delight to all the people; that every man, woman, and child should anticipate its approach with pleasure. On that day, if on no other, let the edifices of the church be open free to all who love its praises, prayers, and instructions. Let the tables and alcoves of the public library be accessible to such persons as feel that they can find suitable mental and spiritual food. If the social science association, now active in promoting good fellowship and liberal feeling, desire to, let it also add its proportion of good things to the feast of the day. Let the art museums, halls of science, academies of music, public parks, and galleries of paintings disclose their treasures on Sundays freely to visitors. Let all persons be unmolested on that day to seek the enjoyment and kind of rest they may respectively need, they alone being judges thereof, always provided that no one shall infringe on the equal liberty of any other person.

> "Rest is not quitting
>   The busy career—
> Rest is the fitting
>   Of self to its sphere;
> 'Tis loving and serving
>   The highest and best—
> 'Tis onward, unswerving,
>   And that is true rest."

WHAT IS CIVILIZATION?

Very many regard it as an *entity*, a *thing*, rather than a *process*. It can no more be called a thing or an entity, than life, growth, or thinking, but like these, it is a process. "Dr. Whately speaks of it as if it were a 'thing' which could be handed about from one nation to another, or hidden away in some dark corner." (Fiske's "Cosmic Philosophy," vol. 2, p. 175.) In general terms we may define it as a progressive movement of the individual and of society. Its results are the highest attainments, the acquisition of the best things, as wealth, culture, and morality. But these "best things" must be shared liberally by the laboring classes or the civilization cannot long survive. Every civilization of the past has been false in this respect. The pyramids of Egypt have a record of kings possessing millions of slaves. Greece produced a civilization inspired by a love of the beautiful, and has consequently contributed more toward the civilization of mankind than any other people. But no nation has conspicuously sought to secure to its people the rights of liberty and justice. And until the time comes when the people get these rights, there can be no true civilization. Humanity must become the supreme purpose of life. The augean stables of legislation must be renovated for the presence of better men who shall take the places of the corrupt demagogues who now fill our highest offices of public trust. The very fact that a dozen of our United States senators represent $160,000,000 speaks volumes of itself.

Many of these men have secured the most if not all their great wealth since they have been the custodians of the people's public interests.

A true civilization has never yet appeared in the world. Much that is written in proof of our boasted civilization is twaddle. We are living in many respects as barbarians lived thousands of years ago. But to return to our definitions. It should be borne in mind that civilization is not an end, but a means to higher ends; the results are not therefore fixed and final, as they in turn become causes of other results. If we regard civilization as a refined and cultured state of society, we shall find that it means more than this —that it is rather the activity of mind which leads to higher refinements, to investigation, invention, discovery, and that it constantly inspires man with desires for still nobler achievements. Civilization is the onward and upward movement of the human race. This fermentation of humanity is the product of many factors, and has been effected by all sorts of human activities. War, commerce, agriculture, inventions, crusades, discoveries, literature, art, religion, skepticism, government, languages, science, manufactures, climate, soil, food, and many other things have assisted in developing the mind and heart of man, and in improving his physical condition. In the present century, science has worked wonders by way of discovery and invention, increasing the intellectual activities, thereby widening the knowledge of men and augmenting the sum of human happiness.

We should not overlook the fact that the world's advancement has been vastly more in the line of intellectual improvement and material prosperity than in the development of man's moral nature. Our civilization is much like our dress, it abounds in shoddy and tinsel. There is much in the dome of modern civilization that glares in the sunlight, while its foundations, which are out of sight, are rotten. Our great cities show us that the rich are becoming richer and the poor poorer. Where will this end? Can a splendid civilization be established on such a basis?

Distinguished men have entertained widely different notions of the causes of human progress. One writer thinks that government possesses the secret power of progress; another claims all advancement for Christianity, and others that morality is the cause, while yet others attribute the magic power to the forces of nature. Mr. Buckle maintains that man's progress is due to his physical environment. And a moment's reflection will show us that there is much truth in his claim. We know that it is utterly impossible to establish a grand civilization in the tropics or in the polar regions. Suppose we should send all the ministers in the country, all the gold and silver in the United States treasury and millions of our best citizens to Greenland, could they build up a splendid civilization there? Not at all. Nature is too inhospitable. Society flourishes only in a temperate climate. If it were the church that created civilization then we should see similar results in different latitudes and among different races. But the facts are opposed to this claim. Wherever there is a high civilization there is good soil and temperate climate. As an illustration of this fact I may refer the reader to the Abyssinians, who have had the Bible in their possession about twice as long as the Anglo-Saxons; and yet they are all a race of barbarians still.

 Christianity was introduced in that country about A.D. 330. The people still remain rude and barbarous.
 Bruce relates how he saw the people cut steaks from living cattle and eat them raw. (Ency. Brit.)

Mr. Buckle claims that the favorable environment produces progress in the race, and that as man progresses he gains more control over nature and utilizes her forces. He makes the desert to blossom, he overcomes diseases, as plague, leprosy, and prevents famine, and because of his increased knowledge wars are becoming less frequent and less barbarous. From these facts he claims that the advance of civilization is characterized by a diminishing influence of physical laws, and an increasing influence of **mental laws**. In proof of his position that climate, soil, and food are the determining influences of progress, he refers us to the climate of Asia and Africa as compared with the climate of Europe and America, pointing out the latter as having vast mineral resources and great facilities of travel over highways, rivers, and lakes. The temperate climate is in every way therefore most favorable to the highest civilization.

In the tropics man does not have to exhaust himself in obtaining his food, as it grows spontaneously and in abundance, but the burning sun takes out of him his energy and enterprise; while on the other hand the inhabitant of Greenland has to fight for life against the severe cold. His efforts and manner of life are exhausting, and tend to dwarf him physically, morally, and mentally. However much man may do in overcoming nature, these two hindrances of extreme heat and excessive cold remain insuperable barriers in his way.

War has been a civilizing power, although it has been fearful expensive of blood, treasure, and public morals. The American revolution of 1776 secured the independence of this country. The French revolution of 1789, transformed the whole of Europe. The recent great rebellion in this country emancipated the slave, and has made a more perfect union of the North and South. The crusades were a great revolutionary movement in Europe, beginning in 1096, and lasting about two hundred years. In fact there was no such a thing as Europe before this great epoch. The different countries which constitute Europe, had, prior to the crusades, almost no intercourse with one another, and consequently each was comparatively ignorant of the manners and customs of the others. The uprising of millions of men, women, and children, as warriors of Christ, who set out from time to time, from England, France, Germany, and Spain to rescue the Holy Land from the Infidel, the Mohammedan, brought wonderful experiences to the few thousand who survived to tell their stories. The pathways over which these deluded people thronged were whitened with the bleached bones of those who had fallen victims of disease, exposure, hunger, and the sword. What a monstrous blind sacrifice this was, offered up on the altar of ignorance! Of course it could do the world no good to rescue the Holy Land. If God wanted that land rescued he could do it himself. And that he did not do so is self-evident that he did not want it rescued, besides, he would not allow even his own peculiar people to rescue it. The church is still offering its sacrifices of public weal, of blood, and treasure in trying to rescue, abroad, the Pagan from his Paganism, and at home, the Infidel from his Infidelity, while God could do it himself if he so desired, but he does not, neither does he permit his own "peculiar" people to do it.

The crusaders had no commission from heaven for this business—they were not the agents of God, but only pretenders—and the church of to-day has no more right to pretend to save the world than the crusaders had to deliver the holy sepulchre from the so-called Pagans. The one and the others are alike impostors upon a credulous world. The crusades did nothing in the matter of rescuing the Holy Land. In this respect they were failures. The God of hosts did not lead them on to certain victory. But if they did not secure what they aimed at, they found something infinitely better—a wider knowledge of the world.

The intercourse between these different peoples which was occasioned by the marching of armies through their lands, gave new ideas to all; broke up the feudal system, and serfdom, secured the supremacy of a common law over the independent jurisdiction of the chiefs who claimed the right of private wars. In a word, it was the origin of Europe, the first great awakening of the intellect of the masses.

Not only were the old manners and customs changed, but there was stimulated in society an increased mental activity; and the narrow routine in which it had been accustomed to move was destroyed. Society began its new transformations into governments and nations, which says Guizot, is the characteristic of modern civilization.

Industrial Influences.

The causes which mostly disturbed or accelerated the normal progress of society in antiquity were the appearance of great men. In modern times the appearance of great inventions. Printing has secured the intellectual achievements of the past, and furnished a sure guarantee of future progress. Gunpowder and military machinery have rendered the triumph of barbarians impossible. Steam has united nations in the closest bonds. Innumerable mechanical contrivances have given a decisive preponderance to that industrial element which has colored all the developments of our civilization. The leading characteristics of modern societies are in consequence marked out much more by the triumphs of inventive skill than by the sustained energy of moral causes. ("Lecky's History of European Morals," vol. 1, p. 126.)

It is not necessary to point in what way the printing press, art, commerce, and science, have promoted the progress of the race. It is so apparent to every intelligent reader that these have been the stepping stones over which we have passed from barbarism to civilization, that amplification is unnecessary.

The splendid results of science are everywhere so manifest that we hardly need refer to them. What transformations the world has undergone through the uses of the steam engine, the spinning jenny, telegraph, ocean cable, railroads, sewing machines, photography, spectrum analysis, and thousands of other useful inventions. We see advancement achieved in free government, free schools, free libraries, free trade, labor reform, prison reform, and reform in the treatment of lunatics, paupers and criminals, and reform seeking to adjust the wrongs perpetrated upon women.

Besides all these improvements there is every indication in the spirit of to-day that we are soon to witness greater improvements, if not radical changes in government; changes affecting capital and labor.

Skepticism.

Skepticism played a prominent part in the eighteenth century. Doubt instead of faith, possessed the minds of many of the most distinguished men of thought, such as Voltaire, Hume, Diderot, Rousseau, D'Holbach, Gibbon, and others. Some of the more prominent skeptics rejected Christianity on the common ground of incredibility of the scriptures. But as they had no form of belief or knowledge to substitute in place of the dogmas they rejected, it was not difficult for the clergy with specious explanations to cover up the doubts and disbeliefs which the skeptics raised. Something more was needed to break the spell of superstition and arouse the minds of men to thought and action. In the first part of the present century the philosophy of Evolution began to find place in the minds of most profound thinkers. Science has done what skepticism failed to accomplish; it has given *knowledge* instead of *faith*. It has cultivated intense intellectual habits in modern society and given mankind a sure test of truth, in its method of verification, by means of experiment, observation and deduction.

Science.

Science is inexorably hostile to supernaturalism—cannot recognize a particle of it. It knows nothing of a *super*-nature; with science all is nature, and nature is all. From pre-historic times the race has been under the control of ignorance and superstition, the parents of fear and cruelty; but now that science begins to dispel ignorance and superstition, we find courage, kindness, and other humanities taking their places. And we should say just here that Infidelity is no longer synonymous with mere disbelief; it means more than this. It stands for all that reason approves. Freethought is the first fruits of skepticism, and this means honest inquiry on all subjects, old and new. It means independence and manhood in private as well as public life—the right of everyone to think and express his thought regardless of creeds and customs, the right to live his own life in the enjoyment of the broadest possible liberty compatible with the liberty of others. Freethinkers are the prophets of this age, proclaiming justice as the right of all, and predicting a day of wrath to those who trample upon the rights of a long-suffering people. In the light of science, priestcraft must fade away like snow under the increasing heat of the sun.

Metaphysical Method.

The church made no progress in science and art for a thousand years. The energies of the mind had no outlet except in a few channels which were not fruitful. The scholars of the middle ages exerted great mental force upon empty questions, as "quiddities," "entities," "occult virtues," "efficient causes," "realism and nominalism," and the "essence of things." Were any of these problems ever solved? What corresponding benefit has resulted from these long and zealous discussions? What general conclusions have been reached? What first principles have been established by them?

The speculative philosophy created violent agitation in the church; but from its very nature it offered no positive truth, no verifiable facts to take the place of theology. The metaphysical method was fruitless, because its supporters sought to explain every problem by the process of thought alone.

Tennemann has fairly stated the good and bad of scholastic philosophy. It gave rise to a great display of address, subtlety, sagacity in the explanations and distinction of abstract ideas, but at the same time to many trifling and minute speculations, to a contempt of positive knowledge and too much unnecessary refinement. (Hallam, "Middle Ages," vol. 1, p. 33.)

For centuries the church maintained metaphysical discussions about the nature of Christ, one party arguing that he was of the same substance (homoousion) as the Father, and an another as strongly argued that he was of like substance (homoiusion) as the Father. These controversies were attended with bloody conflicts. If one party were in possession of the revealed will of God, it was quite natural that all other parties should listen to them. If they would not they incurred the wrath of God, and if God was angry his people ought to imitate him; if God was going to damn heretics in the next world, his saints, who are his agents here, ought to damn them in this.

RECAPITULATION.

No writer of distinction has been able, publicly, to show that Christianity has been a powerful factor for good in the civilization of the world. The definitions of civilization necessarily exclude superstition. We have seen that civilization is not an "entity" but a progressive movement produced by favorable conditions, for example, temperate climate, good soil, abundance of lakes, rivers, and mineral resources. Human activities upon a large scale have evolved still higher and better conditions for parts of the race. We have shown how war, commerce, agriculture, inventions, crusades, discoveries, literature, art, skepticism, government, languages, science, and philosophy have added to the sum of human well-being in one way and another.

The revival of learning did not spring from the church, but from Pagan literature, and Mohammedan schools. And it requires no great research to learn that the church has never been favorably inclined toward true learning, that is, toward science. It has insisted upon teaching an ignorant world the unknown and unknowable. "Carnal reason" and "blasphemous science" were never pet lessons for its subjects. It chose rather the motto, "Ignorance is the mother of devotion."

Some things Christianity has Not Done.

It has professed to offer the world a revelation of the will of God. And what has this book, the Bible, revealed? What information does it give man of the nature of this earth, of geology, geography, or of the millions of stars seen and unseen; of agriculture? Is it not true that he who invented the plow was a greater man than Moses? What does the Bible teach about government, agriculture, mining, inventions, discoveries, arts, printing, morals, liberty, and all other branches of useful learning? It contains no instructions upon the most important and useful subjects. And of itself, the Bible makes no claim to be an inspired revelation from God. The church, with all its assumptions and presumptions, is not the teacher of the world, as it has nothing but superstition to teach.

The Conflict between Christianity and Civilization.

Christianity is conservative, and, like the bourbon, never gets a new idea or forgets an old one, and it is in its very nature, therefore, non-progressive. The advancement of humanity has been achieved not by and through Christianity, but in conflict with and triumph over it. Christianity itself has been subject to modification and progress from forces without, rather than virtues within itself. The savage doctrine "believe or be damned," is no longer a popular pulpit theme. Eternal torment has ceased to torment or terrify the living, election and reprobation are no longer a commodity greatly in demand, and the divine right of kings is rapidly fading out of mind. Infant damnation is not mentioned—babes do not go to hell in these days—they all crowd into Abraham's capacious bosom. The Devil is not so black as he used to be—it was reported lately that he is dead. Taking it all in all, there has been a great improvement in the doctrines of the church. It should never be forgotten, however, that it professes to save the world, while the truth is just the opposite, that is, the world *saves* the church. Common sense has taught the church the foolishness and wickedness of these absurd and cruel doctrines, and has saved it from immediate decay by forcing it to give them up. The church makes progress because it must, not because it seeks to do so. The sanity of man is saving him from the insanity of religion. The world moves and Christianity, though it hangs back, must nevertheless move with it. The progressive element is in man, and when he is outside of the church he advances in knowledge and morality; but within its walls he is sure to be conservative and non-progressive. For why should he seek to make any progress? Has he not the revealed will of God—a complete guide to duty here and to destiny hereafter? Surely he needs no books to supersede the Bible or other virtues than those awakened by the grace of God.

The Bible Sanctions Great Crimes.

We come now to look at the crimes perpetrated by the people of God, to show how the Bible and Christianity lie as insuperable obstructions in the pathway of progress.

Wars of Extermination.

And when thou comest nigh unto a city to fight against it, and it shall be, if it make the answer of peace, and open unto thee, then it shall be, that all the people that is found therein shall be tributaries unto thee and shall serve thee. And if it will make no peace with thee, but will make war against thee (that is, by defending their wives and children) then thou shalt besiege it.

And when the Lord God hath delivered it into thine hands, thou shalt smite every male thereof with the edge of the sword; but the women and the little ones, and the cattle, and all that is in the city, even all the spoil thereof, shalt thou take unto thyself, and thou shalt eat of the spoil of thine enemies, which the Lord thy God hath given thee. Thus shalt thou do unto all the cities which are very far off from thee, which are not of the cities of these nations. But of the cities of these people, which the Lord thy God doth give thee for an inheritance, thou shalt save alive nothing that breatheth. (Deut. 20: 10–17.)

So Joshua smote all the country of the hills, and of the south, and of the vale, and of the springs and all their kings; he left none remaining, but utterly destroyed all that breathed as the Lord God of Israel had commanded. (Joshua 10: 40.)

Thus saith the Lord of hosts, I remember that which Amelek did to Israel (some three hundred years previous), how he laid wait for him in the way when he came up from Egypt. Now go and smite Amelek, and utterly destroy all that they have and spare them not, but slay both man and woman, infant and suckling, ox and sheep, camel and ass. (1 Sam. 15: 2, 3.)

Now, therefore, kill every male among the little ones, and kill every woman that hath known man by lying with him.

But all the women children that have not known a man by lying with him, keep alive for yourselves. (Numbers 31: 17, 18.)

To believe these bloody massacres to have been done by the express command of the supreme ruler of the universe, made man brutal and despotic. And it is for this very reason that we have had so many wars among Christian nations. The Old Testament is a record of cruelty and blood; and if we fall back in time on this side of the cross of Christ, we shall find the same spirit, and the same bloody deeds perpetrated upon all those who were not numbered as the peculiar people of God. Constantine established Christianity in the Roman empire by the sword; and his holy successors have maintained it by the same power ever since.

Polygamy.

Although Christians now condemn polygamy, they uphold a Bible that not only approves it, but also shows distinctly that God instituted it.

Solomon had seven hundred wives and three hundred concubines, and was not condemned for his polygamy or concubinage, but was condemned for going after other Gods:

And the Lord was angry with Solomon because his heart was turned away from the Lord. (1 Kings 11: 9.)

There is nowhere any condemnation of Solomon for his polygamy to be found in the Bible. On the contrary, he is extolled to the highest degree. God is represented as saying: "I have found David, a man after mine own heart." (Acts 13: 22.) "Yet among many nations was there no king like unto him (Solomon) who was beloved of God." (Neh. 13: 26.)

David, although he was a man after God's own heart, was not so highly esteemed as Solomon who was blest with a thousand wives. David did not have quite as many wives, and consequently did not achieve the royal grandeur of his son Solomon. The Lord gave David a number of wives: "And Abigail hasted and arose, and rode upon an ass with five damsels of her's that went with her; and she went after the messengers of David and became his wife. David also took Ahinoam, of Jezreel, and they were also, both of them, his wives. (1 Sam. 25: 42, 43.)

And David took him more wives out of Jerusalem. (2 Sam. 5: 13.)

And I gave thee (David) thy master's house and thy master's wives into thy bosom. (2 Sam. 12: 8.)

The Christian apologist says that "the Lord endured them to practice polygamy in consequence of the hardness of their hearts." But it is explicitly shown in the above passage that the Lord gave David a number of wives. "I *gave* thee thy master's wives into thy bosom," certainly exonerates David, and throws the responsibility on Jehovah. David is not censured for his polygamy, but is uniformly spoken of with approval except in one instance. In counseling Solomon Jehovah said: "And if thou wilt walk in my ways to keep my statutes and commandments as thy father David *did walk*, then I will lengthen thy days." (1 Kings 3: 14.)

Because David did that which was right in the eyes of the Lord and turned not aside from anything that he commanded him all the days of his life, save only in the matter of Uriah the Hittite. (1 Kings 15: 5.)

The truth is that nearly all the patriarchs and prophets were polygamists. They had not the faintest idea of true marriage, but took women according to their caprice, and kept them as long as they were pleased with them and cast them off when tired of them. It is a remarkable fact that we do not often read of any marriage ceremony when these men after God's own heart took them wives. A man in these days who "takes up" with a woman without marriage is called a free-lover. Were the patriarchs who took a number of women as wives without a marriage ceremony free-lovers? Just now the Christians cannot endure polygamy among the Mormons. They indorse it as a Bible institution, good enough for Abraham, Isaac, and all the rest, but out of fashion just now. The worst of it all is, the Christian sends missionaries and Bibles to the heathens and afterward reports wonderful success in converting them from their Paganism and polygamy through the means of preaching, praying, and missionary work; but when he thinks of the Mormon he forgets what wonders the missionary has done abroad in converting the polygamists, and insists that our Congress send Winchester rifles to Utah rather than missionaries. The Holy Ghost is of no account there. The gospel of peace must now as ever resort to the divine efficacy of bullets rather than Bibles, to secure a victory for truth, justice, and love. Christianity shows the same brutal instincts of war in its treatment of the Mormons that Constantine exhibited in establishing the church by the sword.

The Subjection of Woman.

The Bible nowhere teaches the equality of man and woman, but from Genesis to Revelation it treats her as man's inferior. The mythology of the ancient Hebrew story of the Garden of Eden has proved to be a veritable curse to her. "And thy desire shall be to thy *husband*, and he shall *rule over* thee" (Gen. 3: 16), has been the poisoned chalice put to her lips for over two thousand years. Paul the founder of the church, insists upon the subjection of woman. "Likewise ye wives be in *subjection* to your own *husbands*." (1 Peter 3: 1.)

Wives *submit* yourselves to your own husbands." (Col. 3: 18.)

As the church is *subject* unto Christ, so let the *wives* be to their own husbands in *everything*. (Eph. 5: 24.)

The church has uniformly maintained this doctrine, and demanded in the marriage ceremony that she promise to love, honor, and *obey* her husband.

For the man is not of the woman, but the woman of the man. Neither was the man created for the woman but the woman (was created) *for* the man. (1 Cor. 11: 8, 9.)

Divorce.

Woman is unjustly treated in the matter of divorce, in both the Old and the New Testament. In the Old Testament the husband had the power to divorce his wife if she failed to please him, while the wife could not divorce her husband for any cause.

When a man hath taken a wife and marries her, and it come to pass that she find no favor in his eye, then let him write her a bill of divorcement, and give it into her hand and send her out of his house. (Deut. 24: 1.)

When thou goest forth to war against thine enemies and the Lord thy God hath delivered them into thine hands, and thou hast taken them captives and seest among the captives a beautiful woman, and hast a desire unto her that thou wouldst have her to be thy wife, then thou shalt bring her home to thine house, she shall shave her head and pare her nails and she shall put the raiment of her captivity from off her, and shall remain in thine house and bewail her father and mother a full month, and after that thou shalt go in unto her and be her husband, and she shall be thy wife. And it shall be, if thou have no delight in her, then thou shalt let her go whither she will, but thou shalt not sell her at all for money; thou shalt not make merchandise of her because thou hast humbled her. (Deut. 21: 10-14.)

Jesus says, "Whosoever putteth away his wife, and marrieth another, committeth adultery; and whosoever marrieth her that is put away from her husband, committeth adultery." (Luke 16: 18.)

In this case there is a lack of qualification as to whether the man be innocent or not; and there is no allowance made in case the man who married her who was put away should be ignorant of her being a divorced woman.

Again, "But I say unto you, that whosoever shall put away his wife, saving for the cause of fornication, causeth her to commit adultery, and whosoever shall marry her that is divorced, committeth adultery." (Mat. 5: 32.)

Here we find not a word about the fornication of the husband. In short, there is no equality of rights and duties taught in these passages. Jesus, in the gospels of Matthew, Mark, and Luke teaches that it is adultery to marry a divorced woman. No matter what the crime of the husband has been, a wife is not allowed to put him away and marry another. If he is a fornicator, and his wife is divorced from him and remarries, she commits adultery. This is only a slight modification of the divorce law—that old law according to which the husband had only to write his wife a bill of divorcement and send her off; but it was not lawful for the wife to write a bill and send the husband away. All Christian nations have repudiated the teachings of both the Old and the New Testament on the question of divorce.

Marriage is now rapidly losing its sacramental character. If matches are made in heaven, it is evident that the work is poorly done, and for all practical purposes they might as well be made on earth; and the general opinion is inclined so strongly in that direction that greater attention is now given to the laws of life, which instruct us how to make happy earthly matches, leaving the matches of heaven to be formed when we get there.

The Jews practiced the sale of their daughters:

And if any man shall sell his daughter to be a maid-servant, she shall not go out as the man-servants do. If she pleases not her master who hath betrothed her to himself. (Ex. 21: 7.)

Jacob purchased Leah and Rachel, by serving Laban their father seven years for each of them. He agreed to serve seven years for Rachel, and after he had fulfilled his obligation, Laban deceived him by palming off Leah in the dark upon him as Rachel. But though so deeply wronged Jacob did not dispair, but served another seven years for her whom he loved. See Genesis twenty-ninth chapter.

In the purchase of wives there was usually no ceremony, more than the witnessing of the sale. We read of David and Solomon *taking* wives, but no mention is made of any marriage ceremony.

A jealous husband could torture his wife, by having her poisoned. See Numbers 5: 11–31. There was no such law for a jealous wife. There was no law of even-handed justice for a greatly wronged and outraged wife. The laws were made for the benefit of man, not for the protection of

The New Testament as well as the Old, Holds Woman in Servile Bondage.

Jesus and Paul were celibates, and their teachings and practice in regard to woman, have done her incalculable wrong.

The man is not of the woman, but the woman is of the man. Neither was the man created for the woman; but the woman (was created) for the man. (1 Cor. 11: 8, 9.)

Paul gets this idea from the mythical story of creation in Genesis.

In that childish story God is represented as making woman as "an help meet," for Adam. Indeed her creation does not seem to have been intended at all, but the Creator seeing that it was not good for man to be alone, "caused a deep sleep to fall upon Adam, and he slept; and he took out one of his ribs, and closed up the flesh instead: And the rib which the Lord God had taken from the man, made he a woman, and brought her unto the man." (Gen. 2: 21, 22.) Woman was an afterthought to the Lords of creation then, and she is an afterthought to the lords of creation now.

In that ancient myth woman was doomed to perpetual servitude because she was of an investigating turn of mind, and sought to know good and evil. The sentence was. "Thy desire shall be to thy husband, and he shall *rule* over thee." (Gen. 3: 16.)

Neither Jesus nor Paul proclaimed the dignity of marriage, or discerned the necessity of enlarging the sphere of woman. Jesus shared the common sentiments of his age, and looked upon the marriage relation as incompatible with the establishment of the kingdom of heaven. He deemed it necessary to call his disciples away from their families, and even to advise the men to make eunuchs of themselves if they were able to do so. (Mat. 19: 12.) In his teachings on the question of divorce, he is far from perceiving the even-handed justice which the case demands. He says (Mark 10: 11, 12) that if either the husband or the wife put away one the other and marry again, **commits** adultery. All second marriages would therefore be unlawful according to this teaching. In Matthew (5: 32) he permits the husband to put away the wife for the crime of fornication, but makes no provision for the wife to put away the husband for the same offense. His disciples received an unfavorable impression of marriage, and after listening to him on this subject, they suggested: "If the case of the man be so with his wife, it is not good to marry." (Mat. 19: 10.) How could these plain people have misunderstood him upon a subject with so little chance for misapprehension?

Paul's teachings were adverse to the marital relations: "Art thou loosed from a wife? seek not a wife." (1 Cor. 7: 27.)

"It is better to marry than to burn." (1 Cor. 7: 9.) What an idea of marriage! He does not have the least conception of love, or of the higher and refining joys of the conjugal relation. But permits him who cannot keep himself from beastliness to marry. In this his judgment is remarkably short-sighted, for he does not regard the sacrifice which the woman must make who marries the beast. He looks upon woman as a mere safety-valve for men's passions,—her rights are not considered: she has no rights. He will permit man to marry, but young widows he denounces as heaping up damnation to themselves in marrying: "But the younger widows refuse, for when they have begun to wax wanton against Christ, they will marry having damnation, because they cast off their first faith." (1 Tim. 5: 11, 12.) To marry was to wax wanton against Christ, which was nothing less than damnation! But old widows who were above sixty years of age could join the church if they had "been the wife of one man" and "had washed the saints' feet." (1 Tim. 5: 9, 10.) I wonder what he thought of rejecting all young widowers, and accepting none under sixty years of age, and only those of them who had washed their grandmother's feet?

Paul not only advocates celibacy which is an evil to **woman, but where the marriage relation exists he insists** upon the *subjection* of woman to her husband: "Likewise, ye wives, be in subjection to your own husbands;" (1 Peter 3: 1.) "Obedient to their own husbands;" (Titus 2: 5.) "Let the woman learn in silence with all subjection;" (1 Tim. 2: 11.) "Therefore as the church is subject unto Christ so let the wives be (subject) to their own husbands *in everything.*" (Eph. 5: 24.)

The reasons given for woman's subjection are, "The man is not of the woman, but the woman is of the man. Neither was the man created for the woman, but the woman (was created) for the man." (1 Cor. 11: 8, 9.) "Let the woman learn in silence with all subjection." Wherefore? Because "Adam was first formed, then Eve." "And Adam was not deceived but the woman being deceived was in the transgression." (1 Tim. 2: 11-14.) Woman has always been the guilty cause of man's great misfortune. Adam was not to blame but Eve was the guilty one. Lot was innocent but his daughters were fearfully wicked. Joseph did not tempt anyone, but his master's wife tempted him. Job, dear man, was all patience, but his wife flew into a rage, and tried to have him curse God and die. Solomon, the pure-hearted and single-minded man of seven hundred wives and three hundred concubines was inspired to say, "One man among a thousand have I found, but a woman among all these have I not found." (Eccl. 7: 28.)

And to this day the Christian marriage ceremony demands of woman that she promise to love, honor, and *obey* her husband.

The Bible Sanctions Slavery.

What driveling idiots we mortals have been to suppose for a moment that a good being, a heavenly father, would let one part of his family hold the other in slavery!

Moreover of the children of the strangers, that do sojourn, of them shall ye buy, and of their families that are with you, which they begat in your land, and they shall be your possession.

And ye shall take as an inheritance for your children after you, to inherit them for a possession; they shall be your bondmen forever, but over your brethren, the children of Israel, ye shall not rule one over another with rigor. (Lev. 25: 45, 46.)

If thou buy a Hebrew servant, six years he shall serve, and in the seventh he shall go out free for nothing. If he came in by himself he shall go out by himself; if he were married, then his wife shall go out with him; if his master has given him a wife, and she has borne him sons or daughters, the wife and her children shall be her master's and he shall go out by himself. (Ex. 21: 2-4.)

The New Testament Sanctions Slavery.

Servants, obey in all things your master according to the flesh; not with eye-service, as men pleasers, but in singleness of heart, fearing God. (Col. 3: 22.)

Servants, be subject to your masters with all fear, not only to the good and gentle, but also to the froward. (1 Peter 2: 18.)

In addition to these positive indorsements of slaveholding, it should be remembered that Jesus never condemned it, and it was not difficult, therefore, for the church also to indorse and support it.

The American Church was the Bulwark of American Slavery.

The slave system in this country always received the support of the church. In the early history of the country it was occasionally condemned by some of the bravest ministers, but as the nation grew powerful, so also did this sum of all villainies. Not only the ministers of the slave states, but ministers of the free states lent their support to this despotism. The Rev. N. Bangs, D.D., of New York, said:

It appears evident that however much the apostles might have deprecated slavery as it then existed throughout the Roman empire, he did not feel it his duty as an embassador of Christ, to disturb those relations which subsisted between master and servants, by denouncing slavery as such a *mortal sin* that they could not be the servants of Christ in such a relation.

Rev. E. D. Simms, professor in Randolph-Macon college, a Methodist institution, affirmed that, "These extracts from Holy writ unequivocally assert the right of property in slaves."

The Rev. Wilbur Fisk, D.D., late president of the (Methodist) Wesleyan university, in Connecticut: "The relation of master and slave may and does in many cases, exist under such circumstances as free the master from the just charge of immorality."

Rev. Moses Stuart, of Andover, insisted that, "the precepts of the New Testament respecting the demeanor of slaves and their masters, beyond all question, recognized the existence of slavery."

The Rev. Dr. Taylor, of Yale college, said: "I have no doubt that if Jesus Christ was now on earth, he would, under certain circumstances, become a slaveholder."

The "Independent" makes an admission. Speaking of the degradation of the Southern negroes, it says: "For this Protestant Christianity solely is to blame. It allowed slavery. It was slow to see its enormity. In the South it supported slavery with all its power. It let the negroes live in ignorance of the word of God. It raised no voice against unchristian laws forbidding slaves to be taught to read, and forbidding marriage."

We could give hundreds of just such quotations from ministers who upheld slavery as a divine institution. And these were the blind leaders of the blind until leaders and people were precipitated into the life and death struggle of the nation. If the preachers had been honest and brave we would never have had to pass through the terrible ordeal of the great rebellion.

The northern churches were almost all in sympathy with the "divine institution." Their ministers did not dare to condemn the system lest they should be deposed for their abolitionism. The writer was pastor of a Methodist church in Brooklyn in 1859, and was dismissed from his pastorate on account of his anti-slavery preaching. After President Lincoln's emancipation proclamation the synods and general conferences arrayed themselves against the system, but not before.

The Reformation.

It is a common belief in Protestant countries that Protestantism has been the cause of all modern enlightenment, "overlooking," says Mr. Buckle, "the important fact that until enlightenment had begun, there was no Protestantism required. Enlightenment was the cause of Protestantism. Many causes had been at work to bring up the public mind to a higher intelligence and a braver love of independence."

The reformation broke out at least twenty times before Luther, and was put down. Arnold, of Brescia was put down; Fra Dolcino was put down; the Albigenses were put down; the Vaudois were put down; the Lollards were put down; the Hussites were put down.—Mill, on Liberty.

The reformation was therefore the result of previous enlightenment, a demand for larger liberty. It was the protest of reason against authority. Liberalism is the full protest against all forms of superstition and despotism. We have greatly over-estimated the work of the reformation. It did not greatly change the humanities of society, as the Protestants so fondly imagine. Protestants were found to be the persecutors when they had the power, just as the Romanists had been; circumstances, however, modified and restrained them from such atrocities as the latter had perpetrated.

Persecution for religious heterodoxy, in all its degrees, was in the sixteenth century, the principle as well as the practice of every church. (Hallam, "Middle Ages," vol. 2, p. 48.)

Christianity Teaches Immorality.

The doctrine of the *atonement* has been the dry rot in our civilization. It has led millions to believe that they could escape the consequences of violated laws of nature. Millions of people believe to-day that they can go through life in utter disregard of all that is right and good, and at the last moment when they come to shuffle off this mortal coil, all they will then need to do will be simply to call upon Jesus and receive his approbation and permission to enter the shining courts above. "Jesus died and paid it all," relieves the votary from the demands of morality, and, "the

Devil tempted me and I sinned," exonerates him from all guilt. This sort of teaching has filled our prisons with those who fully believe it—and they are behind the bars because they have lived according to their belief. The malignant and mendacious cry that Freethought leads the truthseeker always downward to a bad life is refuted by the fact that those who fill the prisons of our country are not Infidels, but believers in the divine revelation who have lived up to the advantages offered by the "gathering them in" doctrine of atonement.

The murderers who are hanged on Friday in the different states almost every week, nearly all Christians, are prepared to go to heaven and there join in the company and songs of innocent children and pure maids and matrons who, by their presence, make heaven worthy the name; but these fiends, if they should happen to be pardoned by the governor, there could not be found a reputable Christian who would want to take one of them home to live in his family of noble wife and lovely children, for a single day. And yet he is fit for heaven, fit for the company of angels and the purified of earth. The dying words of a good religious man were, "I am no Infidel," and that man's name is John D. Lee, of Utah, who, in cold blood, murdered innocent men, women, and children, and after eluding justice for twenty years or more was arrested, tried, found guilty and shot to death, with the words on his lips, "I am no Infidel." But his confession was unnecessary, as Freethinkers do not die that way, and the reason they do not die in that manner is because they do not believe in the great bankrupt act—the atonement. They have no savior, and hence have to save themselves. They have no titles to mansions in the skies but have some claims on earth which they prefer to stay with as long as they can.

The doctrine of the atonement is very immoral and no one can begin to estimate the wickedness it has fostered in society, by leading people to believe they can pass through life committing all sorts of crimes and at last, when they find themselves about to die, can call upon Jesus and find eternal life "by believing on his name."

"Long as the lamp holds out to burn
The vilest sinner may return."

"This couplet has helped many a one to die easy." Oh, yes, it has, but it has encouraged too many to live easy—to live entirely too easy—so easy that they did not need to gain intelligence, to practice morality and pay their honest debts.

"Between the saddle and the ground
Was mercy asked and pardon found."

A salvation so extemporaneously performed, I fear could not endure; it resembles too closely the winter revivals whose fruits have all disappeared before the summer's harvest is over.

"Nothing, either great or small,
Nothing, sinner, no!
Jesus did, did it all
Long, long ago.
Weary, working, burdened one,
Wherefore toil you so?
Cease your doing, all was done
Long, long ago.
Till to Jesus' work you cling
By a simple faith,
Doing is a deadly thing,
Doing ends in death.
Cast your deadly doing down,
Down at Jesus' feet,
Rise in him, in him alone,
Gloriously complete."

Where are those who have risen in him gloriously complete? Show us just one.

Prayer is Immoral.

It is immoral because it seeks to accomplish certain ends without using the proper means, or it tries to do what reason teaches us cannot be done. When some years ago we had yellow fever at Memphis the praying people all over this country united in supplicating the unknown to remove the plague; but notwithstanding their united petitions to a throne of grace and to "a prayer-answering God," they utterly failed. The yellow fever remained until the angel of frost came and touched the air with its white wings of health.

Fred Douglass said he prayed for freedom twenty years, but received no answer until he prayed with his legs.

"Give us this day our daily bread," is a childish superstition. What millions of poor women have starved to death with this prayer on their lips. Jesus made a prayer in the garden of Gethsemane which was not answered. Now if the son of God may pray and receive no answer, what can the common rank and file sinner expect?

When the native African sees an eclipse, he fancies some huge monster is attempting to devour the sun, or the moon, as the case may be. He resorts to his tom-tom, by which he hopes to frighten away the fearful monster. After the eclipse has passed away he turns to his skeptical brethren and says, "I told you so," just as his more civilized brother who prays for rain, and after it comes, no matter whether it is a day or a month afterward, turns upon his incredulous friends, and asks them triumphantly, "Didn't I tell you so?"

The tom-tom business in Africa and Christian prayers for rain, are on a dead level with each other.

Sinner.—Is God infinite in his wisdom?
Parson.—He is.
Sinner.—Does he at all times know just what ought to be done?
Parson.—He does.
Sinner.—Does he always do just what ought to be done?
Parson.—He does.
Sinner.—Why do you pray to him?
Parson.—Because he is unchangeable. ("Ingersoll's Interviews," p. 83.)

Prayer is simply supplication to God. God is a mystery; a mystery so profound that nothing is known of him, save that he is a mystery. Even his existence cannot be demonstrated. His non-existence is equally undemonstrable, because no man has a definite conception of him to use as a starting point for investigation. Some claim that he is a person, others that he is omnipresent. Both of these cannot be; for personality and omnipresence are incompatible. Prayer is based on the supposition of his personality. It implies necessarily a person in a certain place, and possessed of certain attributes. He must be omnipotent, omniscient, unchangeable, and all-good. Nothing less than this will come up to the conception of what a God should be. Christians tell us God possesses all these attributes. We accept their statement because it is impossible to prove the contrary. On this basis, then let us examine prayer.

God is said to be all goodness. Goodness is the performance of duty. Perfect goodness is the performance of all duty, and of nothing beyond. It is also the performance of all duty without reluctance or hesitation. Prayer is an insult to this quality of God's character. It implies that his goodness is not perfect. Every blessing for which man can ask, it is the duty of God either to grant or to withhold. In either case, prayer implies the possibility of imperfection. To ask God to grant a blessing which it is his duty to grant, is to assume that he will not do his duty without being urged. Such an assumption is downright insolence. To ask for a blessing which it is God's duty to withhold, is to assume that he can be persuaded to commit sin. This, too, can only be regarded as an insult. In both cases prayer is useless, because God is not likely to grant a blessing asked in the same breath an insult is given.

We are told that God is pleased with prayer, because it shows our faith in his goodness. It rather shows our lack of faith. To be continually asking for blessings, implies a doubt whether we shall get them if we do ask. He who never prays shows the most faith, for he takes it for granted that God is good, and if he is good, he will provide for his children unasked. The child has faith that his father will provide for him, but he never asks him to do so. Such conduct would prove him unworthy of his father's care.

So with prayer; the praying man is the true skeptic, and the Infidel is the true believer.

Prayer makes God a changeable being. It implies that he will grant any favor we ask, whether he had previously designed to do so or not. If we were privy to his designs, and knew what blessings he intended to bestow, we could ask only for such as he had intended to give us. In the absence of this knowledge we pray blindly for blessings which it may be, he has determined to withhold. This necessarily implies that he may change his designs. If the object pleaded for is a good one, such a change would be perfectly proper in an earthly monarch. In God it would be fanciful in the extreme. It would place his will at the disposal of a million fallible human beings. It would overthrow the harmony of his government, and replace it by the most reckless chance. Our reception of a blessing would depend no longer on God's goodness; it would depend on whether some other person of greater persuasive power, was or was not asking an opposite blessing at the same time. God would be in constant indecision, and we should be in constant doubt. Prayer, then, is based on the changeableness of an unchangeable being, and therefore valueless.

Prayer, in theory, is based on the supposition of God's personality; prayer, in practice, assumes that God is omnipotent. It supposes that he can be in all places at all times. People are praying at all hours of the day and in all quarters of the globe. To hear them all God must be at such places at such times. To do this he must cease to be a personal being, he must cease to be God. He will then have no intelligence, no volition, for these depend on a personal organization. Prayer, therefore, logically annihilates the being to whom it is addressed.

Prayer implies doubt of the wisdom of God. To pray is to ask for a certain blessing. We assume that such a blessing is best for us, and inform God of the fact. After insulting his goodness by asking for a blessing, we insult his intelligence by specifying what that blessing shall be. Prayers are rarely or never asked for general blessings alone. A person who asks for a blessing and leaves the choice of that blessing wholly to God, is liable to be considered a lunatic by all true believers. Yet to do otherwise is to deny God's omniscience. It assumes that God does not know what our wants are. If God is a rational being, he can only treat such an assumption with contempt. Prayer has been tried for two thousand years and with no result. No prayer has ever been directly or indirectly answered by God. On the contrary, he apparently delighted in mocking those who call upon him. When the Ville du Havre went down, over two hundred ministers were praying for their lives, but in vain. Two girls who trusted not in prayers, but in swimming-belts, alone were saved. ("Logic of Prayer," Charles Stevenson.)

Some years ago when the yellow fever raged at Memphis, Tennessee, the pious people of this country prayed most devoutly to have the plague swept away. These prayers were repeated, were offered up by the most faithful in the Christian ranks, but all in vain. They had read in their Bible that the prayers of the righteous availeth much. They had been taught to believe that "all things whatsoever ye shall ask in prayer, believing, ye shall receive." (Mat. 21: 22.) There is no one thing that Jesus taught more explicitly than this; the prayers of those who truly believe shall be answered. He said:

Therefore I say unto you, What things so ever ye desire when ye pray, believe that ye receive them, and ye *shall have* them. (Mark 21: 24.)

But we see that prayers are not answered. And besides, those prayers which it is claimed are answered carry no proof of the fact with them.

Did not millions of Christians pray for the restoration of President Garfield? How utterly delusive it is to palm off as truth the following promise upon credulous minds:

Again I say unto you that if two of you shall agree on earth as touching anything ye shall ask, it shall be done for them of my Father, which is heaven. (Mat. 18: 19.)

Jesus himself offered a prayer that was not answered. In the garden of Gethsemane he prayed:

O my Father, if it be possible, let this cup pass from me; nevertheless, not as I will, but as thou wilt. (Mat. 26: 39.)

There is no evidence that God has ever interfered in the affairs of men. The hand of earth is stretched uselessly toward heaven. From the clouds there comes no help. In vain the shipwrecked cry to God. In vain the imprisoned ask for liberty and light—the world moves on, and the heavens are deaf and dumb and blind. The frost freezes, the fire burns, slander smites, the wrong triumphs, the good suffer, and prayer dies upon the lips of faith. ("Ingersoll's Interviews," p. 49.)

"Ask and it shall be given thee" is an erroneous and immoral teaching. It is false. It is not true that people get what they pray for. We hear pious persons praying, "Give us this day our daily bread," but none of them expect to get their bread in that way. What an irresistible smile would wrinkle the faces of the devout if a poor widow should pray: "Give us this day our daily coal," and another of the praying circle should ask, "Give us this day our daily potatoes," and another should beg, "Give us this day our daily beefsteak."

While no one expects to get his daily supplies in answer to prayer, yet millions of pious souls are scandalized if you doubt the efficacy of prayer. They will admit that they have to work for their "daily bread," "but after all God gives it to us just the same." He gives it to the sinner who does not pray in the same manner, that is, if he labors he earns his own bread.

In vain the seamstress in her sickness and poverty, prays, "Give us this day our daily bread." She dies with these her last words on her lips.

In vain the noble souls who have been thrown into prison for daring to tell and defend the truth, have fervently appealed to the judge of all the earth for freedom.

In vain the martyr looked to heaven for deliverance.

Faith in Prayer.

"I will close this letter with a little incident, the story of which may not be so startling, but it is true. It is a story of child faith. Johnny Quinlan, of Evanston, has the most wonderful confidence in the efficacy of prayer, but he thinks that prayer does not succeed unless it is accompanied with considerable physical strength. He believes that adult prayer is a good thing, but doubts the efficacy of juvenile prayer.

"He has wanted a Jersey cow for a good while, and tried prayer, but it didn't seem to get to the central office. Last week he went to a neighbor who is a Christian and believer in the efficacy of prayer, also the owner of a Jersey cow.

"'Do you believe that prayer will bring me a yaller Jersey cow?' said Johnny.

"'Why, yes, of course. Prayer will remove mountains. It will do anything.'

"'Well, then, suppose you give me the cow you've got and pray for another one.'" (Bill Nye.)

A Specimen Prayer.

"O Lord, our Heavenly Father, thou who dwellest in heaven [flattery] Thou art the creator and preserver of all things; [flattery] we thank Thee that we live and move and have our being; [Imagine a response of, 'You are quite welcome, I am sure,'] that we are neither dead nor damned—for hadst Thou visited one sin in a thousand, we should be beyond the reach of hope and mercy. [He's not just, or He would have done it.] Thousands of our fellow mortals, as good by nature as we, and far better by practice, are now trying the unalterable laws of an unending eternity. [Not a very good comment on His justice.] Yet we have [by His partiality] still another opportunity to make our calling and election sure. We come before Thee, O Lord, to ask the forgiveness of our sins. [Must have indulgence.] O Lord, look in mercy on us and remember us in thy love. O we pray Thee that Thou wouldst prosper Thy cause. [He hadn't thought of that for sometime before.] O send more laborers into the harvest, for the harvest is great and the laborers are few, [another piece of information.] O Lord, hasten the time when all shall know Thee from the least unto the greatest [We are satisfied that you are not dilligent enough in this matter, and we want you to hurry up.] O Lord, check the progress of evil [You ought to know enough to do it without being told,] and promote the cause of truth, [which you would do, if you were as much interested in the matter as we are.] O Lord, hear our prayer [Do pay attention and don't forget in an hour, like a stupid dolt, what we have been telling you,] and answer our petitions. And in the end, when we are called to die, save us [which on account of our unworthiness, you may not do, or on account of your forgetfulness you may neglect, and leave us the subject of one of the devil's infernal jokes,] and the praise, and the honor, and the glory, we will ascribe through endless ages to Thee. [A great consideration, which will certainly be some inducement to you to save,—only just think what an advantage such an arrangement will be to you.] All of which we ask for Jesus' sake, Amen."

(Newspaper Clipping.)

The Boston Man's Prayer.

"Oh God, if there be a God, save my soul if I have a soul, from hell if there is a hell, Amen, if it is necessary."

Prayer an Echo.

'From the earliest dawn of Nature's birth,
Since sorrow and sin first darkened the earth;
From sun to sun, from pole to pole,
Where'er the waves of Humanity roll,
The breezy robe this planet wears
Has quivered and echoed with countless prayers.
Each hour a million knees are bent,
A million prayers to heaven are sent;
There's not a summer beam but sees
Some humble suppliant on his knees;
There's not a breeze that murmurs by
But wafts some faithful prayer on high;

There's not a woe afflicts our race
But someone bears to the Throne of Grace;
And for every temptation our souls may meet
We ask for grace at the Mercy Seat.

* * * * * * * * *

The beams smile on, and heaven serene
Still bends, as though no prayers had been;
And the breezes moan, as still they wave,
When man is powerless, heaven cannot save."
—CHARLES STEVENSON.

Other Worldliness.

It seems to some people selfish for one to attempt to live in the personal enjoyment of this world, but to lend all one's energies toward gaining heaven is to them just right. Caring for one's health and family is selfishness, but struggling to save one's soul is the noblest work of life.

The truth is Christian doctrines are purely selfish. When man does certain duties, as they are called, because he wants to get to heaven, his conduct is intensely selfish. The gospel constantly invites the followers of Jesus to act, from the consideration that "great is your reward in heaven." Very many Christians say that if it were not for the hope of future reward, they would not try to do right. In other words they confess that they do not act from moral motives. They are moved by the selfish motives of other worldliness. To act morally we must do right because it is right and for no other consideration. When we look beyond the act to see how much we are going to make out of it, then our conduct is not moral. He who is going through the performance of duties because he wants to get to heaven, has yet to learn the meaning of morality.

Christianity is Intolerant.

Revelation does not admit of two sides to religious questions. There is only one side say the Moodys and Talmages, and that side is God's side. We have no right to question Holy Writ. We *must* accept it. "Believe or be damned," does not admit of the latitude of free thought, or the right of reason to question the authority of the Bible.

"Reason is 'carnal' says the Christian idolator, and you cannot rely upon it—only trust in Jesus and you are saved."

The following historical facts prove beyond question that intolerance is the very soul of Christianity:

"When any step was taken to establish a system of permanent institutions, which might effectually protect liberty from the invasions of power in general, the church *always* ranged herself on the side of *despotism*." (Guizot's "History of Civilization in Europe," p. 154.)

"Persecution for religious heterodoxy, in all its degrees, was in the sixteenth century, the principle as well as the practice of every church." (Hallam's "Middle Ages," vol. 2, p. 48.)

When Queen Mary, the first queen of England, had burned Latimer, Ridley and others, and her ministers had chided her for it, she replied that she did not think God could be angry with her for burning the heretics a few hours in this world, for their heresy, since he was going to burn them eternally in the next world for the same thing.

Here you have the unadulerated article. It is nothing, if not intolerant, and in every age and country, with sword and hand, has commanded the trembling people to believe or be damned. And the Christian who does not do his utmost toward having heretics and infidels burned at the stake, is trying to be better than his God.

Hell, Hades, Gehenna, Sheol.

How many mortals have been frightened out of their senses by the false alarm of fire in the next world. Preachers have pictured to mothers their children who died without the sacraments of the church being administered to them, as rolling on the fiery billows of hell. Parents have been demented by such descriptions, and have gone to lunatic asylums, or to their graves in consequence. Millions thus frightened have joined the church, and confessed belief in the creed, although they may not have known the meaning of a single article of it. But once having avowed their adherence to the church have lived lives of hypocrisy ever afterward because they had not the honor and the courage to break away from their bondage. What stories the pulpit has related of Infidels being struck dead for profanity and blasphemy. These holy pulpit alarmists will have much to answer for if there is any such thing as a judgment day or a God in Israel.

It is plain that Jesus taught the doctrine of future, if not endless punishment. It was endless punishment to those who committed the unpardonable sin: "And whosoever speaketh a word against the Son of man, it shall be forgiven him; but whosoever speaketh against the Holy Ghost, it shall not be forgiven him, neither in this world, neither in the world to come." (Mat. 12: 32.)

Other passages may be cited to show that Jesus taught the horrible doctrine of eternal torment, and all efforts on the part of modern commentators to explain away hell are in vain. "And these shall go away into everlasting punishment, but the righteous into life eternal." (Mat. 25: 46.)

If these words do not teach the doctrine of endless torment, it would be a hard matter to express it in the vernacular.

Pictures of Hell.

John Bunyan describes this interesting locality, and its inhabitants thus: "All the devils in hell will be with thee howling and roaring, screeching and yelling in such a manner that thou wilt be at thy wits end, and be ready to run stark mad from anguish and torment. * * *Here* thou must lie and *fry*, and *scorch*, and *broil*, and *burn forevermore*."

The father of New England theology, Jonathan Edwards, portrays his own imagination after this fashion:

"The saints in glory will be far more sensible, how dreadful the wrath of God is, and will better understand how terrible the sufferings of the damned are, yet this will be no occasion of grief to them, but *rejoicings*. They will not be sorry for the damned: it will cause no uneasiness or disatisfaction to them, but on the contrary when they see this sight, it will occasion *rejoicing*, and excite them to *joyful praises*."

Dr. Emmons reveals his own "true inwardness" by giving it the following description:

"The happiness of the elect in heaven will in part consist of watching the torment of the damned in hell. Among these it may be their own children, parents, husbands, wives and friends on earth. One part of the business of the blest is to celebrate the doctrine of reprobation. While the decree of reprobation is eternally executing on the vessels of wrath, the smoke of their torment will be eternally ascending in view of the vessels of mercy who instead of taking the part of those miserable objects will sing, *Amen, hallelujah: praise the Lord.*"

Again, he says: "When they (the saints) see how great the misery is from which God hath saved them and how great a difference he hath made between their state and the state of others who were by nature, and perhaps by practice no more sinful and ill deserving than they, it will give them more a sense of the wonderfulness of God's grace to them in making them so to differ. The sight of *hell-torments* will exalt the *happiness* of the *saints forever*."

> "Where saints and angels from their blest abode,
> Chanting loud hallelujahs to their God.
> Look down on sinners in the realm of woe
> And draw fresh *pleasures* from the scenes *below*."

The Rev. Thomas Button, describes the bottomless character of his fancies thus:

"The godly wife shall applaud the justice of the judge in the condemnation of her ungodly husband. The godly husband shall say, Amen! to the damnation of her who lay in his bosom. The godly parent shall say hallelujah! at the passing of the sentence upon the ungodly child. And the godly child, shall from his heart, approve the damnation of his wicked parents who begot him, and the mother who bore him."

Thomas Vincent, a reverend, raves after this fashion: "This will fill them, the saints, with astonishing *admiration* and *joy*, when they see some of their near relatives going to hell; their fathers, their mothers, their children, their husbands, their wives, their human friends, and companions while they themselves are saved. * * * Those affections they now have for relatives *out* of Christ will *cease*, and they will not have the least trouble to see them sentenced to hell and thrust into the fiery furnace."

> My thoughts on awful subjects roll,
>   Damnation and the dead;
> What horrors seize the guilty soul
>   Upon a dying bed.
>
> Where endless crowds of sinners lie,
>   And darkness makes their chains;
> Tortured with keen despair they cry,
>   Yet wait for fiercer pains.
>
> Then swift and dreadful she descends
>   Down to the fiery coast
> Amongst abominable fiends,
>   Herself a frighted ghost.

> Adore and tremble, for your God
>   Is a consuming fire;
> His jealous eyes with wrath inflame,
>   And raise his vengeance higher.
> Almighty vengeance, how it burns!
>   Vast magazines of plagues and storms
> Lie treasured for his foes.

These grisly rhymes full of horrors are found in one of Watt's hymn books written in England in the early part of the last century, but they are omitted from all modern hymn books.

Tertullian finds great joy in the idea of seeing his enemies in hell.

"What shall be the magnitude of that scene! How shall I laugh! How shall I rejoice! How shall I triumph when I behold so many and such illustrious kings, who were said to have mounted into heaven, groaning with Jupiter their god, in the lowest darkness of hell." (Quoted by Lecky, "Rationalism in Europe," vol. 1, p. 329.)

"One great objection to the Old Testament is the cruelty said to have been commanded by God, but all the cruelties recounted in the Old Testament ceased with death. The vengeance of Jehovah stopped at the portal of the tomb. He never threatened to avenge himself upon the dead; and not one word, from the first mistake in Genesis to the last curse of Malachi, contains the slightest intimation that God will punish in another world. It was reserved for the New Testament to make known the frightful doctrine of eternal pain. It was the teacher of universal benevolence who rent the vail between time and eternity, and fixed the horrified gaze of man on the lurid gulfs of hell. Within the breast of non-resistance was coiled the worm that never dies." (Ingersoll's Reply to Black.)

"Is it necessary that heaven should borrow its light from the glare of hell? Infinite punishment is infinite cruelty, endless injustice, immortal meanness. To worship an eternal gaoler hardens, debases, and pollutes the soul. While there is one sad and breaking heart in the universe, no perfectly good being can be perfectly happy. Against the heartlessness of this doctrine every grand and generous soul should enter its solemn protest. I want no part in any heaven where the saved, the ransomed, and the redeemed drown with merry shout the cries and sobs of hell—in which happiness forgets misery—where the tears of the lost increase laughter and deepen the dimples of joy. The idea of hell was born of ignorance, brutality, fear, cowardice, and revenge. This idea tends to show that our remote ancestors were the lowest beasts. Only from dens, lairs, and caves—only from mouths filled with cruel fangs—only from hearts of fear and hatred—only from the conscience of hunger and lust—only from the lowest and most debased, could come this most cruel, heartless, and absurd of all dogmas." (Ingersoll's Reply to Black.)

"A religion that teaches a mother that she can be happy in heaven, with her children in hell—in everlasting torment—strikes at the very roots of family affection. It makes the human heart stone. Love that means no more than that, is not love at all. No heart that has ever loved can see the object of its affection in pain, and itself be happy. The thing is impossible. Any religion that can make that possible is more to be dreaded than war or famine or pestilence or death. It would eat out all that is great and beautiful and good in this life. It would make life a mockery and love a curse." (Helen H. Gardener's "Men, Women, and Gods.")

"They divided the world into saints and sinners, and all the saints were going to heaven, and all the sinners yonder. Now, then, you stand in the presence of a great disaster. A house is on fire, and there is seen at a window the frightened face of a woman with a babe in her arms, appealing for help; humanity cries out, "Will some one go to the rescue?" They do not ask for a Methodist, Baptist, or a Catholic; they ask for a man. All at once there starts from the crowd one that nobody ever suspected of being a saint; one may be, with a bad reputation; but he goes up the ladder and is lost in the smoke and flame; and a moment after he emerges, and the great circles of flames hiss around him; in a moment more he has reached the window; in another moment, with the woman and child in his arms, he reaches the ground and gives his fainting burden to the bystanders, and the people all stand hushed for a moment, as they always do at such times, and then the air is rent with acclamations. Tell me that that man is going to be sent to hell, to eternal flames, who is willing to risk his life rather than a woman and child should suffer from the fire one moment! I despise that doctrine of hell! Any man that believes in eternal hell is afflicted with at least two diseases petrifaction of the heart and putrefaction of the brain." (Ingersoll's "Ghosts.")

The Church Opposed to Progress.

"The church has opposed every reform and until quite recently, almost every useful invention. In the England of Elizabeth it was declared from the pulpit that the introduction of forks would demoralize the people and provoke the divine wrath." ("Martyrdom of Man," p. 38.)

In the year 1444 Caxton published the first book ever printed in England. In 1474 the then bishop of London, in a convocation of his clergy, said, "If we do not destroy this dangerous invention it will one day destroy us." That bishop was a prophet.

Hume says: "It was remarkable that no physician in Europe, who had reached the age of forty years, ever to the end of his life adopted Harvey's doctrine of the circulation of the blood, and that his practice in London diminished extremely, from the reproach drawn on him by that great and signal discovery. So slow is the progress in every science even when not opposed by factitious and superstitious prejudices." (Hume's "History of England.")

When Buffon had published Natural History, in which was included his "Theory of the Earth," he was officially informed by the faculty of theology in Paris that several of his propositions were "reprehensible and contrary to the creed of the church."

And when Columbus asserted the rotundity of the earth, he was ridiculed by the clergy, who maintained that "everything would roll off on the other side and be consumed in the fires of hell, if the world should turn over."

Benjamin Franklin's experiments with the lightning, were condemned, as he was only invoking upon himself the wrath of an angry God.

Professor Morse was freely ridiculed by the clergy for his attempt to construct a telegraph.

Roger Bacon, who invented spectacles and improved the telescope, was accused of having "sold himself to the devil."

It is scarcely necessary to recall the persecutions of Copernicus, Bruno, and Galileo on account of their discoveries in astronomy.

At Eaton, in Shelly's time, "Chemistry was a forbidden thing."

We read in the life of Locke that "there was a meeting of the heads of the houses of Oxford, where it was proposed to censure and discourage the reading of this essay (On the Human Understanding) and after various debates, it was concluded that without any public censure each head of a house should endeavor to prevent its being read in his own college." (Spencer's "Social Statics," p. 375.)

"With respect to the last, the grandest of all human undertakings (that is the circumnavigation of the earth) it is to be remembered that Catholicism had irrevocably committed itself to the dogma of a flat earth, with the sky as a floor of heaven, and hell in the under world." (Draper's "Conflict," p. 294.)

The clergy for years have ridiculed Darwinism, and scouted the philosophy of evolution, even after the best minds of Europe had accepted it. But after all their ridicule of Darwinism, when Darwin had passed away the great heart of England did not fail to show the esteem in which the people at large held him, but lovingly laid his remains to rest in Westminster abbey with the dust of her noblest dead.

It is in the very nature of Christianity to persecute. It cannot live on terms of equality with anything on earth. It must rule. It must be supreme, and all institutions and all individuals must obey its mandates. It has in all of its vocabulary no such word as liberty. Every knee must bow to it, every tongue confess its authority, and every pocket —pay it tithes. And so gigantic has been its power that its power that obedience in every age has been almost universal. Millions have professed to obey the despot who have had no idea of what they were professing, and hence had not so much even as a dream of liberty. Poor man has been trampled in the dust, and sometimes used as food for cannon, to satisfy the ambition of pope or king, and when not serviceable in that way, he was forced to worship God and serve the priests.

"Let every soul be subject unto the higher powers." (Rom. 13: 1.) That is, the higher powers are the priests. The commandments of these higher powers are expressed in such words as "submit," "obey," "serve," "pay tithes," "believe,"—and to heed them is to lose the higher opportunities of manhood.

PROTESTANT PERSECUTIONS.

William Cobbett on the English Church.—A Letter to Lord Tenderten, Lord Chief Justice of England, April 6, 1829.

"*My Lord:* I have read the report of your lordship's speech made on the 4th inst. on the second reading of the Catholic bill; and there is one passage of it on which I think it my duty thus publicly to remark. The passage to which I allude relates to the *character* of the *law* established church, and also to the probable fate that will, in consequence of this bill, attend her in Ireland.

"First, then, my lord, let us take your proposition 'that there is no church so tolerant as this.' I am sure your lordship has never read her history; I am sure you have not. If you had you never would have uttered these words. Not being content to deal in general terms, I will not say she has been, and was from the outset, the most intolerant church that the world ever saw; that she started at first armed with halters, ripping-knives, axes, and racks; that her footsteps were marked with blood, while her back bent under the plunder of her innumerable innocent victims; and that for refinement in cruelty and extent of rapacity she never had an equal, whether corporate or sole. I will not thus speak of her in general terms, but I will lay before your lordship some historical *facts*, to make good that *contradiction* which I have given to your words. I assert that this law-church is the most *intolerant* church I ever read or heard of; and this assertion I now proceed to make good.

"This church began to exist in 1547, and in the reign of Edward VI. Until now the religion of the country had been for several years, under the tyrant Henry VIII., a sort of mongrel; but now it became wholly Protestant by *law*. The Articles of Religion and the Common Prayer-book were now drawn up, and were established by acts of Parliament. The Catholic altars were pull down in all the churches; the priests, on pain of ouster and fine, were compelled to teach the new religion, that is to say, to be apostates; and the people who had been born and bred Catholics were not only punished if they heard mass, but were also punished if they did not go to hear the new parsons; that is to say, if they refused to become apostates. The people, smarting under this tyranny, rose in insurrection in several parts, and, indeed, all over the country. They complained that they had been robbed of their religion, and of the relief to the poor which the old church gave; and they demanded that the mass and the monasteries should be restored, and that the priests should not be allowed to marry. And how were they answered? The bullet and bayonet at the hands of German troops slaughtered a part, caused another part to be imprisoned and flogged, and the remainder to submit, outwardly, at least, to the law-church. And now mark this tolerant and merciful church. Many of the old monastics and priests, who had been expelled from their convents and livings, were compelled to beg their bread about the country, and thus found subsistence among the pious Catholics. This was an eye-sore to the law-church, who deemed the very existence of these men, who refused to apostatize, a libel on her. Therefore, in company, actually in company with the law that founded the new church came forth a law to punish beggars, by burning them in the face with a red-hot iron and by making them slaves for two years, with power in their masters to make them wear an iron collar. Your lordship must have read this act of Parliament, passed in the first year of the first Protestant reign, and coming forth in company with the Common Prayer-book. This was tolerant work, to be sure; and fine proof we have here of this church being 'favorable to civil and religious liberty.' Not content with stripping these faithful Catholic priests of their livings; not content with turning them out upon the wide world; this tolerant church must cause them to perish with hunger or be branded slaves.

"Such was the tolerant spirit of this church when she was young. As to her burnings under Cranmer (who made the prayer book), they are hardly worthy of particular notice, when we have before us the sweeping cruelties of this first Protestant reign, during which, short as it was, the people of England suffered so much that the suffering actually thinned their numbers; it was a people partly destroyed, and that, too, in the space of about six years; and this is acknowledged even in acts of Parliament of that day. But this law-church was established in reality during the reign of Elizabeth, which lasted forty-five years; that is, from 1558 to 1603; and though this church has always kept up its character, even to the present day, its deeds during this long reign are the most remarkable.

"Elizabeth established what she called 'a court of high commission' consisting chiefly of bishops of your lordship's 'most tolerant church,' in order to punish all who did not conform to her religious creed, she being 'the head of the church.' This commission was empowered to have control over the 'opinions' of all men, and to punish all men according to their 'discretion, short of death.' They had power to extort evidence by prison or the rack. They had power to compel a man (on oath) to 'reveal his thoughts,' and to 'accuse his friend, brother, parent, wife, or child;' and this, too, on 'pain of death.' These monsters, in order to 'discover priests,' and to crush the old religion, 'fined, imprisoned, racked,' and did such things as would have made Nero shudder to think of. They sent hundreds to the rack in order to get from them confessions, 'on which confession many of them were put to death.'

"I have not room to make even an enumeration of the deeds of religious persecution during this long and 'tolerant' reign; but I will state a few of them:

1. It was *death* to make a new Catholic priest within the kingdom.

2. It was *death* for a Catholic priest to come into the kingdom from abroad.

3. It was *death* to harbor a Catholic priest coming from abroad.

4. It was *death* to confess to such a priest.

5. It was *death* for any priest to say mass.

6. It was *death* for any one to hear mass.

7. It was *death* to *deny*, or *not* to swear, if called on, that this woman was the head of the church of Christ.

8. It was an offense (punishable by heavy fine) *not* to go to the *Protestant* church. This fine was £20 a lunar month, or £250 a year, and of our present money £3,250 a year. Thousands upon thousands refused to go to the law-church; and thus the *head* of the church sacked thousands upon thousands of estates! The poor conscientious Catholics who refused to go to the 'most tolerant church,' and who had no money to pay fines, were crammed into the jails until the counties petitioned to be relieved from keeping them. They were then discharged, being first publicly whipped, and having their ears bored with a red-hot iron. But this very great 'toleration' not answering the purpose, an act was passed to banish for life all these non-goers to church, if they were not worth twenty pounds, and, in case of return they were to be punished with death.

"I am, my lord, not making loose assertions here; I am all along stating from acts of Parliament, and the above form a small sample of the whole; and this your lordship must know well. I am not declaiming, but relating undeni-

PROTESTANT PERSECUTIONS. 325

ble facts; with facts of the same character, with a *bare list*, made in the above manner, I could fill a considerable volume. The names of the persons put to death merely for being Catholics, during this long and dreary reign, would, especially if we were to include Ireland, form a list ten times as long as that of our army and navy, both taken together. The usual mode of inflicting death was to hang the victim for a short time, just to benumb his or her faculties, then cut down and instantly rip open the belly, and tear out the heart, and hold it up, fling the bowels into the fire, then chop off the head, and cut the body into quarters, then boil the head and quarters, and then hang them up at the gates of cities, or other conspicuous places. This was done, including Ireland, to many hundreds of persons, merely for adhering to the church in which they had been born and bred. There were one hundred and eighty-seven ripped up and boiled in England in the years from 1577 to 1603; that is to say, in the last twenty-six years of Elizabeth's reign; and these might all have been spared if they would have agreed to go to church and hear the Common Prayer! All, or nearly all of them were racked before they were put to death; and the cruelties in prison, and the manner of execution, were the most horrible that can be conceived. They were flung into dungeons, kept in their filth, and fed on bullock's liver, boiled and unwashed tripe, and such things as dogs are fed on. Edwards Genings, a priest, detected in saying mass in Holborn, was after sentence of death offered his pardon if he would go to church; but having refused to do this, and having at the place of execution boldly said that he would die a thousand deaths rather than acknowledge the Queen to be the spiritual head of the church, Topliffe, the attorney-general, ordered the rope to be cut the moment the victim was turned off, 'so that' (says this historian) 'the priest being little or nothing stunned, stood on his feet casting his eyes toward heaven, till the hangman tripped up his heels, and flung him on the block, where he was ripped up and quartered.' **He was so** much alive even after the boweling that he cried with a loud voice, 'Oh! it smarts!' And then he exclaimed, '*Sancte Gregorie, ora pro me*,' while the hangman having sworn a most wicked oath cried, 'Zounds! his heart is in my hand, and yet Gregory is in his mouth!'"—Wm. Cobbett.

"For centuries the Irish were killed like game. We know not a few good Englishmen who would be convulsed with the story of the murder of Smith or Jones, but whom the killing of an O'Tool or O'Dacherty, or any 'O'' or 'Mac' would not move in the least. That be it remembered in 1825. The collection of tithes alone cost a million lives. Henry VIII. aggravated all the outrages ever committed, and was determined the faith of the Irish should undergo a radical Protestant conversion. Raleigh butchered Limerick garrison in cold blood after Lord Grey had selected seven hundred to be hanged. James I. confiscated one-tenth of all the land in Ireland and destroyed thousands of lives for religion's sake. Protestant rectors kept private prisons for confining all who dissented from their faith. Dr. Leland, a Protestant clergyman, wrote that the favorite object of the English Parliament was the total extermination of all the Catholics in Ireland.

"Cromwell began by massacreing for three days the garrison of Drogheda after quarter had been promised. Whole towns were put up and sold. The Catholics were banished from three-fourths of Ireland and confined to Connaught, and after a certain day every one found outside were shot or hung. Fleetwood, the reverend, said the Lord will appear in this work. On every wolf's scalp and priest's head a premium of £5 was offered! Young girls and boys were gathered up by the thousands and carried to the West Indies. So by 1652 was once populous Ireland so devastated that an occupied house was a curiosity and commented on. Says one writer, S. W. Petry, 'There perished in 1641 over six hunderd thousand lives whose blood somebody must atone to God for.'" (Newspaper article.)

"The sword of the church was unsheathed and the world was at the mercy of ignorant and infuriated priests, whose eyes feasted on the agonies they inflicted. Acting as they believed, or pretended to believe, under the command of God; stimulated by the hope of infinite reward in another world—hating heretics with every drop of their bestial blood; savage beyond description; merciless beyond conception—these infamous priests in a kind of frenzied joy, leaped upon the helpless victims of their rage. They crushed their bones in iron boots; tore their quivering flesh with iron hooks and pincers; cut off their lips and eyelids; pulled out their nails, and into the bleeding quick thrust needles; tore out their tongues; extinguished their eyes; stretched them upon racks; flayed them alive; crucified them with their heads downward; exposed them to wild beasts; burned them at the stake; mocked their cries and groans; ravished their wives; robbed their children, and then prayed God to finish the holy work in hell. Millions upon millions were sacrificed upon the altars of bigotry. The Catholic burned the Lutheran, the Lutheran burned the Catholic, the Episcopalian tortured the Presbyterian, the Presbyterian tortured the Episcopalian. Every denomination killed all it could of every other, and each Christian felt in duty bound to exterminate every other Christian who denied the smallest fraction of his creed. . . . . They have imprisoned and murdered each other, and the wives and children of each other. In the name of God every possible crime has been committed, every conceivable outrage has been perpetrated. Brave men, tender and loving women, beautiful girls, and prattling babes have been exterminated in the name of Jesus Christ. For more than fifty generations the church has carried the black flag. Her vengeance has been measured only by her power. During all these years of infamy no heretic has ever been forgiven. With the heart of a fiend she has hated; with the clutch of avarice she has grasped; with the jaws of a dragon she has devoured; pitiless as famine; merciless as fire; with conscience of a serpent; such is the history of the church of God." (Ingersoll's "Heretics and Heresies.")

THE PURITANS INTOLERANT.

Capital Laws of Connecticut, Established by the General Court, December 1, 1642.

1. If any man after legal conviction shall have or worship any other God but the Lord God, he shall be put to death. (Deut. 13: 6; 17: 2, 3, and Ex. 22: 20.)

2. If any man or woman be a witch (that is, hath or consulteth with a familiar spirit) they shall be put to death." (Ex. 20: 18; Lev. 20: 27; Deut. 18: 10, 11.)

3. If any person shall blaspheme the name of God, the Father, Son or Holy Ghost, with direct, express, presumptuous, or high-handed blasphemy, or shall curse God in the like manner, he shall be put to death. (Lev. 24: 15, 16.)

4. If any person shall commit any wilful murder, which is manslaughter committed upon malice, hatred, or cruelty, not in a man's necessary and just defense nor by mere casualty against his will, he shall be put to death. (Ex. 21: 12, 13, 14; Numb. 35: 30, 31.)

5. If any person shall slay another through guile, either by poisoning, or other such devilish practice, he shall be put to death. (Ex. 21: 14.)

6. If any man or woman shall lie with a beast or brute creature, by carnal copulation, they shall surely be put to death, and the beast shall be slain and buried. (Lev. 20: 15, 16.)

7. If any man lie with mankind as he lieth with a woman, both of them have committed abomination, they both shall surely be put to death. (Lev. 20: 13.)

8. If any person committeth adultery with a married or espoused wife, the adulterer and the adulteress shall surely be put to death. (Lev. 20: 10; 18: 20; Deut. 22: 23, 24.)

9. If any man shall forcibly and without consent ravish a maid or woman, that is lawfully married or contracted, he shall be put to death. (Deut. 22: 25.)

10. If any man shall steal a man or mankind, he shall be put to death. (Ex. 21: 16.)

11. If any man rise up by false witnesses, wittingly and of purpose to take away any man's life he shall be put to death. (Deut. 19: 16, 18, 19.)

12. If any man shall conspire or attempt any invasion, insurrection, or rebellion against the commonwealth, he shall be put to death.

"All these are copied from the capital laws of Massachusetts, established (with her Body of Liberties) December, 1641,—except the ninth (against rape of a married or betrothed woman), which was enacted by Massachusetts in June, 1642. One of the Massachusetts laws punished *manslaughter* with death, was not adopted by Connecticut, and only the first clause of the Massachusetts law against *conspiracy*, *rebellion*, etc. was taken." ("Blue Laws, True and False," by Trumbull.)

"December 1642, two additional capital laws were added to the statute of Connecticut." (Ibid. p. 59.)

13. If any child or children about 16 years old and of sufficient understanding, shall curse or smite their natural father or mother, he, or they shall be put to death, unless it can be sufficiently testified that the parents have been unchristianly negligent in the education of such children or so provoke them by extreme and cruel correction that they have been forced thereunto, to *preserve* themselves from death or maiming. (Ex. 21: 17, 15; Lev. 20: 9.)

14. If a man have a stubborn and rebellious son of sufficient years and understanding, namely, 16 years of age, which will not obey the voice of his father or mother, and that when they have chastened him, will not hearken to them, then may his father and mother, being his natural parents, lay hold on him, and bring him to the magistrates assembled in court and testify unto them that their son is stubborn and rebellious and will not obey their voice and chastisement, but lives in sundry notorious crimes, such a son shall be put to death. (Deut. 21: 20, 21.)

"Persuade men that when ascribing to the Deity justice and mercy, they are speaking of qualities generally distinct from those which exist among mankind—qualities which we are altogether unable to conceive, and which may be compatible with acts which men would term grossly unjust and unmerciful; tell them that guilt may be entirely unconnected with a personal act that millions of infants may be called into existence for a moment to be precipitated into a place of torment, that vast nations may live and die, and then be rased again to endure never-ending punishment, because they did not believe in a religion of which they never heard, or because a crime was committed thousands of years before they were in existence; convince them that all this is part of a transcendentally perfect and righteous scheme, and there is no imaginable abyss to which such a doctrine would not lead." (Lecky's "Rationalism in Europe," vol. 1, p. 384.)

Lecky proceeds to show that men who believe in salvation by the church will always persecute dissenters, and all history attests the truth of his remarks. Catholics persecuted Protestants; Protestants persecuted Puritans; and Puritans, in there turn, persecuted other dissenters. Nor did the work stop here; though limited in their power, yet these dissenters even to-day find ways by which they can persecute dissenters from them without resort to physical means. There was not, two centuries ago, a single sect that did not uphold persecution.

Galileo.

"For sixteen years the church had rest. But in 1632 Galileo ventured on the publication of his work entitled 'The System of the World,' its object being the vindication of the Copernican doctrine. He was again summoned before the Inquisition at Rome, accused of having asserted that the earth moves around the sun. He was declared to have brought upon himself the penalty of heresy. On his knees with his hand on the Bible, he was compelled to abjure, and curse the doctrine of the movement of the earth. What a spectacle! This venerable man, the most illustrous of his age, forced by the threat of death to deny facts which his judges as well as himself knew to be true! He was then committed to prison, treated with remorseless severity during the remaining ten years of his life, and he was denied burial in consecrated ground. Must not that be false which requires for its support so much imposture, so much barbarity? The opinions thus defended by the Inquisition are now objects of derision to the whole civilized world." (Draper's "Conflict Between Religion and Science.")

Bruno.

"On the 17th of February, 1600, a vast concourse of people was assembled in the largest open space in Rome, gathered together by the irresistible sympathy which men always feel, with the terrible and tragic in human existence. In the center stood a huge pile of faggots, from out its logs and branches rose a stake, crowding around the pile were eager and expectant faces, men of various ages and of various characters, but all for one moment united in a common feeling of malignant triumph, religion was about to be avenged; a heretic was coming to expiate on that spot the crime of open defiance to the dogmas proclaimed by the church—the crime of teaching that the earth moved, and that there was an infinity of worlds. The stake is erected for the 'maintenance and defense of the holy church, and the rights and liberties of the same.' Whom does the crowd await? Giordano Bruno—the poet, philosopher, and heretic—the teacher of Galileo's heresy—the friend of Sir Philip Sidney, and the open antagonist of Aristotle. A hush comes over the crowd. The procession solemnly advances, the soldiers peremptorily clearing the way for it. His face is placid though pale. They offer him the crucifix; he turns his head; he *refuses to kiss it!* 'The heretic!' They show him the image of him who died upon the cross for the sake of the living truth—he refuses the symbol! A yell bursts from the multitude.

"They chain him to the stake. He remains silent. Will he not pray for mercy? Will he not recant? Now the last hour has arrived—will he die in his obstinacy, when a little hypocracy would save him from so much agony? It is even so; he is stubborn and unalterable. They light the faggots; the branches crackle; the flame ascends; the victim writhes—and now we see him no more. The smoke envelopes him; but not a prayer, not a plaint, not a single cry escapes him. In a little while the wind has scattered the ashes of Giordano Bruno." (G. H. Lewes's "History of Philosophy.")

"What a contrast between this scene of manly honor, of unshaken firmness, of inflexible adherence to the truth, and that other scene which took place more than fifteen centuries previously by the fireside in the hall of Caiaphas the high priest, when the cock crew, and 'the Lord turned and looked upon Peter.' (Luke 22: 61.) And yet it is upon Peter that the church has grounded her right to act as she did to Bruno.

"But perhaps the day is approaching when posterity will offer an expiation for this great ecclesiastical crime, and a statue of Bruno be unveiled under the dome of St. Peter's at Rome." (Draper's "Conflict Between Religion and Science.")

"A divine revelation must necessarily be intolerant of contradiction; it must repudiate all improvement in itself, and view with disdain that arising from the progressive intellectual development of man." (Draper's "Conflict Between Religion and Science.")

Torture.

"The system (of mediæval tortures) was matured under the mediæval habit of thought, it was adopted by the inquistors, and it received its finishing touches from their ingenuity. *In every prison the crucifix and the rack stood side by side, and in almost every country the abolition of torture was at last effected by a movement which the church opposed, and by men whom she cursed.*" (Lecky's "Rationalism in Europe," vol. 1, p. 333.)

"But the most powerful consideration with a truly benevolent man, if he be a Christian, for the extirpation of heresy by force, is the belief that its unfortunate victims will suffer unending torments in hell. Not for a few days, not for a few years must they suffer, but *forever*. Under the burden of such an awful thought can the sincere, kindhearted Christian fold his arms and look calmly upon the efforts of men who are spreading unbelief or heresy in every direction, who are not only going to hell themselves, but are taking with them thousands of their fellow men. Is it not natural that the sincere Christian, having the power, should suppress such opinions? that if necessary he should resort to coercive measures? that if new heresies are constantly springing up he should punish some of the offenders with severity, and thereby endeavor to deter others from leaving the true faith? Under the influence of such a faith, must not the desire for the suppression of the heresy be a measure of the desire for the suppression of the most injurious and dangerous errors? and will not the zeal to destroy them be in proportion to the love of truth and regard for the welfare of humanity? Will not, therefore, the most sincere, earnest, and devoted Christians, in an age of unquestioning faith, be the most active and zealous persecutors? On *a priori* grounds we cannot help arriving at such a conclusion, and the facts of history attest the correctness of the conclusion thus arrived at from a consideration of the natural effects of the doctrine that certain opinions involve merit and others guilt.

It has been shown by Llorente that the men who founded the Inquisition were men whose characters were free from the stains of vice, and who were actuated in their cruel work of torturing and burning men, by the most philanthropic motives. Many of the worst persecutors, Catholic and Protestant alike, as Mr. Buckle has mentioned, have been among the most conscientious of men and women.

Their cruelty was the result of their faith. What, they argued, are the fleeting pains of a few thousand men compared with the eternal agony of the thousands and tens of thousands they will, unless checked, lead to hell. Thus argued the Christians when they first obtained power and used it in killing Pagans; thus argued the Catholics of the Middle Ages; thus argued the Protestants of Geneva; thus argued the advocates of Episcopacy, the defenders of the Kirk of Scotland, and the pious Puritans of New England. In proportion as men believe that correct theological beliefs involve merit and are essential to salvation, and that theological errors involve guilt and are punished with torments in hell, and have power, they must be persecutors. Such has been the case in the past. It was only when rationalism, acting in opposition to the church, rendered persecution impossible, that theologians discovered that the punishment of men was at variance with their religion. 'With the merits of this pleasing though tardy conversion,' says Lecky, 'I am not now concerned; but few persons, I think, can follow the history of Christian persecution without a feeling of extreme astonishment that some modern writer, not content with maintaining that the doctrine of exclusive salvation ought not to have produced persecution, have ventured, in defiance of unanimous testimony of theologians of so many centuries, to dispute the plain historical fact that it did produce it." ("History of Morals," vol. 1, p. 422.)

"But independently of the influence of the Old Testament teachings, the Christian system makes persecution inevitable in proportion as the system is believed. Intolerance and persecution are a natural result of the doctrine that certain religious opinions involve moral guilt. The Bible declares, 'He that believeth and is baptized shall be saved; he that believeth not shall be damned.' This makes unbelief and heresy a crime, and unbelievers and heretics criminals. It makes it the religious duty of Christians to legislate for the extirpation of the former and the punishment of the latter. Can men treat with charity and kindness those with whom they believe God is displeased—those who are spreading doctrines that are regarded as plainly an offense to God? Is it not the wish of God that unbelief and heresy should be destroyed, and, as an obedient subject, is it not natural that the Christian should, as far as possible, carry out the wishes of the God he worships?

The New Testament Teaches Intolerance.

"'He that believeth not shall be damned.' (Mark 16: 16.) St. Paul exclaims (Galatians 1), 'If any man preach any other gospel unto you than that ye have received, let him be accursed.' He also says (1 Tim. 6), 'If any man teach otherwise, and consent not to the wholesome words, even the words of our Lord Jesus Christ . . he is proud, knowing nothing . . from such withdraw thyself.' 'Of whom (1 Tim. 1) is Hymenæus and Alexander; whom I have delivered unto Satan, that they may learn not to blaspheme.' In these passages persecution and punishment are clearly taught for disbelief. And that such teaching has had an immoral tendency the excommunications, the imprisonments, and sacrifice of the lives of heretics in connection with the history of Christianity abundantly prove."—B. F. Underwood.

"Are men restrained by superstition? Are men restrained by what you call religion? I used to think they were not; now I admit they are. No man has ever been restrained from the commission of a real crime, but from an artificial one he has. There was a man who committed murder. They got the evidence, but he confessed that he did it. 'What did you do it for?' 'Money.' 'Did you get any money?' 'Yes.' 'How much?' 'Fifteen cents.' 'What kind of a man was he?' 'A laboring man I killed.' 'What did you do with the money?' 'I bought liquor with it.' 'Did he have anything else?' 'I think he had some meat and bread.' 'What did you do with that?' 'I ate the bread and threw away the meat; it was Friday.' So you see it will restrain in some things."—Ingersoll.

The Inquisition in Spain, 1568.

"Upon the 16th of February, 1568, a sentence of the Holy Office condemned *all* the *inhabitants* of the Netherlands *to death* as heretics. From this universal doom, only a few persons, *especially* named, were excepted. A proclamation of the king, dated ten days later, confirmed this decree of the Inquisition, and ordered it to be carried into instant execution, without regard to age, sex or condition. This is probably the most concise death-warrant that was ever framed. Three millions of people, men, women, and children, were sentenced to the scaffold in three lines." (John L. Motley, "The Rise of the Dutch Republic," vol. 2, p. 158.)

The Inquisition.

"In 1208. Innocent III. established the Inquisition. In 1209 De Montfoot began the massacre of the Albigenses. In 1215 the Fourth Council of the Lateran enjoined all rulers, 'as they desired to be esteemed faithful, to swear a public oath that they would labor earnestly and to the full extent of their power, to exterminate from their dominions all those who were branded as heretics by the church.'" (Lecky's "Rationalism in Europe," vol. 1, p. 38.)

"Llorente, who had free access to the archives of the Spanish Inquisition, assures us that by that tribunal alone more than 31,000 persons were burnt, and more than 290,000 condemned to punishment less severe than death. The number of those put to death for their religion in the Netherlands alone, in the reign of Charles V. has been estimated by a very high authority at 50,000, and at least half as many perished under his son. (Ibid. pp., 40, 41.)

The Church Opposed to Liberty.

"How has the church in every age, when in authority, defended itself? Always by a statute against blasphemy, against argument, against free speech. And there never was such a statute that did not stain the book that it was in and that did not certify to the savagery of the men who passed it. Never. By making a statute and by defining blasphemy, the church sought to prevent discussion—sought to prevent argument, sought to prevent a man from giving his honest opinion. Certainly a tenet, a dogma, a doctrine, is safe when hedged about by a statute that prevents your speaking against it. In the silence of slavery it exists. It lives because lips are locked. It lives because men are slaves." (Ingersoll, "The Reynolds Blasphemy Trial.")

"So I say if you believe the Bible say so; if you do not believe it say so. And here is the vital mistake, I might almost say, in Protestantism itself. The Protestants when they fought the Catholics, said: 'Read the Bible for yourselves—stop taking it from your priests—read the sacred volume with your own eyes. It is a revelation from God to his children, and you are the children,' and then they said: 'If after you read it you do not believe it, and you say anything against it, we will put you in jail, and God will put you in hell.' That is a fine position to get a man in. It is like a man who invited his neighbor to come and look at his pictures, saying: 'They are the finest in the place, and I want your candid opinion. A man who looked at them the other day said they were daubs, and I kicked him down stairs—now I want your candid judgment.'" (Ibid.)

The Bible Opposed to Liberty.

To-day we say that every man has a right to worship God or not, to worship him as he pleases. Is it the doctrine of the Bible? Let us see:

"If thy brother, the son of thy mother, or thy son, or thy daughter, or the wife of thy bosom, or thy friend, which is as thine own soul, entice thee secretly, saying, Let us go and serve other gods, which thou hast not known, thou, nor thy fathers;

"Namely, of the gods of the people which are round about you, nigh unto thee, or far off from thee, from the one end of the earth even unto the other end of the earth;

"Thou shalt not consent unto him, nor hearken unto him; neither shall thine eye pity him; neither shalt thou conceal him;

"But thou shalt surely kill him; thine hand shall be first upon him to put him to death, and afterward the hand of all the people.

"And thou shalt stone him with stones, that he die; because he hath sought to thrust thee away from the Lord thy God, which brought thee out of the land of Egypt, from the house of bondage." (Deut. 13: 6.)

And do you know according to that, if your wife—your wife that you love as your own soul—if you had lived in Palestine, and your wife had said to you, "Let us worship a sun whose golden beams clothe the world in glory; let us worship the sun; let us bow to that great luminary; I love the sun because it gave me your face; because it gave me the features of my babe; let us worship the sun,"—it was then your duty to lay your hands upon her, your eye must not pity her, but it was your duty to cast the first stone against that tender and loving breast. I hate such doctrine! I hate such books! I hate gods that will write such books! I tell you that it is infamous.

"If there be found among you, within any of thy gates which the Lord thy God giveth thee, man or woman, that hath wrought wickedness in the sight of the Lord thy God, in transgressing his covenant,

"And hath gone and served other gods, and worshiped them, either the sun, moon, or any of the host of heaven, which I have not commanded;

"And it be told thee, and thou hast heard of it, and inquired diligently, and, behold, it be true, and the thing certain, that such abomination is wrought in Israel;

"Then shalt thou bring forth that man, or that woman, which have committed that wicked thing, unto thy gates even that man or that woman, and shalt stone them with stones, till they die." (Deut. 17: 2–5.)—Ingersoll.

SECULARISM.

"Secularism has no mysteries, no mummeries, no priests, no ceremonies, no falsehoods, no miracles and no persecutions.

"It is a protest against theological oppression, against ecclesiastical tyranny, against being the serf, subject or slave of any phantom, or the priest of any phantom. It is a protest against wasting this life for the sake of one we know not of. It proposes to let the gods take care of themselves.

"It means the destruction of the business of those who trade in fear. It proposes to give serenity and content to the human soul. It will put out the fires of enternal pain. It is striving to do away with violence and vice, with ignorance, poverty, and disease. It lives for the ever present *to-day*, and the ever coming *to-morrow*. It does not believe in praying and receiving, but in earning and deserving. It regards work as worship, labor as prayer, and wisdom as the savior of mankind."—Robert G. Ingersoll.

Popular Questions and Objections.

1. It is objected that Freethought is destructive, not constructive.

(*a*) It is destructive of error, crime, cruelty, superstition and all kinds of wrong and oppression.

(*b*) It is constructive in its defense and support of the rights of man, woman, and child.

(*c*) It is constructive in seeking to establish the highest form of morality, that is, rational morality.

(*d*) It is constructive, because it inspires man with a thirst for knowledge, and puts him in sympathy with science.

(c) It is positive and reconstructive in inspiring man with moral courage.

"What will you give us in place of religion?"

(a) We would put in place of religion, liberty, morality, honesty, courage, knowledge, and manliness.

(b) We do not wish to take away the Golden Rule; but we insist that it is not a Christian precept. It was in the world long before Jesus, before Moses, and before Abraham. Long before the pyramids were built mothers called their children to their knees and said to them, "Children be good to each other to-day." This is the Golden Rule. We see then that it is of human origin, and not a part of Christianity, as Christianity is founded upon the supernatural. It is the old, old way that religions have of borrowing human virtues and ascribing them to the gods.

(c) We do not teach men to dispise charity, but to so improve human conditions that charity and charitable institutions shall not be needed.

(d) "What will you give us in place of the Bible?"

We do not propose to take it away. We only ask people to read it as they do other books—accepting the good and rejecting the bad.

"What are we to have in place of the consolation of the gospel?"

The gospel means glad tidings. What are the glad tidings?

1. That man is totally depraved and polluted. Good news!

2. That he deserves eternal torment. Glad tidings!

3. And that nine tenths of the human race will get their deserts. "Many are called, but few are chosen." Glorious news!

4. That hell is in view,—near at hand. Delightful tidings!

5. That the reprobate cannot escape. Glorious gospel!

6. That God hates the most of the race and has from eternity doomed them to eternal woe.

And all this is the gospel of glad tidings!

Suppose we expose the delusion of eternal torments, what does man want in its place? Does he need a smaller hell to taper off on, before he can give up hell altogether? What does any one want in place of *infant damnation?* And so also with witchcraft, polygamy, slavery, and many other wrongs—must we have something to take their place? I heard of a kid gloved dude, who put his finger into a bucket of water, and after taking it out looked for the hole in the water. As well might the poor fellow sick in the hospital ask the doctor, who promises to cure him of the small pox, what he will give him in its stead. Does he want the itch or measles in place of the small pox?

"How does the Freethinker come to know so much more than millions of good and great men who for eighteen centuries have believed in Christianity?"

(a) Here we have the old question of majorities.

Millions of good and great men once firmly believed in witchcraft.

Luther said: "I would have no compassion on these witches, I would burn them all."

John Wesley said: "Giving up witchcraft is giving up the Bible."

Sir Matthew Hale believed in witchcraft.

(b) The good and great men of many ages believed in hell—that is, for somebody else. Practically hell is now in the lower case, if not entirely closed up for repairs.

(c) Millions of good and wise men for many centuries believed that this earth was flat, and that the sun went daily round it. And these good and wise people burned all those who did not agree with them.

(d) Millions of the best of earth at one time believed that it was right and proper to hang a man for stealing a sheep.

(e) At one time almost every body believed that it was well-pleasing to God, for Christians to torture and murder heretics.

(*f*) Millions of the wisest and best men have at different times believed that the world was speedily coming to an end.

(*g*) The great men of the past *professed* to believe in Christianity because they were *compelled* to do so through fear of persecution, torture, and death. Millions of prominent men in society to-day, have to *pretend* to believe in the doctrines of the church in order to be *respectable*.

(*h*) In every country under the sun people believe in their own religion.—The good and great Mohammedans, believe in Islamism. The good and great Buddhists believe in Buddhism, and the good and great Brahmins, believe in Brahminism.

(*i*) The wise men of to-day in Europe and America do not believe in Christianity. The men of science do not attempt to prove the claims of Christianity.

It is claimed that Infidelity is demoralizing in its tendency.

(*a*) With such lives before us as those of Paine, Ingersoll, Palmer, Bennett, Wright, Seaver, and many others this charge proves to be groundless.

(*b*) Liberal principles are not degrading. Truth, liberty, and justice cannot demoralize, but blind faith does.

"Infidels always repent on their death bed."

(*a*) Paine did not. Bennett did not. Dr. T. Brown did not. Courtlandt Palmer, Horace Seaver, Elizur Wright, did not—and millions of other good men have died tranquilly without any belief whatever in another world.

"Can Infidelity save the world?"

One thing is certain, namely, that Christianity cannot do it, as it has been trying to do so for eighteen centuries.

There is no such thing as salvation possible.

The world can be improved most rapidly by allowing everyone to mind his own business—by giving man his natural and equal rights, by inspiring him with liberty, for nothing so fully prepares people for liberty as liberty itself.

"What has Freethought done for the world?"

(*a*) What has Christianity done for the world? Why it has built schools, churches, and charitable institutions.

(*b*) It is true that Christianity instituted schools, colleges, and universities; but not for the purpose of educating the people in truth, but in only such knowledge as would not conflict with its own superstitions. Christian schools have been for ages at war with science and liberty.

(*c*) It is true that the church builds asylums for the poor—but it is the church that is in a large degree responsible for the impoverished condition of the people. And the very money that builds the almshouse was begged from the poor, by the church. The church has nothing of itself to give except preaching. When the church builds an institution it first becomes a beggar.

(*d*) The church builds insane asylums. And the church has filled them with her own people. There are more people made crazy and insane by religious excitements than by any other one thing.

"What have Infidels given for education, charity, and science?"

We will give the names of six noted Freethinkers, and could give more, but give these six to begin with: Stephen Girard, Robert Owen, James Lick, William Maclure, John Rodman, and Peter Brigham. These gentleman who were all Infidels, gave at least fifteen millions of dollars for education, science, and charity. The vast sum given by Stephen Girard for a secular education of orphan children has been stolen by Christians and put to another use.

Orthodoxy and Liberalism Compared.

1. Orthodoxy has a creed, but Liberalism has none. A creed is something you do not understand, but it is nevertheless necessary for you to profess that you believe it—and the more unreasonable and impossible this something is the greater merit you have in saying you believe it.

2. Orthodoxy has a Bible. Liberalism accepts all bibles and books for what they are worth.

3. Orthodoxy has a savior—Liberalism seeks to make all men saviors.

It should not be forgotten that the orthodox savior has failed after trying for eighteen centuries. He even fails to save his own professed people and to make them any better than other folks.

4. Orthodoxy has a prospective heaven. Liberalism takes no stock in harps and crowns in the sky country—and is not terrorized by smoke from the sulphur lake.

5. Orthodoxy insists that the most imperative duty is to *believe*, while Liberalism teaches that man should think, question, and investigate, and always be governed by reason.

The one preaches "he that hath ears to hear, let him hear (us the preachers); the other teaches that "he who has brains to think, let him think."

6. Orthodoxy commands you to obey. Liberalism inspires you to defy despotism and to love liberty.

7. Orthodoxy tells you that there is merit in believing. Liberalism shows you that there is no merit in belief.

8. Orthodoxy maintains that belief is subject to one's will. Liberalism proves that intelligent belief depends upon *evidence*, and that religious beliefs are inherited.

9. Orthodoxy hinges most of its teachings upon the *traditions* of the past, the mysteries of the present and the hopes of an *imaginary* future.

Liberalism admits of no postponement. "One world at a time," and now is the time.

10. Orthodoxy is opposed to the teachings of science. See the lives of Galileo, Bruno, Copernicus.

11. Orthodoxy persecutes her own followers; for example: Dr. Thomas, Professor Swing, Professor William Robertson Smith of Aberdeen College, Scotland, Professor Winchell of Vanderbilt University, Professor Blauvelt, Professor John Miller of Princeton, New Jersey, and hosts of others.

12. Orthodoxy seeks to guide men by authority, mottoes, and texts. Liberalism inspires man to govern and guide himself through the exercise of his own reason.

13. Orthodoxy teaches that the innocent must suffer that the guilty may escape. Liberalism teaches that *justice* should be meted out to all. The great scheme of salvation failed because it was a "scheme." It is now pretty well known as a "bankrupt scheme."

14. "The Bible has stood the attack of Infidelity during eighteen centuries." Ignorance has stood the attack of knowledge for a much longer time, and yet ignorance has not so very materially suffered—it is still ignorance.

Vice has stood the attacks of virtue ever since the world began. Superstition has been besieged by science for many centuries, and yet superstition seems hale and hearty and bids fair to have a long life. Is it true that those who believe in the Bible are willing to have it tested by reason, justice, or humanity? It is not true that it has stood the test of science. Christians are not willing to have the Bible tested.

"The Infidel rejects the religion of his mother." Not always; but even suppose it were true, did not Jesus reject the religion of his mother? Did not Paul, Peter, Luther, Wesley—did they not all reject the religion of their mothers?

Does not preaching consist in asking people to reject the religion of their mothers and to come over to the preachers's religion?

"Freethinkers are ruthless, and do not care how much they hurt our feelings. They speak coarsely upon sacred subjects." Yes; but do not Christians hurt our feelings? They send us to hell, and then put on a look of injured innocence if we do not sweetly return them "thanks."

It is often charged that Freethinkers do not believe anything. While it is true that we are not strong in any form of religious beliefs, yet it is true that we have most positive and decided convictions in regard to this world. We advocate freedom, truth, justice, equity, and every known human virtue. These all have an existence, we believe in all these present existing virtues. We believe in the realities, but the saint believes in the unrealities. He relishes as the meat and drink of his soul, such airy nothings as: dreams, visions, trances, inspirations, revelations, mysteries, miracles, witches, evil spirits, demons, devils, angels, immaculate conception, raising of the dead, drinking poison with impunity, omens, signs, sorcery, magic, resurrection, and ascension.

"We are fools for Christ sake," says the apostle, and in the language of the Quaker, we must say, we have not the heart to contradict him.

It is objected that "Freethought has no moral standard."—Yes it has—it has Reason the only true lamp to man's path. "But Reason is fallible, you can not always trust it." You cannot always trust the reason of him who is not well developed mentally and well informed. But the Bible is fallible, and always fallible, and you can trust it in but very few places except where it presents truth; and this moral truth is older than it. So we could get along *without* the Bible, but we could hardly get along without Reason, although some people try to.

"There is *no agreement* among *Freethinkers.*" That is their glory. Freethought has no procrustean bed upon which it may bring all of its constituency to one and the same size. The glory of Freethought is that it inspires man to become free and possess his liberty against all invaders. To be free is to be a man, and not to be free is to be a slave.

Is there, let me ask, anything like agreement among the creeds? Have the Bible expounders always seen eye to eye? Do the biblical critics all harmonize? Where, I would like to know, can you find more disagreement than in the Christian church?

Infidelity.

"Infidelity is honest. When it reaches the confines of reason, it says: I know no further.

"Infidelity does not palm its guess upon the ignorant as a demonstration. Infidelity proves nothing by slander—establishes nothing by abuse.

"Infidelity has nothing to hide. It has no 'holy of holies,' except the abode of truth. It has no curtain that the hand of investigation has not the right to draw aside. It lives in the cloudless light, in the very noon of human eyes.

"Infidelity has no bible to be blasphemed. It does not cringe before an angry god.

"Infidelity says to every man: Investigate for yourself. There is no punishment for unbelief.

"Infidelity asks for no protection from legislatures. It wants no man fined because he contradicts its doctrines.

"Infidelity relies simply upon evidence—not evidence of the dead, but of the living.

"Infidelity has no infallible pope. It relies only on infallible fact. It has no priest except the interpreter of nature. The universe is its church. Its bible is everything that is true. It implores every man to verify every word for himself, and it implores him to say if he does not believe it, that he does not.

"Infidelity does not fear contradiction. It is not afraid of being laughed at. It invites the scrutiny of all doubters, of all unbelievers. It does not rely upon awe, but upon reason. It says to the whole world: It is dangerous *not* to think. It is dangerous *not* to be honest. It is dangerous *not* to investigate. It is dangerous *not* to follow where reason leads.

"Infidelity requires every man to judge for himself. Infidelity preserves the manhood of man." (Ingersoll's "Interviews," p. 165.)

Por.—Why, man, what's the matter? Don't tear your hair.

Sir Hugh.—I have been beaten in a discussion, overwhelmed and humiliated.

Por.—Why didn't you call your adversary a fool?

Sir Hugh.—My God! I forgot it!

The Objects of Orthodoxy and Liberalism.

Liberalism, like all reform movements, is poorly understood by all the masses. The more ignorant of the clergy know nothing of its real objects, and the few who do understand it dare not tell the truth, therefore we can not refer to its real objects too often. In this article we propose to place side by side the principle objects of Orthodoxy and Liberalism without comment so that our readers will be able to study them in contrast and see which is the more reasonable.

Orthodoxy seeks first and above all to glorify God; Liberalism seeks first and above all to glorify man.

Orthodoxy seeks to save men from hell; Liberalism seeks to save them from vice, ignorance, and superstition.

Orthodoxy teaches men how to die; Liberalism teaches them how to live.

Orthodoxy says believe and be saved; Liberalism says behave and be saved.

Orthodoxy promises happiness to the elect in another world; Liberalism seeks to make all happy in this one.

Orthodoxy encourages men to seek for mansions in the skies; Liberalism encourages them to secure homes on earth.

Orthodoxy teaches men to rely on God and pray; Liberalism teaches them to rely on themselves and work.

Orthodoxy teaches self-abnegation; Liberalism teaches self-respect.

Orthodoxy tells you what the Bible means; Liberalism takes it for granted the Bible means what it says.

Orthodoxy says salvation is by faith only; Liberalism says it is by honesty, education, and industry.

Orthodoxy offers a substitute for the sins of such as believe; Liberalism expects every man to answer for his own acts. (Independent Pulpit.)

CHRISTIANITY AND MATERIALISM COMPARED.

Christianity Teaches:

1. The existence of a God infinite in presence, yet a personal being; infinite in knowledge, yet a being who cogitates, contrives, plans, and designs, like man; infinite in power, yet the author of a world full of imperfections; infinite in goodness (as well as power), yet permits martyrs to expire amid flames, and patriots and philanthropists to languish in dungeons; unchangeable, yet at a certain time after a beginningless state of inaction, aroused from his idleness and made a universe out of nothing; is not the cause of evil, yet the creator of everything and everybody save himself; is free from infirmities, yet is pleased with some things and displeased with others; is without body, parts, or passions, and yet is of the masculine gender.

2. The original perfection of everything.

3. The existence of a devil—a creature made by God, and the author of evil that will exist forever.

4. That man is a "fallen creature," and unable to improve by his own unassisted efforts.

5. That man can be "saved" only through the blood and merits of Christ.

Materialism Teaches:

1. The self-existence, the eternity, and the sufficiency of nature, and the universality and invariableness of natural law.

2. That in the history of this world there has been an evolution from the simple to the complex, from the special to the general, from the homogeneous to the heterogeneous.

3. That good and evil are relative terms. All morality is founded on utility and evolved by the wants and necessities of human existence. Honesty is right, not because a God has so declared, but because man's security, safety, and happiness are promoted by it.

4. That man's condition, although imperfect, is improvable by his own unaided efforts.

5. That man should look to *himself* and not to a spectacle of suffering and death of eighteen hundred years ago, for improvement and elevation.

6. That belief and unbelief are involuntary and without moral merit or demerit.

7. That instead of worshiping God, we should direct all our efforts to improve ourselves, letting "gods attend on things for gods to know."

8. That man, wherever he may exist, it is rational to believe, will be fitted to his condition.

6. That belief in the Christian system involves moral merit; disbelief, sin.

7. That it is man's duty to worship God by prayer and praise.

8. That a comparatively small portion of mankind in the future will be happy; the greater portion will be in torment eternally.

9. That man has received a book revelation, of which, however, but a comparatively small part of the race has ever obtained information.

10. That reason should be subordinated to the teachings of the Bible.

11. That the acts of the Jews, such as are practiced now by barbarians only, were commanded by God, and were, therefore, right.

12. That there are mysteries contrary to experience and reason, which must nevertheless be believed.

13. Although God has given man a revelation, there is great uncertainty as to what he meant to say on several subjects of great importance.

14. That woman is man's inferior and subordinate, was made for his gratification and convenience, while man was made for himself and the glory of God.

15. That God has approved and sanctioned polygamy, slavery, and despotism.

An unbroken everlasting sleep, which probably awaits us all, affords no ground for fear. And how infinitely preferable to a future state of punishment in which the majority of our race will be forever miserable!

9. That the teachings of reason and the lessons of experience are the only revelations man has received.

10. That the Bible should be tested by the same rules of historical and modern criticism that are applied to other ancient documents.

11. That the barbarous acts of the Israelites, like those of other ancient nations, were the result of their undeveloped, and uncivilized condition.

12. That the universe is full of mysteries, above our comprehension, but none contrary to our reason.

13. That the difference of opinion among Liberals is consistent with their common position that man has no infallible standard. That the enlightened reason of man is the highest and best standard he possesses.

14. That woman is man's equal and natural companion —exists for him only in the sense in which he exists for her.

15. That slavery, polygamy, and despotism are evils whenever and wherever they exist.

16. That man should attend to the affairs of this world, and,

16. That man should take no thought for the morrow. He should pattern after the lilies of the field.

17. That man's ills and sufferings are ascribable largely to the immediate agency of a personal, malicious Devil—a being of extended presence, of almost infinite knowledge, of great strategy, and immense power.

18. That Jesus was God Almighty incased in human flesh.

19. That the golden age of the earth was in the past.

16. contrary to the notion of Jesus, *should* take "thought for the morrow."

17. That evil is due to natural causes. Man can gradually remove the evils that afflict him by becoming acquainted with his nature, relations, and surroundings.

18. Jesus was probably a reformer, a "come-outer," an "Infidel" of his time. We can esteem him as a benefactor without worshiping him as a God.

19. The present is better than the past, and the golden age of the world is in the future.

B. F. UNDERWOOD.

"Safest to Believe."

It has often been argued that credulity is safer than skepticism—that "it is safest to believe;" inasmuch as if a man believes in heaven and hell, and there be no such places, he is, if no gainer, at least no loser; whereas the Infidel may lose, and cannot gain. Upon the same principle, it were safest to believe all the religions of the world at once—Christian, Mohammedan, Jewish, Hindoo, Confucian, and all the rest; because it is but insuring the matter by halves to trust to one only. If Allah be not the only God and Mahomet be an imposter, there is no harm done and nothing lost; and if there be not a paradise in another world, there has been a pleasant dream of anticipated joys in this.

Let us ask, is the balance of profit and loss fairly struck? Are the chances all in favor of the believer and all against the skeptic? Is there nothing to be thrown into the opposite scale? Surely much. If religion be a fallacy, it is a fallacy pregnant with mischief. It excites the fears without foundation; it fosters feelings of separation between the believer and the unbeliever; it consumes valuable time that can never be recalled, and valuable talents that ought to be better employed; it draws money from our pockets to support a delusion; it teaches the elect to look upon their fellow men as heathen and castaways, living in sin here, and doomed to perdition hereafter; it awakens harassing doubts, gloomy despondency, and fitful melancholy; it turns our thoughts from the things of the world, where alone true knowledge is found; it speaks of temporal miseries and temporal pleasures as less than nothing and vanity, and thus fosters indifference to the causes of the weal and woe of mankind; worse than all, it chains us down to an antiquated orthodoxy, and forbids the free discussion of those very subjects which it most concerns us to investigate. If religion be a fallacy, its votaries are slaves. Whereupon, then, rests the assertion, that if the believer does not gain, he cannot lose? Is it nothing to lose time and talents, to waste our labor on that which is not bread, and our money upon that which profiteth not? Is it nothing to feel that the human beings that surround us are children of the devil and heirs of hell? Is it nothing to think that we may perhaps look across the great gulf and see some one we have loved on earth tormented in a fiery lake; and hear him ask us to dip a finger in water that it may cool his parched tongue? Is it no loss to live in disquiet by day, and in fear by night; to pass through dark seasons of doubt and temptation, and to be conscious that we are but as strangers and pilgrims here, toiling through a weary valley of cares and sorrows? Is it no loss to hold back when truth oversteps the line of orthodoxy, and when there ought to be free discussion, to shrink before we know not what? Is all this no loss? Or, is it not rather the loss of all that a free and rational being most values?

Those engaged in the trade of religion, imagine themselves to have a mighty advantage against Infidels upon the strength of the old, worn out argument that whether the Christian religion be true or false there can be no harm in believing; and that belief is, at any rate, the safer side. Now to say nothing of this old popish argument, which a sensible man must see is the very essence of popery, and would oblige us to believe all the absurdities and nonsense in the world: inasmuch as if there be no harm in believing, and there be some harm and danger in not believing, the *more* we believe, the better; and all the argument for any religion whatever would be, that it should frighten us out of our wits; the more terrible, the more true; and it would be our duty to become the converts of that religion, whatever it might be, whose priests could swear the loudest, and damn and curse the fiercest. This is a wolfish argument in sheep's clothing. (Truth Seeker tract.)

The "Safe Side."

"Ours is the safe side," says the Christian; "for if Infidelity be true then both Infidel and Christian have the same destiny, namely to die and end all, but if Christianity be true what will become of the Infidel?" In reply to this we say, that although at death both believer and unbeliever fall asleep side by side upon the bosom of mother earth, yet it does not make yours the safe side; because if Christianity be true then the most of the human race go into eternal torment. Orthodoxy has always taught that "many are called but few are chosen." Now if nine tenths of the race are going to suffer endless pain I do not see how those who are going to constitute a large part of that number and are to be eternally lost, can call it the "safe side." For it should not be forgotten that the vast majority of those who are going to suffer the wrath of God, are professed Christians. "Many will say unto me in that day, Lord, Lord, have we not prophesied in thy name? and in thy name done many wonderful works? And then will I profess unto them—I never knew you, depart from me ye that work iniquity." (Mat. 7: 22, 23.)

No, no, it will not do to trust that side as the "**safe** side" where "many are called but few are chosen."

We need something safer than that.

Again, we do not see how it can be the "safe side," to despise this life, in hopes of another that we know nothing of. If Infidelity be true, all Christians are superstitious idolaters. If Infidelity be true, Christians are deceived and are corrupting the minds of millions of children with superstition which will render them bigoted, cruel, and unhappy. And this is about the size of it. How, then, can it be the safe side. The safe side is always to be fair and honorable. It is safe always to examine both sides. It is safe to be on the alert for more truth. It is safe to accept the truth even when it cuts away old prejudices and old beliefs. It is safe not to be a sectarian. It is not safe to be a partizan, but it is safe to be free, courageous, and honest in all things. It is not safe for you to cling to myths, fables, and superstitions, and to leave them as a blighting inheritance to your children.

Popular Objections to Infidelity Answered, Showing Some Mistakes of Christians.

1. That we are negative, only.—We deny what we deem to be false, we affirm what we believe to be true, Christians do the same; only much that they affirm, we deny, and much that they deny, we affirm. Negation is necessary and healthful. No affirmation is possible that does not presuppose a negation. Negation is but the assailing side of affirmation. We deny the fables of mythology; we affirm the demonstrable truths of science.

2. That we have no incentive to good deeds.—If the Christian acts as he believes, he does good to escape hell and gain heaven—he respects the rights of others through fear of punishment and hope of reward. Hence it is that he cannot understand how the man who rejects his creed can be a good man. We do right because all the experience of the race has shown that what we call "right" is conducive to happiness; because the line of right action is the line

of least resistance; because we believe in the principle of reciprocity, and because every act of every individual becomes a part of the inheritance of the race, and thus as we are, so shall be our children. If we are intemperate, diseased, and criminal, our children shall suffer in consequence thereof. What higher or stronger incentive to right action can be offered?

3. That we are unhappy.—Why should we be more unhappy than the Christian? Why should we not be more happy? We live in the same world; we believe in making the most of its opportunities for obtaining happiness, while he (theoretically, at least,) believes that earthly joy depreciates heavenly bliss; we are cursed by no fear of an angry God, by no dreams of an endless hell and of a revengeful devil; the Christian no more than the Infidel, is exempt from accident, sickness and death, and the agony of parting with loved ones is his no less than ours. He accepts Revelation and Creation, and hence believes that we belong to a falling race; we accept Science and Evolution, and hence believe that we belong to a rising race. Which is the most rational and hope inspiring belief?

4. That it is "safest to believe."—If this proves anything it proves too much. If our future (if we have one) can be rendered more secure by pretending to believe when we do not, then the Protestant should accept Catholicism, and the Catholic, Protestantism, while the members of every sect should believe all that is taught by all other sectarists and Christians of every school should believe all that is contained in the sacred books of other religions.

5. That we hurt the feelings of those who cherish the old faith.—Why should the Christian complain that we disturb settled convictions and cut loose the anchored bark of faith? Has not Christianity ever been a missionary religion? It seeks to disturb the religion of the whole world. Christians attack all religions other than their own—our offence is that we include Christianity in the category of false faiths. (Lucifer.)

"All Owing to the Bible."

"It is a very common argument with Christians, that only those nations which have had the Bible are refined, civilized and learned. The following is the boastful manner in which Christians set forth the claims of their religion: 'Take a map of the world, draw a line around those countries that have enjoyed the highest degree of refinement, and you will encircle just those nations that have received the Bible as their authority in religion.'" In refutation of this assumption Horace Seaver writes: "From this language the plain inference is, that those nations have been indebted to the influence of the Bible *for* the positions to which they have attained. Let us follow out a little this line of argument and see where it will lead.

"The ancient Egyptians stood as far in advance of their contemporaries as do the nations of Christendom at the present day, as the remains of their cities and temples fully attest. And if the argument is good, they were indebted for that superiority to their worship of cats, crocodiles, and onions!

"The ancient Greek might have exclaimed, as he beheld the proud position to which Greece attained—'See what we owe to a belief in our glorious mythology; we have reached the highest point of enlightenment the world has ever witnessed; we stand unequaled in power, wealth, the cultivation of the arts, and all that makes a nation refined, polished, and great!'

"How immeasurably would his faith in the elevating tendency of *his* religion have been increased could he have looked with prophetic eye into the distant ages of the future, and beheld the enlightened and *Christianized* nations of the nineteenth century adopting the remains of Grecian architecture, sculpture, painting, oratory, music and literature as their models! Pagan Rome, too, once mistress of the world and arbitress of nations—the home of philosophers and sages—the land in which the title 'I am a Roman citizen,' was the proudest that mortal could wear—Rome, by the above Christian argument, should have ascribed all her honor, praise, and glory to her mythology.

"The Turk and the Saracen, likewise, have had their day of power and renown. Bagdad was the seat of science and learning at a time when the nations of Europe were sunk in darkness and superstition. The Turk and Saracen should have pointed to the Koran as the source of their refinement.

"Thus we see that the Christian argument we are noticing, if it proves anything, it proves too much. If the nations of Christendom are indebted to the Bible for their enlightenment, likewise were the Egyptians indebted to their cat and crocodile and onion worship, the Greeks and Romans to their mythology and the Turks and Saracens to their Koran."—Seaver.

The following is from William Denton's "Common Sense Thoughts on the Bible:"

"'But it is well known, that in those countries where the Bible is read, studied, and believed in, there is more knowledge and greater freedom, more virtue and happiness, than in any other countries.'"

"If true, and if all this was the result of reading and believing the Bible, it would not prove the Bible to be divine. A book may be useful, though merely human. But where is the proof that we owe our virtue, liberty, and enlightment to the Bible? The Abyssinians have had the Bible in their possession twice as long as the Anglo-Saxons, and yet they are a race of barbarians still. What did the Bible accomplish for the people of Syria, and Asia Minor, who were first blessed with it? So little, that the Koran superseded it; the Mohammedans being superior in almost every respect, to the Christians whom they conquered and converted. The Greeks and Romans were as far in advance of surrounding nations as we are or profess to be. Was it the Bible that elevated and made them and made their unsurpassed poets, painters, sculptors, and orators? Their priests, doubtless, attributed their superiority to the superior religion they possessed. So Bible believers oppose science and reform to the last; but when they triumph in spite of their opposition, they are the first to shout glory to the Bible for what it has accomplished."—Denton.

"I had a conversation with a gentleman once—and these gentlemen are always mistaking something that goes along with a thing for the cause of the thing—and he stated to me that his particular religion was the cause of all advancement. I said to him, 'No, sir; the causes of all advancement in my judgment, are plug hats and suspenders.' And I said to him, 'You go to Turkey, where they are semi-barbarians, and you won't find a pair of suspenders or a plug hat in all that country; you go to Russia, and you will find now and then a pair of suspenders at Moscow or St. Petersburg; but you go on down until you strike Austria, and black hats begin; then you go to Paris, Berlin, and New York, and you will find everybody wears suspenders and everybody wears black hats. Wherever you find education and music, there you will find black hats and suspenders.' He said that any man who said to him that plug hats and suspenders had done more for mankind than the Bible and religion he would not talk to." (Ingersoll's "Ghosts.")

THE BIBLE ON TEMPERANCE.

Passages Commending or Enjoining the Use of Wine or Strong Drink, or Both, or including a Plentiful supply of Wine among the Blessings to be Bestowed upon Favored individuals or tribes, etc.; or including the Deprivation of it among the Punishments inflicted upon the Disobedient.

"Jacob, blessing Judah, said: (Gen. 49: 11, 12): 'Binding his foal unto to the vine, and his ass's colt unto the choice vine; he washed his garments in wine, and his clothes in the blood of grapes. His eyes shall be red with wine, and his teeth white with milk.'

"Doesn't look as though Yahweh, the 'God of Jacob,' thought wine a very bad article.

"Num. 6: 20: 'After that the Nazarite may drink wine.'

"In Deut. 7: 13, God, through Moses, said to his chosen people: 'And he will love thee, and bless thee, and multiply thee; and he will also bless the fruit of thy womb, and the fruit of thy land, thy corn, and thy wine, and thine oil,' etc., etc.

"Just think of it, Woman's Christian Temperance Union people, God has solemnly promised to bless his faithful children with an especially large vintage, a better vintage than that of their unbelieving neighbors! Rather rough on the heretic French and the Infidel Germans!

"Deut. 11: 14: 'That I will give you the rain of your land in his due season, the first rain and the latter rain, that thou mayest gather in thy corn, and thy wine, and thy oil.'

"Yahweh is determined that the supply of wine shall not fall short.

"Deut. 14: 26: 'And thou shalt bestow that money for whatsoever thy soul lusteth after, for oxen, or for sheep, or for wine, or for strong drink, or for whatsoever thy soul desireth; and thou shalt eat there before the Lord thy God, and thou shalt rejoice, thou and thine household.'

"Rev. Mr. Stevenson to the box! Repeat your testimony, please. 'I said that, The education of the children of the republic in temperance principles logically involves the maintenance in those schools of the Bible as the great text book in morals.'

"Deut. 15: 14: 'Thou shalt furnish him liberally out of thy flock, and out of thy floor, and out of thy wine-press of that wherewith the Lord thy God hath blessed thee thou shalt give unto him.'

"This is said regarding the manumitted Hebrew slave. And so it is a *blessing* for God to give the fruit of the wine-press to his children? And we are to emulate him?

"It seems that God punishes his people by blasting their vineyards, and thus cutting short their supply of wine, as below:

"Deut. 28: 39: 'Thou shalt plant vineyards, and dress them, but thou shalt either drink of the wine, nor gather the grapes, for the worms shall eat them.'

"Verse 51 of the same chapter tells the people that their cattle and wine and oil shall be taken from them if they disobey God's commands. This is the famous 'cursing chapter' of the Bible, and is just the reading calculated to make a man believe that God was the first pope of Rome.

"Deuteronomy is a very good book for the Woman's *Christian* Temperance Union, and I suggest that it hold a special meeting to pray for the evidently 'rum'-loving god who wrote it. There is much other matter in it that helps to make it an admirable work for use in the schools.

"Judges 9: 13: 'And the vine said unto them, Should I leave my wine, which cheereth God and man, and go to be promoted over the trees?'

"Ah! so it appears that God, the 'original prohibitionist,' according to the Woman's Christian Temperance Union drinks wine, else how could it cheer him?'

"Second Sam. 6: 19: 'And he dealt among all the people, even among the whole multitude of Israel, as well to the women as men, to every one a cake of bread, and a good piece of flesh, and a flagon of wine.'

"Query: What would the *Christian* temperance ladies have done with that wine had they been present when David, the man after God's own heart, dealt it out to all, men as well as women?

"Second Sam. 16: 2: 'And Ziba said, The asses be for the king's household to ride on; and the bread and summer fruit for the young men to eat; and the wine that such as faint in the wilderness may drink.'

"In Kansas and Iowa many get 'faint in the wilderness,' judging by the business of the drugstores. No doubt they have all seen this prescription given by God.

"Second Chron. 2: 10: 'And behold, I will give to thy servants, the hewers that cut timber, twenty thousand measures of beaten wheat, and twenty thousand measures of barley, and twenty thousand baths of wine, and twenty thousand baths of oil.'

"The article which Solomon, 'the wisest of all men,' gave to the servants of the king of Tyre in one-fourth payment for their labor in preparing the temple which he built to the Lord, was probably especially blessed by the Lord for that use, and so rendered non-intoxicating, else we must conclude that he pays those who build houses for him in what friend St. John would call 'liquid damnation.'

"And inasmuch as Solomon was the wisest of all men (or God made a mistake when he so said), and the temple was for the said

God, I am justified in concluding that this God regards wine as a legal tender, and so I put the above passage in this category as one in which God has sanctified the use of wine.

"Neh. 5: 11: (To the usurers): 'Restore, I pray you, to them, even this day, their lands, their vineyards, their olive yards, and their houses, also the hundreth part of the money, and of the corn, the wine, and the oil, that ye exact of them.'

"Neh. 10: 39: 'For the children of Israel and the children of Levi shall bring the offering of the corn, of the new wine, and the oil . . . and we will not forsake the house of our God.'

"Wine, old or 'new,' seems to have been always acceptable to 'our God,' whether tendered as a holy offering or otherwise.

"The Lord' makes wine, according to the Psalmist:

"Psalm 104: 15: 'And wine that maketh glad the heart of man, and oil to make his face to shine, and bread which strengtheneth man's heart.'

"If 'the Lord' lived in Iowa, Lozier and Foster would have him arrested for violation of the new iron-clad prohibitory law.

"Prov. 3: 10: 'So shall thy barns be filled with plenty, and thy presses shall burst out with new wine.'

"Prov. 31: 6, 7: 'Give strong drink unto him that is ready to perish, and wine unto those that be of heavy heart. Let him drink and forget his poverty and remember his misery no more.'

"In these two verses, the author of Proverbs has more than nullified all the good things he said in his earlier chapters, and which I have quoted in List A. I am quite sure that where *they* have prevented the drinking of one glass of wine or strong drink, these passages have led to the drinking of one thousand. And this is a mild statement of the case.

"Eccl. 9: 7: 'Go thy way, eat thy bread with joy, and drink thy wine with a merry heart; for God now accepteth thy works.'

"Song of Sol. 1: 2: 'Let him kiss me with the kisses of his mouth; for thy love is better than wine.'

"From this we gather that, next to love wine is the best thing in the world. This is the opinion of most bacchanalian experts, I believe. Solomon seems to have had much experience.

"Song of Sol. 5: 1: 'I have drunk my wine with my milk; eat, O friends; drink, yea, drink abundantly, O believers.'

"Is this the earliest mention of milk punch?

"Song of Sol. 8: 2: 'I would cause thee to drink of spiced wine of the juice of my pomegranate.' Metaphorical, undoubtedly.

"Isa. 1: 22: 'Thy silver is become dross, thy wine mixed with water.'

"Have your wine full strength, as much as you would have your silver unalloyed, is the admonition of God's prophet.

"Isa. 24: 7: 'The new wine mourneth, the vine languisheth; all the merry-hearted do sigh.'

"One more in the long list of passages wherein it is said that God punished his chosen people by cutting off their vintage. What God regards as a real deprivation to lose must be good to have and to keep, in his opinion, whatever the Woman's Christian Temperance Union people may think about it. Verse 9 says: 'They shall not drink wine with a song; strong drink shall be bitter to them that drink it.' Verse 11: 'There is a crying for wine in the streets; all joy is darkened; the mirth of the land is gone.'

"God thus punished them by taking away their wine, on the same principle that he punishes us by killing our children, as Christians say that he does. Will they contend that children are inherently an evil? They must if they follow the same line of reasoning that they do in interpreting these texts.

"Isa. 27: 2, 3: 'In that day sing ye unto her, a vineyard of red wine. I the Lord do keep it; I will water it every moment; lest any hurt it, I will keep it night and day.'

"Figurative, doubtless! So is the next, but all the influence of these passages is on the side of intemperance, necessarily, for the simple reason that the great mass of the people will take them literally, and for the further reason that the constant association of wine with 'good news' and symbols of religion familiarize the mind with it and serve to give it something of a sacred character. This last mentioned fact helps to explain why the church so long opposed the modern temperance movement. But here is the passage above indicated, Isa. 55: 1: 'Ho, everyone that thirsteth, come ye to the waters, and he that hath no money; come ye, buy and eat: yea, come buy wine and milk without money and without price.'

"Isa. 62: 8: 'The Lord hath sworn by his right hand, and by the arm of his strength, Surely I will no more give thy corn to be meat for thine enemies; and the sons of the stranger shall not drink thy wine, for the which thou hast labored.'

"Rev. Stevenson should suggest to the Lord that, whereas wine is an evil thing, and the Bible a 'great text book of morals,' and the palladium of temperance, essential in the proper training of our children, therefore, he, the Lord, should have clearly shown that he meant that the enemies of his chosen people should take from them their wine that through such deprivation they should be better and happier. But, no! he ranks wine with corn, and registers a mighty oath that the people shall have them both.

"Isa. 65: 8: 'Thus saith the Lord, As the new wine is found in the cluster, and one saith, Destroy it not, for a blessing is in it, so I will do for my servants' sake, that I may not destroy them all.'

"Jer. 31: 12: 'Therefore they shall come and sing in the hight of Zion, and shall flow together to the goodness of the Lord, for wheat, and for wine, and for oil,' etc.

"Jer. 40: 10: 'But ye, gather ye wine, and summer fruits, and oil, and put them in your vessels, and dwell in the cities that ye have taken.'

"Probably 'wine' here means grapes, though it is used in the same construction as 'oil.'

"Jer. 48: 33: 'And joy and gladness is taken from the plentiful field, and from the land of Moab, and I have caused wine to fail from the wine presses.'

"Dan. 1: 5: And the king appointed them a daily provision of the king's meat, and of the wine which he drank, so nourishing them three years, that at the end thereof they might stand before the king.'

"Here God intends, plainly, to convey the impression that wine is nourishing! The only way in which the Christian temperance people can relieve him from the imputation of teaching lessons so opposite to theirs is to enter the plea that he did not inspire the writer!

"Hos. 2: 8, 9: 'For she did not know that I gave her corn, and wine, and oil, and multiplied her silver and gold which they prepared for Baal. Therefore I will return and take away my corn in the time thereof, and my wine in the season thereof, and will recover my wool and my flax given to cover her nakedness.'

"Of course, if these passages and very many of like import, are any argument against wine, they are of equal weight in the scale against corn, wool, and many other useful and necessary articles. The authors of such verses, wherever found, unquestionably looked upon wine as one of God's good gifts to his children, but which he was compelled to sometimes deprive them of because of their disobedience.

"Hos. 9: 2: 'The floor and the wine-press shall not feed them, and the new wine shall fail in her.'

"That is, Israel shall be punished for her transgressions by the destruction of the fertility of the soil.

"Evidently the perfume of wine was pleasing unto the Lord, for he says, in promising his blessing to the repentant people (Hos. 14: 7): 'They shall revive as the corn, and grow as the wine; the scent thereof shall be as the wine of Lebanon.'

"Joel 1: 5: 'Awake, ye drunkards, and howl, all ye drinkers of wine.'

"This, taken by itself, would be an unqualified condemnation of intoxicants, but such was not the prophet's meaning. The verse concludes: 'Because of the new wine, for it is cut off from your mouths.'

"In the vision of the prophet he sees the great evils that have come upon his country; the palmer-worm, and the locust, and the canker-worm have destroyed the crops. 'The meat-offering and the drink-offering is cut off from the house of the Lord, ... the corn is wasted, the oil languisheth,' etc. While in the verse quoted the drinkers are mildly requested to howl, in verse thirteen we have, 'Gird yourselves and lament, ye priests; howl ye ministers of the altar.' No temperance admonition or lesson here, that is plain.

"Joel 3: 18: 'And it shall come to pass in that day that the mountains shall drop down new wine, and the hills shall flow with milk, and all the rivers of Judah shall flow with water,' etc.

"Thus, again, among the great blessings to be bestowed upon the faithful is wine in abundance. One of the facts that strikes me most forcibly, in making such an examination as this, is the almost universal favor with which the Hebrew prophets looked upon wine and wine-drinking; and in prophesying the evils to come upon their people because of their disobedience to God or their oppression of their fellows, they rarely fail to include the cutting off of the wine supply. This they evidently regarded as one of the greatest of calamities. Our *Christian* temperance friends would gladly, so they say, visit wholesale destruction upon the vineyards and barley fields, and they seem almost to seek to convey the impression that God made a mistake when he created grapes and barley. This proves how honest they are when they say that the Bible is a temperance book. In Amos 5: 11, we have another example of the above-mentioned fact in the utterances of the prophet. Denouncing the people for their injustice, he says: 'Ye have planted pleasant vineyards, but ye shall not drink wine of them.' In the preceding sentence he had said: 'Ye have built houses of hewn stone, but ye shall not dwell in them.' Houses were good, wine was good; but because of their sins they should be deprived of both. There is here no argument either direct or implied in behalf of abstinence.

"Amos 9: 14: 'And I will bring again the captivity of my people of Israel, and they shall build the waste cities and inhabit them; and they shall plant vineyards and drink the wine thereof; they shall also make gardens and eat the fruit of them.'

"It does not seem that even Mr. Stevenson would venture to claim this verse as a Bible argument for temperance. They *shall* drink the wine!

"Micah. 6: 15: 'Thou shalt sow, but thou shalt not reap; thou shalt tread the olives, but thou shalt not anoint thee with oil; and sweet wine, but shalt not drink wine.'

"How can apparently honorable men claim that God, as revealed in the Bible, disapproves of the use of intoxicants when he is continually telling his chosen people that he will punish them by destroying their corn, and their wine, and their oil; evidently taking particular pains to impress upon them the fact that they (wine, corn, and oil) are equally good and useful?

"Zeph. 1: 13: 'They shall also build houses, but not inhabit them; and they shall plant vineyards, but not drink the wine thereof.'

"The same old story:

"In chapter 1, verse 11, Haggai calls for a drouth upon the land to punish the people, and he includes, as usual, the corn, and the oil, and the new wine among the things to be destroyed.

"Zech. 9: 17: 'For how great is his goodness, and how great is his beauty; corn shall make the young men cheerful, and new wine the maids.'

"Rather a singular apportionment of his bounty, unless 'corn' means something stronger than wine.

"Matt. 11: 19: 'The Son of man came eating and drinking, and they say, Behold, a man is gluttonous, and a wine-bibber, a friend of publicans and sinners. But wisdom is justified of her children.' But are these her children who claim Jesus as very God and yet fly directly in the face of his precepts and practice? Or is it moral uprightness instead of wisdom that they lack?

"In Mat. 21: 33 to 41, and Mark 12: 1 to 9, Jesus gives us the parable of the vineyard and the husbandman, and in it all there is no hint that there was anything wrong in the business of winemaking.

"The thought that we find expressed in Mat. 11: 19, is given again in Luke 7: 33-4-5, where we read: 'For John the Baptist came neither eating bread nor drinking wine; and ye say, He hath a devil. The Son of man is come eating and drinking, and ye say, Behold a gluttonous man, and a wine-bibber, a friend of publicans and sinners! But wisdom is justified of all her children.'

"Whoever uttered these words, man or god; whoever wrote them, John or some one else one hundred or more years later, there can be no disputing regarding the lesson which is taught. It is that each individual is to determine for himself or herself in all things pertaining to personal conduct and habits. 'Let every man be fully persuaded in his own mind' is the central idea of the various renderings. There is no rebuke, expressed or implied, of intemperance; there is nothing that can be tortured into a condemnation of wine-drinking or into an approval of the principle of total abstinence, or that of prohibition. Here was his opportunity to condemn the drinking of wine, to speak for that which is now called temperance; but from his lips fell no words of warning; to those gathered about him he said nothing in favor of the great reform which Christians of to-day, falsely assuming to speak in his name, declare finds its sanction and inspiration, its bulwark and tower of defense, in the Bible.

"It seems that the good Samaritan (Luke 10: 34) had with him a supply of wine with which he dressed the wounds of the stranger.

"John 2: 3-11: 'And when they wanted wine, the mother of Jesus saith unto him, They have no wine. Jesus saith unto her, Woman, what have I to do with thee? Mine hour is not yet come. His mother saith unto the servants, Whatsoever he saith unto you, do it. And there were set there six water pots of stone, after the manner of the purifying of the Jews, containing two or three firkins apiece. Jesus saith unto them, Fill the water-pots with water. And they filled them up to the brim. And he saith unto them, Draw out now, and bear unto the governor of the feast. And they bare it. When the ruler of the feast had tasted the water that was made wine, and knew not whence it was (but the servants which drew the water knew), the governor of the feast called the bridegroom, and saith unto him, Every man at the beginning doth set forth good wine; and when men have well drunk, then that which is worse; but thou hast kept the good wine until now. This beginning of miracles did Jesus in Cana of Galilee, and manifested forth his glory; and his disciples believed on him.'

"John 4: 46: 'So Jesus came again into Cana of Galilee, where he made the water wine.'

"The first miracle which Jesus performed was to convert six pots of water into wine! And this feat convinced his disciples of his supernatural origin and powers! And he did this to manifest forth his glory! Either this is true or the Bible is false. Whether true or not, it has been a most powerful argument against abstinence; it has resulted directly in making drunkards, as it has indirectly in making hypocrites and Jesuitical sophists. I of course mean by this last sentence that the seeming necessity to prove the Bible a temperance work has made any number of Christian apologists resort to all kinds of specious arguments and make any number of false claims in order to make good their assertions. The assumption that this wine was not of an intoxicating nature is purely gratuitous. There is not even the ghost of a fact to be found in support of it. Hundreds of passages, which I have quoted under their appropriate heads, prove beyond a doubt that the wine so often mentioned in the Bible was intoxicating; the words of the governor prove that this miraculously produced portion of it certainly was of the very best, for it is against all reason to suppose that men accustomed to the taste and effects of wine would pronounce simple grape-juice to be better than all that had already been served to them at the feast; and, finally, the declaration that this act of Jesus was a miracle and that it made his disciples to 'believe on him,' gives the last stroke to the already nearly dead 'non-intoxicating' theory.

"Col. 2: 16: 'Let no man therefore judge you in meat, or in drink, or in respect of a holy day, or of the new moon, or of the Sabbath days.'

"In other words, judge for yourselves in all these matters,

submit to no dictation from without. How does that strike you, Messrs. Bible Prohibitionists?

"1 Tim. 5: 23: 'Drink no longer water, but use a little wine for thy stomach's sake and thine often infirmities.'

"It is probable that this short verse has led to the consumption of more wine and caused more intemperance than any other equal number of words in any language or contained in any book. It has had more potent effect upon the mind of the Christian believer than have twenty passages which have in a hesitating, half-hearted, uncertain way caution against the use of *much* wine.

"Comparing this class of passages with those grouped under 'A,' we find that the Bible pleas for temperance are out voted *more than five to one* by those in favor of the use of intoxicants. The record is an astonishingly bad one for the Bible as a total abstinence and Prohibition work, and should put to the blush all of its worshipers and apologists who have been so foolish or unscrupulous as to claim that it is indispensable to the temperance cause and in the education of our children. Both claims are absurd." (E. C. Walker's "Bible Temperance.")

The Inconsistency of Agnosticism.

"It seems to me as irrational to say there is *no* God as to say there is *a* God."—Editor Twentieth Century.

"But pray, why? Does not that proposition tacitly concede that it is irrational to say there *is* a God? If so, how can it be irrational to deny an irrational proposition or absurdity? Are not the two propositions antithetical? If so, one or the other is, of necessity, false. Conceding then, as he does, the absurdity of the God idea, why will Mr. Pentecost persist, inconsistently, in maintaining that there is no difference between the rationality of Theism and Materialism, with its incidental Atheism?

"Will he kindly tell us the difference in degree of rationality between the position that there is a personal Devil and that there is a God? Are not both notions of the same origin and equally absurd? Are not both transmitted to us from the dark ages, from the same book, and must not both stand or fall together? Yet Mr. Pentecost would not,

INCONSISTENCY OF AGNOSTICISM.

from pure deference and respect for our poor, non-evolved pious friends, assume an Agnostic's attitude and concede that 'it is as irrational to say there is no Devil as to say there is a Devil.' Of course not. He simply denies the existence of His Satanic Majesty without equivocation, and the proof of his existence not being forthcoming his denial is equivalent to proof that such a being does not exist.

"In law and equity the affirmative is obliged to prove its case. If then a proposition is self-evidently absurd, unnatural and absolutely impossible, why concede to those affirming, without a shadow of proof, that their belief is equally rational with our unbelief, that 'it may be so,' 'I don't know,' etc.

"Having discarded as authoritative ancient traditions, there is absolutely no logic, no reason, no science, no analogy that will sustain or demonstrate the existence of a God. And in view of this fact a simple denial is all-sufficient to prove the negative. As the plea of the prisoner at the bar of 'not guilty' is equivalent to proof of his innocence and bound to be respected by court and juror, unless, indeed, the affirmative, beyond a shadow of a doubt, establishes his guilt, so the Atheist's fearless denial, nowadays, must demand profound respect, and is equivalent to proof, unless, indeed, the Church brings proof, outside of a discarded Bible, of the truth of its basic idea.

"Now, though unnecessary to prove a negative, and the God-idea not having been established by history, revelation, science, or reason, yet alleged arguments being continually advanced in the vain endeavor to resuscitate a vanishing religion, a few propositions are here advanced *which prove there is no God*.

"There *is* a universe. This proves there is *no* God.

"The universe is infinite. This excludes anything else of like character—two infinities being an absurdity.

"The universe (nature) is here and there and everywhere. This proves that God cannot be here and there and everywhere.

"Two bodies cannot occupy the same space at the same time. Matter (implying energy and force) monopolizing every point of space, nothing else can occupy it in addition.

"The universe exists now. Something cannot come from nothing, therefore the universe has always existed.

"Being eternal and infinite, this excludes anything anterior, exterior, or superior to it.

"Is God in the universe or the universe in God? If there is a God, either of these propositions must be true, yet both are glaringly absurd.

"Can an engineer drive a locomotive and be a locomotive at the same time? If not, how can a God manipulate an infinite universe and be infinite 'Himself?'

"Yet the universe, *outside of a God*, is an absolute reality, as much so as a locomotive is a reality outside of the engineer. The world is a reality, our planets, the sun, all the countless millions of stars within reach of our telescopes and the infinitude of stars and systems beyond the reach of our strongest lenses, which science infers to exist, all these are a reality and all these, yes, every object of knowledge is a reality, and all these are *not God!* How then, in the name of reason I ask, can a God, of whom we know absolutely nothing, be infinite, when an infinite number of material objects—not God—fill all space?

"But does the universe exist *in God?* If we but imagine for a moment the aspect of the universe to resemble a huge machine of infinite proportions, eternally active in all its vast proportions, the idea of the universe existing within a God will appear equally childish and simple.

"All phenomena are the results of energy co-existent and inseparable from matter. All cosmic motion, change, and life may be traced to this physical and chemical energy pervading all nature—*never to a God.*

"Mind—the so-called infinite as well as finite—implies limit, localization, conditions, etc. This fact tends to prove that while God, perchance, might concentrate his mind on the world or some particular sect or individual, considering their exhortations, the rest of the world and the universe for the time being would be Godless!

"From a late scientific authority I quote in proof: "It is impossible for a person's mind to be in two places at the same time.' Noted chess players may play twenty games simultaneously, but it is done by speedy transfer of thoughts from one game to another and not by considering two moves at once.

"Thus 'Omniscience' is impossible.

"Again; mind implies limit and necessitates organism, brain, nervous force, etc. This again makes impossible a God. Let the Church demonstrate *how a God without a brain can be a God and all it implies, or how a God with a brain can be infinite*, and I will kneel down and worship with them.

"Is this dogmatism? The 'dogmatism of the Infidel' we hear so much about? If it is, then asserting that twice two is four is dogmatism. Then we state all the facts of mathematics, all the truths of history is dogmatism. We simply confine ourselves to fact, to knowledge and demonstrated truth. There we stop and refuse to accept the crude notions transmitted from our ignorant ancestors, which, it is dogmatically asserted, are true in spite of our knowledge and reason.

"I protest against being accused of dogmatism, I studiously endeavor to be fair and make no pretensions to scholarship and learning. But I emphatically protest against the dogmatism of others who, assuming a superior air of knowledge assert notions contrary to fact. Supposing some one should affirm that twice two is five, would it be dogmatism, to deny the proposition, and would thinking minds be justified to assume the attitude of Agnostics and concede that while in their opinion twice two is four, yet twice two may be five, 'I don't know,' 'one proposition is as irrational as the other,' etc.?

"We *know* a universe exists. Existing now proves it

is eternal. This simple fact absolutely makes impossible, yes, needless, a God.

"I simply assert that twice two is four and cannot possibly be five. That the universe filling all space nothing else can fill it in addition. If this be dogmatism all knowledge is a farce."—Wettstein.

God Responsible for the Ills Man Suffers.

"If God fore knew whatever was to come to pass, he must have been perfectly well aware that his whole creation, including the scheme of redemption, would be the most stupendous failure imaginable,—as it certainly has been if the Christian religion be true. For what rational or humane man would raise a family of children, if he knew beforehand that they would all be vagabonds and criminals, ending their days in prison or on the scaffold? What prudent farmer would intentionally sow wheat on land certain to produce a bad crop? What sensible business man would knowingly embark in an enterprise sure to prove disastrous, and to involve himself and his family in irretrievable ruin? And yet such conduct on the part of men would be far less irrational and criminal than that of which the Creator is guilty, if the doctrine of his foreknowledge and omnipotence be true. For, according to this doctrine, he alone is responsible for whatever has occurred and will occur, and for all the suffering in the world, since he had full power to prevent it but did not, and does not; and the conclusion to be drawn from this fact is, that he intended all things to be just as they have been in the past, are now and are to be in the future. For, if he possessed absolute power, he might have placed man under entirely different circumstances, and surrounded him by influences which would have led him into the path of perfect rectitude, but did not choose to do so; and we fail to understand how man can be justly held responsible either for his own creation, for the nature with which he is endowed, or for the environment which determines his conduct." (J. W. Stillman's "God and the Universe.")

The Idea of God Must Go.

"I think it is not a good thing for people to believe in God. I think it is a bad thing for them to do so. I think the belief in God is one of the things that is helping very strongly to keep knaves in power and honest people in weakness; it is one of the things that is preventing the people from thinking for themselves and helping themselves. The human mind will never be perfectly free, and peasants and mechanics and day laborers will never be perfectly fairly treated in this world, until the church is utterly destroyed. I do not want to see the church reformed. I want to see her utterly destroyed, because as long as she exists the ruling classes in society will always have in her a faithful ally to help them carry on their infernal schemes of pillage. I do not want people to have a better idea of God or an idea of a better God. I want the idea of God entirely rooted out of the mind, because I know that as long as any idea of God remains in the mind, the priest and the politician will have something to work upon, and this world will never be free and happy until the priest and the politician are gone.

"One man will tell you that God is a Roman Catholic, another that he is a Presbyterian, another that he is a Baptist, and so on. One man will say that he is a Republican, another that he is a single taxer, another that he is a Socialist, and so on. What we must come to see is, that nothing is done in human society that is not done by men. Poverty must be destroyed, not because it is God's will that it should be, but because it is best for the human race that it should be. And general wealth must be achieved, not because it is God's will that it should be, but because it is best for the human race that it should be. Beware of those men who tell you what is or what is not the will of God. In every case you will find a person who is intellectually asleep, or half asleep, or mentally dishonest, or else you will find—and this is more likely—a priest or a politician, a person who wants to get you to not think about what he is teaching you. We have been dragged through enough mire and blood and darkness doing things according to the will of God. It is now time we began to think things out for ourselves."—Pentecost.

"Mr. Barnum said that Christians had a different way of thinking about God now from that of fifty years ago. 'When I first heard of the doctrine of the Universalists,' said he, 'I felt so utterly astonished that I thought I'd drop dead in my boots. The orthodox faith painted God as so revengeful a being that you could hardly distinguish the difference between God and the Devil. If I had almighty power and could take a pebble and give it life, knowing beforehand that fifty-nine seconds out of every sixty would be extreme misery, I would be a monster. Yet this is how God was described, and people talk about loving such a being.'" (Newspaper clipping.)

Atheism.

1. Something (substance) must have *always* been, or anything could not now be.
2. Then this something was eternal, and hence self-existent.
3. Since self-existent and eternal, it must have been infinite, and hence was everything existing everywhere.
4. Therefore, all that is, has always been; that is, *everything* has eternally existed *everywhere*.

But will you say that this something, this self-existent, eternal everything, is God? Very well. Then nothing but God could be. Then he must be the *all* of everything existing *everywhere*. Then where is your universe? You see you cannot have a universe if you have a God. We have the universe; hence you cannot have a God. "But he *created* the universe," you say. Very well; from what did he create it? *Nothing*? Omnipresent God alone extending on, and on, and forever on through all the *everywheres*, cramming all the immensities full of his essential self. He could not have created the universe beyond himself, since there was *no* beyond. There could have been no place in which to put it outside of himself when created, since there was no *outside*. If created, it must have been from his own essence; and then it would not have been a *creation* of anything, but a changing of himself into something different; and that was not possible, since he was self-existent, and must necessarily exist the same forever, since he was eternal, and must exist unchangeable. So the universe could not have been made from nothing, since all the spaces *everywhere* were crammed completely full of *everything*, and hence there was no unoccupied premises where the raw material could have been stored away. It could not have been *created* from God-substance, since that already was; it could not have been *formed* from God's pre-existing self, since that would have been to change the eternally unchangeable into something else—to annihilate himself as God by working himself over into the universe. You see that there can be but one Eternal All. You cannot have both—a God and the universe. And since we have the universe, that is, everything eternally existing everywhere, we need no God, there is no room for a God, and there has never been anything for a God to do. Therefore, there *is* no God.

As an infinite God must necessarily fill the entirety of space, there could be no room for aught else. God and man could not live together in the same universe. God would necessarily be *everything*; then the universe must be *nothing*. But we *have* the universe, and that is everything; therefore God is *nothing*—existing nowhere. A mote that *is*, is better than a God that is not. If we part with God and obtain a universe, we make a magnificent exchange. The issue has always been God versus matter. When people come to understand that matter has *always* been, that it eternally had the start of everything else, and hence needed no creation, it will be seen that there never has been any necessity for a God, and as the universe is ever governed by law, there is nothing for a God to do. Men must believe in matter, because it is everything, and does everything. *Some-*

thing is always better than *nothing*. If God is not matter he is not anything; and the idea of God is destined to become obsolete, and gradually pass into utter forgetfulness. The God-idea has been the center and foundation of all the superstitions of the world. When men have learned to dispense with it, their emancipation will be great indeed."—Sam Preston.

Jehovah a Failure.

1. He was unsuccessful in creation. He made Adam and Eve and the serpent; but all his plans were frustrated in a short time; and "it repented the Lord that he had made man."

2. In repeopling the world from Noah's family he decidedly failed again. How easy it would have been after drowning the whole world, to create a new man and woman of perfect character, and omit the Devil business.

3. In attempting to save the world through Jesus Christ he made another failure. It is not in the nature of things for this world to be saved. "To be saved" means too much, and it means too little. Man can not be saved entirely from his weakness, ignorance, and selfishness; and hence can never be perfect. Man can be made morally better, intellectually wiser, physically healthier, individually and socially happier; but his betterment cannot be achieved through preaching, Bible-reading, praying and other religious exercises. It must come through liberty. He must have equal rights with his fellow men. He must have justice established between man and man. The toiler must get the fruits of his toil. A good home has a more sacred influence over the hearts of men to make them kind and good, than all the preaching in the world. With a home of his own man has a little heaven of his own, and a truer and better love of his neighbor.

"The character of a god is the character of the people who have made him. When therefore I expose the crimes of Jehovah, I expose the defective morality of Israel; and when I criticise the God of modern Europe, I criticise the defective intellects of Europeans. The reader must endeavor to bear this in mind; for though he may think that his idea of the Creator is actually the Creator, that belief is not shared by me." (Winwood Reade, "Martyrdom of Man.")

ATONEMENT.

Atonement for Sin, an Immoral Doctrine.

1. The doctrine of the atonement is of heathen origin, and is predicated upon the assumption that no sin can be fully expiated without the shedding of blood. In the language of Paul, "Without the shedding of blood there can be no remission of sin." A barbarous and bloody doctrine truly! But this doctrine was almost universally prevalent amongst the orientals long before Paul's time.

2. Christians predicate the dogma of atonement for sin upon the assumption that Christ's death and sufferings were a substitute for Adam's death, incurred by the fall. But as Adam's sentence was death, and he suffered that penalty, this assumption cannot be true.

3. If the penalty for sin was death, as taught in Genesis 3, and Christ suffered that penalty for man, then man should not die; but, as he does, it makes the doctrine preposterous. It could not have meant spiritual death, as some argue, because a part of the penalty was that of being doomed to return to dust (Gen. 3: 19).

4. If crucifixion was indispensably necessary as a penalty, then the punishment should have been inflicted either upon the instigator or perpetrator of the deed; either the serpent or Adam should have been nailed to the cross.

5. We are told in reply, that as an infinite sin was committed, it required an infinite sacrifice. But Adam, being a finite being, could not commit an infinite sin; and Christ's sacrifice and sufferings could not be infinite unless he had continued to suffer to all eternity Therefore the assumption is false.

6. An all-wise God would not let things get into such a condition as to require the murder of his only son from any consideration whatever.

7. And no father, cherishing a proper regard and love for his son, could have required him to be, or consented to have him put to death in a cruel manner; for the claims of mercy and paternal affection are as imperative as justice.

8. To put an intelligent and innocent being to death, for any purpose is a violation of the moral law, and as great a sin as that for which he died. Hecatombs of victims cannot atone for the infraction of the moral law which is engraven upon our souls.

9. If it were necessary for Christ to be put to death, then Judas is entitled to one half the merit of it for inaugurating the act, as it could not have taken place without his aid; and no one who took part in it should be censured, but praised.

10. It is evident, that, if everybody had been Quakers no atonement would have been made, as their religion is opposed to bloodshed.

11. The atonement is either one God putting another to death or God putting himself to death to appease his own wrath; but both assumptions are monstrous absurdities, which no person distinguished for science or reason can indorse.

12. Anger and murder are the two principal features in the doctrine of the atonement; and both are repugnant to our moral sense and feelings of refinement, and indicate a barbarous and heathen origin.

13. The atonement punishes the innocent for the guilty, which is a twofold crime, and a reversal of the spirit of justice. If a father should catch four of his children stealing and the fifth one standing by and remonstrating against the act, and should seize on the innocent one and administer a severe flagellation, he would commit a double crime: 1st, that of punishing an innocent child; 2d, that of exonera-

ting and encouraging the four children in the commission of crime. The atonement involves the same principle.

14. No person with true moral manhood would consent to be be saved on any such terms; but would prefer to suffer for his own sins, rather than let an innocent being suffer for them. And the man who would accept salvation upon such terms must be a sneak and a coward, with a soul not worth saving.

15. Who that possesses any sense of justice would want to swim through blood to get to the heavenly mansion. I want neither animals, men, nor Gods murdered to save my soul·

16. If there is any virtue in the atonement in the way of expiating crime, then there is now another atonement demanded by the principles of moral justice to cancel the sin committed by the first atonement—that of murdering an innocent being, "in whose mouth was no guile;" and then another atonement to wipe out the sin of this atonement, and so on. And thus it would be atonement after atonement, murder after murder, *ad infinitum*. What shocking consequences and absurdities are involved in this ancient heathen superstition!

17. It seems strange that any person can cherish the thought for a moment that the Infinite Father would requre a sacrificial offering for the trifling act of eating a little fruit, and require no atonement for the infinitely greater sin of murdering "his only begotten son." Another monstrous absurdity!

18. The advocates of the atonement tell us that man stands toward his Creator in the relation of a debtor, and the atonement cancels the debt. To be sure! How does it do it?—Graves.

A MINORITY NOT A SECT.

"A Protestant minister of Oakland, California, in a recent address on the public school system of the United

States, expressed himself as follows: 'In one of the schools of San Francisco Herbert Spencer's 'Data of Ethics' was introduced as a text book of morals—as palpable a violation of the law forbidding sectarian instruction as the introduction of the Catholic or Methodist catechism; for Hebert Spencer belongs to a very small and narrow sect which promulgates the creed of Agnosticism.'

"If the reverend speaker had taken the ground that the 'Data of Ethics' was too abstruse to be placed in the hands of public school pupils we should have felt inclined to sustain his objection. But when he says that to introduce such a book is to give a sectarian character to the school in which it is used, we must enter a protest. Science is never sectarian; philosophy is never sectarian. Sectarian teaching begins when you ask a man or a child to assume what cannot be proved, for the sake of keeping within the dogmatic lines that fence round some particular creed. The followers of Mr. Spencer may be in a minority, but they are no more a sect than were the adherents of the Copernican system of astronomy, or than are the believers in the Darwinian theory of natural selection. Mr. Spencer makes no appeal to faith, but finds his premises in the common experience of mankind. A pupil who was being taught out of the 'Data of Ethics' would be quite at liberty to dispute either the premises or the arguments of the author; and he would not be silenced by the declaration that Mr. Spencer is infallible. But when catechisms are taught they are taught, not as containing matter for discussion, but as containing doctrines that must not be disputed, on pain of more or less disagreeable consequences. Similarly when the Bible is read in school it is read not as a fallible record of events, or a fallible guide in morals, but as something absolutely authoritative—the very voice of God. It is perfectly obvious then, where sectarianism in education begins; it begins just at the point where doctrines of any kind accepted on faith by a portion of the community and not discussible on grounds of reason, are made a part of public school instruction. Sectarianism comes in whenever the teacher is obliged to say, 'Hush' to the inquiring scholar who wants his reason satisfied before he will believe. There is no sectarianism, on the other hand, in making use of a book which lays no claim to any kind of privilege, and which, therefore, cannot force the belief of anyone. The followers of Mr. Spencer do not form a sect because they have no beliefs which they wish to exempt from criticism or discussion, and because they hold themselves at full liberty to pass beyond the bounds of Mr. Spencer's thought whenever they can see their way to doing so. Mr. Spencer's 'Data of Ethics' may not contain all the truth on the subject of morals, but the truth which it does contain lends itself to demonstration; and no one can be the worse for being taught demonstrable truths. Upon that foundation he can afterward build what he likes—hay, stubble, or what not; and after his superstructure has been tried by the fire of experience, as it is very likely to be, he will still have something solid left on which to rebuild in perchance wiser fashion. We do not advocate the introduction of the 'Data of Ethics' into the public schools: but we are convinced that it would be a very good thing for the rising generation if some of the ideas contained in that book could be brought home to their minds. (Popular Science Monthly, November 1889.)

INDEX

A curse pronounced upon the earth, 24.
Adam gives names to every living creature, 20.
Agnosticism, 368.
All owing to the Bible, 356.
Atheism, 374.
Atonement, 302, 377.
A minority not a sect, 379.
Blue Laws of Connecticut, 328.
Bruno, 331.
Bible, sanctions crime, 291.
    intemperance, 358.
    polygamy, 292.
    slavery, 300.
    the subjection of woman, 294.
    wars of extermination, 291.
    not an inspired revelation, 133.
    opposed to liberty, 337.
Creation, 5.
    completed in six days of twenty-four hours each, 8.
Christianity without historical basis, 119.
    teaches immorality, 302.
    compared with Materialism, 349.
Civilization, 281.

Devil, God creates him, 201.
    serpent knows more about the nature of man than God does, 202-3.
    serpent tells the truth, 203.
    the book of Job speaks of the serpent as Satan; it caricatures him, 206.
Design argument, 239.
Divorce, 294.
Eve made out of a rib, 21.
Eusebius the father of church history, 131.
    a noted liar, 131.
First Cause, 253.
    infinite and absolute, 27.
God cannot use reason, 28.
    is responsible for the ills man suffers, 372.
God's ways not our ways, 141.
Galileo, 330.
Heaven, 69.
Hell, hades, gehenna, sheol, 313.
Immortality, 229.
Inquisition, 336.
In the beginning, 5.
Jehovah a failure, 376.
Jesus Christ, when was he born? 73.
    Christianity rests upon Joseph's dream, 76.
    the golden rule, 77.

Jesus an Essene, 79.
his teaching not up to the moral standard of to-day, 81.
he exhibits an imperfect sense of justice, 83.
he teaches the duty of submission to wrong, 86.
immoral teachings, 87.
bitter and unreasonable, 88.
a false prophet, 89.
curses the fig tree, 90.
history silent concerning Jesus, 91.
not a historical character, 127.
LABOR not a curse, 20.
Light separated from darkness, 7.
MAN created in God's image, 17.
Materialism, 232.
Matter uncreatable, 6.
Miracles, 36, 68.
OTHER worldliness, 312.
PENTATEUCH, 140.
Pictures of hell, 314.

Polygamy, 292.
Prayer, 304, 311.
Prophecy, 31.
Protestant persecutions, 321.
Providence, 247.
Puritans persecute, 321.
SAFEST to believe, 351.
Secularism, 339.
Self-contradictions of the Bible, 145.
Soul questions, 216, 237.
Spurious writings of the early church, 129.
Sunday question, 255.
The church opposed to progress, 319.
The idea of God must go, 373.
The Lord comes down from heaven, 24.
The New Testament teaches intolerance, 335.
The Reformation, 302.
The serpent tempts Eve, 22.
Two cosmogonies, 29.
VAST age of the universe, 30.
WOMAN, subjection of, 294.

www.ingramcontent.com/pod-product-compliance
Lightning Source LLC
Chambersburg PA
CBHW021336300426
44114CB00012B/974